DICTIONARY
OF
BRITISH
PLACE NAMES

DICTIONARY OF BRITISH PLACE NAMES

Andrew M Currie

TIGER BOOKS INTERNATIONAL
LONDON

This edition published in 1994 by
Tiger Books International PLC, London

ISBN 1-85501-376-2

Printed and bound in Slovenia

A

Abbeyleix (Laois) Simply 'abbey of Laois'. *Abeie* (Old French form of Church Latin *abbatia*) 'abbey, monastery'; *Laeighis* (Irish Gaelic tribal territory name) elided to *Leix*. The original monastery, founded here in 1183 by Conor O'More, has long since disappeared. *See* LAOIS.

Abbots Langley *see* **Langley**.

Abbotsbury (Dorset) Place at the 'fortified house or manor of the abbot'. *Abbod* (Old English) 'abbot'; *byrig* (Old English dative of *burh*) 'fortified place'. The name of this village by the CHESIL BEACH reflects the early foundation of a Benedictine abbey here in the 10th century. Records show *Abbodesburie* 945; *Abbodesbyrig* 1045; *Abedesberie* 1086 (Domesday Book).

Aberaeron (Dyfed) 'Mouth of the River Aeron'. *Aber* (Old Welsh) 'river mouth'; *aeron* (Old Welsh river name adapted from aer, meaning 'battle') 'goddess of war'. This small harbour town, developed in the early 19th century by the Rev. Alban Thomas Jones Gwynne, lies on CARDIGAN Bay, southwest of ABERYSTWYTH. The estuary here is cited as *Ayron* in a Latin text of 1184.

Aberchirder (Grampian) 'Mouth of the dark water'. *Aber* (Brythonic Celtic-Pictish) 'mouth of a river'; *chiar* (Scottish Gaelic) 'dark'; *dobhar* (Brythonic Celtic) 'water'. The name of Scotland's smallest royal burgh, southwest of BANFF, refers to the confluence of the peaty Auchintoul stream with the River Deveron.

Aberdare (Mid Glamorgan) 'Confluence of the Dâr and the Cynon rivers'. *Aber* (Old Welsh) 'river mouth'; *dar* (Old Welsh) 'oak'. The modern Welsh name for this former coal-mining town in South Wales is Aberdar, the same rendering as was recorded in a document of 1203.

Aberdeen (Grampian) 'Mouth of the River Don'. *Aber* (Brythonic Celtic-Pictish) 'mouth of a river'; the second element would reasonably suggest that the river is the DEE, which flows into the North Sea at the centre of modern Aberdeen, but the name was recorded as *Aberdon* in the early 12th century and at that time referred to the original settlement, now Old Aberdeen, situated immediately to the north at the mouth of the River Don. By the 13th century the current name form was emerging: *Aberdoen* 1178; *Aberden* 1214.

Aberdour (Fife) 'Mouth of the River Dour'. *Aber* (Brythonic Celtic-Pictish) 'mouth of a river'; *dobhar, dor, dur* (Brythonic Celtic) 'waters', as in DOVER and ANDOVER. The name of this coastal town on the Firth of FORTH west of BURNTISLAND is pronounced 'Aber-dower'.

Aberdyfi (Gwynedd) 'Mouth of the River Dyfi'. *Aber* (Old Welsh) 'river mouth'; *Dyfi* (Old Welsh river name) of uncertain origin. Suggestions made for the derivation of the latter element include *du* (Welsh) 'black' and *dyfn* (Welsh) 'deep'. As with many similar 'aber' places, the name Aberdyfi originally applied to the estuary itself, in this case the large sea inlet north of ABERYSTWYTH. For long known as Aberdovey.

Aberfeldy (Tayside) 'Confluence of Pallidius or Paldoc'. *Aber* (Brythonic Celtic-Pictish) 'river confluence'; *phellaidh* (Brythonic Celtic) refers not to a stream of that name but St Paldoc, Romish missionary to the Picts in the 5th century, or alternatively, a water sprite believed to live where the local Urlar Burn meets the River TAY here, upstream and northwest of PERTH.

Aberfoyle (Central) 'Confluence of the pool'. *Aber* (Brythonic Celtic-Pictish) 'river confluence' or 'mouth'; *phuill* (common Gaelic) a 'pool' or 'bog'.

Abergavenny (Gwent) 'Confluence of the Gavenny and Usk rivers'. *Aber* (Old Welsh) 'river mouth'; *Gobann* (Welsh genitive of *goibniu*) 'the smith'. In a late Welsh legend, Gofannon is the patron of metal-workers. The Roman Latin name for the early settlement here was *Gobannium*. The modern Welsh form, *Y Fenni*, has simply lost the first syllable of the river name.

Abergele (Clwyd) 'Mouth of the River Gele'. *Aber* (Old Welsh) 'river mouth'; and probably *gelau* (Old Welsh) 'spear', 'blade', reflecting the nature of this short but rapid river 'cutting' its way straight to the North Wales coast, where the 19th-century town grew up.

Aberlady (Lothian) Possibly 'mouth of the lady', as in the Virgin Lady. *Aber* (Brythonic Celtic-Pictish) 'mouth'; *hlaedig* (Old English) 'lady' or 'loaf-kneader'. The ruins of Mary's Chapel are found here southwest of Gullane.

Aberlemno (Tayside) 'River confluence of the elmwood'. *Aber* (Brythonic Celtic-Pictish) 'confluence', 'mouth'; *leamhanach* (Scottish Gaelic) 'elmwood'. Well-preserved Pictish sculptured stones are found here and in the locality northwest of FORFAR.

Abernethy (Tayside) 'Mouth of the Nethy' (river). *Aber* (Brythonic Celtic-Pictish) 'mouth;' the second part is possibly derived from *an eitighich* (Scottish Gaelic) 'gullet', signifying water rushing through a gorge. The village was also a capital of *Nechtan*, king of the Picts around AD700. More likely is the old Celtic river name *Nedd*, which means 'glistening'.

Abersoch (Gwynedd) 'Mouth of the River Soch'. *Aber* (Old Welsh) 'river mouth'; *sychu* (Welsh) 'drain'. This small but popular sailing resort on the south side of the LLEYN peninsula, stands at he mouth of a river whose muddy waters still reflect its descriptive name.

Abertillery (Gwent) 'Confluence of the Teleri'. *Aber* (Old Welsh) 'river mouth'; *Eleri* (Old Welsh personal name) a 5th-century female saint. This South Wales 'valley town' developed at the point where the Teleri Brook meets the River Ebwy Fach.

Aberystwyth (Dyfed) 'Mouth of the Ystwyth'. *Aber* (Old Welsh) 'river mouth'; *Ystwyth* (Old Welsh river name) meaning 'winding'. This university town and resort, sometimes referred to as the 'capital of Mid-Wales', lies halfway down the coast of CARDIGAN Bay at the mouth of the River Rheidol, not the River Ystwyth, which is to the south of the present town. This misnomer is similar to that of ABERDEEN. In this case, the original focus of the town was a Norman castle built in 1110 in the Ystwyth valley but it was replaced by another in 1211 where the town now stands.

Abingdon (Oxfordshire) 'Hill of Aebba or Aebbe'. *Aebba / Aebbe* (Old English personal names, male/female respectively) unidentified; *dun* (Old English) 'down' or 'hill'. The modern town of Abingdon lies on flat land by the banks of the River THAMES south of OXFORD, but the original settlement was founded on the nearby upland ridge of Boar's Hill, and moved later to its present site. Early records show *Abbandune* 968; *Abbendone* 1086 (Domesday Book).

Abington (Strathclyde) 'Albin's village'. *Ael-wine* (Old English) 'noble friend'; *tun* (Old English) 'enclosure' or 'settlement'.

Aboyne (Grampian) 'White cow river'. *Abh* (Old Gaelic) 'river'; *bo* (Scottish Gaelic) 'cow'; *fionn* (Scottish Gaelic) 'white'. Reference here, is not to the River Dee on which this town stands, west of BANCHORY, but to a small stream just to the north.

Accrington (Lancashire) 'Acorn farmstead or village'. *Aecern* (Old English) 'acorn'; *tun* (Old English) 'farmstead' or village. This textile town lies north of the Forest of ROSSENDALE which originally extended to here and would have been a source of acorns, once important for the feeding of pigs. Recorded as *Akarinton* 1194; *Akerynton* 1258; *Acrinton* 1277.

Achil Island (Mayo) Probably 'place of the cliffs'. *Achadh* (Irish Gaelic elided to *ach*) 'place', 'open space', 'field'; *aill* (Irish Gaelic) 'cliff'. The largest of Ireland's offshore islands, separated by the very narrow Achil Sound which has been bridged, it rises to over 2200 ft (675 m), dramatically ending in a four-mile stretch of sheer precipices overlooking the Atlantic Ocean, the highest sea cliffs in the BRITISH ISLES.

Achiltibuie (Highland) Possibly 'field of the yellow stream'. *Achadh* (Scottish Gaelic) 'field'; *allt* / *uillt* (Scottish Gaelic) 'stream'; *buidhe* (Scottish Gaelic) 'yellow'. Locally, the preferred explanation is 'field of the yellow(-haired) lad', derived from *Achadh-a-gille-buidhe*; with *gille* (Scottish Gaelic) denoting a lad or a young man.

Achnasheen (Highland) 'Field of the storms'. *Achadh* (Scottish Gaelic) 'field'; *na* (Scottish Gaelic) 'of the'; *sian* (Scottish Gaelic) 'storm'. This remote inland and elevated village in northern Scotland is exposed to much severe weather.

Acton (Greater London) 'Oak farmstead or village'. *Ac* (Old English) 'oak'; *tun* (Old English) 'farmstead', 'village'. This district of the Borough of EALING has a common English place name that was recorded as its current rendering in 1181.

Adare (Limerick) 'Ford of the oaks'. *Ath* (Irish Gaelic) 'ford'; *doire* (Irish Gaelic) 'oak wood'. There are still oaks by the River Maigue in this village, southwest of LIMERICK. The Irish name is *Ath Dara*.

Adlington (Lancashire) 'Estate associated with a man called Eadwulf'. *Eadwulf* (Old English personal name) meaning 'happy wolf'; *ing* (Old English connective particle) 'associated with'; *tun* (Old English) 'farmstead', 'estate'. The name of this town northwest of BOLTON is repeated elsewhere, including a village in CHESHIRE. It was recorded as *Edeluinton* around 1190.

Adwick le Street (South Yorkshire) 'Adda's dwelling or (dairy) farm'. *Adda* or *Eadda* (Old English personal name); *wic* (Old English) 'dwelling' or 'specialised farm', often involved in dairying. The name of this now coal-mining town northwest of DONCASTER has an affix derived from *straet* (Old English) indicating its location on a 'Roman road', and to distinguish it from **Adwick upon Dearne**, a village only 6 miles (10 km) to the southwest, on the latter river. In the Domesday Book of 1086 the name was documented as *Adewic*.

Affric (Highland) Possibly 'ford of the speckled trout or boar'. *Ath* (Scottish Gaelic) 'ford'; *breac* (Scottish Gaelic) 'speckled trout'; or *bhraich* (Scottish Gaelic) 'boar'.

Ailsa Craig (Strathclyde) 'Fairy rock'. *Aillse* (Scottish Gaelic) 'fairy'; *creag* (Scottish Gaelic) 'rock'. Also, *ail* (Old Gaelic) 'steep rock'. All such legendary and geological associations are appropriate to this prominent and isolated island landmark in the Firth of CLYDE.

Aintree (Merseyside) Place of the 'solitary tree'. *Einn* (Old Norse) 'one'; *tre* (Old Norse) 'tree'. This northern suburb of LIVERPOOL, and home of the famous 'Grand National' racecourse, was originally part of the Viking domain accessed from the Irish Sea by means of the MERSEY estuary. A record of 1220 shows *Ayntre*.

Airdrie (Strathclyde) 'High hill pasture'. *Aird* (Scottish Gaelic) 'high'; *ruighe* (Scottish Gaelic) 'slope' or 'shieling'. This industrial town, east of GLASGOW, is situated on an elevated slope.

Alcester (Warwickshire) 'Roman settlement on the River Alne'. *Ceaster* (Old English adaptation of Latin *castra*) 'Roman camp'; *Alne* (Brythonic Celtic river name) possibly meaning 'very white'. This small town south of REDDITCH, lies on the old Roman road, known as Icknield Street (now the A435), that runs roughly north-south. The Roman camp here was called *Alauna*, after the river. The town's name was *Alencestre* in 1138.

Aldeburgh (Suffolk) Place of the 'old fort'. *Ald* (Old English) 'old'; *burg* (Old English) 'fort'. This coastal resort northeast of IPSWICH, internationally famous for its annual music festival, is located at the mouth of the River Alde, near the former site of an 'old fort' apparently destroyed by the sea in early times. The name was recorded as *Aldeburc* in 1086 (Domesday Book).

Alderley Edge (Cheshire) 'Aldred's woodland or clearing on an escarpment'. *Aldred* (Old English personal name); *leah* (Old English) 'woodland', 'clearing'. The name of this residential town south of WILMSLOW reflects its situation on a wooded escarpment, the latter emphasised by the later affix. Recorded as *Aldredelie* in 1086.

Aldermaston (Berkshire) 'Alderman's homestead'. *Ealdormann* (Old English) 'chief officer of a shire', 'nobleman with administrative powers'; *tun* (Old English) 'homestead', 'settlement'. The name of this village, otherwise famous as the home of the Atomic Energy Research Establishment, originally reflected the nearby presence of NEWBURY as a long-time important centre for the county. It was recorded in the Domesday Book in 1086 as *AEldremanestone*.

Alderney (Channel Islands) Possibly 'alder island'. *Alr* (Old Norse) 'alder'; *ey* (Old Norse) 'island'. This, the third largest and northernmost of the Channel Islands, is almost certain to have a name of Scandinavian origin as is the case for most of the others in the group. Its French name is *Aurigny*.

Aldershot (Hampshire) 'Projecting piece of land where alder trees grow'. *Alor* (Old English) 'alder'; *sceat* (Old English) 'a projecting land form'. This 'army camp' town west of GUILDFORD lies immediately below the very abrupt HOGS BACK ridge, on the lower slopes of which the original alder woodlands would have grown. In this area of east HAMPSHIRE and west SURREY there are several similarly situated places with the '-shot' ending in their names: BAGSHOT, Bramshott, Grayshott, and also Sheet as a related manifestation.

Aldgate (Greater London) The 'ale gate'. *Ealu* (Old English) 'ale'; *geat* (Old English) 'gap', 'gate'. This area immediately east of the City of LONDON was the site of the old town's east gate, or entrance, built originally as part of the late-2nd-century city walls of Roman Londinium. Indeed, prior to the 11th century its former name, *AEst Geat*, reflected this situation. Subsequently it became a place where 'ale' was given as a dole to needful wayfarers, and was recorded as *Ealsegate* in 1075 and *Alegate* in 1108 and 1275.

Aldridge (West Midlands) 'Dwelling or farm among alder trees'. *Alor* (Old English) 'alder tree'; *wic* (Old English) 'small settlement', 'dwelling' or 'farm'. The present corrupted form of the name of this small town on the northern edge of the WEST MIDLANDS conurbation is misleading. Early records show its original roots and development: *Aldrewic* in the 1086 Domesday Book; *Alrewich* and *Allerwych* around 1200. *Compare* ALDWYCH.

Aldwych (Greater London) 'Old farm'. *Eald* (Old English) 'old': *wic* (Old English) 'farm', 'settlement'. The name of this part of LONDON's 'West End' has the sense of 'disused farm'. It was originally given to the street that passed it by, and in turn to the urban district that eventually grew up here. It is recorded as *Aldewich* in the 13th century.

Alexandria (Strathclyde) This town in the Vale of Leven lying to the north of DUMBARTON was named after the local member of parliament in 1760, Alexander Smollett.

Alford (Grampian) 'High ford'. Pronounced locally as 'Afherd', the most probable derivation of the name of this small town, northwest of ABERDEEN, is from *ath* (Scottish Gaelic) 'ford'; *aird* (Scottish Gaelic) 'high'. Compare ALFORD (Lincolnshire).

Alford (Lincolnshire) Possibly 'alder ford'. *Alor* (Old English) 'alder'; *ford* (Old English) 'ford'. Other suggestions for the derivation of the name of this small town lying between The WOLDS and the coast include: *alh* + *ford* (Old English) 'ford by the heathen temple'; and *ael* + *ford* (Old English) 'ford of the eels'. In the Domesday Book of 1086 it was recorded as *Alforde*.

Alloa (Central) 'Rocky plain'. Derived from a compound word *ail-mhagh* (Scottish Gaelic) meaning 'rocky plain', most apposite to the town's location on a flood plain on the north bank of the River FORTH.

Alloway (Strathclyde) 'Rocky plain'. This village, made famous as the birthplace of Robert Burns, lies on flat land of the Ayr Basin and owes its name to the same root as ALLOA.

Alness (Grampian) 'Holy or pure river'. This small town, west of INVERGORDON, takes its name from the river on which it stands. Recorded as *Alune* in the 13th century, it probably has the same pre-Celtic river name origin as the River Alun in Wales and River Lune in England.

Alnwick (Northumberland) 'Dwelling or farm on the River Aln'. *Aln* (River name deriving from the Brythonic Celtic root word *alaun*) 'holy' or 'mighty one'; *wic* (Old English) 'dwelling place'. This historic seat of the Percy family thus takes its name from that of the river on which it stands. It was documented around 1180 as *Alnewic*, and is currently pronounced 'Annick'.

Alresford (Hampshire) 'Alder-tree ford'. *Alor* (Old English) 'alder tree'; *ford* (Old English) 'ford'. Lying east of WINCHESTER, the town of **New Alresford**, as it is officially called to distinguish it from the village of **Old Alresford** just to the north, has a straightforward name that was recorded as *Alresforda* in a document of 701.

Alston (Cumbria) Probably 'Aldhun's farmstead'. *Aldhun* (Old Norse personal name) unidentified; *tun* (Old English) 'farmstead'. This small market town, which claims to be the highest in Britain, lies on the western slope of the PENNINES northeast of PENRITH. Its original name, *Aldenby*, was entirely Scandinavian in construction, as recorded between 1164 and 1171. By 1210, under increasing Anglo-Saxon influences, it had become *Aldeneston*, but its meaning was unchanged.

Alton (Hampshire) 'Farmstead at the source of a stream'. *AEwiell* (Old English) 'river source'; *tun* (Old English) 'farmstead'. This town on the southern slopes of the North DOWNS, southwest of GUILDFORD, has a common compound name, signifying the original importance of being located at the source of a stream, in this case that of the River Wey. It was recorded in the Domesday Book of 1086 as *Aultone*.

Alton Towers (Staffordshire) 'Aelfa's farmstead'. *AElfa* (Old English personal name); *tun* (Old English) 'farmstead'. This famous 'theme park' takes the basic name of the nearby village to the east of STOKE-ON-TRENT. The 'Towers' affix refers to the turreted shell of a 19th-century Neo-Gothic mansion here.

Altrincham (Greater Manchester) 'Village of Aldhere's people'. *Aldhere* (Old English personal name; *ing* (Old English connective particle) 'associated with'; *ham* (Old English) 'homestead', 'village'. The name of this residential town, southwest of MANCHESTER, was recorded as *Aldringeham* in 1290.

Alva (Central) ' Rocky plain'. The derivation of this town's name is the same as its nearby neighbour ALLOA.

Alyth (Tayside) 'Steep bank or rugged place'. This small town derives, northwest of BLAIRGOWRIE, its descriptive name from the Hill of Alyth that rises steeply on its northern edge. *Aileach* (Scottish Gaelic) 'mound' or 'bank': alternatively, *aill* (Old Gaelic) 'steep rock'.

Amble (Northumberland) 'Anna's promontory'. *Anna* (Old English personal name); *bile* (Old English) 'promontory'. This small coastal town, southeast of ALNWICK, has a name that refers to the point here at the mouth of the River Coquet, and a second element root that is the same as in the 'bill' of PORTLAND BILL. Early records show: *Ambell* 1204; *Anebell* 1256.

Ambleside (Cumbria) 'Summer pasture by the river sandbank'. *A* (Old Norse) 'river'; *melr* (Old Norse) 'sandbank'; *saetr* (Old Norse) 'sheiling'. The name of this Lake District town, set amongst the hills at the head of WINDERMERE, reflects the pastoral tradition of 'transhumance', or the seasonal migration of livestock to suitable summer grazing grounds, which would involve the setting up of temporary huts or sheilings. It was documented as *Ameleseta* in 1095, and its corruption to a 'side' ending was first noted about 1400 as *Amylside*.

Amersham (Buckinghamshire) 'Ealhmund's village'. *Ealhmund* (Old English personal name); *ham* (Old English) 'village'. The name of this small town, to the northeast of HIGH WYCOMBE, has been much corrupted, as records show: *Agmodesham* 1066; *Elmodesham* 1086; *Augmodesham* 1197; *Aumodeshame* 1222; *Amundesham* 1227.

Amesbury (Wiltshire) 'Ambr's place by the fortified stronghold'. *Ambr* (Old English personal name) probably refers to Aurelius Ambrosius, a 5th-century Romano-British tribal chief who is said to have established his capital here; *byrig* (Old English dative of *burh*) 'fortified stronghold'. The latter part of the name of this small town, to the north of SALISBURY, almost certainly refers to the Iron Age hill-fort here, called Vespasian's Camp after a later Roman Emperor. Records show *Ambresbyrig* in about 880 and *Ambresberie* in 1086.

Amisfield (Dumfries and Galloway) 'Amyas's field'. One Amyas de Charteris was a medieval lord of the local manor, Amyas deriving from *amatus* (Latin) 'beloved'. Lying northwest of DUMFRIES, the name of the village and the 16th-century tower seat of the Charteris family is pronounced 'Aimsfield'.

Amlwch (Gwynedd) 'Near to the swamp'. *Am* (Welsh) 'near to the', 'about the'; *llwch* (Welsh) 'swamp'. The 'swamp' of this small town on the north coast of ANGLESEY was probably the little creek that was here prior to the town developing as the world's greatest copper port in the late 18th century, exporting ore extracted from the nearby Parys Mountain.

Ammanford (Dyfed) 'The ford over the River Amman'. This town, which developed in the 19th century on the western edge of the South Wales coalfield, has a relatively recent and straightforward name, the Welsh form of which, *Rhydaman*, is an exact translation.

Ampthill (Bedfordshire) Literally 'ant hill' or more likely 'a hill infested with ants'. *AEmette* (Old English) 'ant'; *hyll* (Old English) 'hill'. This town south of BEDFORD has this somewhat surprising derivation, but such a feature must have been significant here originally. The 1086 Domesday Book entry is *Ammetelle*.

Amurlee (Tayside) 'Ford of Maelrubha'. *Ath* (Scottish Gaelic) 'ford'; the second element of the name of the village, north of CRIEFF, refers to the 7th-century monk who became the local patron saint.

An Uaimh *see* **Navan**

Andover (Hampshire) Place by the 'ash-tree waters'. *Ann* (Brythonic Celtic derivative of root word *onno*) 'ash tree'; *dover* (Brythonic Celtic derivative of root word *dubro*) 'water'. This town west of BASINGSTOKE is called after a former name of the River Anton, on which it stands. The names of the town and the river are recorded as *Andovere*, in the Domesday Book of 1086. *Compare* DOVER.

Anglesey (Gwynedd) Probably 'Ongull's island'. *Ongul* (Old Norse personal name) unidentified; *ey* (Old Norse) 'island'. Although the name of this well-known large island off the northwest coast of the Welsh mainland has been traditionally derived as being 'the island of the Angles', it seems more plausible that it is Scandinavian in origin, as are most of the names of the other Welsh islands. A 13th-century record shows it as *Ongulsey*. The Welsh name is *Mon*, meaning 'mountain' or 'hill'.

Angus (Tayside) This former country and now administrative district is named after the 8th-century king of the Picts, *Aonghus* (Scottish Gaelic) 'unique choice'.

Annan (Dumfries and Galloway) 'The water' or possibly 'waters'. *An* (Scottish Gaelic) 'the'; *ann* (Scottish Gaelic) 'water'. Alternatively, as the town lies on the River Annan near to the point where it enters the SOLWAY Firth, the name could be literally *ann-an* (Scottish Gaelic) 'waters'.

Annat (Highland; Strathclyde) 'Watery place'. In both cases *annait* (Scottish Gaelic) 'watery', describes well the situations of these villages: the one on Upper Loch TORRIDON, the other on a burn near the north shore of Loch Awe.

Anstruther (Fife) 'The little stream'. *An* (Scottish Gaelic) 'the'; *sruthair* (Scottish Gaelic) 'little stream'. Recorded as *Anestrothir* 1205, *Anstrother* 1231, but with current local pronunciation of the name of this FIFE fishing port as 'Ainster'.

Antonine Wall (Lothian/Strathclyde) A Roman fortification of the 1st century AD that extended from the FORTH to the CLYDE. It was named after the then reigning Roman emperor Antoninus Pius (AD86-161). *See* HADRIAN'S WALL.

Antrim (Antrim) Place of 'one house'. *Aon* (Irish Gaelic) 'one'; *treabh* (Irish Gaelic) 'house'. It is assumed that this town, lying on the northeast corner of Lough NEAGH in Northern Ireland, was so named after an isolated dwelling that originally stood here. The historic county is named after the town. In Irish the name is *Aontroim*.

Aonach Eagach (Highland) 'Airy notched ridge'. *Aonach* (Scottish Gaelic) 'open space' (as on a mountain); *eagach* (Scottish Gaelic) 'notched'. An aptly descriptive name for this classic, exposed mountain ridge of rock spires and pinnacles in the climber's mecca of GLENCOE.

Aonach Mor (Highland) 'Big open ridge'. *Aonach* (as above); *mor, mhor, moire* (Scottish Gaelic) 'big'. This mountain near BEN NEVIS, where a ski centre has recently been developed, is the fulcrum summit of a two-mile open ridge that ends to the south with the slightly higher and thus curiously named **Aonach Beag**—'little open ridge'.

Appin (Strathclyde) 'Abbey lands'. *Apuinn* (Scottish Gaelic) 'abbey lands'. The name probably refers to the land that was owned here in west-central mainland Scotland in medieval times by St Moluag's foundation on the nearby Isle of LISMORE, across the Lynn of LORN.

Appleby in Westmorland (Cumbria) 'Apple farm'. *Appel* (Old English possibly replacing Old Norse *epli*) 'apple'; *by* (Old Norse) 'farmstead'. The common name of this town southeast of PENRITH has had the distinguishing affix added recently to re-promote the former county name of WESTMORLAND, of which it was the main centre. Early records include: *Aplebi* 1130; *Appelbi* 1190.

Applecross (Highland) 'Mouth of the Crossan' (river). *Aber* (Brythonic Celtic) 'mouth of a river'; *crossain* (Scottish Gaelic) 'little cross'. The second element may be associated with the monastery founded here northwestern Scotland in AD673 by St Maelrubha. *See* AMURLEE

Aran Islands (Donegal; Galway) 'Kidney-shaped islands'. *Arainn* (Irish Gaelic dative of *ara*) 'shaped like a kidney', 'arched-backed'. Both the **Aran Islands**, off GALWAY Bay, and **Aran Island**, to the south of the BLOODY FORELAND on the west coast of DONEGAL, have contour outlines that fit this description, even if their wild Atlantic seaboard in both cases appears to have been sliced off. *Compare* ARRAN.

Arbroath (Tayside) 'Mouth of the Brothock Water'. *Aber* (Brythonic Celtic-Pictish) 'mouth of a river'; the second element of the name of this town, northeast of DUNDEE, refers to the name of the local burn, the root of which is *brothach* (Scottish Gaelic) 'boiling/turbulent', referring to its waters.

Ardee (Louth) Place of 'Ferdia's ford'. *Ath* (Irish Gaelic) 'ford'; *Fhirdia* (Irish Gaelic personal name) a warrior apparently killed here in the 1st century AD. The Irish name of the town is *Baile Ath Fhirdia*.

Ardersier (Highland) Possibly 'high west promontory'. *Aird* (Scottish Gaelic) 'high'; *ros* (Scottish Gaelic) 'promontory'; *iar* (Scottish Gaelic) 'west'. This oil-rig construction town lies on the west side of a pronounced promotory, northeast of INVERNESS.

Ardglass (Down) Place of the 'green height'. *Ard* (Irish Gaelic) 'height', 'steep place'; *ghlais* (Irish Gaelic) 'green'. This small coastal resort lies on a green slope running down to the Irish Sea, just south of the entrance to STRANGFORD Lough.

Ardgour (Highland) Possibly 'promontory of Gabran'. *Ard* (Scottish Gaelic) 'promontory'; the second element refers to Gabran, favourite son of King Fergus of ULSTER in ancient times. More plausible alternatives include 'promontory of the goat' from the (Scottish Gaelic) *gobhar*; or 'promontory' of sloping/crooked (a landscape descriptive of this area) derived from the (Brythonic Celtic) *gwyr*. *See* GOWER.

Ardmore (Waterford) 'Big headland'. *Ard* (Irish Gaelic) 'promontory', 'height'; *mor* (Irish Gaelic) 'big'. This name is common in Ireland and Scotland and is usually associated with a prominent coastal headland. Here the small resort lies on Ardmore Bay, immediately north of Ram Head.

Ardnamurchan (Highland) Probably 'promontory of the otters'. *Ard* (Scottish Gaelic) 'promontory'; *na* (Scottish Gaelic) 'of the'; *muir-chon* (Scottish Gaelic) 'sea dogs'. A less likely derivation of the last two parts of this name suggest 'piracy', which may have been associated with this wild westernmost peninsula of Scotland: *muir-chol* (Scottish Gaelic) 'sea villany'.

Ardrishaig (Strathclyde) 'Promontory of thorny brambles by the bay'. *Ard* (Scottish Gaelic) 'promontory'; *dris* (Scottish Gaelic) 'thorns', 'brambles'; *aig* (corrupt form of Old Norse *vik*) 'bay'. An apt description for this town on the Loch Gilp indentation of Loch Fyne and entry point to the Crinan Canal, has thorny banks even today.

Ardrossan (Strathclyde) 'Height of the little cape'. *Ard* (Scottish Gaelic) 'promontory', 'height'; *ros* (Scottish Gaelic) 'cape', 'headland'; *-an* (Scottish Gaelic) 'little'. This ferry port on the Firth of CLYDE is located on the north side of a promotory.

Ards Peninsula (Down) 'Headland peninsula'. *Ard* (Irish Gaelic) 'headland'. The name of this long peninsula running south between STRANGFORD Lough and the Irish Sea really has the same meaning in both its Gaelic and English elements. The latter and the plural *s* have clearly been added as part of its anglicisation.

Argyll (Strathclyde) 'District or land of the Gaels'. *Oirer* (Scottish Gaelic) 'coastland'; *Gaidheal* (Scottish Gaelic) 'of the Gaels'. The Gaels originating in Ireland colonised much of the western seaboard of Scotland during the 6th-9th centuries AD. The name was first recorded as *Arregaithel* in a 10th-century manuscript. The archaic form, Argyle, was used for many centuries.

Arisaig (Highland) 'River-mouth bay'. *Ar-os* (Old Norse) 'river mouth'; *aig* (corrupt form of Old Norse *vik*) 'bay'. Like many coastal names in this area the origin is Scandinavian.

Arklow (Wicklow) 'Arnkel's meadow'. *Arnkel* (Old Norse personal name) unidentified; *lo* (Old Norse) 'meadow'. This resort town south of WICKLOW lies on the Irish Sea coast, which was the area of Ireland most settled by the Vikings over 1000 years ago.

Armadale (Lothian; Highland) This town in LOTHIAN is named after a local landowner, Lord Armadale , who took his title from his village of Armadale on the north coast of SUTHERLAND. The name's likely meaning, 'arm-shaped valley', is Scandinavian in origin and also applies to the Armadale on the Isle of SKYE, another place on the Viking coast. *Arm-r* (Old Norse) 'arm', arm-shaped'; *dalr* (Old Norse) 'dale', 'valley'.

Arnold (Nottinghamshire) 'Eagles' nook'. *Earn* (Old English) 'eagle'; *halh* (Old English) 'corner of land', 'a nook'. The name of this former village, and now northern suburb of NOTTINGHAM, is a corruption of its original form; the Domesday Book entry of 1086 was *Ernehale*.

Arran (Strathclyde) Possibly 'place of peaked hills'. *Aran* (related to *Ard* but Brythonic Celtic) 'height', 'peaked hill'. Alternatively, the derivation of the name of this mountainous island in the Firth of CLYDE may be related to the Irish ARAN Islands where *arainn*, (Irish Gaelic) 'kidney', implies an arched ridge. However, this is only true of Arran when viewed from the mainland to the north, from where it assumes the commonplace description of the 'sleeping warrior'. Some authorities have also supported this meaning in respect of the island's distinctive kidney shape.

Arrington *see* **Ermine Street**.

Arrochar (Strathclyde) 'The aratrum'-an ancient Scottish square land measure of 104 acres, called a ploughgate in Scots, this being the area of land eight oxen could plough in a year at 13 acres each. Derived as a Gaelic corruption of *aratrum* (Latin) 'plough', early medieval recordings of the name of this village at the head of Loch LONG, include *Arathor* 1248; *Arachor* 1350. Alternatively, a local hill spelt as Ben Arrochar on an early map is derived from *Beinn Airigh-chiarr* (Scottish Gaelic) 'mount sheiling-dark'. *Compare* HADDO, KIRRIEMUIR.

Arundel (West Sussex) 'Valley where the hoarhound grows'. *Harhune* (Old English) 'hoarhound' or 'horehound' nettle plant; *dell* (Old English) 'valley'. This town, north of LITTLEHAMPTON, with its mighty 11th-century castle guarding the southern approaches to the Arun Gap in the South DOWNS, could well have been the site of such nettle beds, especially by the river the below castle battlements. It was recorded as *Harundel* in the Domesday Book of 1086.

Ascot (Berkshire) 'Eastern cottages'. *East* (Old English) 'east', 'eastern'; *cot* (Old English) 'cottage', 'hut' or 'shelter'. It was the latter sense, as a shelter for animals, that gave rise to the name of this town with its famous race course, east of BRACKNELL. The name was documented as *Estcota* in 1177.

Ashbourne (Derbyshire; Meath) 'Stream where the ash trees grow'. *AEsc* (Old English) 'ash tree'; *burna* (Old English) 'stream'. This straightforward derivation applies equally to the market town northwest of DERBY and the large village northwest of DUBLIN. The English Ashbourne was recorded as *Esseburne* in the Domesday Book of 1086. *Cill Dheaglain* is the Irish name of the other, and its meaning—'St Declan's Church—is quite unrelated to its English name.

Ashburton (Devon) 'Farmstead by the stream where the ash trees grow'. *AEsc* (Old English) 'ash tree'; *burna* (Old English) 'stream'; *tun* (Old English) 'farmstead', 'settlement'. The name of this market town west of NEWTON ABBOT is an embellished form of ASHBOURNE that appeared in the Domesday Book in 1086 as *Essebretone*.

Ashby de la Zouch (Leicestershire) 'Ash-tree farmstead of de la Zouch's family'. *Askr* (Old Danish) 'ash tree'; *by* (Old Danish) 'farmstead'; *de la Zuche* (Norman French manorial name) refers to the 13th-century 'lord of the manor', Roger de la Zuche. The latter affix was added subsequently to the common Midlands basic name by way of distinction. The name was recorded as simply *Ascebi* in the Domesday Book of 1086, and as *Esseby la Zusche* in 1241.

Ashdown Forest (East Sussex) 'Hill overgrown with ash trees'. *AEscen* (Old English) 'ash trees'; *dun* (Old English) 'down', 'hill'. This former large forested area, now largely heathland, that occupies the central WEALD north of UCKFIELD has a descriptive name that was recorded as *Essendon* in 1207.

Ashford (Kent) 'Ford by a clump of ash trees'. *AEscet* (Old English compound name derived from *aesc* + *sceat*) 'ash copse on a projecting piece of land' *ford* (Old English) 'river crossing point'. The name of this market town and centre of light industry, to the southwest of CANTERBURY, was recorded as *Essetesford* in the 1086 Domesday Book.

Ashington (Northumberland) 'Ash-tree valley'. *AEscen* (Old English) 'ash trees'; *denu* (Old English) 'valley'. The '-ington' ending of the current name of this town, which lies east of MORPETH, turns out to be a misleading corruption. The name was documented as *Essenden* in 1205.

Ashton-in-Makerfield (Greater Manchester) 'Ash-tree farmstead by open land with a ruin'. *AEsc* (Old English) 'ash tree'; *tun* (Old English) 'farmstead'; *macre* (Brythonic Celtic derived from Latin *maceria*) 'ruin', 'wall'; *feld* (Old English) 'field'. This town, west of MANCHESTER, distinguishes its common basic form with the addition of the old district name, recorded as *Macrefeld* in 1121, which itself may allude to the (then as now) 'ruined' Roman fort nearby at WIGAN.

Ashton-under-Lyne (Greater Manchester) 'Ash-tree farmstead near the elm-tree region'. *AEsc* (Old English) 'ash tree'; *tun* (Old English) 'farmstead'; *under* (Old English related to Old Saxon *undar*) 'near'; *Lyme* (Brythonic Celtic district name) 'place of el ms'. This town, on the eastern edge of the Greater MANCHESTER conurbation, distinguishes its basic 'Ashton' name by an affix that refers to a vast elm forest that once extended southwards from here, through CHESHIRE, to northern STAFFORDSHIRE. Recorded as *Asshton under Lyme* in 1305. *Compare* NEWCASTLE-UNDER-LYME.

Aspatria (Cumbria) Place of 'St Patrick's ash tree'. *Askr* (Old Norse) 'ash tree'; *Padraig* (Irish Gaelic personal name) patron saint of Ireland. This small town, on the edge of the CUMBRIAN MOUNTAINS northwest of MARYPORT, has a name of Scandinavian origin but with strong Celtic influences, including the word order. A record of *c*.1230 indicated *Ascpatric*.

Aspull (Greater Manchester) 'Hill where aspen trees grow'. *AEspe* (Old English) 'aspen tree'; *hyll* (Old English) 'hill'. This small town, on the high ground between BOLTON and WIGAN, was named *Aspul* in a document of 1212.

Assynt (Highland) A difficult word which perhaps means '(land) seen from afar'. *Asynt* (Old Norse) 'visible', referring to a Viking view of the area's many isolated and distinctive peaks as seen from out at sea in The MINCH. Alternatively, it could indicate the heavily indented coastline, or even the peaks and troughs of the rugged ancient landscape of this remote part of the northwest Highlands, in the derivation *As-agus-int* (Scottish Gaelic) 'outs-and-ins'.

Athboy (Meath) Place of the 'yellow ford'. *Ath* (Irish Gaelic) 'ford'; *buidhe* (Irish Gaelic) 'yellow'. This must be a reference to the colour of the river bed of the original fording point of what is now a market town west of NAVAN. The current Irish name is *Baile Atha Bui*. The river here is also the Athboy, taking its name from that of the town rather than the other way round, as was a more common practice.

Athelstaneford (Lothian) 'Athelstan's ford'. King Athelstan of Mercia and WESSEX, grandson of Alfred the Great, took Northumbria and invaded LOTHIAN in the early 10th century. In AD937 his troops were defeated near this village west of EAST LINTON, which possibly commemorates his name, which means 'noble stone' (Old English). Legend has it that during another battle near here about a hundred years earlier, the Scots facing a Northumbrian army, led by a General Athelstane, saw a St Andrew's saltire in the sky. Inspired on to victory, they took Andrew as their patron saint and his cross as their national flag. One commentator has even suggested that the origin of this placename has no connection with the Anglo-Saxon name Athelstan(e), but represents a tautology of *ath-ail* (Scottish Gaelic) 'stone ford'.

Athenry (Galway) 'Ford of the kings'. *Ath* (Irish gaelic) 'ford'; *na* (Irish Gaelic) 'of the'; *riogh* (Irish Gaelic—pronounced 'ree') 'king'. This town to the east of GALWAY is the site of a 13th-century Anglo-Norman castle, which was the principal seat of the De Burgs and Berminghams, and the regal reference in its name almost certainly has its roots in these medieval connections.

Atherstone (Warwickshire) 'AEthelred's farmstead'. *AEthelred* (Old English personal name); *tun* (Old English) 'farmstead'. This small town, located on the Roman WATLING STREET north of NUNEATON, was recorded in the Domesday Book of 1086 as *Aderestone*, and in a document of 1221 as *Atheredstone*.

Atherton (Greater Manchester) 'Aethelhere's farmstead'. *AEthelhere* (Old English personal name) *tun* (Old English) 'farmstead'. The name of this town southwest of BOLTON was recorded, as it is now, in 1322.

Athlone (Westmeath) 'Ford of Luan'. *Ath* (Irish Gaelic) ford; *Luain* (Irish Gaelic personal name) unidentified. This town is situated at an important crossing point of the River SHANNON, immediately south of Lough Dee. It is assumed that Luan must have been someone of high standing and of authority here. The Irish name for the town is *Baile Atha Luain*.

Atholl *see* **Blair Atholl**

Athy (Kildare) 'Ford of Ae'. *Ath* (Irish Gaelic) 'ford'; *Ae* (Irish Gaelic personal name) 11th-century MUNSTER chief slain by Lugaid Laigne in a battle here at the old ford over the River Barrow. *Athl* is the modern Irish name for the town. *See* LAOISE.

Attleborough (Norfolk) 'Aetla's stronghold'. *AEtla* (Old English personal name); *burh* (Old English) 'stronghold', 'fortified place'. This food-processing town southwest of NORWICH was noted as *Atleburc* in 1086.

Auchinleck (Strathclyde) 'Field of the flat stones'. *Achadh* (Scottish Gaelic) 'field'; *na* (Scottish Gaelic) 'of the'; *leac* (Scottish Gaelic) 'flat stones'.

Auchterader (Tayside) 'Upland of high water'. *Uachdar* (Scottish Gaelic) 'upper' (land); *ard* (Scottish Gaelic) 'high'; *dobhar* (Brythonic Celtic) 'water'. This description is apt for this town in the elevated part of STRATHMORE.

Auchtermuchty (Fife) 'Upper pig enclosure'. *Uachdar* (Scottish Gaelic) 'upper'; *muc* (Scottish Gaelic) 'pig'; *garadh* (Scottish Gaelic) 'enclosure'. Early records of the name of this town north of FALKLAND show closer renderings to its origins: *Huedirdmukedi* 1250; *Utermokerdy* 1293; *Utremukerty* 1294.

Auckland, Bishop; St Helen; West (Durham) Curiously 'the cliff on the CLYDE'. The basic name of this string of settlements northwest of DARLINGTON is probably of a Brythonic Celtic origin, transferred from an old name for DUMBARTON, *Alclyde*, which later was associated with *aukland* (Old Norse) 'additional land'. The distinguishing affix of the main town refers to the 12th-century residence of the bishops of DURHAM here.

Audenshaw (Greater Manchester) 'Aldwine's copse'. *Aldwine* (Old English personal name); *sceaga* (Old English) 'copse'. This industrial town, to the east of MANCHESTER, was recorded as *Aldwynshawe* around 1200.

Augher (Tyrone) Place on the 'border'. *Eochair* (Irish Gaelic) 'border'. This rustic village lies just north of the border between the Republic of Ireland and Northern Ireland, as well as being only 3 miles (5 km) from MONAGHAN. Its name is presumably associated with the latter county border rather than the early 20th-century international boundary created here. Indeed, it may reflect an even earlier line of demarkation.

Avebury (Wiltshire) Probably 'Afa's place by the fortified stronghold'. *Afa* (Old English personal name); *byrig* (Old English dative of *burh*) 'fortified stronghold'. This village to the west of MARLBOROUGH is regarded by many as Europe's most important Bronze Age site. It includes the famous Avebury Stone Circle and the Silbury Hill mound, but its name's latter element probably refers to the earlier Neolithic fort on nearby Windmill Hill. In the 1086 Domesday Book the entry is *Avreberie*.

Aviemore (Highland) 'Big pass'. *Agaidh* (Scottish Gaelic) 'pass'; *mor* (Scottish Gaelic) 'big'. This popular mountain and ski resort lies at the centre of the wide

STRATHSPEY (or Spey Valley as it is corrupted today) at a strategic entry point into the CAIRNGORMS.

Avon (British Isles) 'The river'. The most common river name that occurs in Britain and Ireland derives from an ancient Brythonic Celtic root word that simply means 'river'. It is represented in modern Welsh as *afon*, and in both Irish and Scottish Gaelic as *abhainn*. The county of Avon, created in 1974, takes its name directly from the best-known Avon, which flows through BRISTOL, on which it is centred.

Avonmouth (Avon) Simply 'at the mouth of the River Avon'. *Afon* (Brythonic Celtic) 'river'; *mutha* (Old English) 'river mouth', 'estuary'. Developed in the 19th century as BRISTOL's main port, this town is on an ancient site on the north bank of the River AVON at the point where the latter flows into the SEVERN estuary. An early document of 918 records *Afenmuthan*.

Axminster (Devon) ' Monastery by the River Axe'. *Axe* (Brythonic Celtic river name derived from the root word *isca*) 'water', 'river'; *mynster* (Old English) 'monastery'. This ancient West Saxon town southeast of HONITON, long famous for the making of carpets, to which it has given its name, is the site of a former monastery. The name was recorded as *Ascanmynster* in 755.

Aycliffe *see* **Newton Aycliffe**.

Aylesbury (Buckinghamshire) Aegel's place by the fortified stronghold'. *AEgel* (Old English personal name); *byrig* (Old English dative of burh) 'by the fort'. This ancient Saxon town, northwest of LONDON and the CHILTERN HILLS, must have been the site of an early fort prior to its reference in the Anglo-Saxon Chronicle of 571, in which the name is recorded as *AEgelesburg*. In a later document of 921 the name form is *AEglesbyrig*.

Aylsham (Norfolk) 'Aegel's village'. *AEgel* (Old English personal name); *ham* (Old English) 'village'. The name of this small town, to the north of NORWICH, includes the same personal name as ALESBURY. It was recorded as *Ailesham* in the Domesday Book of 1086.

Ayr (Strathclyde) The town takes its name from the river at whose mouth it stands on the Firth of CLYDE. An ancient pre-Celtic river name that possibly means 'smooth-running', and which has many variants in England (Aire; Oare; Ore) and elsewhere in Europe (Aar; Ahr; Ahre; Ara; Ohre; Ore).

B

Bacup (Lancashire) 'Valley by a ridge'. *Baec* (Old English) 'ridge'; *hop* (Old English) 'valley'. This industrial town south of BURNLEY lies at the head of the Irwell valley and its name aptly describes its situation. Records show that in 1324 its name was as it is now, but around 1200 the form *Fulebachope* indicated that conditions on the valley floor here must have been particularly muddy; *ful* is Old English for 'foul' or 'dirty'.

Badenoch (Highland) 'Marshy land'. *Baidhteanach* (Scottish Gaelic) 'liable to flooding' (land). So called because this area name originally referred more specifically to the broad STRATHSPEY than to the wider mountainous terrain it encompasses today.

Badminton, Great and Little (Avon) 'Estate associated with a man called Beadumund'. *Beadumund* (Old English personal name); *ing* (Old English connective particle) 'associated with'; *tun* (Old English) 'estate', 'village'. These two neighbouring villages lie east of CHIPPING SODBURY, with the former, commonly referred to simply as Badminton, being the seat of the Dukes of Beaufort for over 300 years. It is this place that gave its name to the sport of badminton, and it is also the annual venue for the famous Badminton Horse Trials. The name was documented as *Badimynctun* in 972, but just over a century later it is misrecorded in the Domesday Book as *Madmintune*.

Bagenalstown *see* **Muine Bheag**

Bagshot (Surrey) 'Projecting piece of land where badgers live'. *Bagga* (Old English) 'badger'; *sceat* (Old English) 'protruding landform'. This small town to the northeast of CAMBERLY is on a part of the LONDON Basin where the underlying clay is capped with harder rock known as the 'Bagshot Sands', giving rise to a noticably projected area of land here, which includes Surrey Hill. It was recorded as *Bagsheta* in 1165. *Compare* Aldershot.

Bailieborough (Cavan) 'Bailie's town'. *Bailie* (Anglo-Norman personal name derived from Old French *baillif*); *burh* (Old English) 'stronghold', 'town'. The name of this town southeast of CAVAN appears at first sight to be a corrupted tautology, with the first element being derived from *baile* (Irish Gaelic) 'town'. However, the origin of this name clearly dates from medieval times, and Bailie (predecessor of the common English surname, Bailey) must have been an Anglo-Norman landowner here.

Bala (Gwynedd) 'The outlet'. *Bala* (Welsh) 'efflux of a river from a lake'. The simple name thus exactly describes the location of this market town to the northeast of Lake Bala, which is named after it, rather than the other way round. The Welsh name for the lake is *Llyn Tegid*, the latter being a personal name.

Balbriggan (Dublin) 'Brigin's town'. *Baile* (Irish Gaelic) 'homestead', 'town'; *Brigan* (Irish Gaelic personal name) unidentified. This seaside resort on the coast north of DUBLIN has been known for the making of stockings for over 200 years; Americans sometimes call them 'balbrigans' to this day.

Baldock (Hertfordshire) This small town, immediately northeast of LETCHWORTH, has a most unusual name in that it represents 'Bagdad'! It was founded in the 12th century by the Knights Templars, who named it after the ancient Mesopotamian city, known then as *Baldac* (Old French). A record of *c.*1168 shows *Baldac*.

Balerno (Lothian) 'Village of the sloe tree'. *Baile* (Scottish Gaelic) 'homestead', 'hamlet'; *airneach* (Scottish Gaelic) 'sloe tree'. The name of this suburb of Edinburgh was first recorded in the 13th century as *Balhernoch* and has since been further anglicised to its present form.

Balham (Greater London) Probably 'Baelga's riverside land'. *Baelga* (Old English personal name); *hamm* (Old English) 'land enclosed by a river bend', 'water meadow'. This district of WANDSWORTH would have originally referred to the riverside land between the two branches of the Falcon Brook, now underground. A document of 957 recorded the name as *Baelgenham*.

Ballachulish (Highland) 'Village of the narrows'. *Baile* (Scottish Gaelic) 'homestead', 'hamlet'; *caolas* (Scottish Gaelic) 'narrows', 'straits'. This name is noticably descriptive of this Highland village's location on Loch Leven at the typical narrow fiord entrance by which it stands, and over which the main road north now crosses by a modern bridge.

Ballantrae (Strathclyde) 'Village on the shore'. *Baile* (Scottish Gaelic) 'homestead', 'hamlet'; *an* (Scottish Gaelic) 'of the', 'on the'; *traighe* (Scottish Gaelic) 'tidal beach'. A long stretch of open sandy shore is found here where the River Stinchar flows into the Firth of CLYDE.

Ballater (Grampian) Possibly 'broom land'. *Bealaidh* (Scottish Gaelic) 'broom'; *tir* (Scottish Gaelic) 'land'. Alternatively, it could be 'pass of the water', which describes well the situation of this Royal Deeside village. *Bealach* (Scottish Gaelic) 'mountain pass'; *dobhar* (Brythonic Celtic) 'water'. Certainly, 18th-century records would suggest the latter derivation: Balader 1704; *Ballader* 1716.

Ballina (Mayo) Place at the 'mouth of the ford'. *Beal* (Irish Gaelic) 'mouth'; *an* (Irish Gaelic) 'of the'; *atha* (Irish Gaelic) 'ford'. The name credibly describes the original situation of this old cathedral town, lying at the first fordable point of the River Moy estuary.

Ballinasloe (Galway) Place at the 'ford-mouth of the gatherings'. *Beal* (Irish Gaelic) 'mouth'; *atha* (Irish Gaelic) 'ford'; *na* (Irish Gaelic) 'of the'; *sluaigheadh* (Irish Gaelic) 'hosts', 'gatherings'. This town, at a crossing over the River Suck, southwest of ATHLONE, has long been the site of regular 'gatherings' of people and animals, today represented by the livestock fair held here each October. The current Irish name of the town is *Beal Atha na Sluaighe*.

Ballybofey (Donegal) Possibly the 'homestead of Fiach's cows'. *Baile* (Irish Gaelic) 'homestead', 'town'; *bo* (Irish Gaelic) 'cow'; *Fiach* (Irish Gaelic personal name) or Fay—unidentified. Apparently the old name for this small town that lies in a wide valley by the Blue Stack Mountains was *Srathbofey*, which would derive as *Srath-bo-Fiach*, meaning 'the river holm of Fiach's cows'.

Ballybunion (Kerry) 'Bunion's town'. *Baile* (Irish Gaelic) 'town', 'homestead'; *na* (Irish Gaelic) 'of the'; *Bhuinneanaigh* (Irish Gaelic personal name) Bunion. This popular Atlantic resort at the mouth of the SHANNON takes the name of some early local landowner, who remains unidentifed.

Ballycastle (Antrim) 'Homestead by the castle'. *Baile* (Irish Gaelic) 'homestead'; *caislean* (Irish Gaelic) 'castle'. This resort on the north ANTRIM coast, called *Baile na Chaistil* in Irish, takes its name from the castle that once stood in the old town here.

Ballycastle (Mayo) 'Homestead by the cashel'. *Baile* (Irish Gaelic) 'homestead'; *caiseal* (Irish Gaelic) 'cashel' or circular round fort. The name of this small seaside town, north of BALLINA, although the same as the Antrim Ballycastle in English, is derived slightly differently through its Irish root. *Compare* CASHEL.

Ballyclare (Antrim) 'The road of the plain'. *Bealach* (Irish Gaelic) 'road', 'pass': *clar* (Irish Gaelic) 'plain'. On the 'road', halfway between ANTRIM and LARNE, this town is situated on relatively low-lying land south of the Antrim Plateau. Its current Irish name, *Bealach Clair*, confirms the above derivation, rather than one with the more common meaning of the *Baile*-'homestead' first element.

Ballyjamesduff (Cavan) 'James Duff's town'. *Baile* (Irish Gaelic) 'town'; *James Duff* (English personal name) an

English officer who fought in Ireland during the Rising of 1798. This small town, southeast of CAVAN, would appear to have had an association of some kind with this soldier. The Irish name is *Baile Sheamais Dhuibh*.

Ballymena (Antrim) 'The middle town'. *Baile* (Irish Gaelic) 'town'; *meanach* (Irish Gaelic) 'middle'. This major town of Northern Ireland is situated on broad lowlands in the centre of ANTRIM, and in consequence is at the meeting of many roads. In Irish it is *An Baile Meanach*.

Ballymoney (Antrim) 'Homestead of the thicket'. *Baile* (Irish Gaelic) 'homestead', 'town'; *muine* (Irish Gaelic) 'thicket', 'shrubbery'. Alternatively, it could mean 'homestead of the moor': *monaidh* (Irish Gaelic) 'moor'. Both of these Gaelic derivations have been attributed to this small town to the southeast of COLERAINE, and either could have been appropriate to the situation of the original settlement.

Ballynahinch (Down) 'Homestead of the island'. *Baile* (Irish Gaelic) 'homestead'; *na* (Irish Gaelic) 'of the'; *inis* (Irish Gaelic) 'island'. In the case of this small town, south of BELFAST, the 'island' in its name was probably a significant area of originally higher and therefore drier land between streams, rather than an island in the middle of a river as such. The current Irish name is *Baile na Hinse*.

Ballyshannon (Donegal) Place at the 'ford-mouth of the hillside'. *Beal* (Irish Gaelic) 'mouth'; *atha* (Irish Gaelic) 'ford'; *seanaidh* (Irish Gaelic) 'hillside'. The name of this town does not have anything to do with the River SHANNON, as might be expected. It does, however, reflect well the town's hilly location near DONEGAL Bay and at the last fordable point of the short section of the River ERNE, flowing out of Lough Erne. The *on* ending is a later corruption, and the local pronunciation of 'Ballyshanny' is nearer the original.

Balmoral (Grampian) Probably 'homestead in the big clearing'. *Baile* (Scottish Gaelic) 'homestead', 'settlement'; *mor* (Scottish Gaelic) 'big'; *ial* (Brythonic Celtic) 'clearing' . Some authorities consider such a mixture of Scottish Gaelic and Brythonic Celtic root elements as being unconvincing here for this Royal Deeside village.

Balquhidder (Central) Apparently 'settlement of fodder'. *Baile* (Scottish Gaelic) 'homestead', 'hamlet'; *foidir* (corrupt Gaelic form of Old Norse *fothr*) 'fodder'. This traditional, long, straggling Highland clachan north-west of CALLANDER has long been associated with cattle rearing. Pronounced 'Balwhidder'.

Baltinglass (Wicklow) 'The road of Cúglas'. *Bealach* (Irish Gaelic) 'road', 'pass'; *Chonglais* (Irish Gaelic personal name, derived from *Cú-ghlas* meaning 'grey hound') of whom there is a very ancient legend. This small town in the Slaney valley, where there is a ruined 12th-century Cistercian abbey, has a name whose origin is much earlier and signifies its strategic position 'on the road' that follows the course of the River Slaney to ENNISCORTHY and eventually to WEXFORD. The current name is the result of an anglised corruption.

Bamburgh (Northumberland) 'Bebba's stronghold'. *Bebba* (Old English personal name) queen of King Aethelfrith (593-617); *burh* (Old English) 'fortified stronghold'. This coastal resort opposite the FARNE ISLANDS, famous for its associations with St Aidan and the heroine Grace Darling, is dominated by a large Norman castle on an elevated site that was the ancient seat of the early kings of Northumbria. It is cited in an 8th-century Latin text as *Bebbanburge*.

Banbridge (Down) Simply, 'bridge over the Bann'. The name of this town midway between NEWRY and LISBURN reflects its location on the River Bann. The river name here has an ancient root and may mean 'goddess', and as such could be related to the River BANDON.

Banbury (Oxfordshire) 'Bana's stronghold'. *Bana* (Old English personal name) unidentified; *byrig* (Old English dative of *burh*) 'fortified stronghold'. This market town north of OXFORD, best known for its celebrated cross and cakes, dates back to early Saxon times, but there is no evidence for a 'fort'. *Bansberie* was recorded in 1086.

Banchory (Grampian) 'Mountain place'. *Beann* (Scottish Gaelic) 'mountain', 'peak'; *achar* (Scottish Gaelic elision of *achadh*) 'place'. Although this small town lies on the valley floor of Royal Deeside, it is surrounded by high hills.

Bandon (Cork) This town lying to the southwest of CORK, takes its name from the river on which it stands. The river name is believed to derive from an ancient Celtic root meaning 'goddess'. *See* BANBRIDGE.

Banff (Grampian) The origins of this ancient coastal Royal burgh's name remain a mystery. Some authorities have suggested 'land left fallow for a year': *banbh* (Scottish Gaelic). Others have made the tentative connection with a Gaelic poetic word for Ireland: *Banba*. Alternatively, there may be more possibility in the derivation of *banbh* (Irish Gaelic) 'piglet'. This also may have been a pre-Celtic name once given to the river here, now called the Deveron. Medieval documents record the development of the name form: *Banb* 1150; *Banef* 1160; *Bamphe* 1290; *Banffe* 1291.

Bangor (Gwynedd; Down) 'The upper row of rods in a wattle fence'. *Bangor* (Old Welsh) ditto, or commonly 'a monastery', these terms possibly being associated in that the early monastic buildings were almost certainly wattle constructed. In any event, the Welsh town, at the eastern mainland end of the MENAI Strait, has its origin in the 6th century as a the oldest monastic foundation in the British Isles apart from WHITHORN. The Irish Bangor, at the north end of the ARDS PENINSULA, was established as a daughter monastery shortly afterwards.

Bannockburn (Central) 'Little shining stream'. *Ban* (Brythonic Celtic) 'shining', 'fair', 'white'; *ock* (Brythonic

Celtic diminutive) 'little'; *burn* (Middle English) 'stream'. This village, now a southern suburb of STIRLING, stands on the banks of the Bannock Burn, which was the site of the famous battle in 1314, when the Scots, led by Robert the Bruce, routed the English army.

Banstead (Surrey) 'Bean place'. *Bean* (Old English) 'bean'; *stede* (Old English) 'place'. This satellite town on the southern edge of the LONDON conurbation was presumably originally a favoured site where beans grew. It is noted in the Domesday Book of 1086 as *Benestede.*

Bantry (Cork) Place of 'Beann's people'. *Beanntrai* (Irish Gaelic tribal name) 'Beann's people'. This town near the head of the renownedly beautiful bay of the same name is probably called after Beann, reputedly one of the sons of Conor Mac Nessa, king of ULSTER in the 1st century. A part of the tribe settled in WEXFORD, and the other part here in County CORK, where their name is retained in these places. Alternatively, some prefer the derivation: *Beann-traigh* (Irish Gaelic) 'headland-shore', which aptly describes the location.

Barking (Greater London) Place of 'Berica's people'. *Berica* (Old English personal name); *ingas* (Old English suffix) 'people of'. This town north of DAGENHAM, with which it now forms a Greater LONDON borough, was first settled in early Saxon times as records show: *Berecingas* 695; *Bercingum* 730; *Berchinges* 1086.

Barlinnie (Strathclyde) 'Hilltop by the pool'. *Barr* (Scottish Gaelic) 'summit', 'top'; *linne* (Scottish Gaelic) 'pool'. An eastern suburb of GLASGOW, it is (in)famous for its prison, which also bears the name that aptly describes its location on top of one of the city's many drumlin hills and close to Hogganfield Loch, both geographical features left after the retreat of the last Ice Age glaciers.

Barmouth (Gwynedd) 'Mouth of the River Mawddach'. *Bar* (anglicised corruption of Old Welsh *aber*) 'river mouth'; *Mawdd* (Old Welsh personal come river name assimilated to English *mouth*). The name of this resort on the north side of the Mawddach estuary on CARDIGAN Bay is a English corruption of *Abermawaddach* officially adopted in 1768. Its Welsh name *Abermo* (often colloquially clipped to just Bermo) confirms this derivation.

Barnard Castle (Durham) This fortified market town, west of DARLINGTON, was rebuilt in 1112 by the Norman baron Bernard de Balliol to guard the crossing of the River Tees here. *Castellum Bernardi* was cited in 1200.

Barnes (Greater London) Place of the 'barn(s)'. *Bere-aern* (Old English) literally 'barley building', 'barn'. This district of the borough of Richmond upon Thames was evidently in early times the site of riverside barns upstream of the old City of LONDON. Records show: *Berne* 939 and 1086; *Bernes* 1222.

Barnet (Greater London) 'Burnt place'. *Baernet* (Old English) 'land cleared by burning'. This borough of north LONDON, which includes the several districts bearing the same basic name but with distinguishing affixes (**Chipping Barnet**; **East Barnet**; **Friern Barnet**; **High Barnet**; **New Barnet**), was the scene of early major woodland clearing by burning. Many of the names of neighbouring districts confirm the former widespread presence of woodlands in the area (BOREHAMWOOD; FINCHLEY; Hadley Wood; WALTHAM FOREST; Wood Green, etc). Recorded as *Bernet* and *Barnet* in 1196.

Barnsley (South Yorkshire) 'Beorn's woodland clearing'. *Beorn* (Old English personal name); *leah* (Old English) 'woodland clearing'. The name of this now coal-mining and industrial town north of SHEFFIELD was recorded in the Domesday Book of 1086 as *Bernslai*.

Barnstaple (Devon) Place of the 'bearded post'. *Beard* (Old English) 'besom'; *stapol* (Old English) 'post'. The name of this market town at the head of the Taw estuary in north DEVON evidently refers to the ancient custom of erecting a post marked with a besom as a landmark or, more likely here, a seamark for approaching ships. Records show: *Beardastapol* 979; *Barnestaple* 1086.

Barra (Western Isles) 'Isle of St Barr'. Although as Bishop of Cork, St Barr (*c*.560-615) never travelled out of Ireland, missionaries from his much-respected monastery carried his fame to many parts of northern Scotland, and there are the ruins of a church dedicated to him on this island at Cille-bharra.

Barrhead (Strathclyde) 'Hilltop'. *Barr* (Scottish Gaelic) 'summit', 'top'; *head* (Middle English) 'summit', 'top'. Thus the name of this industrial town on the outer southwestern edge of the Greater GLASGOW conurbation is really a tautology. This appears somewhat suprising as the original village was only founded as late as in the 1770s. Not situated on a hilltop, it lies in a valley between two lofty moorlands, which might be a clue to the doubled meaning.

Barrow-in-Furness (Cumbria) Place by the 'island off the rump-shaped promontory'. *Barro* (Celtic root word) 'headland'; *ey* (Old Norse) 'island'; *futh* (Old Norse genitive *-ar*) 'rump'; *nes* (Old Norse) 'promontory'. Both the basic name and distinguishing affix of this port and shipbuilding town describe its promontory location opposite the Isle of WALNEY. Documents of the 12th century record both *Barrai* and *Fuththernessa*.

Barry (South Glamorgan) 'The hill place'. *Barr* (Old Welsh) 'hill'. This resort southwest of CARDIFF, mainly developed in the 19th century as a coal-exporting port, takes its name from the small 'hilly' so-called Barry Island that lies in front of it. Its Welsh form is *Barri*.

Barton-upon-Humber (Humberside) 'Barley farm by the Humber'. *Bere* (Old English) 'barley'; *tun* (Old English) 'farm'. This small town at the south end of the Humber Bridge has a basic name that is common in the grain-growing counties of eastern and southern England, and hence the later distinguishing affix. It was recorded as *Bertone* in the Domesday Book of 1086. *See* HUMBER.

Basildon (Essex) Probably 'Beorhtel's hill'. *Beorhtel* (Old English personal name): *dun* (Old English) 'hill'. This name of the New Town designated in 1947 and the surrounding administrative district set up in 1974 on the north bank of the THAMES estuary, has an ancient Anglo-Saxon origin. It appears in the Domesday Book of 1086 as *Berlesduna* and in 1194 as *Bert(h)lesdon*.

Basingstoke (Hampshire) 'Secondary settlement' or 'outlying farm of Basa's people'. *Basa* (Old English personal name); *ingas* (Old English) 'people of'; *stoc* (Old English) 'secondary settlement'. Lying northeast of WINCHESTER, this town possibly derives its name from the early Anglo-Saxon feudal tenanting of secondary fiefs that often would retain an element of the title of the principal place or seat of the landowner. In this case the latter was Basing, a village now an eastward extension of the main town, called Old Basing. The town's name was recorded as *Basingastoc* in 990.

Bassenthwaite (Cumbria) 'Bastun's clearing'. *Bastun* (Middle English personal name); *thveit* (Old Norse) 'clearing' or 'meadow'. The northernmost and only so-called 'lake' in the LAKE DISTRICT is named after the village near its northeast shore; 13th-century records show *Bastunwater* and *Bastunthuait* respectively.

Bath (Avon) Place at 'the baths'. *Baeth* (Old English in dative plural form) 'the baths'. Thus the name of this city southeast of BRISTOL simply refers to the famous spa founded here by the Romans in AD44 as *Aquae Sulis*, meaning 'waters of the Celtic goddess Sulis'. Early records include: *Bathum* 796; *Bade* 1086 (Domesday Book).

Bathgate (Lothian) 'Boar wood' or 'House in the wood'. Recorded in the 12th century as *Batket*, the meaning of the name of the town, southwest of LINLITHGOW,is not what it first seems today. *Baedd* (Brythonic Celtic) 'boar'; *coed* (Brythonic Celtic) 'wood'. According to some authorities, the first element could be derived as *bod* (Brythonic Celtic) 'house'.

Batley (West Yorkshire) 'Bata's woodland clearing'. *Bata* (Old English personal name); *leah* (Old English) 'woodland clearing'. This woollen textiles town southwest of LEEDS was in what was originally a heavily wooded area, as the '-wood' and '-ley' ending names of many of the neighbouring places testify. The entry in the Domesday Book of 1086 is *Bathelie*.

Battersea (Greater London) 'Beaduric's island'. *Beaduric* (Old English personal name); *eg* (Old English) 'island'. Originally the name of this district of WANDSWORTH probably would have had the sense of a slightly elevated and hence drier area amongst the then marshes of the low-lying land here on the south bank of the Thames, rather than a river island as such. It was recorded as *Badriceseg* in 693, and misrecorded as *Patricesy* in the Domesday Book of 1086.

Battle (East Sussex) Place of 'the battle'. *Bataile* (Old French) 'battle'. This village 5 miles (8 km) northwest of HASTINGS has a name that means exactly what it says, for this is the site of William the Conqueror's famous victory in the Norman invasion of England in 1066, which was commemorated by the founding of the Abbey of St Martins here in 1094. Eight years earlier the entry in the Domesday Book had recorded the name in its Norman French form of *La batailge*.

Bayswater (Greater London) 'Bayard's' or "Bayards' watering place'. Thus a document of 1380 referred to this district of the City of WESTMINSTER, denoting the presence here in pre-urban days of the Westbourne River, across which passed the main road to OXFORD. The 'Bayards' may represent a Norman French personal name, but more likely it simply means bay horses.

Beachy Head (East Sussex) 'Fine headland'. *Beau chef* (Old French) 'beautiful headland'. The spectacular chalk headland at the eastern end of the South DOWNS was thus appreciated by early Norman sailors who gave it this name; the 'Head' was unnecessarily added later.

Beaconsfield (Buckinghamshire) 'Open land near a signal fire site'. *Beacon* (Old English) 'signal fire'; *feld* (Old English) 'open land'. This town southeast of HIGH WYCOMBE is reasonably close to Beacon Hill to its north. In a document of 1185 it was *Bekensfelde*.

Bealach na Ba (Highland) 'Pass of the Cattle'. Simply *Bealach* (Scottish Gaelic) 'pass' (between mountains); *na* (Scottish Gaelic) 'of the'; *ba* (Scottish Gaelic) 'cattle'. This scenic but tortuous pass, rising steeply from sea level to over 2000 ft (600 m) on the APPLECROSS peninsula, was in the past one of the Highland drove roads along which cattle were driven to the market trysts.

Beaminster (Dorset) 'Large church associated with a woman called Bebbe'. *Bebbe* (Old English personal name); *ing* (Old English connective particle) 'associated with'; *mynster* (Old English) 'large church'. The name of this small town north of BRIDPORT was recorded as *Bebingmynster* in 872.

Bearsden (Strathclyde) This satellite residential town developed to the northwest of GLASGOW in Victorian times has a deceptively difficult name to explain. Apparently, it was named after a house built near the local railway station in 1863.

Beattock (Dumfries and Galloway) Probably 'sharp-topped (hills)'. *Biodach* (Scottish Gaelic) 'sharp-topped'. The village is well known for Beattock Summit, over which passes the main Glasgow to London road and rail links.

Beaufort (Gwent) This town at the head of the EBBW VALE is named after the Duke of Beaufort who was the landowner here in the late 18th century. Its Welsh name, *Cendl*, is a rendering of the surname of Edward Kendall, an ironmaster who acquired a lease here in 1780.

Beaulieu (Hampshire) 'Beautiful place'. *Beau* (Old French) 'beautiful'; *lieu* (Old French) 'place'. This aptly named village at the head of the Beaulieu estuary south of SOUTHAMPTON, best known today for the National Motor Museum set up here by Lord Montagu in 1952, originally had a Royal connection, as manifest in its Latin description as *Bellus Locus Regis*, recorded in a text of 1205. *Compare* BEAULY; BEWDLEY.

Beauly (Highland) 'Beautiful Place'. *Beau* (Old French) 'beautiful'; *lieu* (Old French) 'place'. *Compare* BEAULIEU in Hampshire. It is recorded in 1230 as *Prioratus de Bello Loco* (Latin) 'priory of the lovely spot', with reference to the then newly founded eccesiastical establishment here.

Beaumaris (Gwynedd) 'The fine marsh'. *Beau* (Old French) 'fine'; *marais* (Old French) 'marsh'. The origin of this ANGLESEY resort's name is said to refer to the suitability of the low-lying site by the shore here for the building of its castle in 1293 by Edward I, who is supposed to have called it 'Beau marais'. Even if the latter claim is suspect, the basic sense of this derivation remains correct.

Bebington (Merseyside) 'Estate associated with a woman called Bebbe'. *Bebbe* (Old English personal name); *ing* (Old English connective particle) 'associated with'; *tun* (Old English) 'estate', 'farmstead'. The name of this town south of BIRKENHEAD was recorded as *Bebinton* in around 1100. *Compare* BEAMINSTER.

Beccles (Suffolk) 'Pasture by a stream'. *Bece* (Old English) 'stream', 'beck'; *laes* (Old English) 'pasture', 'meadow land'. This small market town, lying on the River Waveney west of LOWESTOFT, had the very similar form of *Becles* recorded in the Domesday Book of 1086.

Beddgelert (Gwynedd) 'Celert's grave'. *Bedd* (Welsh) 'grave'; *Celert* (Old Welsh personal name) someone of note, but unidentified. However the name of this mountain resort, lying on the south side of the SNOWDON range, has traditionally been associated with the legend that here is the supposed grave of Gelert, the faithful dog of Prince Llewellyn, killed by him by mistake. It was recorded as *Bedkelert* in 1281.

Bedford (Bedfordshire) 'Bieda's ford'. *Bieda* or *Beda*

(Old English personal name); *ford* (Old English) 'river crossing'. This county town, lying on the Great Ouse river north of LONDON and midway between CAMBRIDGE and NORTHAMPTON, was established as an early nodal and river crossing point, and records show: the town name *Bedanford* 880; the county name *Bedanfordscir* 1011.

Bedwas (Mid Glamorgan) 'Birch-tree grove'. *Bedguas* (Old Welsh) 'Birches'. This 19th-century coal-mining town in the Rhymney Valley just northeast of CAERPHILLY was developed where, presumably, birch had been the natural tree cover.

Bedworth (Warwickshire) 'Beada's enclosure'. *Beada* or *Beda* (Old English personal name); *worth* (Old English) 'enclosure'. The simple name of this town, situated between COVENTRY and NUNEATON, was recorded in the Domesday Book of 1086 as *Bedeword*.

Beeston (Nottinghamshire) 'Farmstead where the bent-grass grows'. *Beos* (Old English) 'bent-grass': *tun* (Old English) 'farmstead', 'settlement'. This fairly common English placename applies to this now manufacturing town, immediately southwest of NOTTINGHAM, by the low-lying valley of the River TRENT, which probably was a good source of bent-grass for thatching in early times. The Domesday Book entry of 1086 is *Bestune*.

Beith (Strathclyde) 'The place of the birch tree'. *Beithe* (Scottish Gaelic) 'birch tree'. Thus this small town southwest of PAISLEY has a simple name derivation.

Belcoo (Fermanagh) 'The mouth of the narrows'. *Beal* (Irish Gaelic) 'mouth'; *caol* (Irish Gaelic) 'narrows'. This village to the west of ENNISKILLEN and on the border with the Republic of Ireland, derives its name from the Irish description of its location on the narrow isthmus between Upper and Lower Loughs Macnean.

Belfast (Antrim) 'Mouth of the sandbank'. *Beal* (Irish Gaelic) 'mouth'; *fearsad* (Irish Gaelic) 'sandbank'. The name of the capital city of NORTHERN IRELAND reflects the importance of an ancient ford crossing point of the tidal River LAGAN, made possible by the presence of a sandbank formed at the mouth of its Farset tributary (of same derivation). The Irish name is *Beal Feirste*.

Belgravia (Greater London) This stately, opulent district of Central LONDON, spaciously laid out in the Regency period by its landowner, the Duke of Westminster, takes its name from his Belgrave estate in CHESHIRE. The original name, as also evidenced in the former village and now northern suburb of LEICESTER, was recorded in the Domesday Book as *Merdegrave*, which derives: *mearth* + *graf* (Old English) 'weasel grove', but because it was associated with *merde* (Old French) 'faeces', 'filth', 'dung', the first element was replaced by the more desirable opposite: *bel* (Old French) 'fine'.

Bellahouston (Strathclyde) 'Settlement of the crucifix'. *Baile* (Scottish Gaelic) 'settlement', 'hamlet'; *cheusadain* (Scottish Gaelic) 'crucifix'. Although now a southside suburb of GLASGOW, it is assumed that the original place manifested a holy cross in some form.

Belleek (Fermanagh) 'Ford-mouth of flagstones'. *Beal* (Irish Gaelic) 'mouth'; *leac* (Irish gaelic) 'flagstone'. The name of this border village, which is synonymous with the distinctive porcelain produced here, lies east of BALLYSHANNON on the River ERNE, at a point where it broadens into a narrow estuary and where also the stones on the river bed were noticably flat.

Belper (Derbyshire) 'Beautiful retreat'. *Beau* (Old French) 'beautiful'; *repaire* (Old French) 'retreat'. The present-day form of the name of this industrial town north of DERBY disguises its origins, which would have been associated with the naming of an Anglo-Norman estate here in the once very attractive valley of the River Derwent. It was recorded as *Beurepeir* in 1231.

Belvoir, Vale of (Leicestershire) 'Beautiful view'. *Beau* (Old French) 'beautiful'; *vedeir* (Old French) 'view'. This broad valley east of GRANTHAM, associated with hunting and coalmines, is named after the nearby

11th-century Belvoir Castle of William I's standard bearer. Pronounced 'Beaver', it was noted as *Belveder* in 1130.

Bembridge (Isle of Wight) Place lying 'within the bridge'. *Binnan* (Old English) 'within'; *brycg* (Old English) 'bridge'. This somewhat curious derivation becomes clearer on examination of the location of this sailing resort at the extreme eastern tip of the island, where it is on a peninsula virtually cut off by the River Yar but for a bridge on the main route into the town. A record of 1316 gives it as *Bynnebrygg*.

Ben Lomond *see* **Lomond**

Ben Nevis *see* **Nevis**

Benagher (Offaly) Place of the 'pointed rocks'. *Beannchar* (Irish Gaelic) 'horns', 'pointed rocks' or 'hills'. In the case of this town, lying in the low central plain of Ireland, it is said to be a reference to the sharp rocks to be found here in the River SHANNON.

Benbecula (Western Isles) 'Hill of the salt-water fords'. *Beinn* (Scottish Gaelic) 'hill', 'mountain', 'peak'; *na* (Scottish Gaelic) 'of the'; *faoghail* (adapted Scottish Gaelic form of *fadhail*) 'salt-water ford'. Alternatively, the last element may have been *faoghlach* (Scottish Gaelic) 'strand', 'beach'. Both these possible derivations are appropriate to this low-lying island which, until earlier this century, could be reached on foot only by fording the sand banks, exposed at low tide, that divide its generally flat plain of lochs (*machair*) from North and South UIST; the only feature rising above the flat bog is the hill of Rueval (410 ft/124 m). The name is recorded in early documents as: *Beanbeacla* 1495; *Benvalgha* 1549; *Benbicula* 1660.

Benbulbin (Sligo) 'Gulban's peak'. *Beann* (Irish Gaelic) 'peak', 'horned-hill'; *Gulbain* (Irish Gaelic personal name) unidentified. This spectacular tabletop mountain to the north of SLIGO, with its truncated craggy slopes, is steeped in legend and is particularly renowned as the place where the great Celtic folklore champion Finn mac Cool exacted revenge on Dermot, who had eloped with his intended bride Grania.

Bentley (South Yorkshire) 'Woodland clearing where bent-grass grows'. *Beonet* (Old English) 'bent-grass'; *leah* (Old English) 'woodland clearing'. This northern suburb of DONCASTER has a common name that reflects the importance of bent-grass as both livestock feed and thatching material in early times. This Bentley was recorded as *Benedleia* in 1086. *Compare* Beeston.

Berkeley (Gloucestershire) 'Birch-tree clearing or wood'. *Beorc* (Old English) 'birch tree'; *leah* (Old English) 'clearing', 'wood'. This name, associated with the 12th-century Berkeley Castle and the Vale of Berkeley, which are situated on the east side of the upper SEVERN estuary, was recorded as *Berclea* in 824, and *Berchelai* in the Domesday Book of 1086.

Berkhamsted (Hertfordshire) Either 'homestead on a hill' or 'homestead where birch trees grow'. *Beorg* (Old English) 'hill'; or *beorc* (Old English) 'birch tree'; and *ham-stede* (Old English) 'homestead'. The name of this town northwest of LONDON was recorded as *Beorchthanstaedae* in the 10th century and *Berchehamstede* in the *Domesday Book* of 1086.

Berkshire (England) Possibly 'hilly place'. *Barro* (Brythonic Celtic root word) 'hill'; *scir* (Old English) 'district', 'shire'. The name of this English 'shire' county is unusual in not being named after its county town. The origin of its 'Berk' element is clearly ancient and reflects the importance of the 'downs' here as the main area of settlement and trading routes in prehistoric times. It was noted as *Bearruscir* in 860. It is pronounced 'Bark-sher.'

Bermondsey (Greater London) 'Beornmund's island'. *Beornmund* (Old English personal name); *eg* (Old English) 'island'. The 'island' in the name of this district of SOUTHWARK on the south bank of the THAMES refers to an area of drier land in former riverside marshes here.

Bermundesye was recorded in the *Domesday Book* of 1086. *Compare* Battersea.

Berwick-upon-Tweed (Northumberland) 'Barley farmstead'. *Bere* (Old English) 'barley'; *wic* (Old English) 'farm,' often on an outlying part of a manorial estate. This northernmost town of ENGLAND, was once a great port of SCOTLAND, and as a much-besieged and often fought for 'border outpost' it changed hands 13 times before becoming English territory in 1482. Its common name was recorded simply as *Berewich* in 1167, but 20 years later it was documented as *Suthberwyc*, presumably as a distinction from NORTH BERWICK in LOTHIAN. Its current suffixed form was first noted as *Berewicum super Twedam* in a Latin text of 1229 . *See* TWEED.

Bessbrook (Armagh) This 19th-century 'garden city' northwest of NEWRY took its name from that of an early 1800s house belonging to a local linen manufacturer, John Pollock, who called it Bess Brook after his wife, Elizabeth, and the stream by which he had it built.

Bethesda (Gwynedd) 'House of mercy'. The name of this slate-quarrying town southeast of BANGOR is Biblical in origin, referring to the pool in Jerusalem where Jesus healed the sick. There was a tradition of Welsh chapels being named after such Biblical associations, and in this case a much expanded 19th-century town arose around a Calvinistic Methodist Bethesda Chapel established here in 1820 on a site formerly known as *Y Wern Uchaf*, meaning 'the upper marshland'.

Bethnal Green (Greater London) Probably 'Blitha's nook'. *Blith-an* (Old English personal name-genitive form); *halh* (Old English) 'nook of land'. Alternatively, the basic name of this district of LONDON's 'East End' may derive from *blithe* (Old English river name) meaning 'the gentle one'. Recorded in the 13th century simply as *Blithehale*, it later added *grene* (Old English) for 'village green', to become *Blethenalegrene* in 1443.

Bettyhill (Highland) Named after Elizabeth, Countess of Sutherland, this village was set up on the north coast of Scotland in about 1820 as an agricultural and fishing centre to provide housing and work for some of those evicted during the Highland 'Clearances'.

Betws-y-Coed (Gwynedd) 'Oratory in the wood'. *Betws* (Welsh adaptation of Middle English *bed-hus*) 'oratory'; *y* (Welsh) 'in the'; *coed* (Welsh) 'wood'. This popular tourist resort set in the wooded upper CONWAY valley near the famed Swallow Falls, was originally just called *Betus*, to which various suffixes were added until the current form was adopted in the 18th century.

Beverley (Humberside) 'Beaver stream'. *Beofor* (Old English) 'beaver'; *laecc* (Old English) 'stream', 'bog'. Thus the name of this historic minster town north of HULL has its origins in a former watercourse here that was frequented by beavers. Records show: *Beferlic* *c.*1025; *Bevreli* 1086 (Domesday Book.)

Bewdley (Hereford and Worcester) 'Beautiful place'. *Beau* (Old French) 'beautiful'; *lieu* (Old French) 'place'. This SEVERN town west of KIDDERMINSTER has the same origin as BEAULIEU and was noted as *Beuleu* in 1275.

Bexhill (East Sussex) 'Box-tree wood or clearing'. *Byxe* (Old English) 'box tree'; *leah* (Old English) 'wood', 'clearing'. The suggestion of a 'hill' in the name of this low-lying residential coastal resort is a misnomer, as can be witnessed from early records: *Bixlea* 772: *Bexelei* 1086 (Domesday Book). *See* BEXLEY.

Bexley (Greater London) 'Box-tree wood or clearing'. *Byxe* (Old English) 'box tree'; *leah* (Old English) 'wood', 'clearing'. This former village and current borough of southeast LONDON has a straightforward derivation of the same origin as BEXHILL; it was recorded as *Byxlea* in 814. The name is also manifest locally in the more recent district name of **Bexleyheath**.

Bicester (Oxfordshire) Probably Roman camp by the burial ground'. *Byrgen* (Old English) 'tumulus'; *ceaster* (Old English) 'Roman fortified settlement'. According to one authority, the first element in the name of this historic town north of OXFORD derives as *beorn* (Old

English) for 'warriors', or it may represent a personal name such as *Beorna* from this same root. *Berenecestre* is the entry in the Domesday Book of 1086.

Biddulph (Staffordshire) 'By the quarry'. *Bi* (Old English) 'by'; *dylf* (Old English) 'diggings', 'pit', 'quarry'. This coal-mining and industrial town north of STOKE-ON-TRENT was established by an early diggings in an area that is still quarried and mined. The Domesday Book record of 1086 shows *Bidolf*.

Bideford (Devon) Possibly 'Bieda's ford'. *Bieda* (Old English personal name) unidentified; *ford* (Old English) 'river crossing'. This market town and port to the southwest of BARNSTAPLE is located at the original lowest crossing point on the River Torridge. The name appears as *Bedeford* in the Domesday Book of 1086.

Biggar (Strathclyde) 'Barley field'. *Bygg* (Old Norse) 'barley'; *garthr* (Old Norse) 'enclosure'. Alternatively, the latter part of the name of this small market toen, southeast of LANARK, may be the more specific *geiri* (Old Norse) 'triangular plot'. Early records include: *Bigir*; *Begart*.

Biggin Hill (Greater London) 'Hill with a building'. *Bigging* (Middle English) 'building'; *hyll* (Old English) 'hill'. This famous World War II air base village is located on the North DOWNS southwest of CROYDON.

Biggleswade (Bedfordshire) 'Biccel's ford'. *Biccel* (Old English personal name); *waed* (Old English) 'ford'. The name of this small town southeast of BEDFORD would seem to have been misrecorded in the Domesday Book in 1086 as *Pichelesuuade*, but in 1132 it appeared in a text as *Bichekeswada*.

Billericay (Essex) Probably 'the tannery'. *Bellerica* (Medieval Latin) 'tanhouse', 'dyehouse'. The name of this town east of BRENTWOOD, which in recent times has had the curious notoriety of often being the first declared seat in a General Election, has itself for long been a toponymical curiosity, and it was only a few years ago that the above plausible explanation was proposed by an authority in this field. The name was recorded as *Billerika* in 1313, and *Billerica* in 1343.

Billinge (Merseyside) Probably 'sword-like hill'. *Billing* (Old English derived from *bill*, a sword) 'hill'. This former coal-mining town southwest of WIGAN would appear to take its name from the ridge-like Billinge Hill here. Several 13th-century records indicate the name as *Billing*.

Billingham (Cleveland) Possibly 'village associated with a man called Billa'. *Billa* (Old English personal name); *ing* (Old English connective particle) 'associated with'; *ham* (Old English) 'village', 'homestead'. This Teesside industrial town northwest of MIDDLESBROUGH, noted for its large chemicals complex, was recorded in early pre-urban times as having the same name form as now. As with BILLINGE, an alternative derivation for the first elements may be *billing* (Old English) 'hill'.

Bingley (West Yorkshire) 'Woodland clearing of Bynna's people'. *Bynna* (Old English personal name); *ingas* (Old English) 'people of'; *leah* (Old English) 'woodland clearing'. This woollen textiles and engineering town lies northwest of BRADFORD in Airedale, the valley through which runs the LEEDS AND LIVERPOOL CANAL. Its name was recorded as *Bingelei* in 1086.

Birkenhead (Merseyside) 'Headland overgrown with birch'. *Bircen* (Old English genitive) 'birch tree'; *heafor* (Old English) 'headland', 'promontory'. The name of this industrial port situated on the WIRRAL peninsula opposite LIVERPOOL, although Old English in origin, shows Scandinavian influences in the use of the hard *k* rather than the softer *ch* found in some earlier forms: *Byrkhed c.*1100; *Birkenhed c.*1150; *Bircheuet* 1260.

Birmingham (West Midlands) Homestead of Beorma's people'. *Beorma* (Old English personal name); *ingas* (Old English) 'people of'; *ham* (Old English) 'homestead', 'village'. Although today Birmingham is BRITAIN's second largest city, and located at the heart of ENGLAND, its name has an ordinary and relatively humble Anglo-Saxon origin. It was recorded in the Domesday Book of 1086 as *Bermingeham*.

Birnam (Tayside) 'Village of the warrior'. *Beorn* (Old English) 'warrior'; *ham* (Old English) 'homestead', 'hamlet'. The name of this village, on the south bank of the River TAY opposite DUNKELD, shows that in Middle English, *beorn* had mutated to *birn*. Little remains of the Birnam Wood immortalised by Shakespeare in his tragedy about the warrior king *Macbeth*.

Birr (Offaly) 'Watery' place. *Biorra* (Irish Gaelic) 'watery'. The Irish name is appropriate to the situation of this former garrison town lying to the south of ATHLONE in the well-watered central lowlands. *Compare* ANNAT. Founded as a 'plantation town' in 1620, it was originally called Parsonstown, after Sir Thomas Parsons of LEICESTERSHIRE, who had been given the lands here in the 'King's County' by King James I of ENGLAND and IRELAND. *See* OFFALY.

Bishop Auckland *see* **Auckland, Bishop; St Helen; West.**

Bishop's Stortford (Hertfordshire) 'Ford by the tongues of land'. *Steort* (Old English) 'tail', 'tongue of land lying between streams'; *ford* (Old English) 'river crossing'. The ecclesiastic affix of this town, lying on the River Stort north of HARLOW, is an indication of its early possession by the bishops of LONDON. It was recorded as simply *Storteford* in the Domesday Book.

Bishopbriggs (Strathclyde) 'Bishop's lands'. The 'bishop' (English) is presumably 'of nearby GLASGOW'; *riggs* (Scots) 'fields'. The *b* has crept in through confusion with the word *brig* (Scots) 'bridge'. There is no local river of significance, and there was no bridge here until the FORTH and CLYDE canal was constructed (1770-90)—well after the name was established.

Black Isle, The (Highland) This broad and fertile peninsula between the BEAULY and CROMARTY Firths has adopted its (English) descriptive name possibly on account of the fact that when seen from afar this area appears to be almost an island and particularly from the higher land to the west appearing generally darkish.

Black Mountains (Gwent/Powys) This range of hills that lies to the north of ABERGAVENNY and extends over the border into England is so called because it generally appears dark when viewed from afar, especially from the eastern and southern side. *Compare* BLACK ISLE.

Blackburn (Lancashire) Simply, the place of the 'dark-coloured stream'. *Blaec* (Old English) 'dark-coloured', 'black'; *burna* (Old English) 'stream'. This industrial town, that has been associated with cotton weaving since medieval times, lies on the Blackwater stream east of PRESTON. Its uncomplicated name was recorded in 1086 as *Blacheburne*, and *Blakeburn* a century later.

Blackheath (Greater London) 'Dark-coloured heathland'. *Blaec* (Old English) 'dark-coloured', 'black'; *haeth* (Old English) 'heathland'. This district of LEWISHAM is so called after the black peat underlying the heath, part of which is still public 'open land', the latter aspect being added to its 12th-century name, *Blachehedfeld*.

Blackpool (Lancashire) 'Dark-coloured pool'. *Blaec* (Old English) 'dark-coloured'; *pull* (Old English) 'pool'. The name of this famous seaside resort, with its 'Tower' and 'Illuminations', reflects the less glittering site of the early settlement by a dark peaty pool behind the sandy shore of the FLYDE peninsula. As recorded in 1260, its original name was simply Pul, and the current form only came into being early in the 17th century.

Blackrod (Greater Manchester) 'Black clearing'. *Blaec* (Old English) 'black'; *rodu* (Old English) 'clearing'. This former coal-mining and textile town west of BOLTON has a name that presumably reflects the 'blackened' state of the 'clearing' site after the woodland had been burnt. It was recorded in a document of 1201 as *Blakerode*.

Blaenau Ffestiniog (Gwynedd) 'Headwaters and defensive position'. *Blaenau* (Welsh plural of *blaen*) 'headwaters'; *ffestin-iog* (Welsh with adjectival ending) 'defensive position'. This slate-quarrying town, northeast of PORTHMADOG, has a duplex name referring to the village of Ffestiniog some three miles (5 km) to the south. The headwaters of the River Dwyryd rise above Blaenau (as it is locally known) which then flows through Ffestiniog, the latter originally occupying a good strategic site on a hill in the river valley.

Blaenavon (Gwent) 'Head of the river'. *Blaen* (Welsh) 'headwater'; *afon* (Welsh) 'river'. This coal-mining and heavy industrial town is situated at the head of the Afon Lwyd north of PONTYPOOL. The Welsh form of its name is, not surprisingly, *Blaenafon*.

Blair Atholl (Tayside) 'Plain of the New Ireland'. *Blar* (Scottish Gaelic) 'plain', 'level clearing'; *ath* (Scottish Gaelic) 'new', 'second'; *Fhodla* (Scottish Gaelic) poetic name for Ireland, linked with the legendary Irish goddess *Fodla*. Atholl, which still today covers a large tract of the east-central Highlands, was thus at least part of the 'New Ireland' that the original Scots settled in the 5th century. Blair Castle, near the village, has been the seat of the Dukes of Atholl since 1269, and is sited on the most cultivated part of the lands.

Blairgowrie (Tayside) 'Plain of Gabran'. *Blar* (Scottish Gaelic) 'plain', 'level clearing'; the second element *gowrie* (Scottish Gaelic) is an elided form of the personal name Gabran, son of King Fergus, and one of the pioneering Celtic invaders from Ireland in the 6th century, who held the land here. northeast of PERTH.

Blanchardstown (Dublin) This former village, and now a satellite residential area on the northwestern fringes of DUBLIN City, was named after an Anglo-Norman family called Blanchard, who acquired lands here in medieval times.

Blandford Forum (Dorset) Probably 'ford where gudgeon fish are found'. *Blaegna* (Old English genitive plural of blaege) 'gudgeon' or 'blay-fish' often used as bait; *ford* (Old English) 'river crossing'. Thus this ancient 'market' town, as affirmed by the Medieval Latin *Forum* affix, was recognised in early times not only as an important crossing point on the River Stour northwest of POOLE, but also as an anglers' source of bait. It was recorded as *Blaneford* in 1086, and *Blaneford Forum* in 1297. Nearby, satellite villages having the same basic name are distinguished by affixes: **Blandford St Mary** and **Langton Long Blandford**.

Blantyre (Strathclyde) 'Edge-land'. *Blaen* (Brythonic Gaelic) 'edge'; *tir* (Brythonic Gaelic) 'land'. The name of this town south of Glasgow, and famous as the birthplace of the 19th-century explorer David Livingstone, is descriptive of its situation above the steeply incised River CLYDE.

Blarney (Cork) place of 'the small field'. *An* (Irish Gaelic) 'the'; *bhlar-na* (Irish Gaelic with a diminutive suffix) 'little field'. The name of this plain village northwest of CORK is world-famous on account of the 'Blarney Stone' in the castle here, once a MacCarthy stronghold.

Bletchley (Buckinghamshire) 'Blecca's clearing'. *Blecca* (Old English personal name); *leah* (Old English) 'woodland clearing'. This town, located by WATLING STREET at the south end of the MILTON KEYNES New Town, was established as an early 'clearing' settlement in a once heavily forested area, the latter being testified by the many nearby placenames with '-ley' or '-wood' endings. It was recorded as *Blechelai* in the early 13th century.

Bloody Foreland (Donegal) This notable Atlantic headland, the most northwesterly point of Donegal, is so named not in memory of some legendary or real local battle or messy event but simply because of the brilliance of the sunsets here, which can colour the surrounding mountains dramatically golden, if not red, and makes, with the sea strewn with rocks and islands, a magnificent sight.

Bloomsbury (Greater London) 'Fortified manor of the de Blémund family'. *De Blémund* (Anglo-Norman family name); *byrig* (Old English dative of *burh*) 'fortified manor'. The name of this district of CAMDEN, which has literary associations in more recent times, had its origins in the 13th century with the consolidation of Anglo-Norman power; a document of 1281 shows *Blemondiberi*, and by 1335 its form was recorded as *Blemundisbury*.

Blyth (Northumberland) Place of 'the pleasant or cheerful one'. *Blithe* (Old English) 'gentle', 'merry', 'pleasant', 'cheerful'. This small North Sea port northwest of TYNEMOUTH, which expanded greatly during the 19th century coal-exporting boom, takes its name from the River Blyth, at the mouth of which it stands on the south side. Although its name in 1130, *Blida*, consisted of a single element as now, its full river-mouth situation is reflected in its recorded name of 1234 as *Blithmuth* and again in 1250 as *Blithemuth*.

Bo'ness (Central) 'Royal burgh on the promontory'. This officially accepted abbreviated place name is a contraction of Borrowstounness, from *Borrowstoun* (Scots) 'Royal burgh'; *naes* (Old Engish) 'promontory'. It is an apt description for this long-established coastal Royal burgh, which is situated on a headland protruding into the Firth of FORTH.

Boat of Garten (Highland) The somewhat odd name for this village, which is situated well inland, is explained as the place of a ferryboat crossing of the River Spey, close to its confluence with the tributary River Garten. The need for the ferry was ended in 1898 when a bridge was built here.

Bodmin (Cornwall) Probably 'house of the monks'. *Bod* (Old Cornish) 'house'; *meneich* (Old Cornish plural of *manach*) 'monks'. The county town of CORNWALL, although TRURO is the main administrative centre, Bodmin is steeply situated on the edge of **Bodmin Moor**, itself named after the town. Its name is said to denote a monastery founded here in the 10th century by King Athelstan and was recorded as *Bodmine* in 975 and in the Domesday Book of 1086.

Bog of Allen (Kildare/Meath/Offaly) Possibly 'peat bed of the little cliff'. *Bogach* (Irish Gaelic) 'swampy/mossy peat bed'; *aillin* (Irish Gaelic) 'little cliff'. This vast ill-defined area of flat bog spanning large parts of three counties in east-central Ireland is a major peat bed created out of the humid decay of mosses, rushes, grasses and trees in the basin of what was once a lake. The specific last element of its name would appear to be a reference to a small cliff that defines the southern edge of this otherwise relatively featureless area. To the north of KILDARE are two villages, one called Allen, the other Allenwood, there being a giant peat-fired power station located at the latter.

Bognor Regis (West Sussex) 'Bucge's landing place on the shore'. *Bucge* (Old English personal name) 'female'; *ora* (Old English) 'shore'. Thus the basic name of this coastal resort, southeast of CHICESTER, has its ancient origins in a Saxon woman's landing place on the shore here, and it was recorded as *Bucganora* as early as 680. The *Regis* (Latin) royal affix was only added earlier this century, after King George V convalesced at the nearby village of Aldwick in 1928.

Bolsover (Derbyshire) Probably 'Boll's scarp'. *Boll* Old English personal name) unidentified; *ofer* (Old English) 'edge', 'slope'. This coal-mining and industrial town, which developed mainly in the 19th century east of CHESTERFIELD, has an ancient name that refers to the prominent escarpment spur immediately east of the town, that also gives rise to the nearby village names of Hills Town and Scarcliffe. However, the first element is obscure, and apart from the possibility of the above personal name, one leading authority has suggested the alternative derivation of *bulan-laes* (Old English) 'bullock pasture'. Records include: *Belesovre* 1086; *Bolesoura* 1167; *Bulesoures* 1197; *Bolesor* 1230.

Bolton (Greater Manchester) 'Village with a special building'. *Bothl* (Old English) 'special building' or 'house'; *tun* (Old English) 'village', 'settlement'. The name of this large industrial town, northwest of MANCHESTER, is a common form in the north of England, and has the implied sense of referring to the village proper as opposed to the outlying parts. It was recorded as *Boelton* in 1135. Other instances of this name form, but with distinguishing affixes, include: **Bolton Abbey** (North Yorkshire); **Bolton-le-Sands** (Lancashire); **Bolton-upon-Dearne** (South Yorkshire).

Bootle (Merseyside) Place of the 'special building'. *Botl* (Old English) 'special building'. This docklands town, adjoining LIVERPOOL to the north and sited at the entrance to the MERSEY estuary, has a name that is similar in origin to that of BOLTON, except in this case the 'special building' may be an outlying one and not necessarily a dwelling house. Records show: *Boltelai* 1086 Domesday Book; *Botle* 1212.

Borders (Scotland) Although since 1975 the 'Borders' name has been officially associated with the most southeastern administrative region in Scotland, the term has long been used to describe the area straddling the border with England. The designation almost certainly originated 'north of the border', there being only one for Scotland, and as such the name has more currency there.

Borehamwood (Hertfordshire) 'Wood of the hill settlement'. *Bor* (Old English) 'hill'; *ham* (Old English) 'homestead'; *wudu* (Old English) 'wood'. The name of this residential satellite town just north of the LONDON conurbation is a back-formation of the local wood name.

Borrowdale (Cumbria) 'River valley of the fort'. *Borgar* (Old Norse genitive of *borg*) 'fort'; *a* (Old Norse) 'river';

dalr (Old Norse) 'valley'. This scenic mountain valley upstream of DERWENT WATER, and in turn the high village near its head, take their name from the Borghra, as the upper Derwent river was originally called after an ancient Iron Age fort site at Castle Crag, last used by the Romano-British tribesmen of the Brigantes federation. *Borgordale* was noted in *c.*1170.

Boston (Lincolnshire) 'Botwulf's stone'. *Botwulf* (Old English personal name) unidentified; *stan* (Old English) 'stone'. The name of this Fenland town and former medieval seaport, southeast of LINCOLN, apparently refers to a boundary marker stone of an early Saxon landowner, and has nothing to do with the 7th-century missionary, St Botolph, whose local tall church tower is the renowned 'Boston Stump'. The famous American city of Boston owes its name to inhabitants from this town who emigrated in 1630. The original name, *Botolfston*, was recorded in 1130.

Bourne (Lincolnshire) Place by 'the stream'. *Burna* (Old English from an earlier form *brunna*) 'stream'. This small town, on the edge of The FENS west of SPALDING, has the singular form of a common English place-name ending that simply reflects a location on a stream, in this case the Bourne Eau. Early records show: *Brunne c.*960; *Brune* 1086; *Brunna* 1138.

Bournemouth (Dorset) 'Mouth of the stream'. *Burna* (Old English) 'stream' *mutha* (Old English) 'mouth'. This large fashionable seaside resort, which owes its development to the coming of the railway in the mid-19th century, has a simple ancient name that was recorded in a Latin text of 1407 as *la Bournemouthe*.

Bournville (West Midlands) This southwestern suburb of BIRMINGHAM, developed as a garden-city estate for the workers of Cadburys' chocolate factory, was given this 'ville' name, which was fashionable when it was founded in 1879.

Bowes (Durham) Place of 'the bend' in the river. *Boga* (Old English) or *bogi* (Old Norse) 'bow', 'bend'. This high village on the crest of the PENNINES, here known as Bowes Moor, probably derives its name from bends in the River Greta that afforded a good defensive site for the now ruined 12th-century Norman keep, which was built where the Roman camp of *Lavartris* had once stood. It was recorded as *Bogas* in 1148; *Bogis* in 1171.

Bowland, Forest of (Lancashire) 'District of bends'. *Boga* (Old English) 'bend'; *land* (Old English) 'district'. The name of this upland area southeast of LANCASTER reflects the twisting nature of the valleys that run between the fells here. *Boelanda* was recorded in 1102.

Bowmore (Strathclyde) Place of the 'big bothy'. *Both* (Scottish Gaelic—silent *th*) 'bothy' (a farm cottage); *mor* (Scottish Gaelic) 'big'. Presumably the name refers to the situation of its site prior to 1767, when the local laird Daniel Campbell founded ISLAY's planned capital here.

Boyle (Roscommon) This town lying to the southeast of SLIGO takes its name from the river on which it stands, the meaning of this river name remaining obscure. The Irish Gaelic name for the town is *Mainistir na Buille*, 'monastery of the Boyle'.

Boyne (Kildare/Offaly/Meath) Probably 'white cow'. *Bo* (Irish Gaelic) 'cow'; *bhán* (Irish Gaelic) 'white'. This river, which flows northeastwards from the BOG OF ALLEN to enter the Irish Sea at DROGHEDA, acts like a running pageant of Irish history. It is associated with many events, but none more famous than the Battle of the Boyne in 1690, when William III defeated the deposed James II.

Brackley (Northamptonshire) 'Bracca's clearing'. *Bracca* (Old English personal name); *leah* (Old English) 'woodland clearing'. The simple name of this small town northwest of BUCKINGHAM was *Brachelai* in 1086.

Bracknell (Berkshire) 'Bracca's nook'. *Bracca-n* (Old English personal name—genitive form); *halh* (Old English) 'nook', 'corner of land'. This New Town, designated in 1949 east of WOKINGHAM, has an ancient name that was documented as *Braccan heal* in 942.

Bradford (West Yorkshire) 'Place at the broad ford'. *Brad* (Old English) broad; *ford* (Old English) 'river crossing'. The best-known example of this common and straightforward English place-name is that of the large city west of LEEDS, which is the centre of the British wool industry, and which was recorded in the Domesday Book of 1086 as *Bradeford*. Many other places so called take a distiguishing affix, such as Bradford-on-Avon (Wiltshire), southeast of BATH; documented in about 900 as *Bradanforda be Afne*.

Braemar (Grampian) 'The upper part of Mar'. *Braighe* (Scottish Gaelic) 'upper part'; the second element, *Mar*, is a personal name of unknown derivation. Early records include: *Bray of Marre* 1560; *Brae of Mar* 1610; *Breamarr* 1682.

Braintree (Essex) 'Branuc's tree'. *Branuc* (Old English personal name); *treow* (Old English) 'tree', 'cross'. This town, northeast of CHELMSFORD, has the common '-tree' or '-try' ending that often signified a meeting place. It was recorded as *Branchetreu* in 1086.

Brampton (Cumbria) 'Farmstead where broom grows'. *Brom* (Old English) 'broom'; *tun* (Old English) 'farmstead', 'village'. This small market town northeast of CARLISLE has a common English place-name, which was recorded in 1169 exactly as now.

Brandon Mountain (Kerry) Ireland's second highest peak, which dramatically rises to 3127 ft (953 m) on the DINGLE peninsula, is named after the adventurous 6th-century pilgrim St Brendan, or Brandon, who had a vision that compelled him to sail the Atlantic in search of God and the Promised Land. He had a retreat on this hill, where the remains of his oratory and cell can still be seen.

Bray (Wicklow) Place of 'the hill'. *Bri* (Irish Gaelic) 'hill'. This sizable resort to the south of DUBLIN is named after the rocky headland, Bray Head, at the south end of the town. It is recorded as *Bree* in early documents.

The name of Bray Head at the tip of VALENTIA Island is similarly derived.

Breadalbane (Central/Grampian/Tayside) 'Upper part of Albyn'. *Braghad* (Scottish Gaelic) 'higher', 'upper part', 'hill district'; *Albainn* (Scottish Gaelic) Scotland (minus ARGYLL). Today Breadalbane is an area name applied to a large tract of the central Highlands lying to the south of ATHOLL.

Brechin (Tayside) 'Brychan's place'. This town, west of MONTROSE, has the personal name of a legendary character who is common to Celtic mythologies (*see* BRECON; WREKIN). In Scottish Gaelic, Brychan may mean 'holy' or 'high' and is related to the Celtic river and tribal name *Brigant*.

Brecon (Powys) 'Brychan's place'. *Brychan* (Old Welsh personal name) 5th-century Welsh prince. An early alternative anglicisation that was commonly used for the town and now retained in the name of the local administrative district is *Brecknock*, derived from the Old Welsh form *Brycheinioc* which manifests the territorial *-ioc* ending. The modern Welsh name for this market town, lying north of 'the valleys' of South Wales, is *Aberhonddu*, which simply describes its location at the confluence of the Honddu and Usk rivers. *Compare* BRECHIN; WREKIN.

Brecon Beacons (Powys) This range of mountains, rising to almost 3000 ft (900m), lie south and southwest of BRECON, after which they take the first part of their name. The 'Beacons' tag is a reference to their use in medieval times as signal fire sites. Their Welsh name, *Bannau Brycheinioc* , means the 'Peaks of Brychan's land'.

Brent (Greater London) Place of 'the almighty one'. *Brigantia* (Brythonic Celtic river name) 'high', 'holy' or 'mighty one'. This LONDON borough northwest of the City of WESTMINSTER takes the name of the THAMES tributary river which flows through it, and which in turn relates to the tribal name Brigantes, the late Iron

Age peoples who occupied northern England. The name was recorded as *Braegente* in 959.

Brentford (Greater London) 'Ford over the River Brent'. The name of this district of HOUNSLOW derives from the same root as BRENT, with the addition of *ford* (Old English) referring to the ancient crossing point of the River Brent near to where it joins the THAMES. This name appears in a document of 705 as *Breguntford*.

Brentwood (Essex) 'The burnt wood'. *Brende* (Middle English) 'burnt'; *wudu* (Old English) 'wood'. This town, lying just northeast of the Greater LONDON conurbation, appears to be named after the site of a major fire that accidentally destroyed a former wood here. The earliest documentation of this name is a Latin text of 1176 in which it was recorded as *Boscus arsus*, followed in 1227 by a Norman French citation of *Bois Ars*, and later, in 1274, in a reference in English as *Brendewode*.

Bressay (Shetland) 'Probably breast-shaped island'. *Brjóst* (Old Norse) 'breast'; *ey* (Old Norse) 'island'. This may refer to its main conical shaped hill, the Ward of Bressay, or a Viking impression of its outline, all the more so if viewed together with 'nipple-like' NOSS.

Bridgend (Mid Glamorgan) 'Bridge at the end of the estate'. *Brycg* (Old English) 'bridge'; *ende* (Old English) 'end'. This iron-making town, west of CARDIFF, originally arose around the 'estate' of a 12th-century Norman castle protecting a 'bridge' crossing point of the lower River Ogmore, and thus giving its English name, which was recorded as *Bryge End* in 1535. Its corresponding Welsh name, *Pen-y-bont ar Ogwr*, is a literal translation of the 'Head of the bridge over the Ogmore'.

Bridgnorth (Shropshire) 'The north bridge'. *Brycg* (Old English) 'bridge'; *north* (Old English related to Old Norse *northr*) 'north'. This town and surrounding administrative district, to the west of Wolverhampton, take their simple name from a medieval bridge built over the River SEVERN here, north of the former Quatbridge. Records show: *Brug* 1156; *Brugg* Norht 1282.

Bridge of Allan (Central) Simply 'bridge over the Allan Water'. This example of the common Scottish 'Bridge of' name form reflects the location of this residential and 19th-century spa town at the lower end of Strath Allan, north of STIRLING and home of the modern Stirling University. The river name derives from Brythonic Celtic root word *alaun*, meaning 'mighty or holy one'. *See* ALNWICK.

Bridge of Weir (Strathclyde) Unlike the above entity, the name of this small residential town west of PAISLEY does not derive from the local stream, which in this case is the River Gryfe. The town, and its name, owe their existence to the establishment of two large cotton mills in the vicinity in the 1790s, in connection with which both a bridge and a weir were built across the river here.

Bridgewater (Somerset) 'Walter's bridge'. *Brycg* (Old English) 'bridge'; *Walter* (Anglo-Norman personal name) Walter de Dowai. This town, northeast of TAUNTON, is at an important crossing point over the River Parrett just before it widens into its estuary. Originally the town was simply referred to as 'The Bridge', the Domesday Book entry being *Brugie*. By 1194 a record showed *Brigewaltire*, reflecting its manorial ownership.

Bridlington (Humberside) 'Settlement associated with Beorhtel'. *Beorhtel* (Old English personal name); *ing* (Old English connective particle) 'associated with'; *tun* (Old English) 'settlement', 'estate'. The name of this seaside resort and former fishing port north of HULL was recorded as *Bretlinton* in the 1086 Domesday Book.

Bridport (Dorset) 'Bredy port'. *Bredy* (former borough name derived from River Bride—Brythonic Celtic river name) 'boiling one'; *port* (Old English) 'harbour'. The name of this market town close to the coast, east of LYME REGIS, is in the Domesday Book as *Brideport*.

Brigg (Humberside) This small agricultural town, east

of SCUNTHORPE, was formerly *Glanford Brigg*, meaning 'bridge by the ford where games are played'. *Gleam* (Old English) 'merriment'; *ford* (Old English) 'river crossing'; *brycg* (Old English) 'bridge'. Records show: *Glanford* 1183; *Punt de Glanford* 1218; *Glanford Brigg* 1235.

Brighouse (West Yorkshire) Place of the 'houses by the bridge'. *Brycg* (Old English) 'bridge'; *hus* (Old English) 'house'. Lying on the River Calder southeast of HALIFAX, this textiles town was recorded as *Brighuses* in 1240; the latter element being in plural form.

Brighton (East Sussex) 'Beorhthelm's farmstead'. *Beorhthelm* (Old English personal name); *ton* (Old English) 'farmstead'. This famous 18th-century seaside resort due south of LONDON, noted as the village of *Bristelmestune* in the Domesday Book of 1086, was known as *Brighthelstone* until the 19th century, although the pronunciation by then was as the now shortened name.

Bristol (Avon) 'Assembly place by the bridge'. *Brycg* (Old English) 'bridge'; *stow* (Old English) 'assembly place'. The name of this well-known city and former major port on the River AVON near to the mouth of the SEVERN, has its origins in a place specifically used for public assembly, which in early times would often be sited, as here, by a notable bridge focal point. The change of the final '-ow' to the more liquid '-ol' took place under Norman-French influences, and is reflected as a general feature of local intonation today. Records show: *Brycgstowe* 1063; *Bristou* 1086; *Bricstou* 1169; *Bristoll* 1200.

Britain, Great (British Isles) 'Land of the Britons'. The present form of the name of the main island in the BRITISH ISLES group, derives from *Bretaigne* (Old French adapted from the Latin *Britannia*, which in turn is a version of the Ancient Greek *Prettania)* and the *Great* affix was added to distinguish it from Little Britain, the old name for Britanny, where many Britons had fled at the time of the Anglo-Saxon invasions. Much earlier, in the 4th century BC, the Greeks had recorded the name of the ancient tribe of Britons as *Prettanoi*, meaning 'the figured folk', referring to their custom of tattooing their bodies; it is thought that the initial *P* was later replaced by a *B* due to inexact rendering of the original British form.

British Isles (Europe) This name is the general term given to the group of islands of northwestern Europe, comprising BRITAIN and IRELAND together with many attendant smaller ones, and derives from the dominant British influence, in the modern sense. *See* UNITED KINGDOM.

Brixham (Devon) Probably 'Brioc's village'. *Brioc* (Old English personal name); *ham* (Old English) 'village'. Alternatively, the last element of the name of this fishing port south of TORQUAY may derive as *hamm* (Old English) 'river land'. *Brikesham* was recorded in 1205.

Brixton (Greater London) Probably 'Beorhtsige's stone'. *Beortsige* (Old English personal name); *stan* (Old English) 'stone'. This district of LAMBETH has a name whose origins lie in some ancient landmark or boundary stone that was probably a place of assembly for the 'old hundred' (a medieval administrative unit) of Brixton, recorded in the Domesday Book of 1086 as *Brixiestan*.

Broads, The (Norfolk) This name for the popular boating and tourist area to the east of NORWICH came into use sometime in the 18th century and refers to a network of navigable rivers that connect up over 30 'broads', where the watercourse broadens out to form shallow lakes. Sometimes they are referred to as the NORFOLK BROADS, although one lake is in SUFFOLK.

Broadstairs (Kent) Place of the 'wide steps'. *Brad* (Old English) 'broad', 'wide'; *staeger* (Old English) 'steps', 'ascent', 'stairway'. This coastal resort on the North FORELAND, much associated with Charles Dickens, takes its name from a stepped gateway to the sea that is said to have been built down the steep chalk cliffs here in the 15th century. The earliest known record of 1435 indicates the name as *Brodsteyr*.

Broadway (Hereford and Worcester) Place by the 'broad road'. *Brad* (Old English) 'broad'; *weg* (Old English) 'road'. This charming COTSWOLDS town, at the edge of the Vale of EVESHAM, has a simple name that refers to the 'wide street' around which the original settlement grew. The name was recorded as *Bradanuuege* in 972.

Brockenhurst (Hampshire) Probably 'Broca's wooded hill'. *Broca-n* (Old English personal name—genitive form); *hyrst* (Old English) 'wooded hill'. This town on the southern edge of the NEW FOREST is aptly named. Records show: *Broceste* 1086; *Brocheherst* 1158.

Brodick (Strathclyde) 'Broad Bay'. *Breithr* (Old Norse) 'broad'; *vik* (Old Norse) 'bay'. Early records show: *Brathwik* 1306; *Bradewik* 1488. Ironically, this main ARRAN resort stands now on what is called Brodick Bay.

Bromley (Greater London) 'Clearing where the broom grows'. *Brom* (Old English) 'broom'; *leah* (Old English) 'woodland clearing'. This common name of the south-east LONDON borough was recorded as *Bromleag* in 862.

Bromsgrove (Hereford and Worcester) 'Breme's grove'. *Breme* (Old English personal name); *graefe* (Old English) 'grove', 'copse', 'thicket'. The name of this small town and surrounding administrative district, south-west of BIRMINGHAM, was recorded as the village of *Bremesgrefan* in 804.

Brora (Highland) Place of 'the bridge's river'. *Brú* (Old Norse) 'bridge'; *a* (Old Norse) 'river'. Atypically, a river has been named after a bridge here, presumably because for centuries it was SUTHERLAND's only one, at this place on the east coast north of DORNOCH.

Broughty Ferry (Tayside) This suburb of DUNDEE lies on the north bank of the Firth of TAY at its entrance narrows, across which there was a ferry crossing to FIFE before the opening of the Tay Road Bridge in 1966. *Bruach-taibh* (Scottish Gaelic) 'bank of the Tay', thus provides the first part of the name, and 'ferry' (English) the second. Records show *Brochty* in 1595.

Brown Willy (Cornwall) 'Breast-shaped hill of the swallows'. *Bron* (Old Cornish) 'breast', 'hill'; *guennol* (Old Cornish) 'swallows'. This granite tor on BODMIN MOOR, which rises to 1375 ft (420 m), is the highest place in CORNWALL, and as such has a suitably descriptive Celtic name. *Compare* YES TOR.

Brownhills (Staffordshire) This small town in the former coal-mining district to the north of the West Midlands conurbation has a relatively recent self- explanatory name, reflecting the 'brown-coloured hills' found here just south of CANNOCK CHASE.

Brownsea Island (Dorset) 'Brunoc's island'. *Brunoc* (Old English personal name); *eg* (Old English) 'island'. This, the largest of the islands in POOLE Harbour and famous as the birthplace of the Boy Scout movement founded by Baden-Powell in 1907, was formerly called *Branksea Island* and as such was recorded in 1276 as *Brunkeseye*. The later addition of the 'Island' affix was clearly a case of the original meaning having been lost in the corruption of the name.

Broxbourne (Hertfordshire) 'Badger's stream'. *Brocc* (Old English) 'badger'; *burna* (Old English) 'stream'. This former village, now part of HODDESDON, gave its name to the surrounding administrative district and was entered as *Brochesborne* in the Domesday Book of 1086. *Compare* BROXBURN.

Broxburn (Lothian) 'Badger's stream'. *Brocc-s* (Old English) 'badger's'; *burna* (Old English) 'stream'. *Compare* BROXBOURNE (Hertfordshire)

Bryher (Cornwall) Place of 'hills'. *Bre-yer* (Old Cornish + plural ending) 'hills'. This name of the smallest of the five inhabited Isles of SCILLY is a comparative description that aptly suits the black and yellow hills here. It was recorded in 1319 as *Braer*.

Brynmawr (Gwent) 'Big hill'. *Bryn* (Welsh) 'hill'; *mawr* (Welsh) 'big'. This 19th-century industrial town is located on the upper slopes of the Ebwy Fach valley, northwest of ABERTILLERY.

Buchan (Grampian) Possibly 'place of the cow'. *Buwch*

(Brythonic Celtic, with the suffix *-an*) 'cow place'. An alternative derivation that produces the same meaning is through *baoghan* (Scottish Gaelic) 'calf'. The name was recorded as *Buchan* pre AD1000 in the *Book of Deer*; and *Baugham* 1601. Either way, the description is apt for this northeastern corner of Scotland, which after the great agricultural improvements of the 18th and 19th centuries became a major beef cattle farming area.

Buckfastleigh (Devon) 'Woodland clearing near the place of the bucks' shelter'. *Bucc* (Old English) 'male deer'; *faesten* (Old English) 'secure shelter', 'stronghold'; *leah* (Old English) 'woodland clearing'. This market town on the flank of DARTMOOR northwest of TOTNES has a compound name that refers to the nearby village and famous abbey for its first two elements. It was recorded as *Bucfastenlegh* in 1353.

Buckie (Grampian) Probably place 'of bucks'. *Bocaidh* (Scottish Gaelic) 'of bucks'. This fishing town, on the MORAY coast, has most likely taken its name from the river on which it stands—the Burn of Buckie. It is recorded as *Buky c.*1350.

Buckingham (Buckinghamshire) 'River-bend land of Bucca's people'. *Bucca* (Old English personal name); *inga* (Old English - genitive of *ingas*) 'people of'; *hamm* (Old English) 'land in a river bend'. This ancient and former county town lies on a river bend of the Great Ouse, and its name was documented as *Buccingahamm* in 918, while that of the county as *Buccingahamscir* in 1016.

Buckley (Clwyd) 'Beech forest clearing'. *Boc* (Old English) 'beech'; *leah* (Old English) 'forest clearing'. This town, lying west of the 'border' near CHESTER, has a simple English name. Its Welsh name, *Bwcle*, derives differently, from *bwcl*, meaning 'a buckle'.

Bude (Cornwall) The name of this North Cornish coastal resort, west of HOLSWORTHY, has a Celtic, possibly pre-Celtic, river-name root of uncertain origin and meaning. It was recorded, exactly as now, in a document of 1400.

Budleigh Salterton (Devon) 'Salt works near the manor of Budda's clearing'. *Sealt* (Old English) 'salt'; *aern* (Old English); *tun* (Old English) 'manor'; *Budda* (Old English personal name); *leah* (Old English) 'woodland clearing'. This compound name of the coastal resort east of EXMOUTH indicates the original presence of salt pans here at the mouth of the River Otter. The former situation was described in a text of 1405, which noted *Salterne in the manor of Budddeleghe*.

Builth Wells (Powys) 'Cow pasture spa'. *Bu* (Welsh) 'cow'; *gellt* (Welsh) 'pasture'. The original name of this central Wales town, north of BRECON, was *Buelt*, as recorded around 1000. The 'Wells' was added as a promotional term in the 19th century when the mineral springs here were used to attract visitors. In Welsh, the name *Llanfair-ym-Muallt*, meaning 'St Mary's church in the cow pasture', is an embellishment of the same sense.

Buncrana (Donegal) Apparently the place at 'the mouth of the tree-lined river'. *Bun* (Irish Gaelic) 'mouth', 'end'; *Crann-cha* (Irish Gaelic river name) 'tree-lined'. This description aptly fits the situation of this town on the eastern shore of Lough SWILLY at the point where the River Crann enters it.

Bungay (Suffolk) Probably 'island of Buna's people'. *Buna* (Old English personal name); *inga* (Old English—genitive of *ingas*) 'people of'; *eg* (Old English) 'island'. The name of this town, west of LOWESTOFT, refers to its situation in a loop of the River Waveney. In the Domesday Book of 1086, both *Bongeia* and *Bunghea* are entered for this place.

Burford (Oxfordshire) Possibly 'ford by the hill'. *Beorg* (Old English) 'hill'; *ford* (Old English) 'river crossing'. The name of this attractive COTSWOLD village was recorded as *Beorgfeord* in the Anglo-Saxon Chronicle of 752, and this description seems apt for this place on the River Windrush.

Burgess Hill (West Sussex) This town south of HAYWARDS Heath was a mid-19th-century development directly related to the opening of the LONDON-BRIGHTON Railway, and it took the name of the local hill, which had itself been named after a 13th-century family called Burgeys that lived near here.

Burnham-on-Crouch (Essex) 'Homestead on the stream by the Crouch'. *Burna* (Old English) 'stream'; *ham* (Old English) 'homestead'; *cruc* (Old English) 'cross' of some kind. This small town and sailing centre lies on the Crouch river estuary, although according to one authority the original Burnham lay slightly north on a stream, and its name was borrowed and the affix added, before both places coalesced.

Burnham-on-Sea (Somerset) 'River land by a stream'. *Burna* (Old English) 'stream'; *hamm* (Old English) 'river land'. This small resort south of WESTON-SUPER-MARE lies at the mouth of the River Brue on the BRISTOL Channel. Its derivation, which differs from BURNHAM-ON-CROUCH, can be clearly seen in the record of its name as *Burnhamm* in 880.

Burnley (Lancashire) Clearing by the River Brun'. *Brun* (Old English river name) 'brown one'; *leah* (Old English) 'woodland clearing'. This large industrial town east of PRESTON lies at the confluence of the Brun and Calder rivers; it was recorded as *Brunlaia* in 1124.

Burntisland (Fife) Possibly 'Burnet's land'. *Burnet* (Scots personal name); *land* (Old English) 'estate'. There is no evidence of a fire on any nearby island, despite repeated folk-etymological tales to the contrary that are associated with the name of this industrial port south-west of Kirkcaldy.

Burren, The (Clare) 'The rocky place'. *Boireann* (Irish Gaelic) 'large rock' or 'rocky district'. This simple name describes an extraordinary lunar-like landscape of bare and deeply grooved limestone terraces covering over 300 square miles (800 sq km) of the northwestern portion of County CLARE.

Burry Port (Dyfed) 'Probably the port by the burrows'. *Beorg* (Old English) 'mound', 'hill'. This small port west of LLANELLI, has a name that is said to derive from the sand dunes here, locally known as 'burrows'.

Burscough (Lancashire) 'Wood by the fort'. *Burh* (Old English) 'fortified stronghold'; *skogr* (Old Norse) 'wood'. This small town by the LEEDS and LIVERPOOL Canal, north of ORMSKIRK, is apparently on the site of a early fort and was documented as *Burscogh* around 1190.

Burslem (Staffordshire) 'Burgheard's estate in the elm-tree region'. *Burgheard* (Old English personal name); *Lyme* (Brythonic Celtic district name) 'place of elms'. This, one of the 'Five Towns' that comprise STOKE-ON-TRENT, is a contraction of the derivation elements shown above that appeared as the fuller forms of *Barcardeslim* in the Domesday Book of 1086, and *Borewardeslyme* in a document of 1242. *See* ASHTON-UNDER-LYNE; NEWCASTLE-UNDER-LYME.

Burton-upon-Trent (Staffordshire) 'Farmstead of the fortified place on the Trent'. *Byrh* (Old English—genitive of *burh*) 'of the fortified place'; *tun* (Old English) 'farmstead', 'settlement'. The common name of this famous beer-making town, situated on the River TRENT southwest of DERBY, was recorded as *Brytun* in 1002. The distinguishing affix was added later.

Bury (Greater Manchester) Place by 'the fort'. *Byrig* (Old English—dative of *burh*) 'fortified stronghold'. The simple name of this industrial town north of MANCHESTER was recorded as *Biri* in 1194.

Bury St Edmunds (Suffolk) 'Town associated with St Edmund'. *Byrig* (Old English—dative of *burh*) 'town' rather than 'fort' in this case; *Eadmund* (Old English personal name) 9th-century saint and martyr. This market town, northwest of IPSWICH, was originally known as *Beadriceswyrth* (Old English) meaning 'Beaduric's enclosure'. St Eadmund, who was killed by

Viking invaders in 870, is buried in this place that came to be called *Sancte Eadmundes Byrig*, as recorded in 1038, before assuming its current reversed order form.

Bushmills (Antrim) 'The mill of the (River) Bush'. Its Irish equivalent name, *Muileann na Buaise*, means the same and describes the situation of this former mill town near the mouth of the River Bush, lying midway between BALLYCASTLE and PORTRUSH. The importance of the mill around which the town originally developed has been replaced by the presence of the internationally famous Bushmills Irish Whiskey distillery, which also uses the water from the river.

Bute (Strathclyde) Probably 'patch of land'. *Bot* (Old Norse) 'patch' or 'piece of land'. This derivation could tentatively be explained by the situation of Bute, which although an 'Isle' is all but a 'piece of the (main)-land', separated only by the 400m wide Kyles of Bute. Early records show : *Bot* 1093; *Bote* 1204; *Boot* 1292.

Butetown (South Glamorgan) This dockland area of south CARDIFF is named after the second Marquis of Bute, who in the early 19th century was the owner of much of the land by the River Taff, which he developed as docks for the coal and entrepot trade.

Buttermere (Cumbria) 'Lake whose surrounding pastures produce a high butter yield'. *Butere* (Old English) 'butter'; *mere* (Old English) 'lake'. *Butermere*, as the name was recorded in 1230, is the name of one of the lakes of the LAKE DISTRICT and that of the village named after it on the neck of land that separates it from CRUMMOCK WATER to the northwest.

Buxton (Derbyshire) Place of the 'rocking or logan-stones'. *Bug-stan* (Old English) 'logan-stone'. This graceful spa town, set high in the PEAK DISTRICT, was developed largely in the 18th century on the site of the ancient Roman spa called *Aquae Arnemetiae*, meaning 'waters of Arnemetia'. The existence of a logan-stone, or rocking stone, remains unidentified, but the name was recorded as *Buchestanes* in a document of around 1100.

Byfleet (Surrey) Place 'by the stream'. *Bi* (Old English) 'by'; *fleot* (Old English) 'stream'. This residential satellite town, northeast of WOKING, has a simple English name that indicates its location by the River Wey. Its entry in the Domesday Book of 1086 is *Biflet*.

C

Cadair Idris (Gwynedd) 'The seat of Idris'. *Cadeir* (Old Welsh) 'chair'; *Idris* (Old Welsh personal name) probably a descendant of the ancient Celtic chief Cunedda whose name is the basis of GWYNEDD. This precipitous ridge, which rises to just under 3000 ft (900 m) southwest of DOLGELLAU, is thus described as the 'lofty se at', or 'stronghold', of this historical character, or alternatively as a popular giant and magician of folklore. Formerly spelt as *Cader Idris*.

Caergybi *see* **Holyhead**.

Caerlaverock (Dumfries and Galloway) 'Fort in the elm trees'. *Cathair* (Scottish Gaelic) 'fort'; *leamh-reaich* (Scottish Gaelic) 'elm tree'. The ruins of an impressive 14th-century castle, surrounded by trees, are still to be found on this coastal site at the mouth of the River Nith, downstream and southeast of DUMFRIES.

Caerleon (Gwent) 'Fort of the legion'. *Cair* (Old Welsh) 'fort'; *legionis* (Latin) 'of the legion'. This town northeast of NEWPORT on the River Usk is the site of the Roman camp of *Isca Legionis*, after which both the river and the town names have been separately derived.

Caernarfon (Gwynedd) 'Fort over from Anglesey'. *Caer* (Old Welsh) 'fort'; *yn* (Welsh) 'in (the land)'; *ar* (Welsh) 'over from'; *Fon* (Welsh grammatical form of *Mon*) Angelsey. The origin of the name of this famous fortified town precedes the building of Edward I's mighty fortress in the late 13th century, as this was the site of the Roman camp of *Segontium*, whose own name is reflected in that of the River Seiont here. An early variant name of this place was *Caer Segeint*, but it was the current name form that gained predominance. For a long time the more anglicised spelling of Carnarvon was used, but the Welsh version has been officially readopted of late.

Caerphilly (Mid Glamorgan) 'Ffili's fort'. *Caer* (Old Welsh) 'fort'; *Ffili* (Old Welsh personal name) unidentified. Probably as in the case of CAERNARFON, the first part of the name of this industrial town north of CARDIFF, which is famous for its crumbly cheese, relates to the site of a Roman camp rather than to its castle, which was built in the 13th century. The Welsh name is *Caerffili*, indicating that the now familiar English version is a much distorted form.

Caherciveen (Kerry) 'The stone fort of Sabina'. *Cathair* (Irish Gaelic) 'stone fort'; *Saidhbhin* (Irish Gaelic personal name) Sabina, an unidentified woman's name. KILLARNEY apart, this is the largest settlement on the Iveragh Peninsula, or the so-called 'Ring of KERRY'. The exact reasons for its descriptive name are unclear as there is no evidence of a fort here and the associations with Sabina are obscure. Its Irish name is *Cathair Saidhbhin*.

Cahir (Tipperary) 'The stone fort'. *Cathair* (Irish Gaelic) 'stone fort'. This town, south of CASHEL, is dominated by a vast castle on a rock island in the middle of the River Suir. Although most of this castle is 12th century or later, there is evidence of a fortification on this site from the 3rd century AD. Its Irish name, *An Chathair*, literally means the same.

Cairngorms (Grampian/Highland) 'Blue humped hills'. *Carn* (Scottish Gaelic) 'humped hill'; *gorm* (Scottish Gaelic) 'blue'. An apt description for this significant mountain range, which in spite of rising to a plateau with tops of over 4000 ft (1250 m), is a granite massif that appears from afar as blue, rounded high hills. The collective term derives from the singular CAIRNGORM mountain, now the site of a major skiing developement.

Caister-on-Sea (Norfolk) Place of the 'Roman camp by

the sea'. *Caester* (Old English) 'Roman camp' or 'fort'. This seaside resort north of GREAT YARMOUTH developed on the site of the former Roman settlement known simply by its Latin generic name *Castra*, as recorded in the 11th century. The current distinguishing affix is relatively recent, the town being previously called *Caister-next-Yarmouth*.

Caistor (Lincolnshire) Place of the Roman camp'. *Caester* (Old English adapted from Latin castra) 'Roman camp'. Like CAISTER-ON-SEA, the name of this small town north of MARKET RASEN has its origins in the site of an ancient Roman fort. It was recorded in the Domesday book of 1086 as *Castre*.

Calder (Highland; Lothian; Strathclyde) Possibly 'hard or rapid water'. *Caled* (Brythonic Celtic) 'hard'; *dobhar* (Brythonic Celtic) 'water'. Alternatively, the first part of this common Scottish name may be derived from *callaidh* (Scottish Gaelic) 'rapid'.

Caldey (Dyfed) 'Cold island'. *Kald* (Old Norse) 'cold'; *ey* (Old Norse) 'island'. Like many of the islands off the Welsh coast, the name of this one at the southwestern end of CARMARTHEN Bay is Scandinavian in origin and very descriptive of its exposed location to the full blast of the prevailing winds from the Atlantic. The Welsh name is *Ynys Byr*, 'Pyr's island'.

Calf of Man (Isle of Man) The curious name of the small island lying off the southern tip of the Isle of MAN is derived from the Old Norse *kalfr*, meaning 'calf', and the significance here is that as the only dependent island hugging close to its motherland, it was likened to a 'calf of a cow' by Viking sailors. Another occurrence of this name form can be found in the Calf of Eday in the similarly Nordic influenced ORKNEY Islands.

Callander (Central) Probably as for CALDER, the meaning of this TROSSACHS town's name is 'hard or rapid water'; in this case from the River Teith, which is quite turbulent here. The name was recorded as *Calentare* 1164; *Callanter* 1350.

Calne (Wiltshire) Probably place of 'the noisy one'. *Calaun-* (pre-English river name based on a Brythonic Celtic conjectural root element) 'noisy one'. This small town east of CHIPPENHAM has an ancient name of uncertain origin, but derives from an old name for the local stream recorded as *Calne* in 955. *See* COLNE.

Camberley (Surrey) This residential and military town north of FARNBOROUGH has an arbitrary name of relatively recent origin. Established in 1862, it was at first called Cambridge Town, after the then Duke of Cambridge who was at the time commander-in-chief of the British Army, but following the opening of a railway station here in 1877 its name was altered to Camberley to avoid postal confusion with CAMBRIDGE.

Camberwell (Greater London) Probably 'spring at the crane stream'. *Cran* (Old English) 'crane'; *burna* (Old English) 'stream'; *wella* (Old English) 'spring'. The name of this district of SOUTHWARK was recorded in the 1086 Domesday Book as *Cambrewelle*.

Camborne (Cornwall) Place by the 'crooked hill'. *Cam* (Old Cornish) 'crooked'; *bron* (Old Cornish) 'breast-shaped hill'. The name of this town west of TRURO, probably refers to Camborne Beacon, south of the town.

Cambrian Mountains (Wales) This is a collective term for most, if not all, the mountain ranges of Wales from CLWYD to DYFED. The name is derived from *Cambria*, the Roman Latin name for Wales, itself based on the Welsh people's name for themselves, which in modern Welsh is *Cymry*.

Cambridge (Cambridgeshire) 'Bridge on the River Granta'. *Granta* (Brythonic Celtic river name) 'marshy one'; *brycg* (Old English) 'bridge'. The early settlement of this famous university town was originally called *Grantacaestir*, as recorded in the 8th century, the reference being to the site of the Roman camp of *Duroliponte* by the river here. At about the same time the alternative name *Grontabricc* was also noted, and it was from the latter that the modern name evolved, with the loss of the first *r* and the change of the initial *G* to *C*, caused by Norman influences. The 1086 Domesday Book entry of *Cantebrigie* shows the changing process at the halfway stage. The River Cam, on which the town stands, is a back-formation name, while the original river name of Granta still applies to its southern reaches upstream of here. The county name was first recorded before the Norman Conquest in 1010 as *Grantabrycgscir*, manifesting the earlier form of this place-name.

Cambuslang (Strathclyde) 'River bend of the ship'. *Cambus* (Scottish Gaelic) 'bend in a waterway'; *luinge* (Scottish Gaelic) 'ship'. This town on the meandering River CLYDE upstream of GLASGOW has an name appropriate to its location.

Camden Town (Greater London) This district of the Borough of Camden, which latterly took its name from it, was itself so named in 1795 after Charles Pratt, Earl of Camden, who acquired the estate of KENTISH TOWN, of which this formed part.

Camelford (Cornwall) 'Ford over the crooked stream'. *Cam* (Old Cornish) 'crooked'; *pol* (Old Cornish) 'pool', 'stream'; *ford* (Old English) 'ford', 'river crossing. This small town, north of BODMIN, lies on the upper reaches of the River Camel and takes its basic name from it. The town's name was recorded in 1205, exactly as now.

Campbeltown (Strathclyde) The chief town of KINTYRE was named after Archibald Campbell, Earl of ARGYLL, in 1667. Formerly it had been called Lochhead, and even earlier as Kilkerran.

Campsie Fells (Central/Strathclyde) 'Crooked fairy hills'. *Cam* (Scottish Gaelic) 'crooked'; *sith* (Scottish Gaelic) 'fairy'; *fjall* (Old Norse) 'hill'. Recorded as *Kamsi* 1208; *Camsy* 1300; *Campsy* 1522. The *p* would appear to have crept in through fancied connection with 'camp', as sometimes found in hill names, especially those associated with Iron Age or Roman camps or forts, as is the case with these to the north of GLASGOW.

Canna (Highland) Possibly 'porpoise island'. *Cana* (Scottish Gaelic) 'porpoise'. This small isle, west of RUM, rises out of the sea with a little whale-like humped back.

Cannock (Staffordshire) Place of 'the hillock'. *Cnocc* (Old English) 'small hill'. This apt description of the situation of this 19th-century coal-mining town north of Wolverhampton was recorded in 1156 as *Cnot* and a year later as *Canot*, revealing the point at which the softening Norman influences were introduced by the insertion of an extra vowel.

Cannock Chase (Staffordshire) 'The forest hunting preserve of Cannock'. This elevated woodland area north of CANNOCK is named after the latter together with the 'Chase' generic which derives: *chace* (Old French) an unenclosed woodland where wild animals and fowl are preserved to be hunted. This was a former royal hunting ground whose name has in recent times been adopted as that of the southern administrative district of the county.

Canonbie (Dumfries and Galloway) 'Canons' village'. *Canon* (Middle English based on Norman-French *canunie*) priest; *byr* (Old Norse) 'village'. The name of this 'border' village, south of LANGHOLM, refers to the former Augustinian priory here (1165-1542).

Canterbury (Kent) 'Fortified town of the people of Kent'. *Cant* (Brythonic Celtic) 'Kent', land of the Canti tribe; *ware* (Old English) 'people of', 'dwellers'; *burh* (Old English) 'fortified town' or 'stronghold'. This premier cathedral city of ENGLAND thus has a name that is rooted in the ancient origins of the county in which it is located. The name of the earlier Roman camp here was the Celtic-derived *Durovernum*, and the Old British version, *Dorubernia*, was an alternative name for the town until the 9th century. Records of the prevailing form include: *Cantwaraburg c.*900; *Canterburie* in the Domesday Book of 1086.

Canvey Island (Essex) Probably 'island of Cana's people'. *Cana* (Old English personal name); *inga* (Old English—genitive of *ingas*) 'people of'; *eg* (Old English) 'island'. The name of this island on the north side of the THAMES estuary, and of the relatively recent bungalow town on the island's southern shore, have the superfluous 'Island' affix added. It was recorded as *Caneveye* in 1255.

Cape Wrath (Highland) 'Turning point'. *Cap* (Old French, in turn from Latin *caput*: 'head') 'promontory', 'headland'; *hverfa* (Old Norse) 'to turn'. Despite the seemingly apt suggestion of stormy seas, frequently experienced at this most northwesterly point of mainland Britain, the derivation of this name lies in the geographical significance of this point around which Viking sailors turned direction on route between Scandinavia and western Scotland.

Cappoquin (Waterford) 'Conn's tillage plot'. *Ceapach* (Irish Gaelic) 'a plot of land laid down to tillage'; *Chuinn* (Irish Gaelic personal name) someone called Conn, so far unidentified. This small market town west of DUNGARVAN has the modern Irish name of *Ceapach Coinn*.

Cardiff (South Glamorgan) 'Fort on the Taff'. *Caer* (Old Welsh) 'fort'; *Taf* (Brythonic Celtic river name) Taff. The modern capital city of WALES, located in the south of the principality, derives its name from the site of a Roman station here on the banks of the River Taff. Early records show: *Kardid* c. 1150; *Cardif* 1158; *Kaerdif* 1218. Its modern Welsh name is *Caerdydd*.

Cardigan (Dyfed) 'Ceredig's land'. *Ceredigion* (Old Welsh personal name that manifests the territorial *-ion* ending) 'land of Ceredig', a 5th-century Welsh prince and son of Cunedda. This town on the River Teifi estuary near the southern end of the broad sweep of Cardigan Bay takes its name from the ancient territory (and now an administrative district) around the town rather than the other way round. Its modern Welsh name is simply, *Aberteifi*, denoting the town's location.

Cardross (Strathclyde) 'Wooded promontory'. *Cardden* (Brythonic Celtic) 'wooded'; *rhos* (Brythonic Celtic) 'promontory'. Recorded in the 13th century as *Cardinros*, the name of this village on the north shore of the CLYDE estuary west of DUMBARTON, still aptly describes its situation today.

Carlingford (Louth) Place on the 'fiord of the hag'. *Kerling* (Old Norse) 'hag'; *fjórdr* (Old Norse) 'sea inlet'. This small resort southeast of NEWRY lies on the southern shore of Lough Carlingford , from which it takes its name. The 'hag' here could be a Viking navigator's nickname for a notable hill, such as the Carlingford Mountain, which rises steeply to nearly 2000 ft (615m) above the present-day town, and which could have served as a landmark for ships entering the lough.

Carlisle (Cumbria) 'Fort of Luguvalos'. *Caer* (Brythonic Celtic - Cumbric) 'fort'; *Luguvalos* (Brythonic Celtic-Cumbric personal name). This important Border town and cathedral city in the extreme northwest of ENGLAND was formerly the site of the Roman fort of *Luguvalium*, which was abbreviated to *Luel* by the 11th century when it was prefixed by 'caer' and influenced by the Normans; it was *Carleol* around 1106.

Carlow (Carlow) Place of the 'four lakes'. *Cether* (Irish Gaelic) 'four'; *loch* (Irish Gaelic) 'lake'. This historic cathedral and county town stands at the confluence of the Barrow and Burren rivers, which it is thought may have formed 'four lakes' here, although there is no trace today. There is evidence of drainage work on the Barrow having taken place this century.

Carluke (Strathclyde) Possibly 'Fort on the marsh'. *Caer* (Brythonic Celtic) 'fort'; *lwch* (Brythonic Celtic) 'marshland'. Alternatively, the first element of the name of this town, northwest of LANARK, may be derived from *carn* (Scottish Gaelic) 'cairn', 'humped hill'; and the latter part could be an obscure personal nam e. First recorded in 1320 as *Carneluke*.

Carmarthen (Dyfed) 'Fort seaside-fort'. *Cair* (Old Welsh) 'fort'; *mari* (Brythonic Celtic) 'sea'; *duno* (Brythonic Celtic) 'fort'. The tautologous name of this market and county town at the head of the long sinuous Towy, or Tywi, river estuary off Carmarthen Bay has roots in its ancient Celtic name *Maridunum*, which gave the name of the Roman *Moridunum* camp here as well as the modern Welsh name, *Caerfyrddin*.

Carndonagh (Donegal) 'The church by the cairn'. *Carn* (Irish Gaelic) 'cairn'; *domhnach* (Irish Gaelic) 'church'. This, the main market town for the INISHOWEN peninsula, shows little evidence of the prehistoric cairn, where presumably the original church was established.

Carnforth (Lancashire) 'Cranes' ford'. *Cran* (Old English) 'crane', 'heron'; *ford* (Old English) 'ford', 'river crossing'. This small former railway town north of LANCASTER was recorded as *Chreneford* in the Domesday Book of 1086.

Carnoustie (Tayside) Possibly 'rock of the fir tree'. *Carraig* (Scottish Gaelic) *na*; (Scottish Gaelic) 'of the'; *ghiuthais* (Scottish Gaelic) 'fir tree'. A document of the late 15th century records this coastal town, northeast of DUNDEE, as *Donaldus Carnusy*. The *t* of the name was added at a later date.

Carnwarth (Strathclyde) Apparently 'Kaerandi's ford'. *Kaerandi* (Old Scandinavian personal name); *vath* (Old Scandinavian) 'ford'. The derivation of the name of this small town, northeast of LANARK, remains unauthenticated.

Carrantuohill (Kerry) 'The reversed reaping hook'. *Carran* (Irish Gaelic) 'reaping hook'; *tuathail* (Irish Gaelic) 'left-handed' or anything reversed from its proper direction. This is the highest mountain in Ireland, 3414 ft (1040m), and the dominant peak of the MACGILLYCUDDY REEKS. It can be seen from the KILLARNEY side to have a jagged and serrated profile with great masses of rock projecting like teeth, which, unlike those of a reaping hook, are on the convex rather than the concave edge. Its modern Irish name is Corran Tuathail.

Carrick-on-Shannon (Leitrim) 'Weir of the ridge of the bark'. *Cora* (Irish Gaelic) 'weir'; *droim* (Irish Gaelic) 'ridge'; *rúsc* (Irish Gaelic) 'tree bark'. This town is situated on the upper River SHANNON, as the latter part of its name implies. However it is not really a true 'Carrick' by derivation, as indeed its current Irish name, *Cora Droma Rúisc*, and its former anglicised name of Carrickdrumrusk attest.

Carrick-on-Suir (Tipperary) 'Rock of the Suir'. *Carraig* (Irish Gaelic) rock; *Siuire* (Irish Gaelic river name) meaning uncertain. The name of this town east of CLONMEL refers to a large rock that is to be found in the River Suir at this point. Its Irish name, *Carraig na Siúire*, means the same.

Carrickfergus (Antrim) 'Fergus's rock'. *Carraig* (Irish Gaelic) 'rock'; *Fherghais* (Irish Gaelic personal name) Fergus was the 5th-century chief of the local Dal Riada tribe, who founded the original 'Scots' settlements in ARGYLL. The description here is of the rocky point by the present-day harbour on the north shore of BELFAST Lough, on which its famous Norman castle stands. Its Irish name is *Carraig Fherghais*.

Carrickmacross (Monaghan) 'Rock of the plain of Ross'. *Carraig* (Irish Gaelic) 'rock'; *machaire* (Irish Gaelic) 'plain'; *Ros* (Irish Gaelic) 'wood' or 'point'. 'Ross' here is the name of a lough north of this small market town to the west of DUNDALK. The current Irish name is *Carraig Mhachaire Rois*.

Carrigaline (Cork) 'The rock of O'Lehane'. *Carraig* (Irish Gaelic) 'rock'; *O'Lehane* (Irish Gaelic personal name) unidentified. This much-expanded satellite town just south of CORK has a name whose origins remain obscure.

Carshalton (Greater London) 'Farmstead by the river source where watercress grows'. *Caerse* (Old English) 'watercress'; *aewiell* (Old English) 'river source'; *tun* (Old English) 'farmstead'. This current district of the south LONDON borough of SUTTON was originally a settlement simply called Alton, or *AEuueltone* in an early text of 675, and entered in the Domesday Book as *Aultone*, to which the distinguishing prefix was added subsequently, as later records show: *Kersaulton c.*1150; *Cressalton* 1275. *See* ALTON.

Cashel (Tipperary) Place of 'the circular stone fort'. *Caiseal* (Irish Gaelic) 'stone fort', usually circular. This town, northwest of CLONMEL, is dominated by a limestone outcrop known as the 'Rock of Cashel', upon which are the ancient ruins of a Romanesque church, a medieval Gothic cathedral, a tower house, a unique, early, high cross, a 15th-century hall and a typically Irish round tower. The whole dramatic stronghold, often referred to as the 'Irish acropolis', was the seat of the kings of MUNSTER for over 900 years. This name is found throughout Ireland where such fortified settlements have arisen.

Castle Cary (Somerset) 'Castle by the pleasant stream'. *Castel* (Middle English) 'castle'; *Cary* (Brythonic Celtic or pre-Celtic river name) probably meaning 'pleasant stream'. This small town northeast of YEOVIL is the site of a Norman castle by the River Cary, after which it is named. In the Domesday Book it was recorded simply as *Cari*, while a text of 1237 shows it as *Castelkary*.

Castle Douglas (Dumfries and Galloway) 'Castle (that is the seat of the Clan) Douglas'. This town, northeast of KIRKCUDBRIGHT, was acquired and developed by Sir William Douglas in 1789, having made his fortune trading with Virginia. Previously the settlement here was first known as Causewayend, then Carlingwark.

Castlebar (Mayo) 'Barry's castle'. *Caislean* (Irish Gaelic) 'castle'; *Barry* (English personal name) of the family who held the castle here after the original English invasion. This county town of MAYO, lying at its centre, was established as a 'plantation pown' in the early 17th century. Its Irish name is *Caislean an Bharraigh*.

Castlebay (Western Isles) This surprisingly long-accepted English name simply refers to the prominent castle of Kiessimul, which stands on a rock in the bay around which BARRA's main town lies. The Gaelic rendering, *Bagh a Chaisteil*, is now being officially promoted.

Castleblayney (Monaghan) 'Blayney's castle'. This town to the southeast of MONAGHAN is another 'plantation town' of the early 17th century, and its name arose because King James I of England and Ireland granted its lands to Edward Blayney, who, as governor of Monaghan, built a castle here. Its Irish name is quite different: *Baile na Lorgan*.

Castleford (West Yorkshire) 'Ford by the Roman fort'. *Caester* (Old English) 'Roman fort'; *ford* (Old English) 'river crossing'. This coal-mining town southeast of LEEDS is on the site of the Roman settlement of *Lagentium*, and the ford would have been strategically located here over the River Aire at the point where it is met by the River Calder. The name of the town was recorded in the Anglo-Saxon Chronicle of 948 as *Caesterford*.

Castletown (Isle of Man) Literally, the 'settlement of the castle'. This small town at the south end of the island has grown up around the present 14th-century castle, which is on the site of an earlier 11th-century fortification. The Old Manx name is *Balla Chastal*, which means the same thing.

Caterham (Surrey) Probably 'settlement at the hill called Cadeir'. *Cadeir* (Brythonic Celtic) 'chair-like lofty place'; *ham* (Old English) 'homestead', 'enclosure'. This small town by the North DOWNS south of LONDON was recorded as *Catheham* in 1179. *See* CADAIER IDRIS.

Catford (Greater London) 'Ford frequented by wild cats'. *Catt* (Old English) 'wild cat'; *ford* (Old English) 'ford'. Thus the name of this district of LEWISHAM simply says what it means, and was recorded as such in 1254.

Catterick (North Yorkshire) Probably place of 'the waterfalls'. *Cataracta* (Latin) 'waterfalls' or 'rapids'. Thus the name of this village and large contemporary army camp south of RICHMOND, near the site of the Roman fort of *Cataractonium*, has an unusual derivation, although it aptly relates to the local topographic conditions of Swaledale here. Some authorities consider that such an uncommon root word must have been changed by early Britons, who may have substituted the first element with *catu-* (Brythonic Celtic) 'war', and influenced the form of its ending. It was recorded in the 2nd century by Ptolemy as *Catouraktonion* and in the Domesday Book in 1086 as *Catrice*.

Cavan (Cavan) 'The hollow and/or the grassy hill'. *Cabhán* (Irish Gaelic) 'a hollow', although in northern Ireland, it can also mean 'a round hill'. This is the chief town at the centre of the county of the same name and lies in a hollow with a grassy hill rising above it.

Cawdor (Highland) Possibly 'hard or rapid water'. The derivation of this name is apparently the same as for CALDER. In this case an adapted river name has been transferred to the village, southwest of NAIRN, and the 14th-century castle made famous for its associations with Shakespeare's *Macbeth*.

Ceannanus Mor *see* **Kells**

Celbridge (Kildare) 'The church by the bridge' *Cill* (Irish Gaelic) 'church'; *bridge* (English). The current name of this town, which stands on the River LIFFEY to the west of DUBLIN, is but a half translation from its original Irish name *Kildrohed*, which derives the same meaning in *droichead* (Irish Gaelic) 'bridge'. The latter is retained in the local parish name Kildrought.

Celtic Sea (Ireland-England-Wales) This is a recent name given by politically sensitive oil prospectors to the waters of the continental shelf between southern IRELAND, CORNWALL and southern WALES. *See* KINSALE.

Ceredigion *see* **Cardigan**

Cerne Abbas (Dorset) 'Abbey by the stony river'. *Cern* (Brythonic Celtic river name based on the ancient *car* root word) 'stony one'; *abbas* (Latin) 'abbot'. This village north of DORCHESTER, best known for the site of the 'Cerne Giant', a large Romano-British chalk hill carving, has a basic name that derives from the River Cerne on which it stands. The affix was added after the foundation of an Benedictine abbey here in the 10th century. The full name was recorded as *Cerne Abbatis* in 1297.

Chalfont St Giles, and **St Peter** (Buckinghamshire) 'Spring frequented by calves'. *Cealf* (Old English) 'calf'; *funta* (Old English) 'spring'. These two small towns, which are near neighbours on the Misbourne river east of BEACONSFIELD, have a common basic name with distinguishing affixes relating to the dedicated saints of their respective parishes. A 13th-century text records both places as *Chalfund Sancti Egidii* and *Chalfhunte Sancti Petri* respectively.

Chapel-en-le-Frith (Derbyshire) 'Chapel in the woodland scrub'. *Chapele* (Middle English) 'chapel'; *en +le* (Old French) 'in the'; *fyrhth* (Old English) 'sparse woodland'. This industrial town north of BUXTON has its origins in a 13th-century chapel built here in the PEAK Forest, and its name retains the distinctive Norman connective middle elements. In 1272 it was recorded as *Capella del Frith*.

Chard (Somerset) 'Building on rough common land'. *Ceart* (Old English) 'a rough common'; *renn* (Old English side-form of *aern*) 'house', 'building'. The name of this elevated market town southeast of TAUNTON is the result of the merger and abbreviation of its two root words. Early records show: *Cerdren* 1065; *Cerdre* 1086.

Charing Cross (Greater London) 'Cross by the bend'. *Cierring* (Old English) 'bend', 'turning point'; *cros* (Old English) 'cross'. The reference here is to the commemorative cross erected by Edward I in 1291 to mark the last stage in the funeral procession of his first queen, Eleanor of Castile, from Harby in Nottinghamshire to Westminster Abbey; the bend is either that in the River THAMES here, or more likely in the Roman road that ran west from the old city of LONDON. It was recorded as *Charryngcros* in 1360.

Charlbury (Oxfordshire) 'Fortified place associated with a man called Ceorl'. *Ceorl* (Old English personal name) 'churl', a lower class order; *ing* (Old English connective particle) 'associated with'; *burh* (Old English) 'fortified place'. The name of this small town northwest of OXFORD was recorded as *Ceorlingburh* in about 1000, manifesting the now lost '-ing' element.

Charnwood Forest (Leicestershire) 'Wood in rocky country'. *Carn* (Brythonic Celtic) 'rock', 'stones'; *wudu* (Old English) 'wood'. This 'craggy' elevated district and former densely wooded hunting ground northwest of LEICESTER was recorded in 1276 as *Charnwode*. The later addition of 'Forest' is really a tautology.

Chatham (Kent) 'Village by the wood'. *Ceto* (Brythonic Celtic root word based on Old Celtic *kaito*) 'wood', 'forest'; *ham* (Old English) 'village', 'settlement'. This historic MEDWAY town, developed as a royal naval base by Elizabeth I in the 16th century, has the name of the original village here, which was recorded as *Caetham* in the 10th century.

Chatteris (Cambridgeshire) Probably 'raised strip of land by a wood'. *Ceto* (Brythonic Celtic root word) 'wood'; *ric* (Old English conjectural name) 'raised strip' or 'stream'. This small agricultural town, on The FENS northeast of Ely, was recorded as *Caeateric* in 974 and *Cietriz* in the Domesday Book. Some authorities suggest the alternative of *Ceatta* (Old English personal name) for the first element.

Cheadle (Greater Manchester; Staffordshire) Place of 'the wood'. *Ceto* (Brythonic Celtic root word) 'wood'; *leah* (Old English) 'wood'. Thus the common name of these two towns, one west of STOCKPORT, the other east of STOKE-ON-TRENT, is a tautology, with the second element apparently being added when the meaning of the original Celtic name had been lost. The Domesday Book records the MANCHESTER Cheadle without its second element as *Cedde*, whereas the Staffordshire town appears as *Celle*.

Cheam (Greater London) 'Village by the tree stumps'. *Ceg* (Old English conjectural name) 'tree stump'; *ham* (Old English) 'village', 'homestead'. Early successive records of the name of this district of SUTTON clearly show its evolution: *Cegeham* 675; *Cegham* 819 and 950; *Ceiham* 1086 (Domesday Book); *Cheiham* 1199; *Cheham* 1722.

Cheddar (Somerset) Place of 'the ravine'. *Ceoder* (Old English conjectural name based on *ceod* for a pouch) 'cave', 'ravine'. The reference here is to the Cheddar Gorge and its caves, at the entrance to which this famous cheese-making town lies on the southern edge of the MENDIPS. Records show: *Ceodre c.*880; *Cedre* 1086.

Chelmsford (Essex) 'Ceolmaer's ford'. *Ceolmaer* (Old English personal name); *ford* (Old English) 'river crossing', 'ford'. This cathedral city, northeast of LONDON, is on the site of the old Roman town of *Caesaromagus*, meaning 'Caesar's market', strategically located at this important nodal and crossing point over the River Chelmer (back-formation name). Records show: *Celmeresfort* 1086; *Chelmeresford* 1190.

Chelsea (Greater London) 'Chalk landing place'. *Cealc* (Old English) 'chalk', 'limestone'; *hyth* (Old English) 'landing place'. The name of this riverside district of southwest central LONDON, renowned for its arty associations, was recorded in 789 as *Celchyth* and as *Chelchee* in 1214, thus confirming the main function of the original settlement here.

Cheltenham (Gloucestershire) Probably 'river land by a hill called Celte'. *Celte* (pre-English or even pre-British hill name); *hamm* (Old English) 'land enclosed in the bend of a river'. Such a derivation aptly describes the situation of this elegant town, which was developed as a spa in the 18th century on the banks of the River Chelt (back-formation name) at the foot of the western slope of the COTSWOLDS. The name of the early settlement was recorded as *Celtanhomme* in 803, and during the last 200 years it was often known as *Cheltenham Spa*.

Chepstow (Gwent) 'Market place'. *Ceap* (Old English) 'market'; *stow* (Old English) 'place'. This 'border' market town with its Norman castle, near the mouth of the River Wye and now at the western end of the SEVERN Bridge, would appear to have an earlier but so far unexplained n ame of *Striguill*, as recorded in 1228. Its Welsh name is *Cas-Gwent*, meaning 'castle in GWENT'.

Chertsey (Surrey) 'Cerot's island'. *Cerot* (Brythonic Celtic personal name); *eg* (Old English) 'island'. The original site of this town on the southwest fringe of the LONDON conurbation was probably higher ground between local tributary streams of the THAMES here. Early records include *Cerotaesi c.*730; *Certesy* 1086 (Domesday Book).

Chesham (Buckinghamshire) 'River meadow with a heap of stones'. *Ceastel* (Old English) 'heap of stones'; *hamm* (Old English) 'river land'. This derivation of the name of this small town, north of BEACONSFIELD, is manifest in a record of 1012 as *Caestaeleshamme*.

Cheshire *see* **Chester**.

Cheshunt (Hertfordshire) Probably 'huntsman of the Roman camp'. *Ceaster* (Old English) 'Roman settlement'; *hunta* (Old English) 'huntsman'. The exact meaning of the name of this town, on the northern fringe of the LONDON conurbation, is not clear. Although it stands on ERMINE STREET, there is no evidence of Roman settlement near here. It is recorded in the Domesday Book as *Cestrehunt*.

Chesil Beach (Dorset) 'Shingle bank'. *Cisel* (Old English) 'shingle', 'pebbles'. This long, narrow, and almost straight coastal shingle bank that rises to over 35 ft (10 m) high in places, extends for 16 miles (25 km) between ABBOTSBURY and PORTLAND. It is documented in a text of around 1540 as *Chisille Bank*.

Chessington (Greater London) 'Cissa's hill'. *Cissa-n* (Old English personal name—genitive form); *dun* (Old English) 'hill'. This name of this district of KINGSTON UPON THAMES, famous for its zoo, does not have a normal '-ington' ending derivation. It was recorded in the Domesday Book of 1086 as *Cisendone* and in 1195 as *Chissindon*.

Chester (Cheshire) Place of the 'Roman fort'. *Ceaster* (Old English) 'Roman fortified settlement'. The name of this county town and cathedral city has been shortened to its current generic form. Originally, as recorded by Ptolemy in the 2nd century AD, the Roman town was called *Deva* (Brythonic Celtic root word) meaning 'goddess', from its situation on the lower reaches of the River DEE. Later it was known as *Castra Legionum*, (Latin) for 'camp of the legions', which in turn gave rise to *Legacaestir* (Old English), as noted by the Venerable Bede in the 8th century. Its abbreviated form was first documented as *Cestre* in the Domesday Book of 1086. The county name, **Cheshire**, was first recorded in the Anglo-Saxon Chronicle of 980 as the unabbreviated form of *Legacaesterscir*.

Chester le Street (Durham) 'Roman camp on the Roman road'. *Ceaster* (Old English based on Latin *castra*) 'Roman fortified settlement'; *straet* (Old English based on Latin *strata*) 'street', 'road'. This former coal-mining town, north of DURHAM, lies on the site of the former Roman station of *Concangis*, with partial retention of the latter in *Cunceceastre*, its name as recorded in the 11th century. Its modern name shows Norman influences in the form of its distinguishing affix.

Chesterfield (Derbyshire) 'Open land near a Roman fort'. *Ceaster* (Old English) 'Roman fort'; *feld* (Old English) 'field', 'open land'. This historic and industrial town south of SHEFFIELD, with its famous crooked church spire, has a straightforward derivation referring to the unnamed Roman station recently unearthed here. It was recorded as *Cesterfelda* in 955 and *Cestrefeld* in the 1086 Domesday Book.

Chesters (Northumberland) Place of the 'Roman fort'. *Ceaster* (Old English) 'Roman fortified station'. This name is literally a reference to the well-preserved Roman remains of the fort of *Cilurnum* on HADRIAN'S WALL north of HEXHAM. Like CHESTER, its modern form has been abbreviated, in this case from *Scytlecester*, as recorded around 1105; the first element of the latter probably deriving from *scyttels* (Old English) meaning a 'bar' or 'bolt', and implying that in post-Roman times this fort may have been used as an enclosure for livestock.

Cheviot Hills (Borders/Northumberland) This range of hills that straddles the eastern section of the border between ENGLAND and SCOTLAND has an ancient name of uncertain meaning, and probably of pre-Celtic origin. It takes its name from the single highest hill, the Cheviot, or Great Cheviot, which rises to 2674 ft (815m), and early documentary records show the name as *Chiuiet* 1182; *Chyvietismores* 1244; *Chyviot* 1250; *Chivyet* 1251.

Chichester (West Sussex) 'Cissa's Roman town'. *Cissa* (Old English personal name) late 5th-century Saxon chieftain, son of Aella—the first king of the South Saxons; *ceaster* (Old English) 'Roman fortified settlement'. This cathedral city, north of SELSEY BILL, stands on the site of the Roman station of *Noviomagus*, meaning 'new market'. Following the Saxon invasions of the south coast of ENGLAND in the latter half of the 5th century, this then ruined former Roman town was occupied by Cissa. The town's name is recorded in the Anglo-Saxon Chronicle of 895 as *Cisseceaster*.

Chigwell (Essex) Possibly 'shingly spring'. *Cingel* (Old English conjectural word) 'shingle'; *wella* (Old English) 'well', 'stream'. This small town on the northeastern edge of the LONDON conurbation has a name that appears to have been influenced by that of nearby CHINGFORD. Alternatively, some authorities consider the first element may derive from the conjectural personal name of Cicca. It was recorded as *Cingheuuella* in the Domesday Book of 1086 and *Chiggewell* in 1187.

Chiltern Hills (Buckinghamshire/Hertfordshire/ Oxfordshire) Possibly 'place of the hill slope'. *Celte* or *cilte* (pre-English or even pre-Celtic conjectural element) 'hill slope'; *erno* (Brythonic Celtic suffix). The name of the range of hills that bounds the LONDON Basin to the northwest, between READING and TRING, was recorded as *Ciltemes efes* in 1006, a clear reference to the steep escarpment of their western side.

Chingford (Greater London) 'Shingle ford'. *Cingel* (Old English conjectural word) 'shingle'; *ford* (Old English) 'river crossing'. This district of the Borough of WALTHAM FOREST, which sits astride the River Ching (back-formation name), has a name that was recorded in 1050 as *Cingeford* .

Chippenham (Wiltshire) 'Cippa's riverside meadow'. *Cippa-n* (Old English personal name—genitive form); *hamm* (Old English) 'land in the bend of a river'. The name of this town on a bend of the River AVON, upstream and northeast of BATH, was recorded as *Cippanhamm* in the Anglo-Saxon Chronicle of 878.

Chipping Campden (Gloucestershire) 'Market place in the valley of enclosures'. *Ceping* (Old English based on ceap) 'market place'; *camp* (Old English) 'enclosure'; *denu* (Old English) 'valley'. This small town, situated in a COTSWOLD valley southeast of EVESHAM, was a former market centre for the wool trade. It was recorded simply as *Campedene* in the Domesday Book of 1086, but as *Chepyng Campedene* in 1287, confirming its then acquired trading status.

Chipping Norton (Oxfordshire) 'Market place of the northern homestead'. *Ceping* (Old English) 'market place'; *north* (Old English) 'northern'; *tun* (Old English) 'homestead'. The name of this small COTSWOLD market town, southeast of CHIPPING CAMPDEN, was noted with its 'market' affix in a Medieval Latin text of 1246 as *Norton Mercatoria* and in a English document of 1280 as *Chepyngnorton*.

Chipping Ongar (Essex) Market place by the pasture land'. *Ceping* (Old English) 'market place'; *anger* (Old English conjectural name) 'pasture', 'grassland'. Early records of the name of this small town northwest of BRENTWOOD reflect the situation 'before' and 'after' gaining its market: *Aungre* 1045; *Chepyngaungre* 1314.

Chipping Sodbury (Avon) 'Market at Soppa's fortified place'. *Ceping* (Old English) 'market place'; *Soppa* (Old English personal name); *byrig* (Old English dative of *burh*) 'fortified place'. The records of the name of this town, northeast of BRISTOL, also confirm that it acquired 'market' status around the 12th century: *Soppanbyrg* 872-915; *Sopeberie* 1086 (Domesday Book); *Cheping Sobbyri* 1269; *Sodbury Mercata* 1316 (Latin).

Chislehurst (Greater London) 'Gravelly wooded hill'. *Cisel* (Old English) 'gravel', 'shingle'; *hyrst* (Old English) 'wooded hill'. The simple name of this district of BROMLEY was documented as *Cyselhyrst* in 973. *Compare* CHESIL BEACH.

Chiswick (Greater London) 'Cheese farm'. *Ciese* (Old English) cheese; *wic* (Old English) 'specialised dairy farm'. The name of this THAMES riverside district of HOUNSLOW was recorded as *Ceswican* around 1000. *Compare* KESWICK.

Chorley (Lancashire) 'Churls' woodland clearing'. *Ceorla* (Old English—genitive plural of *ceorl*) 'churls', 'peasants'; *leah* (Old English) 'woodland clearing'. The common name of this industrial town, north of WIGAN, was recorded as *Cherleg* in 1246.

Chorleywood (Hertfordshire) 'Churls' woodland clearing'. *Ceorla* (Old English—genitive plural) 'churls'; *leah* (Old English) 'woodland clearing'; *wudu* (Old English) 'wood'. The name of this residential town west of RICKMANSWORTH has the same basic name as CHORLEY in LANCASHIRE, except for the superfluous later addition of 'wood'. Records show: *Cherle* 1278; *Charlewoode* 1524.

Christchurch Dorset) 'Church dedicated to Christ'. *Crist* (Old English) Christ; *cirice* (Old English) 'church'.

This residential town on the coast to the east of BOURNEMOUTH takes it current name from the foundation of an Augustinian priory here in the early 12th century, first recorded as *Christecerce* in abou t 1125. Previously it had been called *Twynham*, deriving as *betweonan* + *eam* (Old English) meaning 'place between rivers', which aptly describes its position between the Avon and Stour.

Church (Lancashire) Place at 'the church'. *Cirice* (Old English) 'church'. This simple name of the textile town west of ACCRINGTON was recorded as *Chirche* in 1202.

Church Stretton (Shropshire) 'Church of the Roman road settlement'. *Cirice* (Old English) 'church'; *straet* (Old English) 'Roman road'; *tun* (Old English) 'farmstead' or 'village'. Thus the name of this small town, south of SHREWSBURY, directly reflects its location on an old Roman road that parallels the LONG MYND to the west. The 'Church' affix was added to distinguish this Stretton from its neighbouring villages of All Stretton to the north and Little Stretton to the south; records confirm: *Stratun* 1086; *Chirchestretton* 1337.

Cinderford (Gloucestershire) 'Ford built up of cinders'. *Sinder* (Old English) 'cinders'; *ford* (Old English) 'river crossing'. The name of this colliery and former iron-smelting town at the northern end of the FOREST OF DEAN literally means what it says, for here a ford across the local stream was made up of cinders or slag from the ancient iron works. It was recorded as *Sinderford* in 1258.

Cirencester (Gloucester) 'Roman town of Corinium'. *Corinion* (Latin adaptation of Brythonic Celtic tribal name *Cornovii*); *ceaster* (Old English) 'Roman station'. The exact origin of the first element of the name of this major COTSWOLD market town remains uncertain. One leading authority has suggested that if *Korinion*, as recorded by Ptolemy around 150, is indeed a mistake for *Kornion* it may be explained as a shortened form of *Durocornovium*, which derives from the tribal name

Cornovii, whose territory was to the north of the town. In turn, a shortened *Kornion* would thus have developed into an Old English form such as *Ciern*. It was recorded as *Cirenceaster* around 900, and *Cirecestre* in the Domesday Book.

Cissbury Ring (West Sussex) 'Cissa's fort'. *Cissa* (Old English personal name) 5th-century Saxon chieftain; *byrig* (Old English—dative of *burh*) 'fort'. The post-16th century contrived name of this huge Iron Age fort, north of WORTHING, is probably of antiquarian origin.

Clackmannan (Central) 'Stone of Manau or Manan'. *Clach* (Scottish Gaelic) 'stone'; *Manau* or *Manan* is an ancient personal name given to this area at the head of the Firth of FORTH. The 'stone' is a large glacial erratic rock that now stands in the centre of the town of Clackmannan.

Clacton-on-Sea (Essex) 'Estate associated with a man called Clacc'. *Clacc* (Old English personal name); *ing* (Old English connctive particle) 'associated with'; *tun* (Old English) 'estate'. This coastal town, developed as a 19th-century seaside resort for railway-borne trippers from LONDON, added the 'on-Sea' affix partly for promotional reasons but also in contradistinction to the nearby villages of Great and Little Clacton, which would also have formed part of the original manorial estate. The basic name was recorded in a text of around 1000 as *Claccingtune*.

Clapham (Greater London) 'Village on or by a hillock'. *Clop* (Old English conjectural word) 'small hill'; *ham* (Old English) 'village', 'settlement'. The name of this LONDON district south of the THAMES, renowned for its major railway junction, reflects the terrain here, which rises to the south and east with a culmination at Crystal Palace. It was noted as *Cloppaham c.*800.

Clara (Offaly) 'The level place'. *Clar* (Irish Gaelic) 'plain', a level piece of land. This small town, northwest of TULLAMORE, is located almost at the centre of Ireland in an area dominated by flat lowlands.

Clare (Ireland) 'The level place'. *Clar* (Irish Gaelic) 'plank', 'board', 'plain', 'level place'. This county in the west of Ireland takes its name from the small settlement now called Clarecastle, lying to the south of ENNIS, where the land is fairly flat.

Clayton-le-Moors (Lancashire) 'Clayey soil village on the moorland. *Claeg* (Old English) 'clay'; *tun* (Old English) 'village', 'estate'; *le* (Norman French definite article remaining after loss of preposition) 'on the'; *mor* (Old English) 'moorland'. This small industrial town takes its name from the nature of the soil on the high ground between ACCRINGTON and Great Harwood. The affix was added later to distinguish it from the nearby villages of **Clayton-le-Dale**, 4 miles (7 km) to the west, and **Clayton-le-Woods**, 12 miles (20 km) to the southwest. Records show: *Clayton* 1263; *Clayton super Moras* 1284.

Cleator Moor (Cumbria) 'Hill pasture on the rocky moorland'. *Klettr* (Old Norse) 'rock', 'cliff'; *erg* (Old Norse) 'hill pasture', 'sheiling'; *mor* (Old English affix) 'moorland'. This former iron-ore mining town and the nearby original settlement of **Cleator** have a basic name that aptly describes the local terrain in its first element, and the past summer-grazing activity here in its second part. A record of *c.*1200 shows *Cletergh*.

Cleckheaton (West Yorkshire) 'High farmstead on a hill'. *Klakkr* (Old Scandinavian) 'hill'; *heah* (Old English) 'high'; *tun* (Old English) 'farmstead', 'settlement'. The name of this town, southeast of BRADFORD, appeared in the Domesday Book of 1086 as Hetun, and by 1285 the prefix had been added to give *Claketon*, presumably to distinguish it from the nearby village of Kirkheaton.

Cleethorpes (Humberside) 'Hamlets near Clee'. *Claeg* (Old English) 'clayey place'; *thorpe* (Old Danish) 'outlying farm' or 'hamlet'. This resort at the mouth of the Humber lies immediately east of GRIMSBY, which includes the original principal settlement of Clee, recorded as *Cle* in *c.*1115 and now known as Old Clee. All references to Cleethorpes are much later, and the spelling is always as now.

Cleish (Tayside) Possibly 'a trench'. *Clais* (Scottish Gaelic) 'ditch', 'furrow', or even 'narrow valley'. The latter suggestion for the meaning of the name of this viilage, north of DUNFERMLINE, however, is difficult to reconcile with the nearby isolated **Cleish Hills**.

Clerkenwell (Greater London) 'Students' well'. *Clercen* (Middle English with plural ending) 'clerics', 'students', 'scholars'; *wella* (Old English) 'spring', 'well'. This district of the present-day borough of ISLINGTON was clearly an area just outside the walls of the medieval city of LONDON, where students would gather by a favourite 'watering hole'! The name was recorded as it is now in the mid-12th century.

Clevedon (Avon) 'Hilly place by the cliffs'. *Clif* (Old English) 'cliff'; *dun* (Old English) 'hill'. The name of this resort and residential town on the SEVERN estuary west of BRISTOL aptly describes the coastal topography here. In the Domesday Book the entry was *Clivedon*.

Cleveland (England) 'Area of cliffs and crags'. *Clif-a* (Old English—genitive plural) 'cliffs', 'crags'; *land* (Old English) 'tract of land'. This name, adopted in 1974 by the new county centred on lower TEESSIDE, is taken from the Cleveland Hills, which lies to the south as the northwestern flank of the North York Moors; it was recorded as *Clivelanda* in the early 12th century.

Cleveleys (Lancashire) There is no trace of the name of this town on the FYLDE coast between BLACKPOOL and FLEETWOOD before early in the 20th century. In the view of at least one authority it is probably a late transfer of a manorial name from a family called Cleveley, who may have come from Cleveley, 10 miles (16 km) to the east, near GARSTANG. In this case the original name derives: *clif* + *leah* (Old English) which means 'clearing by the cliff or crag', being recorded as *Cliueleye* in about 1180.

Clicklade (Wiltshire) Place of 'the river crossing by a hill'. *Crug* (Brythonic Celtic conjectural root word) 'hill'; *gelad* (Old English) 'river crossing'. The name of this small town northwest of SWINDON, on the upper reaches of the River THAMES near to its source, was recorded as *Crecca gelad* in 905; *Crac-gelad* 975; *Craecilad* 1016; and *Crichelade* in the Domesday Book of 1086.

Clifden (Galway) 'The stepping stones'. *An Clochan* (Irish Gaelic) 'stepping stones'. The current name of this picturesque town on the coast of CONNEMARA, is a corruption of its Irish form, reflecting a crossing point here over the River Owenglin near its mouth.

Cliffs of Moher *see* **Moher**

Clifton (Avon) 'settlement on a cliff or steep hillside'. *Clif* (Old English) 'cliff'; *tun* (Old English) 'settlement'. The meaning of this common English place-name is well demonstrated in this fashionable western residential district of BRISTOL, which occupies a steep hill east of the AVON Gorge that is spanned by the famous Clifton Suspension Bridge of Isambard Kingdom Brunel. This Clifton appears to have been misrecorded in the Domesday Book as *Clistone*.

Clitheroe (Lancashire) Possibly 'the hill of the song thrush'. *Klithra* (Old Scandinavian) 'thrush'; *haugr* (Old Scandinavian) 'hill'. Alternatively, some authorities have suggested the partially conjectural derivation: *clyder + hoh* (Old English) meaning 'hill of loose stones'. Either way, it probably refers to the hill on which the 12th-century Norman keep was built in this town set high above the Ribble valley, upstream and northeast of PRESTON. It was recorded as *Cliderhou* in 1102.

Clogher (Tyrone) 'Stony place'. *Cloch* (Irish Gaelic) 'stone'. This former cathedral town southeast of OMAGH has a simple name that refers to either the stony nature of the ground here or the prevalence of stone buildings. In Irish the name is *An clochar*.

Clonakilty (Cork) 'Stone of the wooded place'. *Cloch* (Irish Gaelic) 'stone'; *na* (Irish Gaelic) 'of the'; *coilltean* (Irish Gaelic) 'wooded'. The name of this small market town on the south coast of Ireland shows that originally it grew up around a fort in the woods. The current Irish rendering is *Cloich na Coillte*.

Clondalkin (Dublin) 'Dolcan's meadow'. *Cluain* (Irish Gaelic) 'meadow', 'a fertile piece of land amongst bog and marsh'; *Dolcain* (Irish Gaelic personal name) unknown. This modern commercial complex and satellite residential area on the western fringes of DUBLIN City originally must have been a favoured piece of agricultural land.

Clones (Monaghan) 'Meadow of Eos'. *Cluain* (Irish Gaelic) 'meadow'; *Eois* (Irish Gaelic personal name) unknown. This busy little agricultural centre north of CAVAN originally developed around the 6th-century monastery founded here by St Tigernach. Its English name is still pronounced with two syllables.

Clonmel (Tipperary) 'Meadow of honey'. *Cluain* (Irish Gaelic) 'meadow'; *meala* (Irish Gaelic) 'honey'. This market town to the west of CARRICK-on-SUIR was probably originally sited on a meadow frequented by wild bees, rather than one with beehives.

Clontarf (Dublin) 'Pasture of bulls'. *Cluain* (Irish Gaelic) 'meadow', 'pasture'; *tarbh* (Irish Gaelic) 'bull'. This pleasant DUBLIN coastal suburb on the northeast of the city has a name clearly indicating its former land use in ancient times. Immediately offshore in Dublin Bay is North Bull Island, the home today of the Royal Dublin Golf Course, which is connected to Clontarf by the Bull Bridge.

Clwyd (Wales) The 'hurdle'. *Clwyd* (Welsh) 'hurdle'. This ancient name, revived in 1974 as the new county name for northeast Wales, derives from the River Clwyd, which may have had a hurdle ford across it. *See* DUBLIN.

Clyde (Strathclyde) 'Cleansing one'. A Brythonic Celtic

river name derived from the root element *clouta*. The Roman name for this famous river was recorded in the 2nd century AD as *Clota*.

Clydebank (Strathclyde) Simply, 'the (River) Clyde's bank'. This (Modern English) name was given to this industrial town, lying on the north bank of the CLYDE immediately to the west of GLASGOW, when it was developed in the late 19th century with the founding of the shipyards that were soon to become world famous.

Coalbrookdale (Shropshire) 'Valley of the cold brook'. *Cald* (Old English) 'cold'; *broc* (Old English) 'brook', 'stream'; *dael* (Old English) 'valley'. Recorded as *Caldebrok* in 1250, the name of this town immediately north of IRONBRIDGE, was aptly corrupted for a place that was to become one of the early 'cradles of the Industrial Revolution', this being the site of the famous 18th-century ironworks of Abraham Darby.

Coalville (Leicestershire) This coal-mining town, which developed in the early 19th century at the western edge of CHARWOOD FOREST, northwest of LEICESTER, has a name created to reflect the main activity of this place, incorporating the then fashionable '-ville' ending. *Compare* BOURNVILLE; WATERLOOVILLE.

Coatbridge (Strathclyde) 'Bridge by the cottages'. The bridge was built here only about 1800 as part of the development of the area, east of Glasgow, as a coal-mining centre around the earlier small settlement of *Cotts* (Old English *cot*), meaning 'shelter'.

Cóbh (Cork) 'The cove'. *An Cóbh* (Irish Gaelic) 'cove'. Exceptionally, the name of this port east of CORK is a latter-day Irish version of its former English name of Cove. Following a visit by Queen Victoria in 1849, it was called Queenstown until 1922.

Cobham (Surrey) 'Cofa's village'. *Cofa-n* (Old English personal name—genitive form); *ham* (Old English) 'village'. This residential satellite town on the south-western edge of the LONDON conurbation, east of WOKING, has a name that was recorded in the Domesday Book as *Covenham*, and whose change of middle consonants appears to have been relatively late.

Cockenzie (Lothian) The meaning of the name of this coastal resort, east of EDINBURGH, is obscure, but a personal name could be involved. Some authorities suggest 'Kenneth's nook'. *Cuil* (Scottish Gaelic) 'nook'. Recorded as *Cowkany* in 1590, and still pronounced today as 'Cockennie'.

Cockermouth (Cumbria) 'Mouth of the crooked one'. *Coker* (Brythonic Celtic river name derived from Old Celtic root word kukro) 'crooked'; *mutha* (Old English) 'river mouth', 'confluence'. This small town at the northern edge of the CUMBRIAN MOUNTAINS east of WORKINGTON lies at the river confluence of the Cocker with the DERWENT, and takes its name from the former. Records show: *Cokyrmoth c.*1150; *Cockermuth* 1253.

Colchester (Essex) 'Roman town on the River Colne'. *Colne* (Brythonic Celtic river name derived from Old Celtic conjectural root word *colauno*) 'water'; *ceaster* (Old English) 'Roman station'. This ancient settlement, at the head of the Colne river estuary southwest of IPSWICH, dates back to the Iron Age. In AD49-50 the Romans founded their first capital of Britain here, under the Romano-British name of *Colonia Camulodunum*; the latter deriving as 'fort of Camulos', a Celtic god of war. Some authorities consider that the first part of the current name may have come from the Roman designation *colonia*, (Latin) 'colony for retired legionaries', as with LINCOLN. In this case, however, it may be mere coincidence. Early records of the name include: *Colneceaster* as in the Anglo-Saxon Chronicle of 921; *Colecestra* as in the Domesday Book of 1086.

Coldstream (Borders) Simply a reference to the 'cold' temperature of the River TWEED at this point, which since it was not bridged until 1766, would have been a fact well aware to all crossing the former deep ford here, northeast of KELSO.

Coleford (Gloucestershire) 'Ford across which charcoal

is transported'. *Col* (Old English) 'charcoal'; *ford* (Old English) 'river crossing'. The name of this small town in the FOREST OF DEAN, reflects the former local importance of charcoal-making in connection with the long history of iron-ore smelting in these parts. It was recorded as *Colford* in 1291.

Coleraine (Londonderry) 'Recess in the ferns'. *Cuil* (Irish Gaelic) 'corner', 'recess'; *rathain* (Irish Gaelic) 'ferns'. This sizable harbour town on the lower reaches of the River Bann was, according to legend, the place where a chieftain named Nadslua presented St Patrick with a piece of land on which to build his church; it was very overgrown with ferns which were cleared miraculously by some boys playing with fire. Other Irish place names are similarly derived: **Cooleraine** (Limerick) and **Coolrainy** (Wexford).

Coleshill (Warwickshire) 'Hill on the River Cole'. *Cole* (Brythonic Celtic river name) 'river of the hazel'; *hyll* (Old English) 'hill'. The straightforward name of this small town, situated on hilly land east of BIRMINGHAM, was recorded as *Colles hyl* in 799.

Coll (Strathclyde) Probably 'barren place'. *Kollr* (Old Norse) 'bald head', 'bare top'. This description is apt for this Inner Hebridean island, which presents a bleak face of gnarled rock protruding through the scant skin of heather. It is in complete contrast to its neighbour, TIREE.

Colne (Lancashire) Probably, place of 'the noisy one'. *Calaun-* (pre-English river name based on Brythonic Celtic conjectural root element) 'noisy'. This textiles town northeast of BURNLEY takes its name from the Colne Water on which it stands, giving it a similar origin to CALNE in WILTSHIRE. It was recorded as *Calna* in 1124.

Colonsay (Strathclyde) Possibly '(St) Columba's Isle'. Alternatively, some commentators suggest 'Kolbein' (Old Scandinavian) as a substitute personal name; the second part is derived from *ey* (Old Norse) 'island'.

Colwyn Bay (Clywd) 'Bay by the puppy stream'. *Colwyn* (Welsh) 'puppy'. This North Wales coastal resort, which developed west of ABERGELE only after 1865, took its basic name from the nearby village, now a eastern suburb of the town, called Old Colwyn, and added the 'Bay' element for distinction and promotion as a seaside holiday centre. The original Colwyn derives its name from the 'puppy' stream on which it stands.

Comrie (Tayside) Place of the 'confluence'. *Comar* (Scottish Gaelic) 'river confluence'. Near here both the Water of Ruchill and the River Lednock meet with the River Earn in a major convergence of valleys which proved a good site for the original settlement, west of CRIEFF.

Congleton (Cheshire) Probably 'farmstead by the round-topped hill'. *Cung* (Old English conjectural word) 'conk-like'; *hyll* (Old English) 'hill'; *tun* (Old English) 'farmstead', 'settlement'. This industrial town southwest of MACCLESFIELD is set amongst such hillocks, and its name was noted as *Cogeltone* in the Domesday Book.

Conisbrough (South Yorkshire) 'The king's stronghold'. *Konungr* (Old Scandinavian) 'king'; *burh* (Old English) 'fortified place', 'manor'. The name of this small town, in the coal-mining area between DONCASTER and ROTHERHAM, was recorded as *Cunungesburh* in 1002.

Coniston (Cumbria) 'The king's farmstead'. *Konungr* (Old Scandinavian) 'king'; *tun* (Old English) 'farmstead', 'estate'. The name of this village, 6 miles (10 km) west of WINDERMERE, gave its name to **Coniston Water**, one of the famous lakes of the LAKE DISTRICT, on which it lies near its head. The village name was recorded as *Coningeston* in the 12th century.

Conn, Lough (Mayo) 'Lake of the hounds'. *Loch* (Irish Gaelic) 'lake'; *con* (Irish Gaelic genitive plural of *cu*) 'of the hounds', or 'fierce dogs'. This large lake in north-central MAYO drains southwards through the linked Lough Cullin before doing a U-turn and flowing north by the River Moy to the Atlantic near BALLINA.

Connacht *see* **Connaught**

Connah's Quay (Clwyd) An industrial town and port on the River Dee just upstream from FLINT. Founded in the early 18th century, it was originally called New Quay on account of a new channel being cut in the river estuary. The Irish personal name was substituted later in the same century. Although it is not known exactly who Connah was, it is clear that there was a notable Irish immigration to the town at that time.

Connaught (Ireland) This is the name, usually spelt Connacht by the Irish, for the ancient kingdom and historic province of western Ireland, that consists of the current counties of GALWAY, LEITRIM, MAYO, ROSCOMMON and SLIGO. It takes its name from the Connachta tribe, in turn thought to have been derived from *connadh* (Irish Gaelic) 'firewood', 'fuel'. *See* LEINSTER; MUNSTER; ULSTER.

Connemara (Galway) 'The seaward lands of Conmac's people'. *Conmacne* (Irish Gaelic tribal and territorial name) descendants of Conmac and their lands; *mara* (Irish Gaelic genitive of *muir*) 'of the sea'. This renowned scenic coastal and mountainous area of western GALWAY derives its name ultimately from Conmac, the son of the legendary Queen Maev of Connacht (*see* CONNAUGHT) and Fergus MacRoy, ex-king of ULSTER. The second part of the name was added to distinguish these lands of the Conmacne that lay to the west of Lough CORRIB and Lough Mask from other territories held by them. The name has been recorded in an early document as *Conmaicne-mara*.

Consett (Durham) 'Prominent hill of Cunuc'. *Cunuc* (Brythonic Celtic hill name based on a conjectural pre-Celtic root element *cunaco*); *heafod* (Old English) 'promontory', 'head', 'hill'. The name of this former iron and steel town, northwest of DURHAM, aptly describes its elevated situation. It was recorded as *Conekesheued* in 1228.

Conwy (Gwynedd) This resort and small port, with its famous 13th-century castle and town walls, lying on the west side of the Conwy estuary south of LLANDUDNO, derives its name from that of the river here, which may have its origins in the conjectural Brythonic Celtic root element *can*, meaning 'famous' or 'the chief one', together with *gwy*, 'river'. A former name of the town was *Aberconwy*, indicating its location, and for a long period, until recently, the name was spelt as Conway.

Cookstown (Tyrone) This 'plantation town' was founded under royal patronage in the early 17th century by an Alan Cook, after whom it is named. Its Irish name has a different derivation: *An Chorr Chriochach* (Irish Gaelic) 'the hill of the boundary', reflecting the town's location close to the TYRONE-LONDONDERRY county boundary.

Corbridge (Northumberland) 'Bridge near Corchester'. *Cor* (Old English shortened form) Corchester; *brycg* (Old English) 'bridge'. The first element of the name of this small town, east of HEXHAM, is probably derived ultimately from the nearby site of the Roman camp of *Corstopitum* at Corchester.

Corby (Northamptonshire) 'Kori's farmstead'. *Kori* (Old Scandinavian personal name); *by* (Old Danish) 'farmstead'. The name of this steel-making town, north of Kettering, was recorded in the Domesday Book of 1086 as *Corbei*.

Corfe Castle (Dorset) 'Castle in the gap'. *Corf* (Old English conjectural name derived from *ceorfan*, 'to cut') 'cutting', 'gap', 'pass'; *castel* (Middle English) 'castle'. The original name of this picturesque village, northwest of SWANAGE, reflects its location at a gap in the PURBECK Hills, later to be strategically commanded by a Norman castle, and giving rise to the particular affix here, as records confirm: *Corf* 955; *Corffe Castell* 1302.

Cork (Cork) 'Marshy place'. *Corcach* (Irish Gaelic) 'marsh'. The name of the 'Republic's second city', and that of the surrounding county, originate in the marshland here at the head of the penetrating sea inlet known today as Cork Harbour. This was first a Viking settlement beside the site of St Finbar's early-7th-century monastery. Like a Dutch canal town, its waterways and quaysides, built to contain the ever-flooding River Lee, remind us of the significance of its name. The current Irish rendering is *An Coraigh*.

Cornwall (England) Territory of 'the Cornovii tribe—the foreigners'. *Cornovii* (Brythonic Celtic tribal name) 'peninsula people'; *walas* (Old English plural of *walh*) 'foreigners', 'strangers'. Like that of WALES, the origin of the name of Britain's southwesternmost county lies in the ethnically discriminating attitudes of the early Anglo-Saxon-speaking invaders, who regarded those of a Celtic tongue, such as the Cornovii tribe of ancient Britons, as foreigners. Records show: *Cornubia c.*705; *Cornwalas* 891; *Cornualia* 1086 (Domesday Book).

Corrib, Lough (Galway/Mayo) 'Oirbsean's lake'. *Loch* (Irish Gaelic) 'lake'; *Oirbsean* (Irish Gaelic personal name) of a legendary hero. The original personal name given to this large lake (Ireland's second largest) has been abbreviated and corrupted from the Irish *An Choirb* into its present form.

Corrievreckan (Strathclyde) 'Whirlpool of Brecon'. *Coire* (Scottish Gaelic) 'whirlpool', 'cauldron'; *Brychan* (a personal name) common to Celtic mythologies —(*See* BRECON; BRECHIN; WREKIN). In Scottish Gaelic legend, the hero Brychan perished with all his fifty ships in the notorious Corrievrekan whirlpool, which lies north of the island of JURA.

Corsham (Hampshire) 'Cossa's village'. *Cossa* (Old English personal name); *ham* (Old English) 'village', 'homestead'. The name of this former town, now a northern district of PORTSMOUTH, was recorded as *Cosseham* in the Domesday Book of 1086, and *Cosham* by 1170.

Corstorphine (Lothian) Possibly 'cross of the fair hill'. *Crois* (Scottish Gaelic) 'cross'; *torr* (Scottish Gaelic) 'hill'; *fionn* (Scottish Gaelic) 'fair'. A cross did stand here by Corstorphine Hill in what is now a western suburb of EDINBURGH. Other less well-founded derivations include one from Torphin (personal name) or from the 11th-century Norse warrior Thorfinn the Mighty. Records show *Crostorfin* 1128; *Corstorphyne* 1508.

Corwen (Clwyd) Apparently 'sacred stone'. This small market town west of LLANGOLLEN, was earlier called *Corfaen*, with the last element deriving as *maen* (Welsh) 'stone'. The *Carrig-y-Big* is such an ancient stone which was found here and is preserved in the local church.

Cotswolds (Gloucestershire/Oxfordshire) 'Cod's high forest land'. *Cod* (Old English personal name); *wald* (Old English) 'upland forest area later cleared'. This scenically renowned range of gently folded hills, extending from BATH to BANBURY, has in the latter generic part of its name a common root element with the WEALD, and such typically forested uplands as the Schwarzwald, the 'Black Forest', in Germany. The basic name was recorded as *Codesuualt* in the 12th century.

Cottingham (Humberside) 'Homestead of Cott's people'. *Cott* (Old English personal name); *inga* (Old English—genitive of ingas) 'people of'; *ham* (Old English) 'homestead'. This settlement, now adjoining HULL to the northwest, was noted in the Domesday Book of 1086 as *Cotingeham*.

Coventry (West Midlands) 'Cofa's tree'. *Cofa* (Old English personal name); *treow* (Old English) 'tree'. The name of this historic city and major industrial centre east of BIRMINGHAM, like similar names with the '-tree' ending, such as BRAINTREE or OSWESTRY, could have its roots as an ancient 'public place of assembly', which was often marked by a distinctive tree or, alternatively, as is more probable here, the 'tree' had the sense of an erected pole or cross. *Couentre* was recorded in 1043.

Cowal (Strathclyde) The name of this large Highland

peninsula lying between Loch Fyne and the Firth of CLYDE is a corruption of Comgall, the name of one of the sons of the King Fergus of Ulster, and himself a chief of the Dalriad Scots in the 6th century.

Cowbridge (South Glamorgan) 'Bridge of the cow'. The name of this market town west of CARDIFF appears to be a straightforward latterday English translation of *Pontyfon* (Old Welsh—where *fon* is by assimilation for *mon*, meaning 'cow'). The name *Pontyfuwch*, of the same meaning, was recorded in 1645. The 'cow' association with this place could be an early one as it is on the site of the Roman station of *Bovium*, deriving from *bovis* (Latin genitive of *bos*) 'of the cow' or 'ox'. The town's modern Welsh name does not preserve the bovine connection; *Y Bont-faen* means 'the stone bridge'.

Cowdenbeath (Fife) Possibly 'Cowden's (land) by the birches'. Cowden (personal name) suggested by the earliest available record in 1626, which refers to this place, northeast of DUNFERMLINE, as *terris de Cowdounesbaithe*; the second element is certainly derived as *beith* (Scottish Gaelic) 'birch'.

Cowes (Isle of Wight) This internationally famous yachting resort, at the north tip of the island, does not have an appropriately nautical name. It derives fro m two offshore sandbanks on either side of the mouth of the River Medina here, that in a text of 1413 were *Estcowe* and *Westcowe* respectively. Later known jointly as 'The Cows', the name was transferred to the town.

Cowley (Oxfordshire) Probably 'Cufa's clearing'. *Cufa* (Old English personal name); *leah* (Old English) 'woodland clearing'. The name of this settlement, now a southeastern suburb of OXFORD that is famous for its car-manufacturing plant, was recorded as *Couelea* in 1004, and in the Domesday Book as *Covelie*.

Craigavon (Armagh) This New Town, designated in 1965 and sited between LURGAN and PORTADOWN, was named after the then prime minister of Northern Ireland, James Craig, later Viscount Craigavon.

Crail (Fife) 'Boulder rock'. *Carr* (Old Gaelic) 'boulder'; *ail* (Old Gaelic) 'rock'. This ancient port of the East Neuk of FIFE has an equally ancient name, which was recorded as *Caraile* in 1153, showing the two elements of this apparent tautology. The dangerous 'Carr Rocks' lie 3 miles offshore to the east in the Firth of FORTH.

Cramond (Lothian) 'Fort (on the River) Almond'. *Caer* (Brythonic Celtic) 'fort'; *amhainn* (Scottish Gaelic corrupted) 'river'. There was a Roman fort here, at this now western suburb of Edinburgh, by the Firth of FORTH.

Cranborne Chase (Dorset/Wiltshire) 'Hunting preserve of the crane's stream'. *Cran* (Old English) 'crane', 'heron'; *burna* (Old English) 'stream'; *chace* (Old French) 'wooded hunting ground'. This partially wooded upland area southeast of SHAFTESBURY, which once was a large forest and hunting preserve, takes its basic name from the manorial village of Cranborne to the southeast of the Chase. The Domesday Book entry for the village was *Cernburna*.

Crawley (West Sussex) 'Crow's wood or clearing'. *Crawe* (Old English) 'crow'; *leah* (Old English) 'wood', 'clearing'. The common name of this 1947-designated New Town, situated midway between LONDON and BRIGHTON, was recorded as *Crauleia* in 1203 for the original settlement here.

Crediton (Devon) 'Farmstead on the River Creedy'. *Creedy* (Brythonic Celtic river name) 'winding one'; *tun* (Old English) 'farmstead', 'settlement'. This small and ancient town, northwest of EXETER, lies beside the River Creedy, which is aptly named. The original settlement's name was recorded as just *Cridie* in 739, but as *Cridiantun* in the Anglo-Saxon Chronicle of 977.

Crewe (Cheshire) Place of 'the fish trap or weir'. *Criu* (Brythonic Celtic related to Welsh *cryw*) 'fish trap', 'weir'. The name of this famous railway-junction town, at the southern edge of the CHESHIRE Plain near NANTWICH, has its origins in a form of fish-catching weir on a local stream here. According to one authority, the sense here may be 'stepping stones', referring to the probable laying of such stones alongside the weir. The name was recorded as *Creu* in the Domesday Book.

Crewkerne (Somerset) Place of 'the building by a hill called Cruc'. *Cruc* (Brythonic Celtic) 'hill'; *aern* (Old English) 'building', 'house'. This small town southwest of YEOVIL is situated in a hollow surrounded by hills, one of which would have been the original Cruc. It was documented as *Crucern* in about 880.

Crianlarich (Central) Possibly 'little pass'. *Crion* (Scottish Gaelic) 'little'; *lairig* (Scottish Gaelic) 'pass'. This would describe the situation of the village at the rise out of Glen Dochart that goes over and into Glen Falloch, north of Loch LOMOND. Some authorities have suggested another (Scottish Gaelic) derivation: *critheann* '(the) aspen tree'; *laraich* '(of the) ruined house'.

Criccieth (Gwynedd) 'Mound of the captives'. *Crug* (Welsh) 'mound', 'motte'; *caith* (Welsh plural of *caeth*) 'captives', 'prisoners'. The name of this seaside resort on the north shore of TREMADOC BAY, south of CAERNARFON, is a direct reference to the now ruined 'Castle of the Welsh Princes', built on a rocky coastal knoll here in the 1230s by Llewelyn the Great. In 1239 Dafydd, the legitimate son of Llewelyn, imprisoned his half-brother, Gruffudd, and Gruffud's son, Owain, in the castle.

Crieff (Tayside) Place 'among the trees'. *Craobh* (Scottish Gaelic—locative) 'tree'. An early record of the name of this town, west of PERTH, shows it as *Craoibh*.

Cromarty (Highland) Apparently 'crooked promontory'. *Crom* (Scottish Gaelic) 'crooked'; *ard* (Scottish Gaelic) 'promontory', 'headland'. An apt description for this town with its two headlands (the Sutors) at the tip of the BLACK ISLE peninsula. Records show its earlier (Old Gaelic) form as *Crumbathyn* in 1263, which had then elided to *Cromardy* in 1398, and *Cromarte* in 1565.

Cromer (Norfolk) 'Crow's pond'. *Crawe* (Old English) 'crow'; *mere* (Old English) 'pond', 'lake', 'marsh'. The name of this small seaside resort north of NORWICH refers to an inland mere rather than any connection with the sea. It was recorded as *Crowemere* in the early 13th century.

Crook (Durham) Place in 'the bend of a river'. *Krok* (Old Danish) 'river-bend land'. This industrial town northwest of DURHAM lies in the broad bend of a tributary of the River Wear and was originally named *Cruketona* in 1267 but shortened to *Crok* in 1304.

Crosby (Merseyside) 'Village with a cross'. *Krossa* (Old Scandinavian) 'cross'; *by* (Old Scandinavian) 'village'. The name of this coastal town next to BOOTLE at the mouth of the MERSEY estuary was recorded as *Crosbi* in the Domesday Book of 1086. Little Crosby village, just to the north, has seven Viking crosses.

Crossmaglen (Armagh) 'The cross of Lionnan's son'. *Cros* (Irish Gaelic) 'cross'; *mhic* (Irish Gaelic) 'son of'; *Loinnain* (Irish Gaelic personal name) unidentified. This border town southwest of NEWRY has a name in which the first element could possibly refer to its situation at a crossroads rather than a crucifix.

Crowborough (East Sussex) 'Hill frequented by crows'. *Crawe* (Old English) 'crow'; *berg* (Old English) 'hill', 'mound'. This small town in an elevated situation east of the ASHDOWN FOREST was misrecorded in 1292 as *Cranbergh* instead of *Craubergh*

Crowland (Lincolnshire) 'Land at the river bend'. *Cruw* (Old English conjectural word) 'bend'; *land* (Old English) 'tract of land', 'estate'. This small 8th-century abbey town on the FENS northeast of PETERBOROUGH was established long before any serious attempt was made to drain and channel the rivers of the area, so it is quite likely that there was once a significant bend in the River Welland here. The name was recorded as *Cruwland* around 745.

Croydon (Greater London) 'Saffron valley'. *Croh* (Old

der Scottish rule before being annexed by William II in 1092 and thereafter formalised as the Anglo-Norman county of CUMBERLAND.

Cumbrian Mountains (Cumbria) This general name for the mountainous area of the LAKE DISTRICT, which includes England's highest peak, SCAFELL PIKE, is derived from the Brythonic Celtic tribal name root *Cymry*, as are the CAMBRIAN MOUNTAINS in WALES.

Cumnock (Strathclyde) Perhaps, 'crooked hill'. *Cam* (Scottish Gaelic) 'crooked', 'sloping'; *cnoc* (Scottish Gaelic) 'hill'. The name of this old Ayrshire town, east of AYR, remains obscure. It was recorded as *Comnocke* 1297; *Cunnok* 1461; *Canknok* 1548.

Cupar (Fife) Possibly, the 'common-(land)'. *Comhpairt* (Scottish Gaelic) 'common pasture'. Some authorities believe that this ancient market town, in the centre of FIFE, has a pre-Celtic derivation. Recorded as *Cupre* 1183.

Curragh, The (Kildare) 'The marsh or the racecourse'. *Currach* (Irish Gaelic) 'marsh'; or *cuirreach* (Irish Gaelic) 'racecourse'. This plain, east of KILDARE, almost certainly began as a marshy area until drained to become the largest area of unfenced arable land in Ireland. Its double meaning is reflected in the fact that a racecourse has been established here for over 2000 years, and its name is synonymous with the world-famous Irish horseracing headquarters.

Currie (Lothian) 'Boggy land'. *Currach* (Scottish Gaelic—locative) 'bogland', 'marshy area'. Now a southwestern suburb of EDINBURGH, the site of the original settlement was on low-lying land by the Water of LEITH, which would have been boggy prior to being drained. *See* CURRAGH, THE.

Cushendall (Antrim) 'The foot of the River Dall'. *Cois* (Irish Gaelic) 'foot of'; *abhainn* (Irish Gaelic) 'river'; *Dhalla* (Irish Gaelic river name) Dall. This coastal resort lies at the foot of one of the scenic 'Glens of Antrim'. In its current Irish form the derivation changes slightly to *Bun Abhann Dalla*, 'the mouth of the River Dall'.

Cushendun (Antrim) 'The foot of the River Dun'. *Cois* (Irish Gaelic) 'foot of'; *abhainn* (Irish Gaelic) 'river'; *Duinne* (Irish Gaelic river name) Dun. This village on the coast to the north of CUSHENDALL is at the foot of another of the 'Glens of Antrim'. Its modern Irish name, *Bun Abhann Duinne*, slightly changes the sense to 'at the mouth of the River Dun'.

Cwmbran (Gwent) 'Valley of the Bran'. *Cwm* (Welsh) 'valley'; *Bran* (Welsh river name) 'raven', implying 'dark waters'. This 19th-century coal-mining and heavy industrial centre, later designated as a New Town in 1949, and since 1974 the county town of GWENT, lies between NEWPORT and PONTYPOOL in the short valley of the River Bran, from which it takes its name.

Cydwelli *see* **Kidwelly**.

D

Dacorum (Hertfordshire) The hundred 'of the Danes'. *Dacorum* (Medieval Latin—genitive plural of *Daci*) 'of the Dacians', as the Danes were erroneously referred to in medieval times. This name of an administrative district formed in 1974 in the west of the county was adopted in recognition of the historic county division or 'hundred' here, recorded in a text of 1196 as *de hundredo Dacorum*. The original name referred to a hundred that was to the west of, and on the Anglo-Saxon side of, the official WATLING STREET boundary of the Danelaw, but still under Danish administration.

Dagenham (Greater London) 'Daecca's homestead'. *Daecca* (Old English personal name); *ham* (Old English) 'homestead'. The name of this district of eastern LONDON, on the north bank of the River THAMES, is today linked to that of a famous car manufacturer, which has a large plant located here. It was originally recorded as *Daeccanhaam* in the late 7th century.

Dalbeattie (Dumfries and Galloway) 'Haugh of the birch trees'. *Dail* (Scottish Gaelic) 'haugh', 'water meadow within the bend of a river'; *beitheach* (Scottish Gaelic) 'birch tree'. It is an apt description for this town, which is enclosed by a bend in the River Urr, east of CASTLE DOUGLAS. Recorded as *Dalbaty* in 1469.

Dalkeith (Lothian) 'Field by the wood'. *Dol* (Brythonic Celtic) 'field'; *coed* (Brythonic Celtic) 'wood'. Early documents show the name of this town, on the South Esk upstream from MUSSELBURGH, as *Dalkied* 1140; *Dolchet* 1144; *Dalketh* 1145.

Dallas (Grampian) Possibly 'Meadow resting place'. *Dol* (Brythonic Celtic) meadow; *as* (Brythonic Celtic source) resting place. The name of this small town in the beef-cattle rearing district, southwest of Elgin, like its famous Texan namesake, is aptly descriptive.

Dalry (Dumfries and Galloway; Strathclyde) Probably both 'field of the heather'. *Dail* (Scottish Gaelic) 'field'; *fhraoich* (Scottish Gaelic) 'heather'. However, the old Dumfriesshire village, known in full as St John's Town of Dalry, had associations with King James IV, and it could be derived as 'the king's meadow': *righ* (Scottish Gaelic) 'king'.

Dalton-in-Furness (Cumbria) 'Valley farmstead'. *Dael* (Old English) 'dale', 'valley'; *tun* (Old English) 'village', 'farmstead'. This descriptive basic name, common in northern England, takes its later distinguishing affix from the local district. *See* BARROW-IN-FURNESS. It was first recorded simply as *Daltune* in the Domesday Book of 1086, and then in 1332 as *Dalton in Founais*.

Dalwhinnie (Highland) Apparently the 'field of the champion'. *Dail* (Scottish Gaelic) 'field'; *cuingid* (Scottish Gaelic) 'champion'. This may refer to some historic or legendary contest that took place at or near this remote BADENOCH village, north of DRUMOCHTER.

Darfield (South Yorkshire) Place by 'the open deer country'. *Deor* (Old English) 'deer'; *feld* (Old English) 'open country', 'tract of land'. This small coal-mining town east of BARNSLEY was recorded in the Domesday Book as *Dereuueld*.

Darlington (Durham) 'Estate associated with Deornoth'. *Deornoth* (Old English personal name); *ing* (Old English connective particle) 'associated with'; *tun* (Old English) 'estate', 'farmstead'. The name of this famous industrial town southwest of MIDDLESBROUGH, synonymous with George Stephenson and the world's first passenger railway, was first recorded as Dearthingtun in *c.*1050.

Dartford (Kent) 'Ford across the River Darent'. *Darent* (Brythonic Celtic river name) 'river beside which oak trees grow'; *ford* (Old English) 'river crossing'. The name of this industrial town east of LONDON, which appropriately is at the southern approach to the modern tunnel and bridge river crossing of the THAMES, reflects the earlier importance of a local stream-fording point. The Darent derives from the same Celtic root origin as the Dart in DARTMOOR and DARTMOUTH, the Darwen in DARWEN and the Derwent as in DERWENT WATER. Records show: *Tarentfort* 1086 (Domesday Book); *Tarentford* 1159; *Darenteford* 1194.

Dartmoor (Devon) 'Moor of the River Dart'. *Dart* (Brythonic Celtic river name) 'river beside which oak trees grow'; *mor* (Old English) 'moorland'. This major upland area of central DEVON, famed for its desolate beauty and a remote prison, takes its name from one of its main rivers, the Dart, which drains to the southeast and flows into the English Channel at DARTMOUTH. It was recorded as *Dertemora* in 1182.

Dartmouth (Devon) Place at 'the mouth of the River Dart'. *Dart* (Brythonic Celtic river name) 'river beside which oak trees grow'; *mutha* (Old English) 'river mouth'. The name of this small port and resort, with its Royal Naval College, is self-explanatory of its location, southeast and downstream of a deeply indented drowned-valley estuary from TOTNES. It appears in texts of the 11th century as *Daerentamutha* and *Dertamutha*; the former manifesting the common root element that gave rise to DARTFORD.

Darwen (Lancashire) Place on 'the River Darwen'. *Darwen* (Brythonic Celtic river name) 'river beside which oak trees grow'. This industrial town, together with the village of **Lower Darwen**, both immediately south of BLACKBURN, take their basic name directly from that of the short river on which they stand. A record as *Derewent* in 1208 shows its common root with DERWENT.

Daventry (Northamptonshire) 'Dafa's tree'. *Dafa-n* (Old English personal name—genitive form); *treow* (Old English) 'tree'. Like other places with a '-tree' ending, such as BRAINTREE and COVENTRY, the name of this town west of NORTHAMPTON may signify a 'meeting place', but more probably an erected cross or marker of some kind. It appears in the Domesday Book of 1086 as *Daventrei*.

Dawley (Shropshire) 'Clearing called after Dalla'. *Dalla* (Old English personal name); *ing* (Old English connective particle) 'associated with'; *leah* (Old English) 'woodland clearing'. This former village, which now forms the central part of TELFORD New Town, has a name for which a record of 1185 as *Dalilega* shows the remanent *i* of the original middle, and now missing 'ing' element.

Dawlish (Devon) Place on 'the Dawlish Water'. *Dawlish* (Brythonic Celtic river name) 'black stream'. The name of this seaside resort south of EXETER is taken from that of the stream at whose mouth it stands. It has a similar derivation to DOUGLAS and was recorded as *Douelis* in the Domesday Book of 1086.

Deal (Kent) Place at 'the hollow'. *Dael* (Old English) 'valley', 'hollow'. The name of this seaside resort on the east coast of KENT, midway between DOVER and RAMSGATE, suggests some former depression in the local terrain here, as there is not a valley as such nearby. It was recorded in the latinised form of *Addelam* in the Domesday Book of 1086, and as *Dela* in a text of 1158.

Dedham (Essex) 'Dydda's homestead or village'. *Dydda* (Old English personal name); *ham* (Old English) 'homestead', 'village'. The name of this village on the River Stour, northeast of COLCHESTER, which has become internationally known as the scene of many of John Constable's revered paintings, was misrecorded in the Domesday Book as *Delham*, but noted as now in 1165.

Deer (Grampian) 'Forest grove'. *Doire* (Scottish Gaelic) 'grove'. There is still today the Forest of Deer beside the remains of the 13th-century Deer Abbey, which is near the village of **Old Deer**, west of PETERHEAD. **New Deer** is a more recent village 6 miles (10 km) further west.

Denbigh (Clwyd) 'Little fortress'. *Din* (Old Welsh) 'hill fortress'; *bych* (Old Welsh) 'little'. This small market town stands on the River CLWYD, some 10 miles (16k) upstream from RHYL. The original fortress would have been on the site of the ruined 13th-century castle that occupies the rocky limestone outcrop known as Castle Hill. The current Welsh name is *Dinbych*, and early records show: *Dinbych* 1269; *Denbiegh* and *Dynbeigh* *c.*1350; *Dynbigh* 1485. The town gave its name to the former county of Denbighshire. *See* TENBY.

Denby Dale (West Yorkshire) 'Village or farmstead of the Danes'. *Dene* (Old English—genitive plural of *Dena*) 'of the Danes'; *by* (Old Danish) 'farmstead', 'village'. This mining town northwest of BARNSLEY had the later affix, deriving as *dael* (Old English) 'valley', added to distinguish it from the villages of **Upper** and **Lower Denby**, lying just to the south. The basic name reflects the location of the original farmstead, which like many places in eastern and northern ENGLAND was probably founded by early Danish settlers during the 9th-11th centuries. It lies in the ancient region known as the Danelaw, where, under an agreement reached during the reign of the Saxon king, Alfred the Great, Danish law and customs were to be observed. *Denebi* is recorded in the Domesday Book of 1086. *Compare* DARCORUM.

Denny (Central) Presumably 'valley'. *Denu* (Old English) 'valley'. This industrial town, northwest of FALKIRK, lies in the Carron Valley near the site of the famous former iron works.

Denton (Greater Manchester) 'Valley farmstead'. *Denu* (Old English) 'valley'; *tun* (Old English) 'farmstead', 'village'. This common English place-name is applied here to this settlement, now an industrial town east of MANCHESTER, which is situated in the valley of the River Tame. It was recorded in its current form in 1255. *Compare* DALTON.

Derby (Derbyshire) 'Deer village'. *Djur* (Old Danish) 'deer'; *by* (Old Danish) 'farmstead', 'village'. This major engineering industries centre and county town southwest of NOTTINGHAM, originally the Saxon settlement of *Northworthig*, was renamed by Danes who came here in the 9th century. However, the earliest records show the form *deor* (Old English) for 'deer': *Deoraby* 917; *Deorby* 959-75. The county name, **Derbyshire**, was recorded in 1049 as *Deorbyscir*, affixing *scir* (Old English) 'district'.

Derg, Lough (Clare/Galway/Tipperary) 'Lake of the red-eye'. *Loch* (Irish Gaelic) 'lake'; *derg* (Irish Gaelic contracted form of *deirg-eirt*) 'red-eye'. According to legend, it was at this large lake on the lower SHANNON where a king gave one of his eyes to a wandering poet and then washed his face in its waters that then ran red. A more logical explanation is probably to be found in the reddish colour of the churned-up waters of a whirlpool somewhere in the lough.

Derry *see* **Londonderry**

Derwent Water (Cumbria) This scenic lake of the LAKE DISTRICT, southwest of KESWICK, takes its name from the River Derwent, which flows through it. It is derived from an ancient Brythonic Celtic root, meaning 'river beside which oak trees grow'. *Compare* DARTFORD; DARTMOOR; DARWEN.

Desborough (Northamptonshire) 'Deor's fortified place'. *Deor* (Old English personal name) meaning 'deer' or simply 'animal'; *burh* (Old English) 'fortified place', 'stronghold'. This small manufacturing town northwest of KETTERING has a relatively straightforward name that has undergone the process of dissimilation—the first *r* of the original name has been dropped as it is represented by the second. Early records show this evolution: *Dereburg* 1086; *Deresburc* 1167; *Desburc* 1197.

Devizes (Wiltshire) Place on 'the boundaries'. *Devises* (Old French derived from Latin *divisae*) 'boundaries'. This historic market town, southeast of CHIPPENHAM, stands on the site of a Norman stronghold built by the bishops of SALISBURY, through which passed the important dividing line, or boundaries, of two former 'hundreds' (medieval administrative units). The name appeared as *Divisas* in 1139.

Devon (England) Territory of 'the Defnas'. *Defnas* (Old English version of Brythonic Celtic tribal name *Dumnonii*) 'Devonians', 'men of Devon'. Thus, the original name of Celtic aborigines was transferred to their Saxon conquerors and eventually became associated with the territory itself. It was recorded as both *Defnum* and *Defnascir* in the late 9th century, the latter translating as **Devonshire**.

Devonport (Devon) This western district of PLYMOUTH, beside the stretch of the Tamar estuary known as the Hamoaze, has a relatively modern and self-explanatory name. Founded by William III in 1689 as a naval dockyard, called then simply Plymouth Dock, it changed its name to its present form when expanded in 1824.

Dewsbury (West Yorkshire) 'Dewi's fortified place'. *Dewi* (Old English personal name); *byrig* (Old English—dative of *burh*) 'fortified place', 'stronghold'. The name of this industrial town west of WAKEFIELD was recorded as *Deusberia* in the Domesday Book of 1086.

Didcot (Oxfordshire) 'Dudda's cottage'. *Dudda* (Old English personal name); *cot* (Old English) 'cottage'. This town south of OXFORD was noted as *Dudecota* in 1206.

Dingle (Kerry) 'The fortress'. *Dingin* (Irish Gaelic elided form of *daingean*) 'fortress'. As common in Irish Gaelic, the final *n* has changed to an *l* in the process of anglicisation. This small town and the mountainous peninsula on which it is located have had a stronghold function from ancient times.

Dingwall (Highland) 'Parliament field'. *Thing* (Old Norse) 'parliament', 'assembly'; *vollr* (Old Norse) 'field', 'open space'. This must indicate that Dingwall, northwest of INVERNESS near the head of the CROMARTY Firth, was the site of an annual meeting to make laws and administer justice in the days of Viking occupation. Exact parallels to the name are found in other areas of Norse influence (e.g. TYNWALD HILL on the ISLE OF MAN, Tingwall on SHETLAND, and Tinwald in DUMFRIES and GALLOWAY).

Diss (Norfolk) Place by 'the ditch or dyke'. *Dic* (Old English) 'ditch', 'man-made water channel'. This small market town, southwest of NORWICH, lies on the flat valley floor of the River Waveney, where much drainage work has taken place in the past. The present name-form manifests the softening Norman influences on the original English name, which was recorded in 1135 simply as *Dic*, which by 1158 had become *Dize*, and later in the 1190s was rendered as *Disze* and *Disce*.

Docklands (Greater London) This name is of very recent origin, having literally come off the planners' drawing board in the 1980s when it assumed official and wide public recognition as a real place. Before then the vast complex of dock basins of LONDON's 'East End', stretching for 5 miles (8 km) downstream of Tower Bridge mainly on the north bank of the THAMES, was a little visited territory of decline and decay. Under the 1976 'London Docklands Strategic Plan' much of the area has now been transformed, and its already renowned name is synonymous with 'new enterprise culture' and 'post-modern architectural development', the latter culminating in the completion of Canary Wharf Tower, Britain's tallest building, which is 800ft (244m) high. *See* DOGS, ISLE OF.

Dodworth (South Yorkshire) 'Dudda's enclosure'. *Dudda* (Old English personal name); *worth* (Old English) 'enclosure'. The name of this coal-mining town west of BARNSLEY was recorded as *Dodesuuorde* in the Domesday Book entry of 1086. *Compare* DIDCOT; DUDLEY.

Dogs, Isle of (Greater London) The origin of this old name for the central part of LONDON's DOCKLANDS remains obscure. Lying within a pronounced U-shaped meander of the THAMES, the area is technically a peninsula, but with early creeks and later dock basins cutting across its neck, it always has felt an island. Records refer to: *Marsh of Stebenhithe* 1365; *Isle of Doges* 1593; the later probably having derogatory roots.

Doking (Surrey) Place of 'Deorc's people'. *Deorc* (Old English personal name); *ingas* (Old English) 'people of'. The name of this North Downs gap town, midway between Guildford and Reigate, was recorded as *Dorchinges* in the Domesday Book of 1086.

Dolgellau (Gwynedd) 'Monastic cells on the meadow'. *Dol* (Welsh) 'meadow'; *cellau* (Welsh plural of *cell*) 'monastic cells'. This market and former county town of Merioneth lies in the broad valley to the north of Cadair Idris at the confluence of the Wnion and Aran rivers and is the possible site of an early monastic foundation that may have been linked with nearby Cymer Abbey. From the 16th century it was known by the anglicised spelling of Dolgelly or Dolgelley until its Welsh form was recently readopted.

Dollar (Central) Place by the 'ploughed field'. *Dol* (Brythonic Celtic) 'field'; *ar* (Brythonic Celtic) 'arable', 'ploughed'. This name would have been apt for the fertile lands here by the River Devon at the foot of the Ochil Hills.

Donaghadee (Down) 'Church of Diach'. *Domhnach* (Irish Gaelic) 'church'; *Daoi* (Irish Gaelic personal name) Diach—conjectural. This name applies to the town and port on the north coast of the Ards Peninsula.

Doncaster (South Yorkshire) 'Roman fort on the River Don'. *Don* (Brythonic Celtic river name) 'water', 'river; *ceaster* (Old English) 'Roman station'. This industrial town northeast of Sheffield lies on the site of the former Roman fort of *Danum*, which itself derived from the name of the river here. The '-caster' ending is a harder-sounding form, possibly Scandinavian influenced, common in the northeastern parts of England, which is represented by '-chester' elsewhere. The name was recorded as *Doneceastre* in 1002; *Donecastre* 1086.

Donegal (Donegal) 'Fortress of the foreigners'. *Dun* (Irish Gaelic) 'fort'; *na* (Irish Gaelic) 'of the'; *gall* (Irish Gaelic) 'foreigner'. This market and county town lies in the south of the territory and at the head of the bay that both bear its name, which refers to the Danes as the foreigners who had a rudimentary fort here in the 10th century. See GALLOWAY.

Dorchester (Dorset) 'Roman town of Durnovaria'. *Dornwaru* (Old English adopted form based on Brythonic Celtic root word *durno*) possibly meaning 'place with fist-sized peebles', *see* DORNOCH; *ceaster* (Old English) 'Roman town'. Thus the name of the county town of DORSET, north of WEYMOUTH, reflects its Roman origins with an abbreviation of its initial specific element. It was recorded in 864 in its fuller form as *Dornwaraceaster*, and by 1086 it had become *Dorecestre*.

Dornie (Highland) Place of 'pebbles'. *Dornach* (Scottish Gaelic) 'with pebbles'. There is a pebbly spit here where the fiord-like Loch Long and Loch Duich empty into Loch Alsh.

Dornoch (Highland) Place of 'pebbles'. *Dornach* (Scottish Gaelic) 'with pebbles' or 'fist-size stones'. The root word *dorn* means 'fist'. Today, the beach here on the Dornoch Firth is mainly sandy. The name was recorded as *Durnach* in 1150.

Douglas (Isle of Man; Strathclyde) Place of 'the black stream'. *Du* (Brythonic Celtic) 'black'; *glas* (Brythonic Celtic) 'stream'. Both places of this name, one the capital of the Isle of MAN, the other a small Scottish town south of LANARK, take the name of the rivers on which they stand; namely the Dhoo and the Glass in the case of the former and the Douglas Water for the latter. The Old Manx form is *Dub Glais*.

Doune (Central) Simply 'castle or fortified place'. *Dun* (Scottish Gaelic) 'fortress'. This town, lying on the River Teith northeast of STIRLING, is dominated by the 14th-century Doune Castle, although earlier fortifications almost certainly existed here.

Dounreay (Highland) Possibly 'fortified pen'. *Dun* (Scottish Gaelic) 'fortified'; *rett* (Old Norse) 'fold'. If correct, the derivation is apt today as this town, on the north coast of Scotland to the west of THURSO, is the site of a large nuclear power installation.

Dover (Kent) Place of 'the waters or the stream'. *Dubras* (Brythonic Celtic conjectural river name) 'waters'. The name of this major Channel ferry port, southeast of CANTERBURY, which is immortalised in the wartime song, 'The White Cliffs of Dover', is derived from that of the local stream here, now called the River Dour. Early records show: *Dubris* 4th century; *Dofras c.*700; *Dovere* 1086 Domesday Book.

Down (Ireland) Place of the 'fort'. *Dun* (Irish Gaelic) 'fort'. This historic county in Northern Ireland takes its name from its county town DOWNPATRICK, originally known simply as Down.

Downham Market (Norfolk) 'Hill settlement'. *Dun* (Old English) 'hill'; *ham* (Old English) 'farmstead'. This town, south of KING'S LYNN, was simply *Dunham* in 1086, but by 1130 it appeared as *Mercatus de Dunham*, confirming the market status conferred in early Norman times.

Downpatrick (Down) 'Patrick's fort'. *Dun* (Irish Gaelic) 'fort'; *Padraig* (Irish Gaelic personal name) Patrick, patron saint of Ireland. This county town southeast of BELFAST, the site of an ancient fort, had Patrick added to its name when his assumed holy relics were found here in the 12th century. *See* DOWN.

Downs, North and **South** (Kent/Surrey; East/West Sussex) Often referred to colloquially as simply 'The Downs', these two parallel ranges of chalk hills, north and south of The WEALD, which to the east end in dramatic white sea cliffs at DOVER and BEACHY HEAD respectively, derive their basic name from *dun* (Old English) 'hill'. Various renderings have been recorded, including: *The Downys* 1460; *The Downes* 1520.

Drayton (Norfolk) 'Farmstead where drays are used or

near a portage slope'. *Draeg* (Old English) 'dragging'; *tun* (Old English) 'farmstead'. This fairly common English placename applies in this case to the now greatly expanded residential satellite town just northwest of NORWICH, whose entry in the Domesday Book of 1086 was *Draituna*. *See* MARKET DRAYTON.

Driffield, Great and **Little** (Humberside) 'Dirty open stubble land'. *Drif/drit* (Old English) 'stubble'/'dirt'; *feld* (Old English) 'open land'. The basic name of this town and attendant village on flat open land southwest of BRIDLINGTON was recorded as *Driffelda* in 705.

Drogheda (Louth) 'Bridge over the ford'. *Droichead* (Irish Gaelic) 'bridge'; *atha* (Irish Gaelic) 'ford'. The name of this industrial port situated near the mouth of the River BOYNE reflects its strategic position of controlling the main east coast routes between north and south. An Anglo-Norman bridge was built here in the 12th century to supercede the ford crossing of the earlier fortified Danish settlement.

Droichead Nua (Kildare) 'New bridge'. *Droichead* (Irish Gaelic) 'bridge'; *nua* (Irish Gaelic) 'new'. This small town on the River LIFFEY southwest of NAAS has a name, like that of COBH, that has in recent times been translated into Irish from its English original form, in this case Newbridge—the 'new bridge' here dating from the early Anglo-Norman period.

Droitwich (Hereford and Worcester) 'Muddy salt works'. *Drit* (Old English) 'dirt', 'mud'; *wic* (Old English) 'salt works'. This town to the northeast of WORCESTER is on the site of the former Roman camp of *Salinae*, a clear reference to the past presence of salt works here. Indeed, it was recorded as *Saltwic* in 888. In the Domesday Book entry it is simply *Wich*, and the first indication of its current form appears as *Drihtwych* in a document of 1347. *See* MIDDLEWICH; NANTWICH; NORTHWICH.

Dromore (Down) 'Big ridge'. *Droim* (Irish Gaelic) 'ridge'; *mor* (Irish Gaelic) 'big'. This historic cathedral town southwest of LISBURN has an apt name that can be found elsewhere in Ireland for similar reasons.

Dronfeield (Derbyshire) 'Open land swarming with drones'. *Dran* (Old English) 'drone'; *feld* (Old English) 'open land'. This town northwest of CHESTERFIELD was recorded as *Dranefeld* in the Domesday Book of 1086.

Droylsden (Greater Manchester) Possibly 'valley of the dry stream'. *Dryge* (Old English) 'dried-up'; *wella* (Old English) 'stream'; *denu* (Old English) 'valley'. This east-MANCHESTER suburb was recorded as *Drilisden c.*1250.

Drumchapel (Strathclyde) 'Ridge of the horse'. *Druim* (Scottish Gaelic) 'ridge'; *chapuill* (Scottish Gaelic) 'horse'. This large housing estate was built in the 1950s on the western edge of GLASGOW as part of the city's post-war 'overspill' programme to relieve overcrowding in the inner areas. The original settlement of the same name was sited on one of the many drumlins—low humpback ridges—that are prevalent here.

Drumnadrochit (Highland) 'Ridge by the bridge'. *Druim* (Scottish Gaelic) 'ridge'; *na* (Scottish Gaelic) 'of the'; *drochaid* (Scottish Gaelic) 'bridge'. An apt description of this place where there has long been a bridge over the River Enrick beneath a very steep ridge on the western bank of Loch NESS.

Drumochter (Highland/Tayside) 'The top of the ridge'. *Druim* (Scottish Gaelic) 'ridge'; *uachdar* (Scottish Gaelic) 'the top of', 'the upper part'. Indeed, this lonely settlement is situated on the watershed ridge between the Garry/Tay river system flowing south and that of the Truim/Spey flowing north. Even at its lowest point on the floor of the Pass of Drumochter the main A9 road and rail links rise to over 1400ft (400m) here.

Dryburgh (Borders) Apparently 'dry town'. *Dryge* (Old English) 'dry'; *burh* (Old English) 'town', 'borough', 'burgh'. Early records of the name of this village and the ruins of its famous mid-century abbey, that lie in the northbank of the River TWEED opposite ST BOSWELLS, show *Drieburh* 1160, *Dryburg* 1211.

Drymen (Central) 'On the ridge'. *Drumein* (Scottish Gaelic—dative/locative of *druim*) 'on the ridge'. An apt description of the situation of this village to the northwest of GLASGOW, which is pronounced 'Drimmin'.

Dublin (Dublin) Place of the 'black pool'. *Dubh* (Irish Gaelic) 'black'; *linn* (Irish Gaelic) 'pool'. The descriptive name of the Irish capital city refers to the noticably dark peat-stained waters of the part of the River LIFFEY by which the original settlement arose in prehistoric times and where the Viking town was built in the 9th and 10th centuries. Its alternative official Irish name, *Baile Atha Cliath*, meaning 'town of the hurdle ford', derives from: *baile* (Irish Gaelic) 'town'; *ath* (Irish Gaelic) 'ford'; *cliath* (Irish Gaelic) 'hurdle'. The latter name form is also ancient, but it was the simpler descriptive name that was to become established by the English during their 800 years of occupation.

Duckinfield (Greater Manchester) 'Ducks' field'. *Ducena* (Old English—genitive plural of *duce*) 'ducks'; *feld* (Old English) 'open space'. This town east of MANCHESTER lies in the valley of the River Tame, which may have been a natural wildfowl breeding ground. The name was documented as *Dokenfeld* in the 12th century.

Dudley (West Midlands) 'Dudda's clearing'. *Dudda* (Old English personal name); *leah* (Old English) 'woodland clearing'. The name of this industrial town west of BIRMINGHAM was recorded in the Domesday book as *Dudelei* and is one of many similar placenames in this area, which indicate the former presence of a large forest and its clearing for industry and settlement. *Compare* DIDCOT; DODWORTH.

Dufftown (Grampian) This town, southeast of ELGIN, was founded and laid out in 1817 by James Duff, the 4th Earl of Fife, after whom it is named. Today it is famous for its whisky distilleries.

Dulwich (Greater London) 'Marshy meadow where dill grows'. *Dile* (Old English) 'dill' herb plant; *wisce* (old English) 'marshy meadowland'. This low-lying district of SOUTHWARK, where in its famous park and on the common there are still ponds and lakes, has a name reflecting the original abundance of wild dill here. Early records show: *Dilwihs* 967; *Dilewisse* c.1210.

Dumbarton (Strathclyde) 'Fortified stronghold of the Britons'. *Dun* (Scottish Gaelic) 'fortified stronghold'; *Breatainn* (Scottish Gaelic) tribe of Britons. Lying on the CLYDE estuary, northwest of GLASGOW, this town with its castle on a steep rock was the capital of the ancient kingdom of Strathclyde, between the 5th and 11th centuries. Records show *Dunbretane* 1300-1450. The old county and postal name, Dunbartonshire, reverted the *m* to *n* only in this century.

Dumfries (Dumfries and Galloway) 'Fortress of the woodland'. *Dun* (Scottish Gaelic) 'fortified stronghold'; *phris* (Scottish Gaelic genitive of *preas*) 'of the woodland copse'. The name of this country town, northwest of CARLISLE, was recorded as DUMFRES around 1190. *See* NITHSDALE.

Dunbar (Lothian) 'Fort on the height'. *Dun* (Scottish Gaelic) 'fort'; *barr* (Scottish Gaelic) 'height'. A castle was built on the high rocks above the port's natural harbour but it was ruined in 1650 by Cromwell's army. Recorded as *Dynbaer* in the early 8th century, the name of this coastal town, northeast of HADDINGTON reflects on even earlier fort on this side.

Dunblane (Central) 'Hill of (St) Blane'. *Dun* (Scottish Gaelic) 'hill', 'mound'; *Blaan* (personal name) son of King Aidan, who founded a monastery here in the 7th century. The name of this town, north of Stirling, was noted as *Dumblann* around 1200.

Dundalk (Louth) 'Fort of Dealga'. *Dun* (Irish Gaelic) 'fort'; *Dealgan* (Irish Gaelic personal name) Dealga, an ancient pre-Celtic Firbolg chieftain, who apparently established a fort on Castletown Hill to the west of the modern town and port at the head of Dundalk Bay.

Dundee (Tayside) Commonly derived as the 'fort of Daig'. *Dun* (Scottish Gaelic) 'fortified place'; *Daig* (personal name) of unknown connection. The fort presumably would have been on the high ground of Dundee Law where the 13th-century Dundee Castle, long since destroyed, once stood. Other possible derivations include *Dun-dubh* (Scottish Gaelic) 'dark hill', or *Dun-De* (Scottish Gaelic genitve of *Dia*) 'hill of God'. One authority considers that there is probably no need to look further than the local river name, the TAY, for a more convincing derivation of the second element. In early records there are various renderings: *Donde* 1177; *Dunde* 1199; *Dundho*, *Dundo* 1200.

Dundonald (Down) 'Fort of Donall'. *Dun* (Irish Gaelic) fort; *Donaill* (Irish Gaelic personal name) Donall, unidentified. This 20th-century industrial and residential estate established on the eastern fringe of BELFAST takes its name from an ancient fort that would have been on the site of the later Anglo-Norman motte.

Dunfermline (Fife) The full explanation of the name of this ancient town, just north of the famous FORTH bridges, remains obscure. The first part is obviously *dun* (Scottish Gaelic) 'hill' or 'fort', this being consistent with both the geography and history of the town—an early capital of the emerging Scottish nation, where Queen Margaret founded an abbey in 1072. Records show *Dumfermelyn* 1100; *Dumferlin* 1124; *Dunferlyne* 1375.

Dungannon (Tyrone) 'Fort of Geanann'. *Dun* (Irish Gaelic) fort; *Geanainn* (Irish Gaelic personal name) Geanann, unidentified. This 17th-century 'plantation town' to the south of COOKSTOWN is where this ancient fort must have been sited, although there is no documentory evidence.

Dungarvan (Waterford) 'Fort of Garbhan'. *Dun* (Irish Gaelic) 'fort'; *Garbhain* (Irish Gaelic personal name) Garbhan, unidentified. This port and administrative centre for County WATERFORD has developed on the site of a former fort by the estuary of the River Colligan, where the remains of the later Anglo-Norman castle and town walls still stand.

Dungeness (Kent) 'Headland of Denge'. *Denu-ge* (Old English) 'valley district'; *naess* (Old English) 'headland'. This prominent headland southeast of LYDD takes its name from the Denge Marsh which occupies most of the low-lying land behind. Records show: *Dengenesse* 1335.

Dunkeld (Tayside) 'Fort of the Caledonians'. *Dun* (Scottish Gaelic) 'fort'; *Chailleainn* (Scottish Gaelic) 'Caledonians'—referring to the tribe of Picts who had a royal stronghold here in t he first millennium AD. Early records reveal the name of this small burgh, northwest of PERTH, as *Duincaillen* 865; *Dun-calden* and *Dunicallenn* *c.*1000.

Dunkery Beacon (Somerset) Probably 'craggy hill'. *Duno* (Brythonic Celtic root word) 'hill'; *careg* (Brythonic Celtic) 'crag', 'cliff'. This name of the highest point of EXMOOR, at 1750 ft (519 m), was recorded as *Duncrey* in the 13th century. The 'beacon' affix is self-evident.

Dun Laoghaire (Dublin) 'Fort of Laoghaire'. *Dun* (Irish Gaelic) 'fort'; *Laoghaire* (Irish Gaelic personal name) of uncertain identity; according to some, he was a 5th-century king of Ireland and follower of St Patrick. The name of this major ferry port on DUBLIN Bay was earlier rendered in English as Dunleary, which is how it is pronounced today. Following a visit by King George IV in 1821, the town was known as Kingstown until 1921, when under the Irish Free State, it reverted to its original Gaelic name. *See* COBH.

Dunmow, Great and **Little** (Essex) 'Hill meadow'. *Dun* (Old English) 'hill'; *mawe* (Old English conjectural word) 'meadow'. The basic name of this small town and attendant village east of BISHOP'S STORTFORD was documented as *Dunemowe* 951; *Duommawa* 1086 (Domesday Book).

Dunmurry (Antrim) 'Fort of Murray'. *Dun* (Irish Gaelic) 'fort'; *Muireadhaigh* (Irish Gaelic personal name) Murray, unidentifed. This satellite suburb in the extreme southwest of the BELFAST built-up area has grown up around the site of this ancient fort of uncertain origin.

Dunoon (Strathclyde) 'Fort (on) the river'. *Dun* (Scottish Gaelic) 'fort'; *obhainn* (Scottish Gaelic—adjectival variant of *abh*) 'river'. Traces of a 12th-century castle, and possibly an even earlier fort, can be found on a rock above the pier of this resort on the CLYDE estuary, northwest of GLASGOW. Recorded as *Dunhoven* 1270; *Dunnovane* 1476.

Duns (Borders) Simply 'fortified hill'. *Dun* (Scottish Gaelic) 'fort', 'hill'; the *s* is a later addition, possibly meant as a plural. The former main town of BERWICKshire, lies at the foot of a hill called Duns Law, west of BERWICK-UPON-TWEED. An older town, on the hill itself, was raised in 1542.

Dunstable (Bedfordshire) 'Dunna's post'. *Dunna* (Old English personal name); *stapol* (Old English) 'post', 'pillar', 'landmark'. This manufacturing town, immediately west of LUTON, has a name that probably reflects its importance as the intersection of two ancient routes established by the Romans. This was the site of the Roman camp of *Durocobrivis*, where WATLING STREET crossed the ICKNIELD WAY. The name *Dunestaple* was documented in 1123.

Dunster (Somerset) 'Dunn's tor'. *Dunn* (Old English personal name); *torr* (Old English) 'craggy hill'. The name of this historic market town, lying below EXMOOR southeast of MINEHEAD, was recorded simply as *Torre* in the Domesday Book of 1086, and with the later personal prefix, as *Dunestore* in 1138.

Dunvegan (Highland) Possibly 'fort of the few'. *Dun* (Scottish Gaelic) 'fort'; *beagain* (Scottish Gaelic) 'few in number'. This place with its spectacular castle in northwest SKYE is the ancestral home of the Macleods. Most historians agree that the original 12th-century fort here was built by Leod, a younger son of Olaf, one of the last Norse kings of Man and the North Isles. Thus Leod (of the Liotr family) would have been one of 'the few' Norse chieftains left in Scotland after the Scots finally crushed the Viking rule of the Western Isles at the battle of Largs in 1263. Recorded as *Dunbegane* 1498; *Dunveggane* 1517; *Dunnevegane* 1553.

Durham (Durham) 'Island with a hill'. *Dun* (Old English) 'hill'; *holmr* (Old Scandinavian) 'holm', 'island'. This name aptly describes the domineering and defensive rocky site of the original town's famous 11th-century cathedral and castle, built high above a horseshoe-shaped meander of the River Wear. Recorded as *Dunholm* around 1000, the name was subsequently influenced by the Normans to evolve into its current form: *Dunhelme* 1122; *Durealme c.*1170; *Duram* 1297. The county name, which never added the '-shire', is comparatively late.

Durness (Highland) 'Headland of the deer'. *Djur* (Old Norse) 'deer'; *nes* (Old Norse) 'headland'. This remote village is the most northwesterly on mainland Britain, situated on a remote headland where certainly today the deer roam wild.

Dursley (Gloucestershire) 'Deorsige's clearing'. *Deorsige* (Old English personal name); *leah* (Old English) 'woodland clearing'. The name of this small town, southwest of STROUD, on the edge of the COTSWOLDS is noted as *Dersilege* in the Domesday Book.

Dyce (Grampian) Possibly 'southwards'. *Deis* (Scottish Gaelic locative of *deas*) 'to the south'. This may have been a reference to the location of the settlement here, with ABERDEEN a few miles to the south. Alternatively, the meaning may be: *dys* (Old Norse) a cairn.

Dee (Grampian; Gwynedd/Cheshire/Merseyside) 'Goddess'. *Deva* (Brythonic Celtic) 'goddess'. This common British river name, exemplified in the Scottish one that flows eastwards through 'Royal Deeside' to discharge into the North Sea at ABERDEEN, and the Anglo-Welsh Dee with its famous wide estuary west of the WIRRAL, has ancient roots. The Roman name for CHES-

TER was *Deva*, the same as the then name for the river Dee on which it stands. In 1196 this same river was recorded as *Deverdoe*, simply meaning 'waters of the Dee', a forerunner of the modern Welsh version *Dyfrdwy*. The first element of the latter derives from the same Celtic root as does DOVER.

Dyfed (Wales) 'Land of the Demetae'. The modern name of the county that was created in 1974 to cover the southwestern region of the principality is a revival of the ancient tribal name that referred to the kingdom of the *Demetae*, which existed here between the 1st and 11th centuries.

Dymchurch (Kent) Probably 'the judge's church'. *Dema* (Old English) 'judge'; *cirice* (Old English) 'church'. Alternatively, some authorities consider that the first element, in the name of this small coastal town by ROMNEY MARSH, may derive: *Diuma* (Old English personal name) 7th-century bishop of Mercia. Records show: *Deman circe* around 1100; *Demecherche* in 1243.

E

Eaglesham (Strathclyde) Possibly 'church village'. *Eaglais* (Scottish Gaelic) 'church'; *ham* (Old English) 'village'. The name of this village, south of GLASGOW, was recorded as *Egilshame* 1158; *Eglishame* 1309.

Ealing (Greater London) Place of 'Gilla's people'. *Gilla* (Old English personal name) possibly a nickname related to *giellan* meaning 'to scream'; *ingas* (Old English) 'people of'. The name of this west-LONDON borough is elided from *Gillingas*, recorded *c.*700, and subsequently documented as *Gilling* 1130; *Ylling* 1254.

Earlston (Borders) Possibly 'Earcil's hill'. *Earcil* (personal name); *dun* (Old English) 'hill'. Early records of the name of this small town, northeast of GALASHIELS, show: *Ercheldon* 1144; *Ercildune* 1180.

Easington (Durham/Tyne and Wear) 'Estate associated with Esa'. *Esa* (Old English personal name); *ing* (Old English connective particle) 'associated with'; *tun* (old English) 'estate'. This common English name is here applied to a string of former coal-mining communities extending northwest from PETERLEE to HOUGHTON LE SPRING, two attendant villages having distinguishing affixes, namely **Easington Colliery** and **Easington Lane**. The basic name was recorded as *Esingtun c.*1050.

East Anglia *see* **England**.

Eastbourne (East Sussex) 'Eastern' place called 'stream'. *East* (Old English) 'eastern'; *burna* (Old English) 'stream'. The original name of this popular coastal resort and conference centre near BEACHY HEAD was simply *Burne*, as entered in the Domesday Book of 1086; the later form *Estburn*, documented in 1279, was in contradistinction to *Westburne* (1302), the name of a village 50 miles (80 km) to the west near Havant.

East Dereham (Norfolk) 'Eastern enclosure for deer'. *East* (Old English) 'east', 'eastern'; *deor* (Old English) 'deer'; *hamm* (Old English) 'pasture', 'riverside land'. Originally *Derham*, as recorded in the Domesday Book of 1086, this town west of Norwich became known as *Estderham*, as noted in 1254, to differentiate it from the village of *Westderham* (1203), 20 miles (32 km) away.

East Grinstead (West Sussex) 'Eastern green place'. *East* (Old English) 'eastern'; *grene* + *stede* (Old English) 'green place'. The basic name of this town east of Crawley, recorded in 1121 simply as *Grensteda*, has the sense of 'grassy land'. *Estgrenested*, as of *c.*1270, contrasted it from *Westgrenested*, 20 miles (32 km) away.

East Ham *see* **West Ham**.

East Kilbride (Strathclyde) 'Church of (St) Brigid'. *Cill* (Scottish Gaelic) 'church'; *Brigid* (personal name) of a saint who may never have actually lived but is the legendary Celtic goddess of fire and poetry. Although East Kilbride was designated as Scotland's first New Town in 1947, the old village here, southeast of Glasgow, was recorded as *Kellebride* in 1180. The 'East' was added later to distinguish it from West Kilbride, 30 miles away near to the Ayrshire coast.

Eastleigh (Hampshire) 'East wood or clearing'. *East* (Old English) 'east'; *leage* (Old English—dative form of *leah*) 'wood' or 'woodland clearing'. This industrial town north of Southampton was recorded as *Estleie* in the Domesday Book of 1086.

East Linton (Lothian) 'Flax enclosure'. *Lin* (Old English) 'flax' (compare 'linen'); *tun* (Old English) 'enclosure', 'village'. The name of this small town, on the River Tyne, downstream and northwest of Haddington, was recorded as *Lintun* in 1127. The 'East' was added later to distinguish it from West Linton, 30 miles southwest, by the Pentland Hills.

East Midlands *see* **West Midlands**

East Sussex *see* **Sussex**

East Wemyss *see* **Wemyss**.

Eastwood (Nottinghamshire) 'Eastern clearing'. *East* (Old English) 'eastern'; *thveit* (Old Scandinavian) 'woodland clearing'. Thus, this common English placename, which normally means what it says, in the case of this town northwest of NOTTINGHAM has the sense of a 'meadow' that arose from a forest clearing. Records show that at some point in medieval or Tudor times the substitution of the English '-wood' ending took place: *Estwic* 1086; *Estweit* 1165; *Estwood* 1575.

Ebbw Vale (Gwent) Place in the 'Ebwy Valley'. This was a 19th-century designation for the then new coal-mining and industrial town that developed around the former ironworks here in the upper valley of the River Ebwy. The origin of the river name may derive from a ancient Celtic root word related to the modern Welsh *ebol*, meaning 'colt' or 'horse' river.

Ecclefechan (Dumfries and Galloway) Possibly 'church of (St) Fechin'. *Eaglais* (Scottish Gaelic) 'church'; *Fechin* (personal name) the saintly 7th-century Irish abbot from Meath, who never came to Scotland but some of whose disciples did. Alternatively, some authorities still support the derivation of the name of this small town, north of ANNAN, as *eglwys-bychan* (Brythonic Celtic) 'little church'.

Eccles (Greater Manchester) Place of 'the ancient church'. *Egles* (Brythonic Celtic conjectural root word) pre-English, Romano-British, 'church'. The name of this town, west of MANCHESTER, was recorded in *c*.1200, exactly as now. *Compare* ECCLEFECHAN; ECCLESHALL; ECCLESTON.

Eccleshall (Staffordshire) 'Church nook'. *Egles* (Brythonic Celtic conjectural root word) pre-English, Romano-British, 'church'; *halh* (Old English) 'nook of land'. The name of this small town, northwest of STAFFORD, was recorded as *Ecleshelle* in 1086; and *Eccleshale* in 1227.

Eccleston (Lancashire) 'Farmstead by the ancient church'. *Egles* (Brythonic Celtic conjectural root word) pre-English, British-Romano, 'church'; *tun* (Old English) 'farmstead', 'settlement'. The name of this small town, west of CHORLEY, documented in 1094 as *Aycleton*, is one of several such 'Eccles' names in LANCASHIRE.

Edenbridge (Kent) 'Eadhelm's bridge'. *Eadhelm* (Old English personal name); *brycg* (Old English) 'bridge'. The name of this small town, west of TONBRIDGE, was recorded as *Eadelmesbregge* in a text of around 1100.

Edenderry (Offaly) 'The hill brow of the oak grove'. *Eadan* (Irish Gaelic) 'brow'; *doire* (Irish Gaelic) 'oak wood'. This small market town west of DUBLIN has hills immediately to the north and south, either of which could be that described in the name. The current Irish name for this town is *Eadan Doire*.

Edgbaston (West Midlands) 'Ecgbald's farmstead'. *Ecgbald* (Old English personal name); *tun* (Old English) 'farmstead'. The name of this south-central district of BIRMINGHAM, famous as the site of the test cricket ground and the city's main university campus, was oddly recorded as *Celboldestone* in the Domesday Book of 1086, but as *Egboldeston* in the early 12th century.

Edgeware (Greater London) 'Ecgi's wier'. *AEcge* (Old English personal name); *wer* (Old English) 'weir', 'fishing enclosure'. This district of BARNET, sitting astride the old Roman road of WATLING STREET, which itself begins as the Edgeware Road in central LONDON, was recorded as *AEcges wer* in a document of 975.

Edgeworthstown (Longford) This small town, lying to the southeast of LONGFORD in Ireland's 'Lakeland' region at the centre of the country, is indeed a 'plantation town' with a clearly imported English name from the Edgeworth family which came to Ireland in 1585 and developed this town here during James I reign. The former name of the settlement was Mostrim, an anglicised version of the Irish *Meathas Troim*, which means:

'frontier of the elder tree', this place being close to the boundary between LONGFORD and WESTMEATH.

Edinburgh (Lothian) 'Fort of the rock face'. *Eideann* (Scottish Gaelic corrupted form of *aodann*) 'rock face'; *burh* (Old English) 'stronghold'. The latter element was a replacement for the original *dun* (Scottish Gaelic) 'stronghold' or 'fort', which preceded what is now the first element (an arrangement later to be transferred to *Dunedin* in New Zealand). Thus, the etymological description is most apt for Scotland's capital city with its famous castle (and earlier fort) on a rock.

Edmonton (Greater London) 'Eadhelm's farmstead'. *Eadhelm* (Old English personal name); *tun* (Old English) 'farmstead'. The name of this northern LONDON district in the borough of ENFIELD appears in the Domesday Book as *Adelmetone*, and later as *Edmeltona* in 1130. *Compare* EDENBRIDGE.

Egham (Surrey) 'Ecga's homestead'. *Ecga* (Old English personal name); *ham* (Old English) 'homestead', 'village'. The name of this now residential satellite town, on the southwestern fringe of the LONDON conurbation, was early recorded as *Egeham* in 933.

Egremont (Cumbria) 'Sharp-pointed hill'. *Aigre* (Old French) 'sharp'; *mont* (Old French) 'hill'. The name of this former iron-ore-mining town, on the site of a late 11th-century Norman keep, was apparently transferred from Aigremont in Normandy, but probably in association with the ridge of sharp-pointed Skiddaw slate found here and partly with the local River Ehen, previously Egne. It was documented as *Egremont* in around 1125. *See* ENNERDALE Water.

Eigg (Highland) Probably '(island with) the notch'. *Eag* (Scottish Gaelic) 'notch', 'nick', 'gap'. On this Inner Hebridean isle, a wide rift or notch runs through from southeast to northwest separating the northern plateau from the An Sgurr ridge in the south. Recorded as *Egge* 1292; *Egg* 1654. Its current pronunciation is 'Egg'.

Eire *see* **Ireland**

Elgin (Grampian) 'Little Ireland'. *Ealg* (Scottish Gaelic) early name for Ireland; *-in* (Scottish Gaelic—diminutive suffix) 'little'. Such a name would have been given by the original Scots settlers from Ireland to remind themselves of the mother country. *Compare* BLAIR ATHOLL and GLENELG.

Elie (Fife) Place of 'the tomb'. *Ealadh* (Scottish Gaelic) 'tomb'; or *ayle* (Scots) 'covered cemetery'. There was once such a cemetery here. The name of this town on the coast southwest of ST MONANS was recorded as *Elye* 1491; *Alie c.*1600. Pronounced today as 'Eelay'.

Elland (West Yorkshire) 'Riverside estate'. *Ea-land* (Old English) 'cultivated land by a river'. This wool-textile town, northwest of HUDDERSFIELD on the River Calder, is noted: *Elant* 1086; *Eiland* 1167; *Elande* 1202.

Ellesmere Port (Cheshire) This 19th-century name of the industrial port at the southeast landward end of the WIRRAL peninsula, where the Ellesmere Canal enters the MERSEY estuary, derives from the former, which in turn refers to the small SHROPSHIRE town of Ellesmere ('Elli's lake') to which it is linked by canal.

Ellon (Grampian) Possibly 'green plain or meadow'. *Ailean* (Scottish Gaelic) 'green spot' or 'enclosure'. This derivation suits the location of the place at the head of the narrow Ythan River estuary. Alternatively, it could be derived as *eilean* (Scottish Gaelic) 'island', referring again to its situation. It was recorded in the mid-12th century as *Eilan*.

Elstree (Hertfordshire) 'Tidwulf's tree'. *Tidwulf* (Old English personal name); *treow* (Old English) 'tree boundary marker'. The name of this residential village southwest of BOREHAMWOOD, famous for its film studios, would appear to have lost its initial *t* due to the wrong division of a 11th-century text in which it was recorded as *aet Tithulfes treow*.

Ely (Cambridgeshire) 'Eel district'. *El* (Old English) 'eel';

ge (Old English) 'district', 'region'. This renowned cathedral city got its name from the great number of eels once caught on The FENS here. Recorded as *Elge* in an 8th-century text of the Venerable Bede, it had become *Elig* by 970, and *Elyg* as entered in the Domesday Book of 1086. The transformation to the latter and current form is believed to have happened with the original second element being taken for *eg*, (Old English) 'island', or, as was apt in this case, having the sense of an elevated drier area surrounded by marshland.

Enfield (Greater London) 'Eana's open land'. *Eana* (Old English personal name); *feld* (Old English) 'tract of land cleared of trees'. The name of this north LONDON borough was recorded as *Enefelde* in 1086.

England (Britain) 'Land of the Angles'. *Engla* (Old English—genitive plural of *Engle*) 'of the Angles'; *land* (Old English) 'land', 'region'. Thus the southern part of BRITAIN was named by the peoples from the Continental homeland of Angel in Schleswig (now northern Germany), who together with the Saxons and Jutes invaded and settled here in the 5th and 6th centuries. It was first documented as *Englaland* around 890. The modern region of **East Anglia** was an ancient kingdom of the Angles.

Ennerdale Water (Cumbria) 'Lake in Anundr's valley'. *Anundar* (Old Norse personal name—genitive); *dalr* (Old Norse) 'valley'; *waeter* (Old English) 'lake'. This, the westernmost lake in the LAKE DISTRICT, takes its name from the valley here, originally *Ananderdala*, as recorded in about 1135. Later, sometime around 1300, the first element was replaced by the river name *Ehen* (of uncertain origin), giving *Eghnerdale* in a document of 1321 and *Eyneswater* in 1338.

Ennis (Clare) 'The island or water meadow'. *Inis* (Irish Gaelic) 'island', 'water meadow', 'haugh'. Either of these river situations would be appropriate to the original settlement of this now small county town that sits astride the River Fergus, in the centre of CLARE.

Enniscorthy (Wexford) The full meaning of the name of this town north of WEXFORD remains in doubt, even if its river situation on the Slaney is appropriate to explaining the first element: *inis* (Irish Gaelic) 'water meadow', 'island'.

Enniskillen (Fermanagh) 'Kethlenn's island'. *Inis* (Irish Gaelic) 'island;' *Ceithleann* (Irish Gaelic personal name) Kethlenn, the semi-legendary wife of Balor, the Fomorian king of TORY ISLAND. This county town is built around an island in the short stretch of the River ERNE connecting Upper and Lower Lough Erne.

Epping (Essex) Place of 'the lookout ridge'. *Yppe* (Old English) 'ridge' or 'elevated land used as a lookout'; *ingas* (Old English) 'people of'. This town to the north-east of LONDON, lying at the north end of Epping Forest, was recorded as *Eppinges* in the Domesday Bookof 1086. *Compare* UPPINGHAM.

Epsom (Surrey) 'Ebbe's homestead'. *Ebbe* (Old English personal name); *ham* (Old English) 'homestead', 'village'. The name of this town, at the southern fringe of the LONDON built-up area on the North DOWNS and famous as the venue of the annual racing classic, 'The Derby', was originally noted as *Ebbesham* in about 973.

Erith (Greater London) 'Gravelly or muddy landing place'. *Ear* (Old English) 'gravel'; *hyth* (Old English) 'landing place'. The name of this THAMES riverside district of BEXLEY, immediately downstream of the Erith Marshes, was recorded in about 960 as simply *Earhyth*.

Ermine Street (England) 'Roman road called after Earna's people'. *Earna* (Old English personal name); *ingas* (Old English) 'people of'; *straet* (Old English) 'Roman road'. Probably originally applying to the stretch of road near the CAMBRIDGESHIRE village of Arrington (*tun* 'of Earna's people'), the name eventually came to be the designation for the entire length between LONDON and YORK. Later it was transferred as the name of another Roman road, running from Silchester, near BASINGSTOKE, to GLOUCESTER.

Erne, Upper and Lower Lough (Fermanagh) This long lake system, that splits the county of Fermanagh in two, is named after the Ernai or Erni, said to be an ancient race living here on a plain that pre-dated the lake.

Errigal Mountain (Donegal) 'The oratory'. *An earagail* (Irish Gaelic) 'oratory'. This brilliant quartzite cone, rising to 2466 ft (752m), is the highest peak in north-west Ireland. As such, it would have been a suitable place for having an oratory or hermitage on it, in common with many other mountains in Ireland. See BRANDON Mountain.

Esher (Surrey) 'Ash-tree district'. *AEsc* (Old English) 'ash tree'; *scearu* (Old English) 'share' or 'division of land', 'district'. Recorded as *AEscaeron* in a document of 1005, the name of this residential town near the outer southwestern edge of the LONDON conurbation had become more recognisable as *Esshere* by 1062.

Eskdale (Cumbria) 'Valley of the River Esk'. *Isca* (Brythonic Celtic conjectural root element) 'water'; *dalr* (Old Norse) 'valley'. This major LAKE DISTRICT valley, whose river flows southwestwards from the slopes of SCAFELL PIKE, is one of the few not to contain a lake; its name was documented in 1294 as *Eskedal*.

Essex (England) Territory of 'the East Saxons'. *East* (Old English) 'east'; *Seaxe* (Old English tribal name) 'Saxon'. A present-day county in southeast ENGLAND, its name, recorded as *East Seaxe* in 894, originally applied to the ancient kingdom of the East Saxons, which between the 5th and 10th centuries included not only the territory of the present county, but also all of the former MIDDLESEX and part of HERTFORDSHIRE. *See* MIDDLESEX; SUSSEX; WESSEX.

Eton (Berkshire) 'Farmstead by the river'. *Ea* (Old English) 'river'; *tun* (Old English) 'farmstead', 'village'. This town and its famous school, which are situated on the north bank of the THAMES opposite WINDSOR, have a common English place name, more often rendered as

Eaton. It was recorded as *Ettone* in the Domesday Book of 1086.

Ettrick (Borders) The name of this village, southwest of Selk, is taken from the river on which it stands, the Ettrick Water. This also applies to other nearby places: Ettrick Forest; Ettrick Pen; Ettrickbridge; etc. One authority has suggested *arte* (Brythonic Celtic) 'playful', as an apt description of the river here. However, the exact origin for this name is unattested, and it may be of an ancient pre-Celtic root.

Evanton (Highland) 'Evan's town'. This village on the shore of the CROMARTY Firth was founded around 1810 by a landowner named Evan Fraser of Balconie.

Everton (Merseyside) 'Farmstead where the wild boar roam'. *Eofor* (Old English) 'wild boar'; *tun* (Old English) 'farmstead', 'village'. This well-known district of LIVERPOOL was recorded as *Evretona* in 1094.

Evesham (Hereford and Worcester) 'Eof's river land'. *Eof* (Old English personal name); *hamm* (Old English) 'land in the bend of a river'. The name of this town, on the River Avon at the centre of the Vale of Evesham horticultural area, was noted as *Eveshomme* in 709.

Ewell (Surrey) Place at 'the river source'. *Aewell* (Old English compound of *ea* and *wella*) 'river source', 'spring', 'well'. This town on the outer southern fringe of the LONDON conurbation, just to the north of EPSOM, has a straightforward name suggesting a well, and does refer to the Hogsmill River, a small THAMES tributary that rises here on the edge of the North DOWNS. It was recorded as *Euuelle* in 933.

Exeter (Devon) 'Roman town on the River Exe'. *Isca* (Brythonic Celtic conjectural river name) 'water'; *ceaster* (Old English) 'Roman station'. This historic cathedral city and county town of DEVON lies near the head of the deeply indented estuary of the River Exe, and derives its name from the latter. The name of the Roman camp here was *Isca Dumnoniorum*, which refers to the river and the local Celtic tribe of the Dumnonii, who had their ancient capital here. Influenced by the French-speaking Normans, the present name is a contraction of the later English form, *Exanceaster*, as recorded around 900. The Domesday Book entry of 1086 was *Excestre*.

Exmoor (Somerset/Devon) 'Moorland of the River Exe'. *Isca* (Brythonic Celtic conjectural river name) 'water'; *mor* (Old English) 'moorland'. This elevated moorland, although situated on the BRISTOL Channel side of England's southwest peninsula, is drained principally southwards by the River Exe, from which it takes its name. It was documented as *Exmora* in 1204.

Exmouth (Devon) Place at 'the mouth of the River Exe'. *Isca* (Brythonic Celtic conjectural river name) 'water'; *mutha* (Old English) 'river mouth'. Like DARTMOUTH, the name of this coastal resort southeast of EXETER clearly denotes its situation at the entrance to one of Devon's typical drowned river-valley estuaries, known as rias. An early manifestation of its name, *Exanmuthan*, was recorded in the Anglo-Saxon Chronicle around 1000.

Eye (Suffolk) 'Elevated land in the marsh'. *Eg* (Old English) 'island'. The name of this small agricultural town, northeast of BURY ST EDMUNDS, simply means an 'island' in the sense of its slightly higher, and hence drier, situation compared to the generally low-lying surrounding land here, drained by the river Dove and other tributaries of the River Waveney, in an area that would almost certainly have been a marshland in early times. It was recorded as *Eia* in the Domesday Book of 1086.

Eyemouth (Borders) 'At the mouth of the Eye Water'. this coastal fishing port northwest of BERWICK-UPON-TWEED takes its name from its river which is tautologically derived from *ea* (Old English) 'river'; 'water' was added when the old meaning was lost.

Eynsham (Oxfordshire) 'Egon's homestead or river land'. *Egon* (Old English personal name); *ham* or *hamm* (Old

English) 'homestead' or 'riverside meadow'. This small town, northwest of OXFORD, lies between the THAMES (or Isis, as this stretch is called) and the Evenlode rivers, and it seems likely that the latter of the two derivations is the more probable. Early records show: *Egonesham* 571 (Anglo-Saxon Chronicle); *Egenes homme* 864; *Eglesham* 1086 (Domesday Book).

F

Failsworth (Greater Manchester) Probably 'fenced enclosure'. *Fegels* (Old English conjectural word) 'fence'; *worth* (Old English) 'enclosure'. The name of this industrial town, northeast of MANCHESTER, was recorded as *Fayleswrthe* in 1212. *See* LETCHWORTH.

Fairford (Gloucestershire) 'Clear water ford'. *Faeger* (Old English) 'fair', 'clear', 'clean'; *ford* (Old English) 'river crossing'. The name of this small COTSWOLD town, east of CIRENCESTER, means exactly what it says. Records include: *Fagranforda* 862; *Fareforde* 1086.

Fair Isle (Shetland) 'Sheep Island'. *Faer* (Old Norse) 'sheep'; *isle* (probably English translation of Old Norse *ay*) 'small island'. The remote Fair Isle, lying midway between SHETLAND and ORKNEY, was settled by the Vikings as a staging post to which they brought sheep. A place-name exactly parallel to this is found in the Faeroe Islands, and for the same reasons. Unsuprisingly, the tradition of distinctive knitwear has arisen here. A record of 1529 shows the 'isle' as *Faray*.

Fakenham (Norfolk) 'Facca's homestead'. *Facca-n* (Old English personal name—genitive form); *ham* (Old English) 'homestead'. Recorded as *Fachenham* in the Domesday Book in 1086, the modern name applies to the agricultural centre northwest of NORWICH.

Falkirk (Central) 'Speckled church'. *Fawe* (Middle English) 'speckled'; *kirke* (Middle English) 'church'. This derivation has been attested, and it is presumed that the original settlement, long predating the industrial town, had a church that was built of varigated stone. The name of this town, southeast of Stirling, was recorded as *Faukirke* in 1298.

Falkland (Fife) The origin of the name FIFE of this small burgh with its medieval Royal palace and hunting forest remains uncertain. Possible associations with falconry have been made from *falca* (Old English) 'falcon'. One authority has drawn another connection with the town's regal status in proposing the derivation *folc* (Old English) 'people's', 'land' (English), i.e. Crown property. (Faulkland in Somerset derives from these sources). Early records show: *Falleland* 1128; *Falecklen* 1165.

Falmouth (Cornwall) Place at 'the mouth of the River Fal'. *Fal* (Ancient river name) of uncertain origin and meaning; *mutha* (Old English) 'river mouth'. The name of this Cornish port, south of TRURO, remains an etymological mystery; it was recorded as *Falemuth* in 1235, and that of the river name as *Faele* in 969.

Fareham (Hampshire) 'Homestead amongst the ferns'. *Fearn* (Old English) 'fern'; *ham* (Old English) 'homestead', 'dwelling house'. The name of this town, at the northeast end of PORTSMOUTH Harbour, was recorded as *Fernham* in the Domesday Book. *Compare* FARNHAM.

Faringdon (Oxfordshire) 'Fern-covered hill'. *Fearn* (Old English) 'fern'; *dun* (Old English) 'hill'. This small town situated by the Vale of the White Horse, west of ABINGDON, is in an area of downland where ferns grow. It was noted as *Fearndun* in 924. *Compare* FARNBOROUGH.

Farnborough (Hampshire) 'Fern-covered hill'. *Fearn* (Old English) 'fern'; *beorg* (Old English) 'mound', 'hill'. This military town north of ALDERSHOT and famous for its air shows at the Royal Aircraft Establishment here, has a name of similar meaning to FARINDON, but of a different derivation. Records show: *Ferneberga* 1086.

Farne Islands (Northumberland) Probably 'Fern islands'. *Fearn* (Old English) 'fern'. Thus the basic name of this group of about 30 islands, lying offshore opposite BAMBURGH, could be derived, although it is suspected that a so-far undiscovered ancient Celtic root may be involved. *See* LINDISFARNE.

Farnham (Surrey) 'Fern homestead or riverside meadow'. *Fearn* (Old English) 'fern'; *ham* or *hamm* (Old English) 'homestead' or 'river land'. In the case of this town, to the west along the HOG'S BACK from GUILDFORD, the latter alternative is the most likely derivation; the name was recorded as *Fearnhamme* in the Anglo-Saxon Chronicle of 894. *Compare* FAREHAM.

Farnworth (Greater Manchester) 'Ferny enclosure'. *Fearn* (Old English) 'fern'; *worth* (Old English) 'enclosure'. The name of this industrial town, southeast of BOLTON, was recorded as *Farnewurd* in 1185.

Fauldhouse (Lothian) 'House on the fallow land'. *Falh* (Old English) 'fallow land'; 'house' (English). Situated on what is still a bleak elevated plateau in central Scotland there would always have been much fallow land.

Faversham (Kent) Probably 'the smith's homestead'. *Faefer* (Old English conjectural word derived from Latin *faber*) 'metal-working smith'; *ham* (Old English) 'homestead', 'village'. Alternatively, the first element may be of an unidentified personal name. This small market town and port, east of CANTERBURY, was noted with the name of *Fefresham* in a document of 811.

Felixstowe (Suffolk) 'Filica's meeting or holy place'. *Filica* (Old English personal name); *stow* (Old English) 'assembly place'. The present form of the name of this major container port and seaside resort, southeast of IPSWICH, would appear to have come about by assimilation of the original personal name to that of St Felix, the first Bishop of EAST ANGLIA in the 7th century. It was recorded as *Filichestou* in 1254.

Feltham (Greater London) Probably 'village on open land'. *Feld* (Old English) 'open country'; *ham* (Old English) 'village'. This HOUNSLOW district was recorded as *Feltha* in 1086, which suggests that the name's first element may derive as *felte*, (Old English) 'wild marjoram'.

Fens, The (Cambridgeshire/Lincolnshire/Norfolk) 'The

marshes'. *Fenn* (Old English) 'fen', 'marsh'. This simple name applies to the major low-lying area of eastern ENGLAND, west and south of The WASH, which consisted of salt marshes until it was dyked, drained and reclaimed in the 17th to 19th centuries. Many individual Fenland placenames are associated with the former conditions and improvements here, including Bedford Level; Fenton; Fosdyke; Holland Fen; Hundred Foot Drain; Marshland Fen; Quadring Eaudike.

Fermanagh (Ireland) 'The men of Monach'. *Feara* (Irish Gaelic) 'men'; *Manach* (Irish Gaelic personal name) Monach was a 2nd-century chieftain of a LEINSTER tribe who lead his people to settle here, in what is now the most southwestern county of NORTHERN IRELAND.

Fermoy (Cork) 'The men of the plain'. *Feara* (Irish Gaelic) 'men'; *machaire* (Irish Gaelic) 'plain'. The fuller sense of this derivation can be seen in the present Irish name, *Mainistir Fhear Mai*, meaning 'monastery of the men of the plain'. However, there is no trace of a monastery in this 'plantation town', which only really developed in the late 18th century as a garrison and a staging post for DUBLIN-CORK travellers.

Ferns (Wexford) Place of the 'alder trees'. *Fearna* (Irish Gaelic) 'alder trees'. The *s* plural ending was added unnecessarily as part of the anglicisation of the name of this small cathedral town and former royal seat of LEINSTER, northeast of ENNISCORTHY.

Ferryhill (Durham) 'Wooded hill'. *Fiergen* (Old English) 'wooded hill'; *hyll* (Old English later addition) 'hill'. The partially tautologous name of this town, south of DURHAM, apparently evolved from the original name of *Feregenne*, as recorded in the 10th century, through the descriptive form of *Ferye on the Hill*, as was documented in 1316.

Fettercairn (Grampian) 'Wooded slope'. *Faithir* (Scottish Gaelic) 'terraced slope', 'gradient'; *cardden* (Brythonic Celtic) 'wood', 'copse'. The name of this small town on the southeastern fringe of the HIGHLANDS was recorded in the *Pictish Chronicle* around AD970 as *Fotherkern*.

Ffestiniog *see* **Blaenau Ffestiniog**

Fife The name of this ancient kingdom, former county and present administrative region of eastern SCOTLAND, has been attributed to Fib, a legendary hero of the Picts. However, the territory predates this personal name, and there must be some other derivation. Recorded *Fib* 1150; *Fif* 1165.

Filey (North Yorkshire) Probably 'five clearings'. *Fif* (Old English) 'five'; *leah* (Old English) 'clearings'. This seaside resort, southeast of SCARBOROUGH, could have such a 'number' name, found elsewhere in places like SEVENOAKS, Sixhills, etc. Records show: *Fiuelac* 1086; *Fivelai c.*1125; *Fifle* 1148.

Filton (Avon) 'Hay farm'. *Filethe* (Old English) 'hay'; *tun* (Old English) 'farmstead'. The name of this northern suburb of BRISTOL, famous as the British production site of 'Concorde', was recorded in 1187 as now.

Finchley (Greater London) 'Wood or clearing of the finches'. *Finc* (Old English) finch; *leah* (Old English) 'wood', 'clearing'. This fairly straightforward name of a district of BARNET was noted as *Finchlee* in *c.*1208.

Findhorn (Grampian) Place of the 'white water'. *Fionn* (Scottish Gaelic) 'white'; *eren* (common pre-Celtic river name often appearing as *earn*). This village, north of FORRESS derives its name from the river at whose mouth it stands.

Fingal's Cave (Strathclyde) Possibly the 'fair (haired) stranger's cave'. *Fionn* (Scottish Gaelic) 'fair', 'white'; *gael* (Scottish Gaelic) 'strangers'; 'cave' (English). Such fair-haired strangers were presumably the blond Vikings. This large cave on the island of STAFFA, which is famous for its large basaltic pillars and which inspired Mendelssohn's overture, is also said to be named after the legendary Celtic giant Fionn MacCaul (or Finn mac Cool).

Fintry (Central; Grampian) Apparently, the 'white

house'. *Fionn* (Scottish Gaelic) 'white'; *tref* (Brythonic Celtic) 'house', 'homestead'. This large village lies in the hills bearing its name to the north of GLASGOW.

Fishbourne (West Sussex) 'Fish stream'. *Fisc* (Old English) 'fish'; *burna* (Old English) 'stream'. Recorded as *Fiseborne* in the Domesday Book of 1086, this relatively straightforward name applies to the village, west of CHICHESTER, that is famous as the site of a large Roman palace, built here in the 1st century AD.

Fishguard (Dyfed) 'Fish yard'. *Fiskr* (Old Norse) 'fish'; *garthr* (Old Norse) 'yard'. The name of this small ferry and fishing port at the head of the large sheltered Fishguard Bay on the north PEMBROKEshire coast clearly has a Scandinavian origin related to its having been a good place for Viking settlers either to catch or store fish. The alternative Welsh name, little used in this English-speaking part of Wales, is *Abergwaun*, which simply describes its location.

Fivemiletown (Tyrone) The somewhat curious name of this small town south of OMAGH apparently was created on account of its five mile equidistance from Clabby, Clogher and Colesbrooke. *Compare* nearby SIXMILECROSS.

Flamborough Head (Humberside) 'Headland of Flein's stronghold'. *Flein* (Old Scandinavian personal name); *burh* (Old English) 'fortified place'; *heafod* (Old English) 'headland', 'promontory'. This major pointed, nose-like headland on the North Sea coast, north of BRIDLINGTON, is named after the nearby village, which was recorded as *Flaneburg* in the Domesday Book of 1086. The description of the actual headland dates from the 14th century.

Fleet (Hampshire) Place of 'the stream'. *Fleot* (Old English) 'stream', 'creek', 'pool'. The simple name of this town, west of FARNBOROUGH, was recorded as *Le Flete* in 1506. The name of the LONDON's famous **Fleet Street** has the same derivation, referring to the River Fleet that flows southwards from HIGHGATE Hill to the

River THAMES, now largely channelled underground.

Fleetwood (Lancashire) This major fishing and ferry port at the tip of the FYLDE peninsula, north of BLACKPOOL, is named after Sir Peter Fleetwood, who established it in 1836.

Flint (Clwyd) 'Hard stone'. *Flint* (Old English related to Old High German *flins*; Old Swedish *flinta*) 'hard rock' in the general sense rather than specifically the quartz as found in chalk. The significance of the name of the former county and now that of an industrial sprawl on the southern shore of the DEE estuary refers back to 1277 when Edward I built the first of his many castles in Wales on an outcrop of 'hard rock'. The current Welsh name, *Y Flint*, has the same meaning.

Fochabers (Grampian) This small town near the mouth of the River Spey, southeast of ELGIN, appears to have a hybrid name meaning 'lake-marsh'. *Fothach* (Brythonic Celtic) 'lake'; *abor* (Scottish Gaelic) 'marsh'. Perhaps the second element was added as the condition of the lake changed.

Folkstone (Kent) Probably 'Folca's stone'. *Folca* (Old English personal name); *stan* (Old English) 'stone'. In the case of this present-day busy Channel port, and entrance point to the Channel Tunnel, the original sense of its name was almost certainly that of a 'stone marking a hundred meeting place'. Some authorities consider that the first element may represent *folc*, (Old English) 'people', implying that this was a 'people's meeting place'. Records show *Folcanstan c.*697.

Foreland, North and **South** (Kent) 'The headland'. *Fore-land* (Old English compound word) 'land that comes to a head', 'cape', 'promontory'. These two headlands, the former lying at the northeast tip of KENT, between BROADSTAIRS and MARGATE, and the other a less pronounced cape just north of DOVER, have this common basic name, which is found elsewhere, such as at the eastern extremity of the ISLE OF WIGHT.

Forest of Bowland *see* **Bowland, Forest of**.

Forest of Dean (Gloucestershire) 'Forest of the valleys'. *Forest* (Middle English) 'woodland area'; *denu* (Old English) 'valley'. This former royal hunting ground, which lies between the lower stretches of the SEVERN and WYE rivers, is characterised by heavily wooded hills, winding valleys and fast-flowing streams, and manifests several places that incorporate the basic 'dean' form, such as Little Dean and MITCHELDEAN. It was recorded as simply *Dena* in a text of 1130. *See* CINDERFORD; COLEFORD.

Forfar (Tayside) Possibly 'watching hill'. *Fothair* (Scottish Gaelic) 'terraced slope'; *faire* (Scottish Gaelic) 'watching', 'spying'. The nearby Hill of Finhaven would have been a suitable place for such a lookout. The name of this market town, north of DUNDEE, was recorded as *Forfare* in a document from around 1200.

Formby (Merseyside) 'Forni's farmstead'. *Forni* (Old Scandinavian personal name); *by* (Old Scandinavian) 'farmstead', 'village'. The name of this residential satellite town situated between LIVERPOOL and SOUTHPORT was recorded as *Fornebei* in the Domesday Book of 1086.

Forres (Grampian) Literally means 'below the shrubs'. *Fo* (Scottish Gaelic) 'below', 'under'; *ras* (Scottish Gaelic) 'shrubs', 'underwood'. The name of this town, east of NAIRN was recorded as *Fores* 1187; *Forais* 1283.

Fort Augustus (Highland) Formerly known as Kilcummin, this town at the south end of LOCH NESS was renamed after the 1715 Rebellion in commemoration of William Augustus, Duke of Cumberland.

Forth (Central/Fife/Lothian) The river name probably derives from the description of its estuary: *fjord* (Old Norse adapted form of *fjordr*) 'deeply indented estuary'.

Fortrose (Highland) 'Beneath the headland'. *Foter* (Scottish Gaelic) 'beneath'; *ros* (Scottish Gaelic) 'cape'. This town lies beneath the ROSEMARKIE headland.

Fort William (Highland) This town at the head of Loch Linnhe was originally the settlement of Inverlochy. A fort was established here by General Monk in 1655, at which time the place was called Gordonsburgh, after the Duke of Gordon on whose land it had been built. Shortly afterwards, its name changed briefly to Maryburgh, after Queen Mary, wife of King William III. Finally, in 1690 the fort was rebuilt as a major garrison, upon which it and the surrounding town were renamed Fort William, after the king.

Fosse Way (England) Trackway with 'the ditch'. *Foss* (Old English conjectural word probably based on Latin *fossa*) 'ditch'. This ancient trackway, sometimes spelt Foss Way, was adapted by the Romans as part of their overall road network of England and is still largely followed by modern highways such as the A37, the A429, and the A46. It runs from near SIDMOUTH in DEVON to the HUMBER, passing through ILCHESTER, CIRENCESTER; LEICESTER and LINCOLN, thereafter coinciding with ERMINE STREET. So called because it had a ditch on either side of the roadway, it was referred to in a document of 956 as *strata publica de Foss*.

Foula (Shetland) 'Bird Island'. *Fugl* (Old Norse) 'fowl', 'bird'; *ey* (Old Norse) 'island'. This remote and isolated small island , lying 14 miles (23 km) due west of the SHETLAND mainland is famed for its very high and sheer cliffs, the sanctuary of thousands of sea birds.

Foulness (Essex) 'Bird promontory'. *Fugol* (Old English) 'bird'; *naess* (Old English) 'promontory'. This peninsula-like low-lying island, separated only by a bridged narrow channel from the mainland northeast of SOUTHEND-ON-SEA, sits between the entrances to the THAMES and Crouch river estuaries and is renowned for its bird life, especially its wildfowl. It was recorded as *Fughelnesse* in 1215. *Compare* FOULA.

Fountains Abbey (North Yorkshire) 'Abbey of the springs'. *Fontein* (Old French) 'spring'; *abeie* (Old French) 'abbey'. This famous abbey, whose ruins lie southwest of RIPON, was so named by Benedictine monks from YORK who apparently discovered springs here when they were founding a newly adopted Cistercian monastic order in the early 12th century; a contemporary text refers to *Sancta Maria de Fontibus*.

Fowey (Cornwall) Probably the place on 'the beech-tree river'. *Faw* (Old Cornish conjectural word possibly derived from Old Breton *fau*) 'beeches'. This coastal resort and china-clay-exporting port, south and downstream of LOSTWITHIEL, lies at the mouth of the River Fowey, from which it takes its name. It was recorded as *Fawe* around 1200.

Foyers (Highland) 'Terraced slope'. *Fothair* (Scottish Gaelic) 'terraced slope', 'stepped gradient'. This name aptly describes the situation of this village on the steeply terraced east side of Loch NESS, in the faulted GLEN MOR.

Foyle, Lough (Donegal/Londonderry) This large sea inlet in the north of Ireland takes the name of the river flowing into it near LONDONDERRY. This is a common Irish river name derived from the Gaelic *faill*, meaning 'cliff', the place of origin of many streams.

Fraserburgh (Grampian) 'Fraser's town'. This major fishing port on the north coast of BUCHAN, originally called Faithlie, was renamed in 1592 to honour Sir Alexander Fraser, the then new landowner and developer of the town. The second element is derived from *burh* (Old English and adapted Scots *burgh*) 'town'.

Freuchie (Fife) 'Heathery place'. *Fraochach* (Scottish Gaelic) 'heathery'. This village on the hills, southeast of FALKLAND, has a name descriptive of its situation.

Frimley (Surrey) 'Fremi's clearing'. *Fremi* (old English personal name); *leah* (Old English) 'woodland clearing'. The name of this town, adjoining CAMBERLEY to the south, which was recorded as *Fremeley* in 933, has the same personal name element as in that of the SURREY village of **Frensham**, 10 miles (16 km) to the south, which itself was documented in 967 as *Fremesham*.

Frinton-on-Sea (Essex) 'Fritha's homestead'. *Fritha* (Old English personal name); *tun* (Old English) 'village', 'homestead'. This seaside resort on the Essex coast, just northeast of CLACTON-on-Sea, similarly developed with the coming of the railways in the mid-19th century, and, like the latter name-form, the '-on-Sea' affix was added by promotional design. The name of the original settlement was recorded in the Domesday book as *Frie(n)tuna*.

Friockheim (Tayside) Originally known simply as Friock (apparently after a baillie from nearby FORFAR by the name of Freke), *heim*, (German) 'home', was added in 1830 as the personal wish of a major tenant of the area, John Andson, who had spent some time in Germany. It is pronounced 'Freakam'.

Frodsham (Cheshire) Simply 'Frod's homestead'. *Frod* (Old English personal name); *ham* (Old English) 'homestead', 'village'. This small town, south of RUNCORN, was recorded as *Frotesham* in the Domesday Book of 1086, and as *Frodesham* in a text a little later, in about 1100.

Frome (Somerset) Place on 'the fair brisk river'. *Fram-* (Brythonic Celtic root element) 'fine', 'fair brisk'. This medieval market town, south of BATH, derives its name from the River Frome, on which it stands; both are recorded as *Froom* in the 8th century, which is their phonetic form today.

Fulham (Greater London) 'Fulla's riverside meadow'. *Fulla* (Old English personal name) unidentified; *hamm* (Old English) 'land in the bend of a river'. Such an origin is most appropriate for the name of this LONDON district, which lies on the low-lying north bank of a broad U-shaped meander of the River THAMES. The name was documented as *Fulanham* around 705.

Furness *see* **Barrow-in-Furness**.

Fylde, The (Lancashire) 'The plain'. *Gefilde* (Old English) 'plain', 'tract of flat land'. This ancient name of the peninsular region between the Irish Sea and the River Wyre, and today adopted as the name of the administrative district centred on BLACKPOOL, aptly and simply describes the low-lying flat land here. It was recorded as *Filde* in 1246.

Fyvie (Grampian) Possibly a 'path'. *Fiamh* (Scottish Gaelic) 'path'. The meaning and sense of the name of this village, with its impressive 15th century turretted castle, northeast of ABERDEEN, however remains uncertain. Some authorities consider that the origin of FIFE comes from the same root.

G

Gainsborough (Lincolnshire) 'Gegn's stronghold'. *Gegn* (Old English personal name—abbreviation of *Gaenbeald* or *Geanburh*); *burh* (Old English) 'fortified place'. The name of this inland port on the River TRENT, northwest of LINCOLN, was recorded as *Gegnesburh* in 1013.

Gairloch (Highland) 'Short loch'. *Gearr* (Scottish Gaelic) 'short'; *loch* (Scottish Gaelic) 'enclosed expanse of water', in this case as a inlet of the sea. The village is situated, northwest of INVERNESS, at the head of this short sea loch, after which it is named.

Galashiels (Borders) 'Shielings by the Gala Water'. *Gala* (river name that means 'gallows stream') refers to the Gala Water on which this town stands southeast of EDINBURGH; *skali-s* (Old Norse) 'sheilings', sheds, or huts used by shepherds as temporary shelters on summer pastures. This town has long been a centre for the BORDERS woollen trade. The name was recorded: *Galuschel* 1237; *Gallowschel* 1416.

Galloway (Dumfries and Galloway) 'Land of the stranger Gaels'. *Gall* (Scottish Gaelic) 'stranger'; *Ghaidhil* (Scottish Gaelic) 'Gaels'. This tribal name was given by the Scots to this extreme southwest part of Scotland, which was once settled by Gaels of mixed Irish and Norse origins, who were thus regarded as 'foreigners'.

Galston (Strathclyde) 'Village of the strangers'. *Gall* (Scottish Gaelic) 'stranger'; *tun* (Old English) 'village'. As in the case of GALLOWAY, the reference to strangers, in the case of this small town east of KILMARNOCK, would have been to settlers of a tribe different from the native Scots.

Galty Mountains (Limerick/Tipperary) 'Mountains of the woods'. *Na* (Irish Gaelic) 'of the'; *gaibhlte* (Irish Gaelic) 'woods'. A mountain range to the west of CAHIR, which rises through woods to 3018 ft (920m) in Galtymore.

Galway (Galway) 'Stony place'. *Gall* (Irish Gaelic) 'stone'. The name of this county town in the west of Ireland, and ultimately that of its surrounding county, stems from the description of its rocky location and probably also to the stony bed of the River CORRIB, at the mouth of which it stands. Its modern Irish name is *Gaillimh*.

Gardenstown (Grampian) Literally, 'Garden's town'. This fishing port on the BANFF-shire coast was set up in 1720 by Alexander Garden of Troup, who gave it his name. Locals call it 'Gamrie' after the parish and bay on which it is situated.

Garelochhead (Strathclyde) At the head of the short loch'. *Gearr* (Scottish Gaelic) 'short'; *loch* (Scottish Gaelic) 'sea loch', 'fiord'; 'head' (English) 'at the top of'. This village is thus situated on the Gareloch, a short fiord-like indentation off the Firth of CLYDE, which is today Britain's nuclear submarine base. See GAIRLOCH.

Garforth (West Yorkshire) Probably 'Gaera's ford'. *Gaera* (Old English personal name—abbreviated form of names such as *Gaerburh* or *Gaerwine*); *ford* (Old English) 'river crossing'. This town in the coal-mining district east of LEEDS was entered in the Domesday Book in 1086 as the settlement of *Gereford*.

Gargunnock (Central) Possibly 'place of the rounded hill'. *Garradh* (Scottish Gaelic) 'enclosure', 'place'; *cnuic* or *duin-ock* (Scottish Gaelic) 'rounded hill' or 'mound'. This village is situated on a small hill, west of STIRLING.

Garscadden (Strathclyde) 'Enclosure for herring'. *Garradh* (Scottish Gaelic) 'enclosure'; *sgadain* (Scottish Gaelic) 'herring'. This now suburb of GLASGOW is situated on the north bank of the CLYDE, downstream from the city centre, where the river is tidal.

Garstang (Lancashire) Place of 'the spear-shaped pole'.

Geirr (Old Norse) 'spear'; *stong* (Old Norse) 'pole'. The name of this small town, midway between LANCASTER and PRESTON, has a name of Scandinavian origin, which probably had the sense of a special marker denoting a boundary or a meeting place. It was documented as *Gairstang* in about 1195.

Gartocharn (Strathclyde) 'Place of the humped hill'. *Garradh* (Scottish Gaelic) 'enclosure', 'place'; *chairn* (Scottish Gaelic corrupt form of *carn*) 'humped hill'. This village is situated beneath the isolated upturned pudding basin-shaped or dumpling-shaped Duncryne Hill on the southern shore of Loch LOMOND.

Garve (Highland) Literally, 'place of rough water'. *Garbh* (Scottish Gaelic) 'rough (water)'. This village is situated on the tumbling Black Water west of DINGWALL.

Gatehouse of Fleet (Dumfries and Galloway) 'Roadhouse on the (Water of) Fleet'. *Geata-hus* (Old English) 'roadhouse'; *Fleet* (Old English river name *fleot*, which means 'stream'). Prior to 1790, when the town was founded, there was only one 'gatehouse' sited here northwest of KIRKCUDBRIGHT.

Gateshead (Tyne and Wear) 'Goat's headland or hill'. *Gat* (Old English) 'goat'; *heafod* (Old English) 'headland'. This industrial town on the south bank of the River TYNE opposite NEWCASTLE UPON TYNE, has a name of relatively straightforward derivation, but the actual sense of its original meaning remains unclear. It was referred to as *Ad Caprae Caput* in the Venerable Bede's 8th-century Latin text 'Historia Ecclesiastica', literally translating as 'at the (place) of the goat's head'. In 1196 it appears in a document as *Gatesheued*.

Gatwick (Surrey/West Sussex) 'Goat farm'. *Gat* (Old English) 'goat'; *wic* (Old English) 'specialised farm'. The name of LONDON's second international airport, which is situated in WEST SUSSEX, north of CRAWLEY, was originally recorded as *Gatwik* in 1241.

Gerrards Cross (Buckinghamshire) This residential satellite town west of the LONDON conurbation is named after a local family called Jarrard or Gerrard. The name was noted as *Gerards Cross* in 1692.

Giant's Causeway (Antrim) This world-famous promontory of columnar basalt on the north coast of ANTRIM is steeped in legend, and it is not suprising that it should have been given such a folk-name. A former Irish name, *Clochan-na-bhFomharaigh*, meaning 'stepping stones of the Fomorians', denoted that these ancient sea rovers from TORY ISLAND were magnified into giants. The current Irish name is simply *Clochan an Aifir*, the 'stepping stones of the giant', and the most popular reference is to Finn mac Cool, who is said to have built a causeway of these curious stones over to Scotland. *See* FINGAL'S CAVE.

Giffnock (Strathclyde) 'Little ridge'. *Cefn* (Brythonic Celtic) 'ridge'; *ock* (Brythonic Celtic diminutive suffix) 'little'. This aptly describes the situation of this place, now a southside suburb of GLASGOW.

Gifford (Lothian) This village, south of HADDINGTON, is only about 200 years old, having been founded by the long-established local landowning Gifford family.

Gigha (Strathclyde) Possibly 'God's Isle'. *Gud* (Old Norse) 'God'; *ey* (Old Norse) 'island'. THe name of this small island off the west coast of KINTYRE was recorded as *Gudey* 1263; *Geday* 1343; *Gya* 1400; *Giga* 1516.

Gillingham (Dorset; Kent) 'Homestead of the people of Gylla'. *Gylla* (Old English personal name); *inga* (Old English—genitive case of *ingas*) 'of the people of'; *ham* (Old English) 'homestead'. Both these places, one a small town northwest of SHAFTESBURY, the other one of the large industrial MEDWAY Towns, have the same derivation but refer to different persons. A 10th-century record for the Kent name shows *Gyllingeham*, while the Domesday Book entry for both is *Gelingeham*.

Girton (Cambridgeshire) 'Settlement on gravelly ground'. *Greot* (Old English) 'gravel'; *tun* (Old English) 'farmstead', 'village'. This relatively common place-name applies here to the now northwest satellite suburb of CAMBRIDGE, known for its women's college of the same name. Records show *Gretton* and *Gryttune* in *c*.1060.

Girvan (Strathclyde) According to one authority, this AYRshire coastal town standing at the mouth of the Water of Girvan takes its name from the latter, which in turn may be derived: *gearr* (Scottish Gaelic) 'short'; *an* or *abhainn* (Scottish Gaelic) 'river'. Another authority prefers: *garan* (Old Gaelic) 'thicket'; *vind* (Old Gaelic) 'white'. It was recorded as *Girven* in 1275.

Glamis (Tayside) 'Wide gap'. *Glamhus* (Scottish Gaelic) 'wide gap', 'vale'. The name is very descriptive of the situation of this village, with its famous 14th-century castle, lying in the centre of the long open vale of STRATHMORE between the SIDLAW HILLS and the edge of the Highlands. Records show *Glammes* 118 7; *Glammis* 1251.

Glamorgan (Wales) 'Morgan's shore'. *Glan* (Welsh) 'shore'; *Morgan* (Welsh personal name) 7th-century prince of GWENT. The name of the former county of South Wales, now subdivided into Mid, South, and West Glamorgan, was in its current Welsh rendering of *Morgannwg*, meaning 'Morgan's land', also the name of the ancient kingdom that was created in the 11th century by the expansion of the kingdom of Gwent (the original lands of the descendants of Morgan) and assimilated the territory of Glywysing, which covered the area of modern Glamorgan. It is in this sense that Glamorgan possibly can be seen to have referred to that part of the ancient Morgan teritory by the shore.

Glasgow (Strathclyde) 'Place of the green hollow', or 'dear green place'. *Glas* (Brythonic Celtic-Cumbric) 'green'; *cau* (Brythonic Celtic-Cumbric) 'hollow'. It is not hard to imagine how this descriptive name was apt to the early settlement here in Cumbric times, for despite the large-scale industrialisation and urban development that has taken place in the last 200 years, Scotland's largest city still lies on the River CLYDE in a vast hollow, with much open green space and parkland, more or less encircled by barren hills and plateaux. Some authorities consider that there is a familiarative sense implied in the derivation, and hence the more commonly accepted meaning of the 'dear green place'. The name was recorded as *Glasgu* in 1116, and *Glasguensis episcopus* in a Latin text of 1130.

Glastonbury (Somerset) Probably 'place at the stronghold of the people where the woad grows'. *Glastonia* (Brythonic Celtic conjectural name derived from Old Celtic root element *glasto-*) 'place where woad grows'; *inga* (Old English—genitive of *ingas*) 'of the people'; *byrig* (Old English—dative of *burh*) 'at the fortified place'. The name of this town east of BRIDGWATER, famous as an ancient centre of Christian culture and pilgrimage and earlier pagan and legendary Arthurian associations, was recorded as *Glastingburi* in 725, and *Glaestingeberia* in the 1086 Domesday Book.

Glenalmond (Tayside) 'Glen of the river'. *Gleann* (Scottish Gaelic) 'glen', 'valley'; *amhainn* (Scottish Gaelic) 'river'. Flowing through this glen, northwest of, the River Almond is thus a back-formation tautology.

Glencoe (Highland) Probably the 'narrow glen'. *Gleann* (Scottish Gaelic) 'glen', 'valley'; *comhann* (Scottish Gaelic) 'narrow'. This spectacular, deep, glaciated valley with its many sheer rock faces is famed today for mountain climbing and in the past for the notorious massacre that took place here in 1692. The village of Glencoe lies at the west end near where the River Coe flows into Loch Leven.

Glendalough (Wicklow) 'Valley of the two lakes'. *Gleann* (Irish Gaelic) 'valley'; *da* (Irish Gaelic) 'two'; *loch* (Irish Gaelic) 'lake'. This popular tourist glen in the WICKLOW Mountains to the south of DUBLIN, where a monastery was founded by St Kevin in 545, has a name that simply describes the picturesque scene; the two lakes are themselves simply called Upper Lake and Lower Lake.

Gleneagles (Tayside) 'Glen of the church'. *Gleann* (Scottish Gaelic) 'glen'; *eaglais* (Scottish Gaelic) 'church'. Famous for its luxury hotel and golf courses, near AUCHTERARDER this 'Glen' does not take the name of its river. It was recorded as *Gleninglese* in *c.*1165

Glenelg (Highland) 'Glen of Ireland'. *Gleann* (Scottish Gaelic) 'glen'; *Ealg* (Scottish Gaelic) early name for Ireland. Like ELGIN and BLAIR ATHOLL the reference here to Ireland was one of commemoration of the motherland by early Irish Gaelic settlers to this place on the west coast of Scotland. Glenelg also has the distinction of being a palindromic place name.

Glenfinnan (Highland) Possibly 'glen of (St) Finan'. *Gleann* (Scottish Gaelic) 'glen'; *Finan* (personal name) a 7th-century abbot from IONA and contemporary of St Columba. The name means 'white-(haired)'.

Glen Garry (Highland/Tayside) 'Glen of the rough water'. *Gleann* (Scottish Gaelic) 'glen'; *Garry* (river name that derives from an ancient root of the Scottish Gaelic *garbh*) 'rough'. This aptly describes this fast-flowing tributary of the TAY as it tumbles down from the Pass of DRUMOCHTER.

Glenlivet (Grampian) Apparently 'glen of the slippery smooth place'. *Gleann* (Scottish Gaelic) 'glen'; *liobh* (Scottish Gaelic) 'slimy', 'slippery', 'smooth'; *aite* (Scottish Gaelic) 'place'. According to one authority, the name of the River Livet has possibly been back-formed. Today, Glenlivet is a name renowned for its 'smooth water', i.e. fine malt whisky.

Glen Mor (Highland) Simply the 'big glen'. *Gleann* (Scottish Gaelic) 'glen'; *mor* (Scottish Gaelic) 'big'. It is sometimes referred to as The Great Glen, Glen More, or Glen Albyn. All these alternatives are appropriate to this major fault valley, which extends 65 miles (105 km) across the width of Scotland, southwest from the MORAY Firth in the east to Loch Linnhe, an arm of the Atlantic Ocean, and which contains on its floor Loch NESS, Loch Oich, Loch Lochy, which were connected in the 19th century to form the Caledonian Canal.

Glenrothes (Fife) As a New Town designated in 1948 it has a completely fabricated name. There is no glen here in Central FIFE. The second part acknowledges the Earls of Rothes as local landowners, and their former Rothes Colliery.

Glossop (Derbyshire) 'Glott's valley'. *Glott* (Old English personal name); *hop* (Old English) 'valley'. This industrial town, east of MANCHESTER, lies in a narrow valley on the edge of the PEAK District. Early records show: *Glosop* 1086; *Glotop* 1219.

Gloucester (Gloucestershire) 'Roman town of Glevum'. *Glev-* (Brythonic Celtic conjectural root element) 'bright place'; *ceaster* (Old English) 'Roman camp'. This cathedral city and industrial county town, at the head of the SEVERN estuary, was recorded as *Gleawecestre* in 804, and the county as *Gleawcestrescir* in 1016.

Glyndebourne (East Sussex) 'Stream near Glynde'. *Glind* (Old English conjectural word) 'fence' 'enclosure'; *burna* (Old English) 'stream'. This Tudor manor house east of LEWES, famous as the setting for an annual summer opera season, takes its name from the local Glynde stream, which in turn is named after the nearby village of Glynde. A text of 1288 refers to both the river and village as *Burne juxta Glynde*.

Godalming (Surrey) Place of 'Godhelm's people'. *Godhelm* (Old English personal name); *ingas* (Old English plural suffix) 'people of'. The name of this town southwest of GUILDFORD was recorded in about 880 as *Godelmingum*.

Godmanchester (Cambridgeshire) 'Roman station associated with a man called Godmund'. *Godmund* (Old English personal name); *ceaster* (Old English) 'Roman camp'. This town, immediately south of HUNTINGDON, was originally the strategically important site of a Roman station established where ERMINE STREET crossed the River Ouse; it was probably known as *Durovigutum*. The name of the later settlement was recorded in the Domesday Book of 1086 as *Godmundcestre*.

Golborne (Greater Manchester) 'Stream where marsh marigolds grow'. *Golde* (Old English) 'marigold'; *burna* (Old English) 'stream'. The name of this coalfield town west of MANCHESTER was noted as *Goldeburn* in 1187.

Golders Green (Greater London) This north LONDON district, in the borough of BARNET, has probably acquired its name from John le Godere, or John Godyer, whose family may have owned or lived by the green here since the 14th century. Records show *Golders Greene* 1612; *Groles* or *Godders Green* 1790.

Goldthorpe (South Yorkshire) 'Golda's outlying settlement'. *Golda* (Old English personal name); *thorp* (Old Danish) 'secondary farmstead' or 'village'. The name of this town, in the coal-mining area west of DONCASTER, was recorded as *Goldetorp* in 1086

Golspie (Highland) Apparently 'Gulli's farm'. *Gulli* (Old Norse personal name); *byr* (Old Norse) 'farmstead'. The name of this small town north of Darnch was recorded as *Goldespy* 1330; *Golspi* 1448.

Goodwin Sands (Kent) Traditionally, the name of these notorious shoals, lying 5 miles (8 km) offshore at DEAL, alludes to a former island here, belonging to Earl Godwine, that was submerged beneath the sea in 1097; waves can still be seen breaking on the shoal at low tide. Alternatively, some authorities consider this Old English name may reflect directly the real or imagined danger that these shoals posed to medieval sailors who may have referred to them as 'good friend' in order to appease any submarine evil spirits. A record of 1371 shows the name *Godewynesonde*.

Goole (Humberside) Place by 'the channel'. *Goule* (Middle English) 'channel', 'ditch', 'sluice'. The name aptly describes this inland port, west of HULL, situated by the tidal lower reaches of the River Ouse, where there is a long history of many man-made channels. It was recorded as *Gulle* in 1362.

Gorbals (Strathclyde) The meaning of the name of this former slum area of GLASGOW remains uncertain. One authority has suggested a derivation with reference to *gorr balk-r* (Old Norse) 'built walls'. It is recorded in a document of 1521 as *Gorbalis*.

Gordonstoun (Grampian) 'Gordon's town'. The well-known school on the MORAYshire coast takes the name of the local estate which had been renamed in 1638 after Sir Robert Gordon. Previously it had been called the Bog of Plewlands.

Gorebridge (Lothian) Possibly the 'bridge at the wedge-shaped land'. *Gora* (Middle English) 'triangular piece of land'; 'bridge' (English).

Gorey (Wexford) Possibly 'wooded' place. *Guaireach* (Irish Gaelic) 'wooded'. This description, it is claimed by one authority, would be more appropriate to the situation of this small town, southwest of ARKLOW, than its current Irish name, *Guaire*, which means 'sandbank'.

Gorseinon (West Glamorgan) Possibly 'Einion's marsh'. *Cors* (Welsh) 'marsh'; *Einion* (Welsh personal name) unidentified, but meaning the 'anvil'. This small town northwest of SWANSEA is situated on low lying land at the point where the Lliw river flows into the Loughor estuary, which was indeed marshy before being drained.

Gort (Galway) Place of the 'tilled field'. *Gort* (Irish Gaelic) 'tilled field'. This small market town southeast of GALWAY takes the simple name of a common Irish descriptive element.

Gosforth (Tyne and Wear) 'Goose ford'. *Gos* (Old English) 'goose'; *ford* (Old English) 'river crossing'. This town, adjoining NEWCASTLE UPON TYNE to the northeast, is a northern variant of the common English placename Gosford; it was recorded in 1166 as *Goseford*.

Gosport (Hampshire) 'Geese market'. *Gos* (Old English) 'goose'; *port* (Old English) 'market town'. Somewhat misleadingly, the name of this sea port, on the west side of PORTSMOUTH Harbour narrows, derives its second element from *porta* (Latin) meaning 'gate', which gave the sense of a market-town gate. It was documented as *Goseport* in 1250. *See* NEWPORT.

Gourock (Strathclyde) Probably the 'place of the hillocks'. *Guirec* (Scottish Gaelic) 'pimple', 'hillock'. The local terrain here is noticably made up of steep hillocks plunging straight into the Firth of CLYDE.

Govan (Strathclyde) Possibly 'dear rock'. *Cu* (Brythonic Celtic) 'dear'; *faen* (Brythonic Celtic mutated form of *maen*) 'stone'. Alternatively, some prefer the derivation *gobhann* (Scottish Gaelic) 'blacksmith', which is appropriate for this shipbuilding suburb of GLASGOW. It was recorded as *Guven* 1147; *Gvuan* 1150; *Gwuan* 1518.

Gower (West Glamorgan) 'Crooked sloping place'. *Gwyr* (Welsh) 'crooked, sloping'. This well-known peninsula, which juts out into the BRISTOL Channel west of SWANSEA, has a name that is descriptive of both its 'crooked' thumb-like shape, and its 'sloping' limestone terrain. Its modern Welsh name is simply *Gwyr*.

Grain, Isle of (Kent) 'Gravelly or gritty ground'. *Greon* (Old English related to greot) 'gravel', 'grit', 'sand'. The name of this peninsula lying to the west of the entrance to the MEDWAY estuary refers directly to the nature of the shore here. The residential development of Grain derives similarly. The name was recorded in around 1100 as *Grean*.

Grampian Mountains (Grampian/Highland/Tayside/Strathclyde) This great mountain range, forming most of the Central Highlands south of the GREAT GLEN, was apparently given its name as the result of a misreading by a 16th-century historian of a citation concerning the Roman victory over the Picts at *Mons Graupius* in AD84. Its earlier name was The Mounth. See MONADHLIATH.

Grange-over-Sands (Cumbria) 'Outlying farm belonging to a religious establishment, across the sands of Morecambe Bay'. *Grange* (Middle English) 'outlying farm'. This resort on the north side of MORECAMBE Bay was originally the grange for the nearby Cartmel Priory; the affix was added later to promote its situation as a seaside holiday town. A document of 1491 records the name as simply *Grange*.

Grangemouth (Central) 'Mouth of the Grange Burn'. This industrial port on the south side of the Firth of FORTH, stands at the mouth of the Grange Burn, itself named after the nearby grange for Newbattle Abbey.

Grantchester (Cambridgeshire) Place of 'the settlers on the River Granta'. *Granta* (Brythonic Celtic river name) probably 'marshy one'; *saete* (Old English) 'settlers'. This village just southeast and upstream of CAMBRIDGE on the River Granta has an etymological link in the latter. It was entered into the Domesday Book as *Granteseta*.

Grantham (Lincolnshire) Probably 'Granta's village'. *Granta* (Old English personal name); *ham* (Old English) 'village', 'homestead'. The name of this town east of NOTTINGHAM on the River Witham may alternatively derive with the first element represented by *grand*, (Old English conjectural word) 'gravel'. It was recorded in the Domesday Book exactly as now.

Grantown-on-Spey (Highland) 'Grant's town by the River Spey'. This town beside the River Spey was originally built in 1766 as a model planned village for the then local landowner Sir James Grant, after whom it is named. The meaning of the river is unknown.

Grasmere (Cumbria) 'Grassy lake'. *Gres* (Old Norse) 'grass'; *saer* (Old Norse) 'lake'; *mere* (Old English) 'lake'. This lake, and the village named after it, are situated in the central part of the LAKE DISTRICT and were recorded in 1245 as *Gressemere*.

Gravesend (Kent) Place at 'the end of a grove'. *Graf* (Old English) 'grove', 'copse'; *ende* (Old English) 'end of an estate'. The name of this industrial town on the south bank of the THAMES, opposite TILBURY, was recorded in the Domesday Book as *Gravesham*, recently adopted as that of the local administrative district.

Grays (Essex) 'Manorial affix of the de Grai family'. Formally known as **Grays Thurrock**, this THAMES river-estuary town, northwest of TILBURY, was recorded as *Turruc* in 1086; *Turrokgreys* in 1248. *See* THURROCK.

Great Britain *see* **Britain, Great**.

Great Driffield *see* **Driffield, Great** and **Little**.

Great Dunmow *see* **Dunmow, Great** and **Little**.

Greater London (England) This recent name applies collectively to 32 new boroughs, surrounding the independent City of LONDON, that functioned under the Greater London Council (GLC) from 1965 to 1985, after which single-tier borough control has operated.

Greater Manchester *see* **Manchester; Merseyside**.

Great Glen, The *see* **Glen Mor**

Great Malvern *see* **Malvern Hills**.

Great Missenden *see* **Missenden, Great** and **Little**.

Great Ormes Head (Gwynedd) 'Big snake's head'. *Ormr* (Old Norse) 'snake', 'worm'; *hofuth* (Old Norse) 'head'. The name of this major headland of the North Wales coast west of LLANDUDNO describes its distinctive shape, which would have been apparent to approaching Viking ships. The 'Great' prefix has been added to distinguish it from Little Ormes Head, which lies to the east.

Great Sankey *see* **Sankey, Great** and **Little**.

Great Torrington *see* **Torrington, Great** and **Little**.

Great Walsingham *see* **Walsingham, Great** and **Little**

Great Yarmouth *see* **Yarmouth**.

Greenock (Strathclyde) Place of the 'sunny hillock'. *Grian-aig* (Scottish Gaelic) 'sunny'; most authorities attribute the last syllable to meaning 'hilly place' or 'hillock'. Certainly, as is the case for the neighbouring town of GOUROCK, the terrain here rises steeply from the Firth of CLYDE, and Lyle Hill is a notable landmark.

Greenwich (Greater London) 'Green harbour'. *Grene* (Old English) 'green'; *wic* (Old English) 'harbour'. This historic LONDON district and borough, on the south bank of the River THAMES opposite the Isle of DOGS, famous for having given us Greenwich Mean Time, has many nautical associations past and present. It appears in an early text of 964 as *Grenewic*.

Gretna Green (Dumfries and Galloway) Possibly place of the 'gravelly haugh'. *Greoten* (Old English) 'gravelly'; *halth* (Old English) 'haugh' or 'fertile land enclosed by the bend of a river'. This 'border' village, made famous by the tradition of marrying eloping couples at the local smiddy, takes its name from the adjacent village of Gretna, both settlements being beside the River Sark. Records show *Gretenho* 1223; *Gretenhowe* 1376; *Gretnay* 1576.

Greystones (Wicklow) This 19th-century seaside resort, developed beside the DUBLIN-WICKLOW railway line, takes its name from the 'grey-stoned' fishermen's cottages of the earlier village. A document of 1760 records the place as Gray Stones.

Grimsby (Humberside) 'Grim's settlement'. *Grim* (Old Danish personal name); *by* (Old Danish) 'farmstead', 'village'. The Scandinavian name of this major port on the south side of the mouth of the Humber is echoed in the great number of placenames in this region with the '-by' ending, and also several incorporating 'Grim' as a personal name. The Domesday Book entry was *Grimesbi*.

Guernsey (Channel Islands) Probably 'Gaern's island'. *Gaern* (Old Norse personal name) unidentified; *ey* (Old Norse) 'island'. Some authorities consider that the alternative derivation of *graenn* (Old Norse) 'green' is at least appropriate for this, the second largest and 'greenest' of the Channel Islands, famed today for its intensive horticulture. The name was recorded as *Guernesi* c.1170; *Gernereye* in 1218; *Guernesey* in 1447.

Guildford (Surrey) Probably 'Golden ford'. *Gylde* (Old English conjectural word) 'gold-coloured'; *ford* (Old English) 'river crossing'. This modern cathedral and university city, as well as county town, is located on the River Wey as it cuts through the HOG'S BACK. It is the latter that is the likely source of this name in the sense of the 'golden-coloured', sandy hillsides exposed here. It was recorded as *Gyldeford* around 880.

Guisborough (Cleveland) Probably 'Gigr's stronghold'. *Gigr* (Old Norse personal name; *burh* (Old English) 'fortified place'. The name of this town, southeast of MIDDLESBROUGH, was recorded as *Ghigesburg* in 1086.

Guiseley (West Yorkshire) 'Gislic's woodland clearing'. *Gislic* (Old English personal name); *leah* (Old English) 'woodland clearing'. The name of this industrial town, northwest of LEEDS, was recorded as *Gislicleh* in about 972, and as *Gisele* in 1086.

Gullane (Lothian) Possibly, place of the 'little loch'. *Gollan* (Scottish Gaelic) small lake. It is said that there was once a small lake here near the coast, north of HADDINGTON.

Gweedore (Donegal) 'Water inlet'. *Gaoth* (Irish Gaelic) 'inlet'; *dobhair* (Irish Gaelic) 'water'. This village and the surrounding spectacular coastal area of great scything sandy bays and estuaries to the south of the BLOODY FORELAND in northwest Ireland has an aptly descriptive name.

Gwent (Wales) 'The place'. The name of the current county in the southeast of Wales, which was formerly MONMOUTHshire, relates to the ancient kingdom of Gwent, and is said to derive from a pre-Celtic root word that implied a 'favoured place'. *See* GLAMORGAN.

Gwynedd (Wales) 'The lands of Cunedda'. This northwestern county of Wales, formed in 1974 out of the former counties of ANGLESEY, CAERNARFONshire and parts of DENBIGHshire and MERIONETHshire, takes the name of the ancient kingdom of Gwynedd that occupied this region from the centuries following the end of Roman rule through to the Anglo-Norman conquest of all Wales by 1300. The name itself derives from *Cunedda* (Old Welsh personal name) 5th-century ruler of the kingdom here. Cunedda's own name means 'good quality', from *cynneddf* (Old Welsh) 'quality'; *dda* (Old Welsh) 'good'. *See* CADAIR IDRIS; CARDIGAN.

H

Hackney (Greater London) 'Haca's island'. *Haca-n* (Old English personal name—genitive form); *eg* (Old English) 'island'. The name of this district and borough, lying on the west side of the Lea Valley northeast of the City of LONDON, became familiar in its use to describe a taxi as a 'Hackney carriage', deriving from the fact that originally many of London's cabs where drawn by hackneys, horses that came from the Hackney Marshes here. It is with reference to an area of higher drier land in or near the latter that this name originates. It was recorded as *Hakeneia* in 1198.

Haddington (Lothian) 'Hada's people's farm'. *Hada* (personal name); *inga* (Old English) 'people's'; *tun* (Old English) 'farm'. This former county town and busy market centre is situated in the River TYNE, at the heart of the rich agrarian land of East LOTHIAN. Recorded as *Hadynton* 1098; *Hadintun* and *Hadingtoun* 1150.

Haddo (Grampian) The name of this village and fine 18th century Adam house, northwest of ELLON, is a corruption of 'half-davoch', an agricultural measure of land reckoned by the number of beasts that worked it. The name is derived as *'healf'* (Old English) 'half'; *dabhach* (Scottish Gaelic) 'land unit'. *Compare* ARROCHAR; KIRRIEMUIR.

Hadleigh (Essex; Suffolk) 'Heather clearing'. *Haeth* (Old English) 'heather', 'heath'; *leah* (Old English) 'clearing'. The names of these two towns, one west of SOUTHEND-ON-SEA and the other west of IPSWICH, have a common origin and could mean either 'a clearing in the heath' or 'a forest clearing where the heather grows'.

Early records show *Haethlege c.*1100 (Essex); *Haedleage c.*995 (Suffolk).

Hadrian's Wall (Cumbria/Northumberland/Tyne and Wear) This most spectacular relic of Roman Britain was built in AD120-123 as a major fortification on the orders of Emperor Hadrian, after whom it is named. Extending for 73 miles (117 km) across northern ENGLAND, from Bowness-on-Solway, near CARLISLE, in the west to the appropriately named town of WALLSEND in the east, it was manned as a defended frontier against the unconquered tribes of Caledonia (SCOTLAND) until it was abandoned in AD383.

Hailsham (East Sussex) 'Haegel's homestead'. *Haegel* (Old English personal name); *ham* (Old English) 'homestead', 'enclosure'. The name of this small town north of EASTBOURNE is recorded as *Hamelesham* in the Domesday Book of 1086. *See* HAYLING ISLAND.

Hale (Greater Manchester) 'The nook'. *Halh* (Old English) 'nook in a river bend'. The common name of this town south of ALTRINCHAM was recorded as now in 1086.

Halesowen (West Midlands) 'The nooks of the Owen manor'. *Halh* (Old English) 'nooks as hollows'; *Owen* (Old English manorial affix) 13th-century Welsh prince who owned land here. The name of this town, southwest of BIRMINGHAM, appeared in a document of 1272 as *Hales Owayn*.

Halesworth (Suffolk) Probably Haele's enclosure'. *Haele* (Old English personal name); *worth* (Old English) 'enclosure'. The Domesday book entry for this small agricultural-industries town northwest of IPSWICH is *Haealesuurda*.

Halifax (West Yorkshire) Probably 'nook of rough grass'. *Halh* (Old English) 'nook'; *gefeaxe* (Old English conjectural word) 'coarse grass'. The origin of the name of this industrial town southwest of BRADFORD remains uncertain; it was recorded in a late 11th-century document as *Halyfax*.

Halstead (Essex) 'Place of refuge or shelter'. *Hald* (Old

English) 'protection'; *stede* (Old English) 'place'. The name of this small town, northeast of BRAINTREE, was documented as *Haltesteda* in the Domesday Book.

Haltwhistle (Northumberland) 'The high confluence'. *Haut* (Old French) 'high'; *twisla* (Old English) 'river confluence'. Despite its location on a railway line, the name of this small market town, west of HEXHAM, has nothing to do with trains. It refers to a confluence of the upper River THYNE here, and was rendered as *Hautwisel* in a document of 1240.

Hambleton Hills (North Yorkshire) 'Crooked hills'. *hamel* (Old English) 'crooked', 'irregularly shaped'; *dun* (Old English) 'hill'. These hills that form a outlying range on the southwest of the North York Moors take their apt name from the individual Hambleton Hill, which was recorded as *Hameldune* in the 13th century. The modern administrative district of Hambleton, which covers this north central part of the county, has adopted in turn its name from these hills.

Hamilton (Strathclyde) Apparently this town on the River CLYDE, upstream and southeast of GLASGOW, was originally a village by the name of Cadzow, which was renamed by the first Lord Hamilton who moved here from England in the 15th century.

Hammersmith (Greater London) Place with 'the hammer smithy'. *Hamor* (Old English) 'hammer'; *smiththe* (Old English) 'smithy', 'blacksmith's shop', 'forge'. This riverside district of west LONDON on the north bank of the THAMES has a name that means exactly what it says, the first element giving descriptive emphasis to its origin. It was recorded as *Hamersmyth* in 1294.

Hamnavoe (Shetland) 'Harbour of the bay'. *Hamn* (Old Norse) 'harbour'; *vagr* (Old Norse) 'bay'. Both the two fishing villages of this name on SHETLAND, one on West Burra, the other on YELL, are thus aptly described.

Hampshire (England) 'Hamptonshire'. The name of this south-central county is thus a contracted form that refers to its main town, SOUTHAMPTON, which was to begin with simply 'Hampton'. It was recorded in the 9th-century Anglo-Saxon Chronicle as *Hamtunscir*. The rendering in the Domesday Book of 1086 already manifests the phonetically softer Norman-influenced *Hantscire*, and it is from the latter that the commonly used county abbreviation of 'Hants' is derived.

Hampstead (Greater London) Simply 'place of the homestead'. *Ham* (Old English) 'homestead'; *stede* (Old English) 'place'. The name of this elevated former village and now district of CAMDEN was recorded as *Hemstede* in 959 and as *Hamstede* in the Domesday Book. *Compare* BERKHAMSTEAD; HEMEL HEMPSTEAD.

Hampton (Greater London) 'Farmstead in a river bend'. *Hamm* (Old English) 'riverside land enclosed by the meander of a river'; *tun* (Old English) 'farmstead'. This name, recorded in the Domesday Book as *Hammtone*, thus aptly describes this suburban village on the THAMES south of HOUNSLOW, famous for Hampton Court Palace. Other derivations of the first element of this common Old English name include *ham* = 'homestead'; *hean* = 'high'.

Handsworth (South Yorkshire; West Midlands) 'Hand's' and 'Hun's enclosure' respectively. *Hand*; *Hun* (Old English personal names); *worth* (Old English) 'enclosure'. These two places, the former being a eastern coal-mining district of SHEFFIELD, the other a western district of BIRMINGHAM, appear in the Domesday Book as *Handeswrde* and *Honesworde* respectively.

Hanley (Staffordshire) Place 'at the high wood or clearing'. *Hean* (Old English—dative form of *heah*) 'high'; *leah* (Old English) 'wood', 'forest clearing'. This, the chief administrative centre for the 'Five Towns' that comprise STOKE-ON TRENT, lies on a hill in the Lyme Forest district. It was recorded as *Henle* in 1212. *See* BURSLEM.

Haringey (Greater London) 'Haering's woodland enclosure'. *Haering* (Old English personal name); *gehaeg* (Old English) 'enclosure' often fenced off. The name of this north LONDON borough is really identical in derivation to HORNSEY, one of its districts. An early record of 1201 shows the original name as *Haringeie*. Today it is sometimes spelt **Harringay**.

Harlech (Gwynedd) 'Beautiful rock'. *Hardd* (Welsh) 'beautiful', 'fine'; *llech* (Welsh) 'rock' or 'slab of smooth stone'. This historic small town, located on a commanding cliff at the southern end of TREMADOC BAY, has a name that refers specifically to the impressive site of its famous castle, built by Edward I in the 1280s on a rocky promontory here. There is no firm evidence for a castle here before the present one, but the site plays a prominent role in the *Mabinogion*, the 12th-century collection of Welsh legends.

Harlesden (Greater London) Probably 'Heoruwulf's or Herewulf's farm'. *Heoruwulf/Herewulf* (Old English personal name); *tun* (Old English) 'farmstead'. The name of this district of BRENT was recorded as *Herulvestune* in the Domesday Book of 1086.

Harleston (Norfolk) 'Heoruwulf's or Herewulf's farm'. The derivation of the name of this small town, north-east and downstream on the River Waveney from DISS, is most likely the same as for HARLESDEN. It appears in the Domesday Book of 1086 as *Heroluestuna*.

Harlow (Essex) 'Army mound'. *Here* (Old English) 'army'; *hlaw* (Old English) 'mound'. Although one of the first designated New Towns in 1947, the original settlement, recorded as *Herlawe* in 1045, now Old Harlow, was a 'hundred' (a medieval administrative centre), and the 'mound' here may have had the sense of a 'meeting place of the people'.

Harpenden (Hertfordshire) Traditionally 'valley of the harp'. *Hearpe* (Old English) *harp*; *denu* (Old English) 'valley'. Some authorities suggest, however, that the first element of the name of this commuter town, north of St ALBANS and near to the track of WATLING STREET, aptly derives *here* + *paeth* (Old English) 'army' or 'military road'. It was noted as *Herpedene* in 1060.

Harris (Western Isles) 'Higher island'. *Har* (Old Norse) 'higher'; *ey* (Old Norse) 'island'. Also *H-earaidh* (Scottish Gaelic) 'higher', although it is more likely that the name has a Norse root, as is more common with island names in these parts. The meaning, however, is clearly descriptive of a topography of high hills, by comparison with LEWIS to the north. Recorded as *Heradh* 1500; *Harrige* 1542; *Harreis* 1588.

Harrogate (North Yorkshire) Place by 'the cairn road'. *Horg* (Old Danish) 'cairn'; *gata* (Old Danish) 'road', 'way'. The name of this spa town and conference centre north of LEEDS had originally the common north-country sense of the 'gata' or gate element that signified a 'right of access to pasturage for cattle'. Hence the 'cairn' would have been a wayside marker connected with the latter. The name was recorded as *Harougat* in the early 14th century.

Harrow-on-the-Hill (Greater London) Place of 'the heathen temple'. *Hearg* (Old English) 'heathen temple' or 'shrine'. This district of the borough of Harrow, in northwest LONDON, whose name has become well-known for its famous public school, probably was the site of a early Saxon shrine on the hill here. Records show that the affix was added later: *Hearge* 825; *Herges* 1086 (Domesday Book); *Haroue on the Hill* 1616.

Hartland Point (Devon) 'Stag peninsula'. *Heorot* (Old English) 'stag'; *eg* (Old English) 'island', 'peninsula'; *tun* (Old English) 'farmstead'; *land* (Old English) 'tract of land'. The current name of this prominent headland on the North DEVON coast, west of BIDEFORD, is much changed from is original postulated form as *Heorot-ieg*, the latter element of which has been lost, while the *tun* and *land* elements have been later added with regard to the nearby village of Hartland. Records show the evolution: *Heortigtun* c.880; *Hertitone* 1086 (Domesday Book); *Hartilanda* 1130; *Hertilaund* 1230.

Hartlepool (Cleveland) Place by 'the stag peninsula bay'. *Heorot* (Old English) 'stag'; *eg* (Old English) 'island', 'peninsula'; *pol* (Old English) 'pool', 'bay'. The name of this industrial coastal port, north of the TEES estuary, aptly describes the geographical situation of the original settlement on the 'Hart' headland that bounds Hartlepool Bay, beside which the 19th-century town, formerly known as West Hartlepool, developed. An early record of *c.*1180 shows *Herterpol*.

Harwich (Essex) Place of 'the army camp'. *Here* (Old English) 'army', 'military'; *wic* (Old English) 'specialised settlement', 'camp'. This major North Sea ferry port, situated on the south side of the mouth of the Orwell estuary opposite FELIXSTOWE, has a name that directly reflects the known presence of a Danish military camp here in the 9th century. Records show: *Herwyz* 1238; *Herewic* 1248; *Herewyk* 1253. *Compare* HARLOW; HARPENDEN.

Haslemere (Surrey) Place of 'the pool by the hazel trees'. *Haesel* (Old English) 'hazel tree'; *mere* (Old English) 'pool', 'lake'. The name of this town, in a heavily wooded part of the county southwest of GUILDFORD, was recorded as *Heselmere* in 1221.

Haslingden (Lancashire) 'Valley where the hazel trees grow'. *Haeslen* (Old English) 'growing with hazel trees'; *denu* (Old English) 'valley'. The name of this industrial town, lying in a sheltered valley surrounded by high moorland southeast of ACCRINGTON, was documented as *Heselingedon* in 1241.

Hassocks (West Sussex) Place of 'the rough grass tussocks'. *Hassuc* (Old English) 'clumps of coarse grass'. This residential satellite, south of BURGESS HILL, was developed as a mid-19th century commuter town with the opening of the LONDON-BRIGHTON railway and takes its name from such a field known locally as 'Hassocks'.

Hastings (East Sussex) Settlement or estate of 'Haesta's people'. *Haesta* (Old English personal name); *ingas* (Old English) 'people of'. The name of this seaside resort, northeast of EASTBOURNE, was first recorded in the early 10th century as *Haestingaceaster*, alluding to a Roman camp here, although there are no remains of this evident. A text from the Anglo-Saxon Chronicle, a century later in 1011, documents the name as *Haestingas*, which in turn had become even more recognisable as *Hastinges* in the Domesday Book of 1086.

Hatfield (Hertfordshire; South Yorkshire) 'Heather covered open land'. *Haeth* (Old English) 'heather'; *feld* (Old English) 'open land'. Both these towns, the former a New Town designated in 1948, and the other a small town on the area of fenland known as Hatfield Chase to the northeast of DONCASTER, have a common English placename of identical origin, both recorded as *Haethfelth* in a text of 731 from the Venerable Bede's 'Historia Ecclesiastica'. *Compare* HEATHFIELD.

Hatton (Grampian) 'Hall farm'. *Hall* (Old English) 'manor house'; *tun* (Old English) 'farmstead'. This was a common name in the 16th and 17th centuries for the large farmhouse in which the laird lived.

Havant (Hampshire) 'Hama's spring'. *Hama-n* (Old English personal name—genitive form); *funta* (Old English conjectural loan-word from Latin *fons* or *fontis*) 'spring'. This town, north of HAYLING ISLAND, has now a much contracted form of its original name, recorded as *Hamanfunta* in 935. By the time of its entry into the Domesday Book in 1086, the changing process was already quite marked as *Havehunte*.

Haverfordwest (Dyfed) Possibly 'goat ford'. The original name of this market town north of MILFORD HAVEN in southwest Wales, was simply *Haverford*. It was recorded as *Haverfordia c.*1188, and according to one authority this means 'goat ford', referring to an early crossing of the Western Cleddau river. The *-west* suffix was added later as a distinction, apparently because misspellings of the original name had confused it with HEREFORD. The Welsh *Hwlffordd* is a rendering, not a translation, of the basic English name.

Haverhill (Suffolk) Probably 'hill where oats are grown'. *Hafri* (Old Scandinavian) 'oats'; *hyll* (Old English) 'hill'. The name of this small industrial town, south-east of CAMBRIDGE, was recorded as *Hauerhella* in the Domesday Book of 1086, and as *Haverhell* in 1158.

Havering (Greater London) Place of 'Haefer's people'. *Haefer* (Old English personal name); *ingas* (Old English) 'people of'. The name of this far-eastern LONDON borough, on the north side of the THAMES, was recorded as *Haueringas* in the Domesday Book. Near the northern edge of the borough, by Havering Forest, is the village of **Havering-atte-Bower**, the distinctive style of affix deriving from *aet*, (Old English) 'at', 'by'; *Bur* (Old English) 'dwelling', having the sense of 'by the bower or royal residence'; Bower House is close by.

Hawarden (Clwyd) 'High enclosure'. *Heah* (Old English) 'high'; *worthign* (Midlands version of Old English *worth*) 'enclosure'. This town, south of QUEENSFERRY, is on rising ground above the River DEE. Its Welsh name also reflects its situation; *Penarlag*, derived from *pennardd* (Welsh) 'height', together with some personal name.

Hawes (North Yorkshire) Place at 'the pass in the hills'. *Hals* (Old Norse) 'neck'. The origin of the name of this small town in WENSLEYDALE has the transferred sense of a narrow neck of land in between the hills, i.e. a pass, or as in the north of England, a 'hause'.

Haweswater (Cumbria) 'Hafr's lake'. *Hafr* (Old Norse personal name); *waeter* (Old English) 'lake'. The name of this, the most easterly lake of the LAKE DISTRICT, now converted into a reservoir, was recorded as *Havereswater* in 1199.

Hawick (Borders) 'Hedged enclosure settlement'. *Haga* (Old English) 'hedge'; *wic* (Old English) 'settlement', 'village'. The name of this 'Border-woollens' town, south of SELKIRK, was recorded as *Hawic* in the 12th century.

Hawkshead (Cumbria) 'Haukr's mountain pasture'. *Haukr* (Old Norse personal name); *saetr* (Old Norse) 'high summer pasture', 'sheiling'. The name of this large village, a popular Lakeland beauty spot near the head of the small Esthwaite Water, indicates the ancient practice of transhumance; it was recorded as *Hovkesete* around 1200. *See* AMBLESIDE.

Haworth (West Yorkshire) 'Hedge enclosure'. *Haga* (Old English) 'hedge'; *worth* (Old English) 'enclosure'. The name of this town, lying at the heart of 'Bronte Country' in a valley southwest of KEIGHLEY, appeared as *Hauewrth* in a document of 1209. Compare HAWICK.

Haydock (Merseyside) Probably 'barley place'. *Haidd* (Brythonic Celtic - Welsh conjectural plus adjectival ending *oc* or *iog*) 'barley place', 'corn farm'. The name of this town, famous for its racecourse, lies in the coal-mining district northeast of ST HELENS. Records show: *Hedoc* 1169; *Heddoch* 1170; *Haidoc* 1212.

Haydon Bridge (Northumberland) 'Bridging point in the hay valley'. *Heg* (Old English) 'hay'; *denu* (Old English) 'valley'; *brycg* (Old English) 'bridge'. The name of this small town bridging the South TYNE river west of HEXHAM was recorded as *Hayden* in 1236.

Hayes (Greater London) 'Land overgrown with brushwood'. *Haes* (Old English conjectural word) 'brushwood'. The name of this district of HILLINGDON was recorded as *Haese* in 831.

Hayle (Cornwall) Place on 'the estuary'. *Heyl* (Old Cornish conjectural word) 'estuary'. The name of this industrial port on the ST IVES Bay inlet is descriptively apt of its situation; it was recorded as *Heyl* in a document of 1265.

Hayling Island (Hampshire) 'Island of Haegel's people'. *Haegel* (Old English personal name); *inga* (Old English—genitive form of *ingas*) 'people of'; *eg* (Old English) 'island'. The name of this island, south of HAVANT to which it is now linked by bridge, was recorded as *Heglingaigae* in 956, and *Halingei* in the Domesday book of 1086. The main settlements here are **North Hayling** and **South Hayling**.

Hay-on-Wye (Powys) 'Fenced enclosure'. *Hege* (Old

English) 'fenced hunting enclosure in a forest'. This small town on the River Wye, northeast of BRECON, was recorded as *Haya c.*1188. The Welsh name is *Y Gelli Gandryll*, literally meaning 'the broken grove'.

Haywards Heath (West Sussex) 'Heathland by the hedged enclosure'. *Hege* (Old English) 'hedge'; *worth* (Old English) 'enclosure'; *haeth* (Old English) 'heath'. This residential town north of BURGESS HILL, which developed, like the latter, in the mid-19th century with the opening of the LONDON-BRIGHTON railway, is on the site of the original settlement simply known as *Heyworth*, as documented in 1261, to which the affix was added later; a record of 1544 shows *Haywards Hoth*.

Hazel Grove (Greater Manchester) Place of 'the hazel copse'. *Haesel* (Old English) 'hazel tree'; *graf* (Old English) 'copse', 'grove'. This town, southwest of STOCKPORT, has a straightforward name that means precisely what it says. It was recorded as *Hesselgrove* in 1690.

Headingley (West Yorkshire) 'The clearing of Hedde's people'. *Hedde* (Old English personal name); *inga* (Old English—genitive form of *ingas*) 'people of'; *leah* (Old English) 'woodland clearing'. The name of this north-western district of LEEDS, well known for its test cricket ground, was recorded as *Hedingeleia* in the Domesday Book of 1086.

Headington (Oxfordshire) Probably 'Hedena's hill'. *Hedena-n* (Old English personal name—genitive form); *dun* (Old English) 'hill'. Although the '-ington ' ending might reasonably suggest a derivation giving the meaning of 'a farmstead associated with', the name of this northern district of OXFORD, which sits on a low hill, was recorded as *Hedenedune* in 1004.

Heanor (Derbyshire) Place at 'the high ridge'. *Hean* (Old English—dative form of heah) 'high': *ofre* (Old English) 'ridge'. This town in the coal-mining district northeast of DERBY is located on a hill, and its name was recorded as *Hainoure* in the Domesday Book of 1086.

Heathfield (East Sussex) 'Heather-covered open land'. *Haeth* (Old English) 'heather'; *feld* (Old English) 'open land'. The name of this small town in the centre of the county, due north of EASTBOURNE, was noted in 1230 as *Hatfeld*; indicating its common origin with HATFIELD.

Heathrow (Greater London) 'Row of dwellings on or near a heath'. *Haeth* (Old English) 'heath'; *raew* (Old English) 'row, line of houses'. The internationally recognised name of LONDON's main airport, situated in the borough of HILLINGDON at the western edge of the metropolitan area, reflects the pre-urban scene here on HOUNSLOW Heath. A document of around 1410 records the name as *La Hetherewe*.

Heaton (Tyne and Wear; West Yorkshire) 'High farm'. *Heah* (Old English) 'high'; *tun* (Old English) 'farmstead'. This fairly common name in the north of England applies here to what has become a northeastern district of NEWCASTLE UPON TYNE and a northwestern district of BRADFORD. In the case of the former, an adjoining suburb of High Heaton creates a comparative tautology. Records show: *Heton* 1256 and *Hetun* 1160 respectively.

Hebburn (Tyne and Wear) 'High burial place'. *Heah* (Old English) 'high'; *byrgen* (Old English) 'tumulus', 'burial chamber'. The name of this industrial town on the south bank of the River TYNE, east of GATESHEAD, was recorded as *Heabyrm* in the early 12th century.

Hebden Bridge (West Yorkshire) 'Bridge over the river of the valley where the rose hips grow'. *Heopa* (Old English) 'rose hips'; *denu* (Old English) 'valley'; *brycg* (Old English) 'bridge'. This industrial town, west of HALIFAX, takes its name from the Hebden Water here Records show *Hebedene* 1086; *Hepden Bridge* 1508.

Hebrides (Scotland) Apparently this name, as is now applied to both the 'Inner' and 'Outer' islands off the west coast of Scotland, resulted from a misprinting of *ri* for *u* in *Haebudes*, the Roman name for the former group.

Heckmondwike (West Yorkshire) 'Heahmund's farm'. *Heahmund* (Old English personal name); *wic* (Old English) 'outlying' or 'specialised farm'. The name of this town, southwest of BATLEY, was recorded as *Hedmundewic* in a document of 1166.

Hedon (Humberside) Probably 'heather-covered hill'. *Haeth* (Old English) 'heather'; *dun* (Old English) 'down', 'hill'. However, there is not much of a hill in the locality of this town east of HULL. The name was recorded in the 12th century exactly as now.

Helensburgh (Strathclyde) 'Helen's town'. This planned residential town on the north shore of the Firth of CLYDE was named in honour of Lady Helen Sutherland, wife of Sir James Colquhoun of LUSS, who in 1752 bought land here, including the former small fishing village of Millig. The renamed town was established in 1776.

Helmsdale (Highland) 'Hjalmund's dale'. *Hjalmund* (Old Norse personal name) 'helmet'; *dalr* (Old Norse) 'valley'; 'dale'. This village lies, southwest of WICK, at the mouth of the Helmsdale River where the valley form is still very steep-sided. Recorded in the *Orkneyinga Saga* of 1225 as *Hjalmunddal*.

Helston (Cornwall) 'farmstead at the ancient court'. *Hen-lys* (Old Cornish conjectural word) 'old court'; *tun* (Old English) 'farmstead', 'village', 'estate'. The compound name of this town at the landward head of the LIZARD Peninsula was documented as *Henlistone* in the Domesday Book of 1086.

Helvellyn (Cumbria) This well-known LAKE DISTRICT mountain, with its popular 'Striding Edge' ridgewalk, appears to have a Celtic name, the origin and meaning of which remain obscure. The earliest record of the name as *Helvillon* in 1577 is too late for an etymology to be suggested.

Hemel Hempstead (Hertfordshire) 'Homestead in the undulating country'. *Hamel* (Old English) 'undulating', 'broken'; *ham-stede* (Old English) 'homestead'.

This New Town, designated in 1947, lying northwest of Watford, in the ancient district of Hemel, itself first recorded in the early 8th century, was documented as the old settlement of *Hamelamestede* in the Domesday Book.

Hemsby (Norfolk) Probably 'Hemer's farm'. *Hemer* (Old Danish personal name); *by* (Old Danish) farmstead. The name of this small coastal town, northwest ofC$$aistor-on-S$$ea, was recorded as *Heimesbei* on the Domesday Book.

Hemsworth (West Yorkshire) 'Hymel's enclosure'. *Hymel* (Old English personal name); *worth* (Old English) 'enclosure'. The name of this coal-mining town, south of Pontefract, was recorded as *Hamelesuurde* in 1086.

Hendon (Greater London) Place 'at the high hill'. *Hean* (Old English—dative form of *heah*) 'high'; *dun* (Old English) 'hill'. The name of this district of Barnet in northwest London was recorded as *Heandun* in *c.*975.

Henfield (West Sussex) 'Stony open land'. *Han* (Old English) 'stone', 'rock'; *feld* (Old English) 'open land'. The name of this small town to the north of the South Downs, in from Shoreham-by-Sea, was recorded as *Hanefeld* in 770.

Henley-in-Arden (Warwickshire) Place 'at the high or chief clearing in the high district'. *Hean* (Old English—dative form of *heah*) 'chief', 'high'; *leah* (Old English) 'woodland clearing'; *Arden* (Brythonic Celtic affix) refers to 'high district' of the medieval Forest of Arden here, recorded as *Eardene* in 1088, which possibly derives from the same root origin as Ardmore, Ards Peninsula, and related to the Ardennes in Belgium. Prior to the distinguishing affix being added, the name of this small market town, east of Reddich, was documented as *Henle* in 1180.

Henley-on-Thames (Oxfordshire) Place 'at the chief clearing by the Thames'. *Hean* (Old English—dative form of *heah*) 'high', 'chief'; *leah* (Old English) 'woodland clearing'. This riverside town on the Thames, upstream and west of MAIDENHEAD, famous for its annual rowing regatta, has a basic name of similar origin to HENLEY-IN-ARDEN, except that the first element here has the sense of 'high' as in 'important'. The name was noted as *Heanlea* in 1168, the affix being added later in contradistinction to other so-named places.

Hereford (Hereford and Worcester) Place of 'the army ford'. *Here* (Old English) 'army'; *ford* (Old English) 'river crossing'. This historic cathedral town midway between MONMOUTH and LEOMINSTER on the former connecting Roman road as it crosses the River Wye, has a name that reflects the suitable passage for an army here. Its name was recorded in 958 precisely as now.

Herm (Channel Islands) This small island in the Bailiwick of GUERNSEY, and lying east of the main island, has an ancient Celtic, or even pre-Celtic, name of obscure origin.

Herne Bay (Kent) Place at 'the angle or corner of land'. *Hyrne* (Old English) 'angle', 'corner'. This north KENT coastal resort takes its name from the nearby village of **Herne**, recorded as *Hyrnan* in about 1100.

Herstmonceux (East Sussex) 'Wooded hill on the Monceux manor estate'. *Hyrst* (Old English) 'wooded hill'; *Monceux* (Anglo-Norman manorial affix) 12th-century possession of the Monceux family, originally from Monceaux in Normandy. Lying inland and north of PEVENSEY BAY, this village, with its 15th-century castle, which is now home to the Royal Observatory, was recorded as simply *Herst* in the Domesday Book of 1086, and by 1287 a document shows it to be *Herstmonceus*.

Hertford (Hertfordshire) Literally and phonetically 'hart ford' or 'ford frequented by harts or stags'. *Heorot* (Old English) 'hart', 'stag'; *ford* (Old English) 'river crossing'. The name of this county town on the River Lea north of LONDON was recorded as *Heorutford* in the

Venerable Bede's 8th-century Historia Ecclesiastica. The county name first appears in a document of 1011 as *Heortfordscir*, the additional ending deriving from *scir*, (Old English) 'district'.

Hessle (Humberside) Place of 'the hazel grove'. *Hesli* (Old Scandinavian) 'copse of hazel trees'. The name of this town on the HUMBER, immediately west of HULL, and now at the north end of the Humber Bridge, appears in the Domesday Book as *Hase*, and as *Hesel* in a document of 1157. *Compare* HASELMERE; HASLINGDEN.

Hetton-le-Hole (Tyne and Wear) 'Hill where the wild rose hips grow'. *Heopa* (Old English) 'rose hips', 'brambles'; *dun* (Old English) 'hill'. Thus the basic name of this former coal-mining town, northeast of DURHAM, is derived. The pre-industrial settlement was recorded as *Heppedun* in 1180. The distinguishing affix, added later, means 'in a hollow'. *Compare* HEBDEN.

Hexham (Northumberland) 'The bachelor homestead'. *Haegsteald* (Old English) 'younger son who has a *haga* or "enclosure" outside the family homestead'; *ham* (Old English) 'homestead'. This market town, west of NEWCASTLE UPON TYNE, was noted as *Hagustaldes ham* in 685, *Hextoldesham* in 1188, and shortened since.

Heysham (Lancashire) 'Brushwood settlement'. *Haes* (Old English conjectural word) 'rough bushes', 'brushwood'; *ham* (Old English) 'homestead', 'village'. This ferry port on the sandy coast immediately southwest of MORECAMBE has a name that would have aptly described early conditions here; it appears in the Domesday Book as *Hessam*, and *Hesham* in a text of 1190. *Compare* HAYES.

Heywood (Greater Manchester) 'High wood'. *Heah* (Old English) 'high', 'chief'; *wudu* (Old English) 'wood'. The origin of the name of this town east of BURY may have had the sense of 'an important or chief wood' rather than being elevated , which is not a feature of its low-lying location. It was recorded as *Hewude* in 1246.

Higham Ferrers (Northamptonshire) 'High homestead of the de Ferariis family'. *Heah* (Old English) 'high'; *ham* (Old English) 'homestead', 'village'; *Ferrers* (Anglo-Norman manorial affix). The common name of this small town east of WELLINGBOROUGH is recorded as *Hehham* 1066; *Hecham* 1086 (Domesday Book); *Heccham Ferrers* 1279.

Highbridge (Somerset) 'High or chief bridge'. *Heah* (Old English) 'high', 'chief'; *brycg* (Old English) 'bridge'. The comparatively simple name of this small industrial town at the mouth of the River Brue, just south of BURNHAM-ON-SEA, probably reflects the importance of this being the furthest downstream crossing point. It was recorded in 1324 exactly as now.

Highgate (Greater London) Place of 'the high tollgate'. *Heah* (Old English) 'high'; *geat* (Old English) 'gate'. The name of this elevated district of HARINGEY directly refers to a former tollgate here on the Great North Road; it was noted as *Le Heighgate* in 1354.

Highland (Scotland) Since 1975 this has been the name of the northernmost administrative region of mainland Scotland. It is derived from the general descriptive term 'the Highlands', long used to distinguish this mountainous area from 'the Lowlands' to the south.

High Wycombe (Buckinghamshire) Place 'at the outlying settlement'. *Heah* (Old English distiguishing affix—later addition) 'high'; *wicum* (Old English—dative plural of *wic*) 'at the dwellings'. This furniture-making town on the south side of the CHILTERNS, noted as *aet Wicumun* in about 970, now incorporates **West Wycombe**.

Hillingdon (Greater London) 'Hilda's hill'. *Hilda-n* (Old English personal name—genitive form) probably shortened version of a man's surname such as Hildwulf; *dun* (Old English) 'hill'. This westernmost LONDON borough has a name that refers to the area of rising ground at the site of the old village northwest of HAYES. It was recorded as *Hildendune* around 1080.

Hillsborough (Down) This 'plantation town' was named after Sir Moyses Hill, an English army officer who obtained lands here between LISBURN and DROMORE in the early 17th century.

Hinckley (Leicestershire) 'Hynca's clearing'. *Hynca* (Old English personal name); *leah* (Old English) 'woodland clearing'. The name of this town, southwest of LEICESTER, appeared in the Domesday Book of 1086 as *Hinchelie.*

Hindhead (Surrey) 'Hill frequented by hinds or does'. *Hind* (Old English) 'doe'; *heafor* (Old English) 'hill', 'ridge'. This 20th-century residential development on the high wooded southern rim of the Devil's Punchbowl, takes its name from this notable physical feature, which is a place still stocked with deer. It was recorded as *Hyndehed* in 1571

Hindley (Greater Manchester) 'Wood frequented by hinds or does'. *Hind* (Old English) 'doe'; *leah* (Old English) 'wood'. The name of this industrial town in the coal-mining district southeast of WIGAN was recorded as *Hindele* in 121 2.

Hitchin (Hertfordshire) Place in the territory 'of the Hicce tribe'. *Hiccum* (Old English tribal name—dative plural of *Hicce*). Although nothing is known about the tribe that gave their name to this town, immediately southwest of LETCHWORTH, it is considered that the name itself may be derived from an old form of the local river **Hiz**, which in turn may have had its origin in an ancient Brythonic Celtic root word meaning 'dry'. Early records include: *Hiccam c.*945; *Hiz* 1086.

Hobkirk (Borders) 'Church in the valley'. *Hop* (Old Norse) 'shelter', 'valley'; *kirkja* (Old Norse) 'church'. Formerly known as *Hopekirk*, the name of this village, southeast of Hawick, was recorded as *Hopechirke* 1220; *Hopeskirk* 1586; *Hoppkirck c.*1610. *See* KIRKHOPE.

Hoddesdon (Hertfordshire) 'Hod's hill'. *Hod* (Old English personal name); *dun* (Old English) 'hill'. The simple name of this town in the Lea valley, downstream and south of WARE, was recorded as *Hodesdone* in 1086.

Hog's Back (Surrey) This long, narrow, symmetrical ridge between GUILDFORD and FARNHAM, created as the result of a vertically upturned underlying stratum of North DOWNS' chalk, has been descriptively so called officially only since 1823. Earlier records indicate its former name as *Geldedon* 1190; *Gildedon* 1251; *Mons Guldedonye* c.1282, suggesting 'Guildford Down', meaning the gold-coloured hill. *See* GUILDFORD.

Holbeach (Lincolnshire) Probably place on the 'hollow ridge'. *Hol* (Old English) 'hollow', 'deep'; *bece* (Old English—locative form of *baec*) 'ridge'. This small town, east of SPALDING, is situated on a gently discernible elevated ridge on The FENS. The name was recorded as *Holebech* in the Domesday Book of 1086.

Holborn (Greater London) 'Stream in a hollow'. *Hol* (Old English) 'hollow'; *burna* (Old English) 'stream'. This LONDON district, to the north of ALDWYCH, lies in the valley of the upper part of the former River FLEET, known as the Holborn. The name appears in the Domesday Book of 1086 as *Holeburne*.

Holderness (Humberside) 'Headland ruled by a high-ranking yeoman'. *Holdr* (Old Norse) 'hold', a man of high rank in the Danelaw; *nes* (Old Scandinavian) 'headland', 'promontory'. This modern-day administrative district takes its name from the low-lying, almost flat peninsula that extends southeast from HULL, ending in the long sand spit of SPURN HEAD at the mouth of the HUMBER estuary. The name was recorded in the Domesday Book as *Heldernesse*.

Holland (Lincolnshire) 'Land bounded by hill spurs'. *Hoh* (Old English) 'hill spur'; *land* (Old English) 'district'. This Fenland area of southeast Lincolnshire, centred on SPALDING, was one of the three former divisions of the county. Also because of its Dutch-like flat, dyked, man-made intensely cultivated landscape it is popularly regarded as 'Little Holland'. It was recorded as *Hoiland* in 1086.

Holloway (Greater London) 'The road in a hollow'. *Hol*

(Old English) 'hollow', 'small valley'; *weg* (Old English) 'way', 'road'. The name of this district of ISLINGTON, well known for its large Victorian prison, has its simple origins in the fact that the 'Great North Road', now the A1, ran across a valley here between Highbury and HIGHGATE. It was documented in 1307 as Le *Holeweye*.

Holmfirth (West Yorkshire) 'The woodland belonging to Holme'. *Holmr* (Old Scandinavian) 'island' of raised drier land in a wet moorland; *fryhth* (Old English) 'sparse woodland'. The name of this industrial town, south of HUDDERSFIELD, makes direct reference to the nearby village of **Holme**, and was recorded as *Holnefrith* in 1274.

Holsworthy (Devon) 'Heald's enclosure'. *Heald* (Old English personal name); *worthig* (Old English variant of *worth*) 'enclosure'. The name of this small town, east of BUDE, was recorded in the Domesday Book as *Haldeword*.

Holt (Norfolk) Place at 'the wood'. *Holt* (Old English) 'wood', 'thicket'. The common and simple name of this small town, lying inland and southwest of SHERINGHAM, has appeared in the Domesday Book exactly as now.

Holyhead (Gwynedd) 'Holy headland'. This industrial port on HOLY ISLAND, lying just off the west coast of ANGLESEY, has had Christian links from the 6th century on. The actual 'head' is Holyhead Mountain to the west of the town. The town's Welsh name, *Caergybi*, refers to St Cybi, to whom the parish is dedicated.

Holy Island (Gwynedd; Northumberland; Strathclyde) All three 'Holy Islands', of Wales, England and Scotland, have long histories of Christian association, that have given rise to the name in each case. Holy Island off ANGLESEY is *Ynys Gybi* in Welsh, meaning 'Cybi's island', so named after the 6th-century saint who founded a monastery here. Holy Island off the NORTHUMBERLAND coast, also known as LINDISFARNE, was the site of oratories established by St Aidan and St Cuthbert, both in the 7th century. The Scottish Holy Island lies off the east coast of ARRAN, and here was the

6th-century cell of St Molaise. In recent times it has become a Buddhist retreat.

Holy Loch (Strathclyde) Apparently so called from its association with St Mund, follower of St Columba, who was reputedly an early Christian missionary at work in this area of the COWAL peninsula. *See* KILMUN.

Holyrood (Lothian) 'Holy cross'. *Halig* (Old English) 'holy'; *rod* (Old English) 'cross'. This name, associated with the royal palace of Holyroodhouse in EDINBURGH, was originally dedicated in the early 12th century foundation of the adjacent abbey by King David I.

Holywell (Clwyd) This industrial town was developed mainly in the 19th century but has a name that relates back to the sacred well of St Winefride, who founded a nunnery here in the 7th century. Its Welsh name, *Treffynnon*, simply refers to the 'village of the well'.

Holywood (Dumfries and Galloway) Literally 'holy wood'. Originally *Darcongall*: 'wood of St Congal' (Scottish Gaelic *doire*: 'copse'), a 12th-century abbey was here. The name of this village north of DUMFRIES means what it says.

Honiton (Devon) 'Huna's Farmstead'. *Huna* (Old English personal name); *tun* (Old English) 'farmstead'. The name of this town east of EXETER, that is locally pronounced 'Hunniton', was recorded as *Honetone* in the Domesday book of 1086.

Horbury (West Yorkshire) Probably 'stronghold on muddy land'. *Horu* (Old English) 'dirt', 'filth'; *byrig* (Old English—dative of *burh*) 'fortified place'. Some authorities, however, consider this derivation as inappropriate to the situation of this manufacturing town to the southwest of WAKEFIELD. An alternative has been suggested: *hordburg* (Old English) 'treasure-stronghold'. It was recorded as *Horberie* in 1086.

Horncastle (Lincolnshire) 'Roman station on a horn of land'. *Horna* (Old English) 'horn-shaped piece of land'; *ceaster* (Old English) 'Roman fortified place'. This small agricultural-services town, east of LINCOLN, has a compound name that reflects both its situation in a 'horn' between two branches of the River Bain, which meet here, and the site of the former Roman camp of *Bannovalium*; the latter itself being derived ultimately from a Brythonic Celtic root that also describes the particular locational feature of this place. The entry in the Domesday Book is *Horncastre*.

Hornchurch (Greater London) Place of 'the church with horn-like gables'. *Horn* or *hornede* (Old English) 'horn-like'; *cirice* (Old English) 'church'. This former ESSEX town, now part of the borough of HAVERING at the extreme eastern end of the LONDON conurbation, has a somewhat surprising name that apparently means precisely what it says. It was recorded as *Hornechurch* in 1233.

Hornsea (Humberside) Place by 'the lake with a horn-shaped promontory'. *Horn* (Old Scandinavian) 'horn'; *nes* (Old Scandinavian) 'promontory'; *saer* (Old Scandinavian) 'sea', 'lake'. Recorded as *Hornessei* in the Domesday Book of 1086, this coastal resort, north-east of HULL, takes its name from the horn-shaped **Hornsea Mere** that lies immediately behind the town.

Hornsey (Greater London) 'Haering's enclosure'. *Haering* (old English personal name); *gehaeg* (Old English) 'enclosure', often fenced off. This district of the borough of HARINGEY has a name of identical origin to the latter, but it has evolved differently as successive records reveal: *Haringeie* 1201; *Harenghaye* 1232; *Haringeshaye* 1243; *Harnesey* 1543; *Hornsey* 1564.

Horsham (West Sussex) 'Village where horses were kept'. *Hors* (Old English) 'horse'; *ham* (Old English) 'homestead', 'village'. The name of this town, south-west of CRAWLEY, was recorded in its present spelling in a document of 947.

Horwich (Greater Manchester) Place at 'the grey wych-elms'. *Har* (Old English) 'grey'; *wice* (Old English) 'wych-elm tree'. This industrial town, west of BOLTON, takes its name from that of a former forest here. It was recorded as *Horewych* in a text of 1254.

Houghton-le-Spring (Tyne and Wear) 'Farmstead on a hill-spur belonging to the Spring family'. *Hoh* (Old English) 'hill-spur'; *tun* (Old English) 'farmstead'; *le* (Old French definite article remaining after the loss of preposition) of the; Spring (Old English manorial affix). This town, in the former coal-mining district southwest of SUNDERLAND, has a common basic name aptly descriptive of its situation, to which the distiguishing affix of an early local landowner has been subsequently added. A record of around 1220 shows both *Hocton* and *Hoghton Springes*.

Hounslow (Greater London) Probably 'Hund's burial mound'. *Hund* (Old English personal name); *hlaw* (Old English) 'burial mound', 'tumulus'. The name of this west LONDON borough was recorded in the Domesday Book as *Honeslaw*.

Houseteads (Northumberland) 'Place of the (Roman) buildings'. *Hus* (Old English) 'houses', 'buildings'; *stede* (Old English) 'place'. This standard English name refers to the major fort of *Vercovicium* on HADRIAN'S WALL.

Houston (Strathclyde) 'Hugo's farmstead'. *Hugo* (Old English personal name); *tun* (Old English) 'farmstead'. This residential village, northwest of PAISLEY, has grown up around the 12th-century farmstead property of Hugo de Paduinan.

Hove (East Sussex) Place of 'the hood-shaped hill or shelter'. *Hufe* (Old English) 'place of shelter' provided by some natural feature. This residential town and coastal resort, immediately west of BRIGHTON, has a unique name that possibly refers to some such place nearby on the South DOWNS. It appears in a text of 1288 as *La Houue*.

Howth (Dublin) 'The headland'. *Hofuth* (Old Norse) 'headland'. This residential northern suburb of DUBLIN is located on a rocky headland that protrudes into the Irish Sea. Its Irish name, *Binn Eadair*, refers to it as 'the peak of Edar', a legendary hero linked with this promontory.

Hoy (Orkney) 'High island'. *Ha* (Old Norse) 'high'; *ey* (Old Norse) 'island'. Hoy is much higher than any of the other ORKNEY islands, and has many dramatic sea cliffs and stacks, including the 'Old Man of Hoy'. It was recorded as Haey in the *c.*1225 *Orkneyinga Saga*. *See* HARRIS.

Hoylake (Merseyside) 'Tidal lake by the sandbank'. *Hygel* (Old English) 'sandbank'; *lake* (Middle English) 'stretch of water'. This 18th-century coastal resort, at the western tip of the WIRRAL peninsula, took its name from the former Hoyle Lake sea inlet, which has totally silted up and been built over. The earliest record of the latter shows a *Hyle Lake* in 1687.

Huddersfield (West Yorkshire) Probably 'Hudraed's open field'. *Hudraed* (Old English personal name); *feld* (Old English) 'open field'. Alternatively, some authorities consider that the first element of the name of this industrial town, south of BRADFORD, may be derived from *huder*, (Old English) 'shelter'. Records show *Oderesfelt* 1086 (Domesday Book); *Hudresfeld* 1121-7; *Huderesfeld* 1297.

Hughenden Valley (Buckinghamshire) 'Huhha's or Hucca's valley'. *Hudda-n* or *Hucca-n* (Old English personal name—dative form); *denu* (Old English) 'valley'. The first part of this tautological name of a village, north of HIGH WYCOMBE, was later transferred to Hughenden Manor, an 18th-century house high on the western valley slope here, that is renowned as the home of Disraeli. The original settlement name was documented as *Hucedene* in the Domesday Book, and as *Huggenden* a 100 years later in 1186.

Hugh Town (Cornwall) Place on 'the ridge'. *Hoh* (Old English) ridge, 'hill', 'spur of land'. The 'capital' of the Isles of SCILLY, situated on the largest island, ST MARY'S, was named after the hill above it on which Star Castle was built in 1593, in which year the name was recorded as *Hew Hill*.

Hull (Humberside) Probably place on 'the muddy one'.

Hul- (Brythonic Celtic root element) 'muddy'. This city and industrial port, located at the point at which the River Hull enters the HUMBER estuary, takes its name from the former river. Its full official name is **Kingston upon Hull**, the royal title being added at the end of the 13th century when Edward I acquired the port here. Records show *Portus de Hull* 1276; *Kyngeston super Hul* 1299.

Humber (Humberside) This major east coast estuary, formed from the TRENT and Ouse rivers, has an ancient pre-English river name of uncertain origin and meaning. The modern county of **Humberside** is named after it.

Hungerford (Berkshire) 'Ford by the unproductive land'. *Hungor* (Old English) 'poor', 'barren', 'unproductive'; *ford* (Old English) 'river crossing'. The name of this town, lying on the River Kennet midway between MARLBOROUGH and NEWBURY, descriptively implies what it says; it was recorded as *Hungreford* in 1011-18, and *Hungerford* by around 1148.

Hunstanton (Norfolk) 'Hunstan's farmstead'. *Hunstan* (Old English personal name); *tun* (Old English) 'farmstead'. The name of this coastal resort on the east side of The WASH was recorded as *Hunstanestun* in around 1035.

Huntingdon (Cambridgeshire) Probably the place on 'the hill of the huntsman'. *Hunta* (Old English) 'huntsman'; *dun* (Old English) 'hill'. Alternatively, it is considered by some authorities that the first element could be that of an Old English personal name. The name of this former county town, situated on a rise above the River Ouse northwest of CAMBRIDGE, was recorded as *Huntadun* in the late 10th century; and the name of the former surrounding county was first documented as *Huntadunscir* in 1011.

Huntly (Grampian) 'Huntsman's wood'. *Hunta* (Old English) 'huntsman'; *leah* (Old English) 'wood'. Originally a BERWICKshire placename, it was transferred north by Alexander Gordon, 4th Duke of Gordon and Earl of Huntly, when in 1769 he founded the town at the confluence of the Deveron and Bogie rivers, north-east of ABERDEEN.

Hurstpierpoint (West Sussex) 'Wooded hill of the Pierpoint estate'. *Hyrst* (Old English) 'wooded hill'; *Pierpoint* (later Anglo-Norman manorial affix) deriving from Roger de Pierpoint, who acquired land here in 1086 on what now is a greatly expanded residential development north of BRIGHTON. Records show: *Herst* 1086 (Domesday Book); *Herst Perepunt* 1279.

Huyton (Merseyside) 'Estate by or with a landing place'. *Hyth* (Old English) 'landing place'; *tun* (Old English) 'estate'. The name of this town, adjoining LIVERPOOL to the east, was noted as *Hitune* in 1086.

Hyde (Greater Manchester) 'Estate assessed as one hide'. *Hid* (Old English) an amount of land that could support one family. The name of this town, northeast of STOCKPORT, was recorded as *Hyde* 1285; *Hide* 1288.

Hythe (Kent) 'The landing place'. *Hyth* (Old English) 'landing place', usually on a river site. The simple and commonplace name of this coastal resort, west of FOLKSTONE, one of the original 'Cinque Ports', was recorded in the Anglo-Saxon Chronicle of the mid-11th century, exactly as now.

I

Ibrox (Strathclyde) 'Ford of the badger'. *Ath* (Scottish Gaelic) 'ford'; *bruic* (Scottish Gaelic) 'badger'. The name of this southside suburb of Glasgow, and home of the famous Rangers football club, manifests a form of brock as still commonly used for a badger in England. *See* BROXBURN.

Icknield Way (England) This prehistoric trackway, that originally ran southwestwards from The WASH in NORFOLK to the DORSET coast, and later was adapted in part by the Romans, has a name of uncertain origin and meaning. Recorded as *Icenhylte* in 903, it can be traced today along the modern highways of the A11 and A505 between THRETFORD and BALDOCK, along the B4009 below the northern escarpment of the CHILTERNS to Streatley, and thence along the 'Ridgeway' to AVEBURY.

Ilfracombe (Devon) 'Valley associated with Ilfred'. *Ilfred* (Old English personal name) West Saxon form of Aelfred; *ing* (Old English connective particle) 'associated with'; *cumb* (Old English) 'valley'. The name was entered in the Domesday Book in 1086 as *Alfreincome*.

Ilkeston (Derbyshire) 'Ealac's hill'. *Ealac* (Old English personal name); *dun* (Old English) 'hill'. The name of this industrial town, lying in the coal-mining district northwest of DERBY, was recorded as *Elchesdona* in 1155-7.

Ilkley (West Yorkshire) Probably 'Illica's woodland clearing'. *Illica* or *Yllica* (Old English personal name); *leah* (Old English) 'woodland clearing'. The name of this town north of BRADFORD, well known from the popular song about 'Ilkley Moor baht 'at', appears in the Domesday Book as *Illiclei*.

Ilminster (Somerset) 'Large church on the River Isle'. *Il-* (Brythonic Celtic conjectural root element) 'swift'; *mynster* (Old English) 'large church'. The name of this small market town, southeast of TAUNTON, was noted in an early record of 995 as *Ilemynister*.

Immingham (Humberside) 'Homestead of Imma's people'. *Imma* (Old English personal name); *inga* (Old English—genitive of *ingas*) 'people of'; *ham* (Old English) 'homestead'. This town with it nearby busy docks on the HUMBER northwest of GRIMSBY was *Imungeham* in 1086.

Inchcolm (Fife) 'Island of (St) Columba'. *Innis* (Scottish Gaelic) 'island'; *Columba* (personal name). This small island in the Firth of FORTH is the site of the now ruined abbey of St Columba, founded here in 1123 by King Alexander I.

Inchmurrin (Strathclyde) 'Island of (St) Mirin'. *Innis* (Scottish Gaelic) 'island'; *Mirin* (personal name) a 7th-century Irish abbot who founded a monastery at PAISLEY where his name is commemorated in that of the local football team of St Mirren. On Inchmurrin, the largest and main inhabited island in Loch LOMOND, there are the ruins of his chapel.

Inchnadamph (Highland) 'Water meadow of the stag'. *Innis* (Scottish Gaelic) 'water meadow'; *na* (Scottish Gaelic) 'of the'; *damh* (Scottish Gaelic) 'stag' or 'oxen', although the latter would be less appropriate here, at the head of Loch ASSYNT, east of LOCHINVER.

Ingilston (Lothian) 'Ingialdr's farm'. *Ingialdr* (Old Norse personal name); *tun* (Old English) 'farm'. This flat and fertile agricultural area to the west of EDINBURGH is now the permanent site of the Royal Highland Show.

Inishowen (Donegal) 'Eoghan's island'. *Inis* (Irish Gaelic) 'island'; *Eoghain* (Irish Gaelic personal name) Eoghan, or Owen, a semi-legendary 4th-century ruler of a kingdom that covered much of the present-day counties of LONDONDERRY and TYRONE. This large rhomboid-shaped peninsula of the far north of Ireland, lying between Lough FOYLE and Lough SWILLY, would have seemed like an 'island' part of this ancient territory. *See* TYRONE.

Innerleithen (Borders) 'Confluence of the River Leithen'. *Inbhir* (Scottish Gaelic); *Leithen* (Scottish Gaelic river name is a corrupted form of *leathann*) 'broad'. This Borders woollen-manufacturing town is sited where the River Leithen meets the River TWEED. Recorded as *Innerlethan* in 1160.

Inveraray (Strathclyde) 'Mouth of the River Aray'. *Inbhir* (Scottish Gaelic) 'river mouth'; *Aray* (Pre-Celtic river name) probably means 'smooth-running'. This 'seat of the Campbells' on Loch FYNE, takes its name from a river name that is widely found throughout Europe in many variant forms: Aar, Ahr, Ahre, Aire, Ara, Ayr, Oare, Ohre, Ore.

Inverbervie (Grampian) 'Mouth of the Bervie Water'. *Inbhir* (Scottish Gaelic) 'river mouth'; *Bervie* (probably Celtic river name similar to Welsh *berw*) 'boiling', 'seething'. The original settlement here, south of STONEHAVEN was *Aberbervie*, more correctly reflecting the strong Brythonic Celtic-Pictish influence on the placenames of this northeast part of Scotland.

Invergarry (Highland) 'Mouth of the River Garry'. *Inbhir* (Scottish Gaelic) 'river mouth'; *Garry* (Scottish Gaelic river name corrupted from *garbh*) 'rough (water)'. The village is sited where the river tumbles into Loch Oich, cutting through the steep-sided GREAT GLEN.

Invergordon (Highland) This town, on the north shore of the CROMARTY Firth, has a fabricated name given in around 1760 to honour its founder, Sir Alexander Gordon, who was the landowner at the time. Previously, the name of the small village here, at the mouth of the local Breckie Burn, was Inverbreckie.

Inverkeithing (Fife) 'Mouth of the Keithing Burn'. *Inbhir* (Scottish Gaelic) 'river mouth'; *Keithing* (Brythonic Celtic river name derived from *coed*) 'wooded'. Early records show the name of this industrial town immediately north of the FORTH bridges, *Hinhirkethy c.*1050; *Innerkethyin* 1114; *Inverchethin c.*1200.

Inverness (Highland) 'Mouth of the River Ness'. *Inbhir* (Scottish Gaelic) 'river mouth'; *Ness* (pre Celtic river name derived from *nesta*) 'roaring', 'rushing (one)'. This town, nominally the 'capital of the Highlands', is situated where the relatively short River Ness, having flowed out of the nearby Loch NESS, discharges into the MORAY Firth. In recent years the normally placid river has lived up to its name, bursting its banks on several occasions, and once in 1988 sweeping away the mainline railway bridge.

Inverurie (Grampian) 'Confluence of the River Urie'. *Inbhir* (Scottish Gaelic) 'river mouth', 'confluence'; *Urie* (Scottish Gaelic river name, probably derived from *uidhre*, genitive of *odhar*) 'drab', 'grey-coloured'. This town is situated, northwest of ABERDEEN, where the River Urie meets the River Don.

Iona (Strathclyde) This small island off the southwest coast of Mull is well known for its long history of association with the Celtic church, and it would seem reasonable that the meaning of its name rests with some Christian connection. The most compelling is with St Columba, who founded a monastery here in the 6th century. A document of around 1100 records the name of *Hiona-Columcille*, and until around 1800 the island was known as *Icolmkill*: *ey* (Old Norse) 'isle'; 'of Columba's' (personal name); *cille* (Scottish Gaelic) 'church'. However, according to some authorities, the present name is the result of a later miscopying of an original document from around AD700, in which the island was referred to as *Ioua insula* —possibly meaning 'island of the yew-tree place'. The first word appears to have been misread as *Iona* —an alternative form of Jonah—and since then the now familiar spelling with the *n* has been repeated without question.

Ipswich (Suffolk) 'Gip's landing place'. *Gip* (Old English personal name) *wic* (Old English) 'landing place'. The name of this town and industrial port, at the point where the River Gipping meets the Orwell river estuary, was noted as *Gipeswic* in the 10th and 11th centuries.

Ireland 'Land called Eire' or 'Eire-land'. *Eire* (Irish Gaelic territorial name probably elided from an ancient root word similar to the modern Irish *iar*) 'western'. Eire was the constitutional name previously applied to the Republic of Ireland between 1937 and 1949, following the change from the Irish Free State (1921-37). The name *Eire* is still used in Irish to describe the whole island of Ireland. The Roman Latin name for Ireland was *Hibernia*.

Ireland's Eye (Dublin) This small island lying off the HOWTH headland has a name that is the result of both a mistranslation and corruption of the original Irish Gaelic *Inis Ereann*, meaning 'Eria's island'. Eria is said to have been a woman who built a church here in the 7th century. However, her Irish personal name was subsequently mistaken as *Eireann*, the genitive of *Eire*, the Irish name for IRELAND, and the Old Norse translation of *ey* for *inis*, meaning 'island', corrupted to *eye*, gave rise to this curious place name.

Irlam (Greater Manchester) 'Homestead on the River Irwell'. *Irre + wella* (Old English) 'winding stream'; *ham* (Old English) 'homestead'. This industrial town, southwest of MANCHESTER, lies on the River Irwell from which it derives its name. It was recorded as *Urwelham* in around 1190.

Ironbridge (Shropshire) This historic town, which now forms part of TELFORD New Town, takes its name directly from the world-famous first cold-blast iron bridge, designed by Abraham Darby, which was built here across the SEVERN gorge in 1778.

Irthlingborough (Northamptonshire) Probably 'the fortified manor of the ploughmen'. *Yrthling* (Old English) 'ploughman'; *burh* (Old English) 'fortified place'.

The name of this town, northeast of WELLINGBOROUGH, is best explained in the sense that there may have been an old fort here that was used for the purpose of keeping cattle. It was noted as *Yrtlingaburg* in 780.

Irvine (Strathclyde) Possibly place of 'the white (river)'. *Yr* (Brythonic Celtic) 'the'; *(g)wyn* (Brythonic Celtic) 'white'. This place, a designated New Town since 1965, almost certainly takes its name originally from the River Irvine, at whose mouth it stands on the Firth of the CLYDE, but the exact meaning of the latter is unknown. Early records show: *Yrewyn c.*1140; *Irvin* 1230.

Isis *see* **Thames, River**.

Islay (Strathclyde) Possibly 'Ile's island'. *Ile* (personal name); *ey* (Old Norse) 'island'. The name of this large and most southerly of the Inner HEBRIDES has at least in part a Norse origin, in common with most of the major islands off the west coast of Scotland. According to many authorities, the insertion of the *s* is relatively recent. Recorded as *Ilea c.*690; *Ile* 800.

Isle of Dogs *see* **Dogs, Isle of.**

Isle of Grain *see* **Grain, Isle of.**

Isle of Man *see* **Man, Isle of**

Isle of Portland *see* **Portland, Isle of.**

Isle of Purbeck *see* **Purbeck, Isle of.**

Isle of Sheppey *see* **Sheppy, Isle of.**

Isle of Thanet *see* **Thanet, Isle of.**

Isle of Walney *see* **Walney, Isle of**

Isle of Wight *see* **Wight, Isle of**

Isles of Scilly *see* **Scilly, Isles of.**

Islington (Greater London) 'Gisla's hill'. *Gisla-n* (Old English personal name—genitive form); *dun* (Old English) 'hill'. This LONDON borough situated north of 'The City', between CAMDEN and HACKNEY, has a name that was recorded in around 1000 as *Gislandune*.

Ivybridge (Devon) 'Ivy-covered bridge'. *Ifig* (Old English) 'ivy'; *brycg* (Old English) 'bridge'. This small town, east of PLYMOUTH, was *Ivebrugge* in 1292.

J

Jarlshof (Shetland) 'Jarl's temple'. *Jarl* (Old Norse personal name); *hof* (Old Norse) 'temple'. The name of this famous archaeological site at the southern tip of SHETLAND's mainland is clearly Norse, but it was Sir Walter Scott in 1816, not the ancient Vikings, who named it as such.

Jarrow (Tyne and Wear) Settlement of 'the fen people'. *Gyrwe* (Old English tribal name derived from *gyr*) 'people of the mud', 'marsh' or 'fen'. The name of this industrial town on the south bank of the River TYNE, famous as the starting point of the Jarrow 'Hunger Marches' in the Depression of the 1930s, was earlier associated with the Venerable Bede, who recorded the name as *Gyruum* in his Historia Ecclesiastica of 730.

Jedburgh (Borders) 'Town by the Jed Water'. The first element of the name of this small BORDERS town, with its famous ruined abbey, is that of its river, which in turn probably is derived from a version of *gweden* (Brythonic Celtic) 'winding', 'twisting' (as of a river meander). The second element has its origins as *burh* (Old English) 'town', but this status must have only been conferred around the mid-12th century. Prior to that time the settlement name was *Jed-worth*, signifying 'an enclosure by the Jed Water'. Records confirm: *Gedwearde c.*800; *Geddewrde* 1100; *Gedword* 1130; *Jaddeuurd c.*1145; *Jeddeburgh* 1160.

Jersey (Channel Islands) Probably 'Geirr's island'. *Geirr* (Old Norse personal, possibly nickname) unidentified but meaning 'spear'; *ey* (Old Norse) 'island'. Traditionally the name of this, the largest of the Channel Islands group, was thought to derive from *Caesarea*, Roman

Latin for 'a place named in honour of Caesar', but this is unsubstantiated. Records show: *Gersus* c.1070; *Gersui* c.1170; *Geresye* 1218; *Gersey* 1454.

Jervaulx Abbey (North Yorkshire) 'Monastery in the valley of the River Ure'. *Jer* (Norman French adaptation) Ure; *val* (Old French) 'valley'; *abeie* (Old French) 'monastery'. The name of this now ruined 12th-century Cistercian abbey in the Ure valley, upstream and northwest of MASHAM, is perhaps a Norman-French translation for 'Ure-dale'. Records show the name as : *Jorvalle* around 1145 and *Girevalle* in about 1200. *Compare* RIEVAULX.

Jethou (Channel Islands) This small island, in the Bailiwick of GUERNSEY and lying to the south of HERM, probably has a name of Scandinavian origin but its derivation remains obscure. The *-ou* ending, which is also present in two other small Channel Islands, namely Brecqhou and Lihou, may represent a possible French-Norman corruption of the Old Norse *ey*, meaning 'island'.

Jodrell Bank (Cheshire) Place by 'the hill-slope of the Jodrell family'. This small village west of MACCLESFIELD, made famous in recent times as the site of the large radio telescope and astronomy laboratory of the University of MANCHESTER, has a field name that derives from the Jodrell family, who where landowners here in the 19th century.

John o' Groats (Highland) This place, which has gained the notable distinction of being the most northeasterly in mainland Britain, was named after John de Groot, a Dutchman who came to live in CAITHNESS in the late 15th century under the patronage of King James IV. The final *s* of the name is the 'possessive' that denotes his house, no longer extant.

Johnstone (Strathclyde) 'John's settlement'. *John* (personal name); *tun* (Old English) 'farm', 'settlement'. This place, as so called, has been in existence to the west of PAISLEY since the late 13th century, but the industrial town as it is now was begun only in 1781, when a large cotton mill was built here.

Joppa (Lothian) The unusual name of this district of EDINBURGH, which lies on the shore of the Firth of FORTH, apparently was derived in the 1780s from that of a farm here, originally having been transferred from the Biblical Joppa (now Jaffa, part of Tel-Aviv, Israel). The name itself is thought to be derived as *yapho* (Hebrew) 'beautiful'.

Joyce's Country (Galway) This scenic area of western Ireland, lying between CONNEMARA and Lough CORRIB, is named after a Welsh family called Joyce that settled here in the 13th century and from which many of the local inhabitants here today are descended. This historic territorial name in Irish Gaelic is *Duiche Sheoigheach*, simply translating back as 'Joyce's district', the first word being elided from *duthaigh*, meaning 'native land'.

Juniper Green (Lothian) 'Village green of the juniper bushes'. This southwestly district of EDINBURGH was formerly a small isolated settlement having the name of *Curriemuirend*, the next place to the west being the village of CURRIE. First recorded in 1812, the renamed village of Juniper Green apparently developed around a green where there had been juniper bushes growing.

Jura (Strathclyde) Apparently 'Doirad's island'. *Doirad* (Scottish Gaelic personal name possibly derived from *deoirid*) 'broken-hearted'; *ey* (Old Norse) 'island'. The latter Old Norse of the name of this largely barren island north of **Islay**, ending may have substituted the earlier Gaelic form, recorded as *Doirad Eilinn* in an early document of 678.

K

Keele (Staffordshire) 'Hill grazed by cows'. *Cy* (Old English—genitive of *cu*) 'cow'; *hyll* (Old English) 'hill'. This simple descriptive name of the village west of NEWCASTLE-UNDER-LYME, which now applies to the modern university here, probably refers to the hill beside the present-day M6 motorway, on which the campus is sited. The name was recorded as *Kiel* in 1169.

Keighley (West Yorkshire) Cyhha's woodland clearing'. *Cyhha* (Old English personal name); *leah* (Old English) 'woodland clearing'. The name of this industrial town northwest of BRADFORD, which is today pronounced as 'Keethly', was recorded as *Chichelai* in 1086.

Keith (Grampian) Simply, the place of 'a wood'. *Coed* (Brythonic Celtic) 'wood'. The name of this town in Strath Isla southeast of ELGIN, was recorded in 1203 as *Ket*.

Kells (Meath) Place of 'cells'. *Cealla* (Irish Gaelic plural of *ci ll*) 'cells', 'churches'. The *s* ending was added somewhat unwittingly in the anglicisation of the original Irish name (*compare* FERNS). This town, northwest of NAVAN, is famous for the 8th-century 'Book of Kells', which was kept here in the prima Columban monastery (the 'cells' of the town's name). The Irish name is *Ceannanas Mor*, meaning 'great head fort' and derived from *ceann* ('head'), *lios* ('round earth fort'), *mor* ('great').

Kelso (Borders) Place of the 'chalk hill'. *Calc* (Old English) 'chalk'; *how* (Old English) 'hill'. There is still a part of this town on the River TWEED, east and downstream of MELROSE, known as 'the chalkheugh'. Early records show *Calkou* 1126; *Kelcou* 1158; *Kelsowe* 1420.

Kelty (Fife) Simply, the place of 'the woods'. *Coilltean*

(Scottish Gaelic) 'woods'. This small town lies on the northern edge of the former FIFE coalfield, north of COWDEN BEATH. A record of 1250 shows *Quilte*. *Compare* KEITH.

Kelvinside (Strathclyde) This leafy district of the West End of GLASGOW takes its name from the River Kelvin, which flows through it, a north bank tributary of the River CLYDE. Some commentators have tentatively suggested that the river name itself derives from *caol abhainn* (Scottish Gaelic) 'narrow river'. Certainly, the latter is very descriptive of the deep gorge that the Kelvin cuts through this area of the city.

Kendal (Cumbria) 'Village with a church in the valley of the Kent' river. Originally, this market town, east of WINDERMERE, was called simply *Kirkby*, deriving as: *kirkju-byr* (Old Norse) 'church village'. Subsequently it became *Kirkby Kendal*, taking the latter distinguishing affix from the local Kent river valley district name which is based on *cunetio* (Brythonic Celtic conjectural root word) 'high' or 'holy one'; *dalr* (Old Norse) 'valley'. Finally, and somewhat unusually, as records show, it was the proper rather than the original descriptive name that has been retained: *Cherchebi* 1086 (Domesday Book); *Kircabikendala c.*1095; *Kendale* 1452.

Kenilworth (Warwickshire) 'Enclosure of a woman called Cynehild'. *Cynehild* (Old English personal name); *worth* (Old English) 'enclosure'. The name of this historic town, southwest of COVENTRY, with the dramatic ruins of its Norman castle popularised by Sir Walter Scott's novel of the same name, was documented as *Chinewrde* in the Domesday Book of 1086, and *Kenildewurda* in 1165.

Kenmare (Kerry) Simply 'head of the sea'. *Ceann* (Irish Gaelic) 'head'; *mara* (Irish Gaelic) 'sea'. The name aptly describes the location of this town at the head of the Kenmare estuary. Its modern Irish name, *Neidin*, meaning 'small nest', also reflects the secluded aspect of its setting amidst the hills of Kerry.

Kennoway (Fife) 'Head field'. *Ceann* (Scottish Gaelic) 'head'; *achadh* (Scottish Gaelic) 'field'. The position of this small agricultural town, lying a few miles inland from the coastal plain at the point where the land begins to rise, is well described in its name. It was recorded as *Kennachyn* in 1250.

Kensington (Greater London) 'Estate associated with a man called Cynesige'. *Cynesige* (Old English personal name); *ing* (Old English connective particle) 'associated with'; *tun* (Old English) 'estate', 'farmstead'. This famous central LONDON district, with its royal palace, gardens and museums, was noted as *Chenesitun* in 1086.

Kent (England) Probably 'the coastal district or land at the edge'. *Canto-* (Brythonic Celtic conjectural root element) 'edge', 'rim', 'coast'. The ancient name of this extreme southeastern peninsular region of Britain possibly applied originally to a narrow coastal strip or even a single headland such as the North Foreland, before it was adopted by Julius Caesar in 51 BC in the form *Cantium* for a larger area that corresponds more to that of the current county. Subsequent sources show the evolution of the modern name *Cantia c.*730; *Chent c.*810; *Cent* 835; *Caent* 871-89.

Kentish Town (Greater London) Probably 'the estate of the Kentish family'. *Le Kentiss(h)* (Middle English surname or nickname); *tun* (Old English) 'estate'. This district of the Borough of CAMDEN, situated immediately north of Camden Town, was known as *Kentisston* in 1208.

Kerry (Ireland) 'The lands of Ciar's people'. *Ciarraidhe* (Irish Gaelic tribal and territorial name) descendants of Ciar and their lands. This southwesternmost county of Ireland ultimately derives its name from Ciar, one of the legendary sons of King Fergus of ULSTER and Queen Maeve of Connacht (*see* CONNAUGHT), whose people progressively took possession of this southwestern territory in ancient times. *Ciarrai* is the modern Irish name. *See* CONNEMARA.

Kesteven (Lincolnshire) 'Meeting place in the wood'. *Ceto-* (Brythonic Celtic root element) 'wood'; *stefna* (Old Scandinavian) 'a meeting'. This name of the former southwestern division of the county, and now represented in the two administrative district names of **North** and **South Kesteven**, was recorded as *Ceoftefne* in about 1000, and *Chetsteven* in the 1086 Domesday Book.

Keswick (Cumbria) 'Cheese farm'. *Cese* (Old English) 'cheese'; *wic* (Old English) 'specialised farm'. This market town in the central LAKE DISTRICT, west of PENRITH, has a name identical in origin and meaning to that of the LONDON district of CHISWICK, but here in the North of England its spelling and harder pronunciation have been subject to Scandinavian influences. It was recorded as *Kesewic* around 1240.

Kettering (Northamptonshire) Probably the settlement of 'Cytra's people'. *Cytra* (Old English personal name); *ingas* (Old English) 'people of'. The name of this town northeast of NORTHAMPTON was recorded as *Cytringan* in 956, and *Cateringe* in the Domesday Book.

Kew (Greater London) Probably 'the quay by the spur of land'. *Caeg*; *key*; *kai* (Old English; Middle English; Old French) 'quay', 'landing place'; *hoh* (Old English) 'spur' or 'projecting piece of land'. The name of this west LONDON district, renowned for its Royal Botanic Gardens, reflects its situation on the south bank of a pronounced meander of the THAMES. It was recorded as *Cayho* in a document of 1327.

Keymer (West Sussex) 'Cow's pond'. *Cy* (Old English—genitive of *cu*) 'cow'; 'mere' (Old English) 'pond', 'lake'. The name of this expanded residential village on the LONDON-BRIGHTON railway, south of BURGESS HILL, was documented in the Domesday Book of 1086 as *Chemere*.

Keynsham (Avon) 'Caegin's riverside land'. *Caegin* (Old English personal name); *hamm* (Old English) 'land in a river bend'. The apt name of this town, on the River AVON between BATH and BRISTOL, appeared in a document of around 1000 as *Caegineshamme*, which by the time of its entry in the Domesday Book in 1086 had been shortened to *Cainsesham*.

Kidderminster (Hereford and Worcester) 'Cydela's monastery'. *Cydela* (Old English personal name); *mynster* (Old English) 'monastery'. This industrial town southwest of BIRMINGHAM on the River Stour has a name that reflects the site of a former monastery that was built here in the 8th century. Early records show *Chideminstre* 1086 (Domesday Book); *Kideministra* 1167.

Kidsgrove (Staffordshire) Probably 'Cyda's grove'. Cyda (Old English personal name) unidentified; *graefe* (Old English) 'grove'. With no early records of the name of this now industrial town northwest of STOKE-ON- TRENT, such a derivation remains speculative.

Kidwelly (Dyfed) Probably the place of 'Cadwal'. *Cydweli* (Welsh personal name with territorial *-i* ending) unidentified, but probably a tribal chief. The name of this small town to the south of CARMARTHEN was recorded in 991 as *Cydweli*, the same as its modern Welsh name.

Kielder Forest (Northumberland) This large area of 20th-century Forestry Commission plantations, which lies south of the CHEVIOT HILLS, derives its name, as does a village and reservoir, from the Brythonic Celtic river name, noted in 1326 as now, meaning 'rapid one'.

Kilbarchan (Strathclyde) Probably the place of 'St Berchan's church'. *Cill* (Scottish Gaelic) 'church'; *Berchan* (personal name) of a 7th-century Irish saint who may have had links with this now small RENFREWshire town, west of JOHNSTONE, that became famous for the weaving of tartan.

Kilbirnie (Strathclyde) Probably the place of 'St Brendan's church'. *Cill* (Scottish Gaelic) 'church'; *Brendan* (Irish Gaelic personal name) of either of two 6th-century Irish saints of this name, both with genuine Scottish links. It is difficult to determine whether the St Brendan here was the famous one who was a friend of St Columba. The name of this town in the upper Garnock Valley, north of IRVINE, was noted as Kilbyrny in 1413.

Kildare (Kildare) 'Church of the oak grove'. *Cill* (Irish Gaelic) 'church'; *doire* (Irish Gaelic) 'oak wood'. This cathedral town, which gave its name to the surrounding county, is where St Brigid built her 5th- or 6th-century church, apparently in the middle of a pagan oak grove. The current Irish name is *Cill Dara*.

Kildrummy (Grampian) 'Head of the ridge'. *Ceann* (Scottish Gaelic) 'head'; *druim* (Scottish Gaelic) 'ridge'. Known earlier as *Kindrummie*, the village and the ruined 13th-century keep are on the edge of the Correen Hills, west of INVERURIE.

Kilkeel (Down) 'Church of the narrows'. *Cill* (Irish Gaelic) 'church'; *caol* (Irish Gaelic) 'narrows'. This town lies on a narrow coastal strip on the southern fringes of the MOURNE MOUNTAINS, and this could well be the sense of the second part of its name. In modern Irish the name is rendered *Cill Chaoil*.

Kilkenny (Kilkenny) 'Church of St Kenneth'. *Cill* (Irish Gaelic) 'church'; *Cainneach* (Irish Gaelic personal name) St Kenneth, a 6th-century monk who worked in Scotland before establishing a monastery here, probably on the hilltop site now occupied by the cathedral of St Canice. The current Irish form is *Cill Chainnigh*.

Killarney (Kerry) 'Church of the sloe trees'. *Cill* (Irish Gaelic) 'church'; *airne* (Irish Gaelic) 'sloe', 'sloe tree'. This popular lakeside town lies in the southwest of Ireland renown for its luxuriant growth in such favoured settings.

Killiecrankie (Tayside) 'Wood of aspen trees'. *Coille* (Scottish Gaelic) 'wood'; *creitheannich* (Scottish Gaelic) 'aspens'. Just south of this village on the River Garry is the still heavily wooded 'Pass of Killicrankie', where in 1689 the troops of King William III were defeated by the Jacobites.

Killin (Central) Possibly place of the 'white church'. *Cill*

(Scottish Gaelic) 'church'; *fionn* (Scottish Gaelic) 'white'. Alternatively, it may be derived from *cilltean* (Scottish Gaelic) 'burying grounds', as this site, at the western head of Loch TAY, has long been a sacred place for the MacNab clan.

Killybegs (Donegal) Place 'of the little churches'. *Na* (Irish Gaelic) 'of the'; *cealla* (Irish Gaelic) 'churches'; *beaga* (Irish Gaelic) 'little'. The name of this small fishing port at the head of a natural harbour on the north shore of the wide DONEGAL Bay probably refers to ancient small monastic cells that may have once been sited here.

Kilmacolm (Strathclyde) 'Church of my Columba'. *Cill* (Scottish Gaelic) 'church'; *ma* (Scottish Gaelic) 'of my'; *Columba* (personal name) referring to the most famous early Irish-Scots saint. The addition of *ma* here denotes dedication to this notable 6th-century saint. Kilmacolme recorded in 1205. The name of this residential town, southeast of Port GLASGOW, is pronounced 'Kil-ma-comb'.

Kilmallock (Limerick) 'Church of St Molach'. *Cill* (Irish Gaelic) 'church'; *Mocheallog* (Irish Gaelic personal name) St Molach, who founded a monastery, in the 7th century, here, southwest of TIPPERARY.

Kilmarnock (Strathclyde) 'Church of my little St Ernan'. *Cill* (Scottish Gaelic) 'church'; *ma* (Scottish Gaelic) 'of my'; *Ernan* (personal name) reputedly priest and uncle of St Columba; *oc* (diminutive suffix). The name of this industrial town, northeast of AYR, that has strong links with Robert Burns, was recorded as *Kelmernoke* in 1299.

Kilmun (Strathclyde) 'Church of St Mund'. *Cill* (Scottish Gaelic) 'church'; *Mundu* (personal name) a disciple and friend of St Columba. The name of this village, on the north shore of the HOLY LOCH, was recorded as *Kilmun* 1240; *Kilmond* 1410.

Kilpatrick *see* **Old Kilpatrick**.

Kilrush (Clare) Probably 'church of the peninsula'. *Cill*

(Irish Gaelic) 'church'; *rois* (Irish Gaelic) 'peninsula', 'headland'. Alternatively, some authorities consider the first element may be derived from *coill* (meaning 'wood') rather than *cill*. Either way, the description is apt for this port and main market town because of the pointed headland to the north of the mouth of the SHANNON.

Kilsyth (Strathclyde) Possibly 'church of St Syth'. *Cill* (Scottish Gaelic) 'church'; *Syth* (personal name). However, there is no saint by such a name. Some authorities consider there may be an alternative derivation in *saighde* (Scottish Gaelic) 'arrows'. The name of this place, northeast of KIRKINTILLOCH,was recorded as *Kelvesyth* in 1210 and *Kelnasythe* in 1217, possibly suggesting some connection with the River Kelvin whose source is nearby at Kelvinhead.

Kilwinning (Strathclyde) 'Church of St Finnian'. *Cill* (Scottish Gaelic Scottish Gaelic) 'church'; *Finnian* (personal name) he learned under St Ninian, and in turn taught St Columba. The name of this town, in the lower Garnock Valley, northwest of IRVINE, was documented as *Killvinin* in 1160.

Kincardine (Fife, Grampian, Highland, Tayside) 'At the head of the wood'. *Cinn* (Scottish Gaelic dative, locative of *ceann*) 'at the head of'; *cardden* (Brythonic Celtic-Pictish) 'wood', 'thicket'. This common descriptive place-name was adopted as that of the former county and present district of Kincardine in the MEARNS area of eastern Scotland. Here the administrative units were named after the 12th-century Kincardine Castle. The largest town of the name is the port officially called **Kincardine-on-Forth**, although the locative suffix is not commonly applied.

Kinder Scout (Derbyshire) Probably 'high hill of the overhanging rock'. *Kinder* (probably Brythonic Celtic hill name derived from *cunetio* and *briga*) 'high' or 'holy one'; *skuti* (Old Norse) 'overhanging rock'. The origin of the first element of the name of this, the highest summit of the High PEAK DISTRICT, remains obscure; it was recorded as *Chendre* in 1086 and *Kynder* in 1285.

King's Lynn (Norfolk) 'The king's manor by the pool'. *King's* (later English royal manorial prefix) after Henry VIII in the 16th century; *lynn* (Brythonic Celtic) 'pool'. This Fenland town and port is situated near the mouth of the Great Ouse river at the southeastern corner of The WASH. Recorded as simply *Lun* in the Domesday Book of 1086, the 'pool' would have been the former mouth of the river, before the seaward lands were reclaimed.

Kinghorn (Fife) 'At the head of the muddy ground'. *Cinn* (Scottish Gaelic) 'at the head of'; *gronn* (Scottish Gaelic) 'muddy land', 'marshland'. Despite the false 'king' associations made by some on account of the fact that it was on the cliffs near here that King Alexander III of Scotland died after falling from his horse in 1286, this place is aptly named, as from its elevated position it overlooks the mudflats on the shore of the Firth of FORTH, east of BURNTISLAND It was recorded as *Kingorn* in 1140.

Kings Langley *see* **Langley, Abbots** and **Kings**.

Kingsbridge (Devon) 'The king's bridge'. *Cyning* (Old English) 'king'; *brycg* (Old English) 'bridge'. This town at the head of the Kingsbridge Estuary, south of TOTNES, is located at a strategic bridging point named after an early Anglo-Saxon king, It was recorded as *Cinges Bricge* in 962.

Kingston upon Hull *see* **Hull**.

Kingston upon Thames (Greater London) 'King's farmstead by the THAMES'. *Cyning* (Old English) 'king'; *tun* (Old English) 'farmstead'. This former SURREY town and now borough of Greater London has had a long history of royal possession, and its name was recorded as *Cynninges tun* in 838 and *Chingestune* in the Domesday Book of 1086. The distinguishing affix was added later.

Kingswood (Avon) Literally 'the king's wood'. *Cyning* (Old English) 'king'; *wudu* (Old English) 'wood'. The relatively common name of this eastern suburb of BRISTOL was recorded in 1231 as *Kingeswode*.

Kington (Hereford and Worcester) 'The king's manor'. *Cyning* (Old English) 'king'; *tun* (Old English) 'manor'. The original form of the name of this small border town northwest of HEREFORD may have been *Cyne-tun*, meaning 'royal manor', but the first element appears to have been subtly changed at an early stage. It was recorded as *Chingtune* in the Domesday Book of 1086.

Kingussie (Highland) 'At the head of the pine wood'. *Cinn* (Scottish Gaelic) 'at the head of'; *ghiuthsaich* (Scottish Gaelic) 'pine wood', 'fir wood'. Forests of fir trees, and especially ancient Caledonian pine woods, are still very much a dominant feature of the STRATHSPEY landscape. Records show: *Kinguscy* 1210; *Kyngucy* 1380.

Kinlochleven (Highland) 'Head of Loch Leven'. *Ceann* (Scottish Gaelic) 'head'; *loch* (Scottish Gaelic) 'arm of the sea'; *leven* (Brythonic Celtic derivation) 'likely to flood'. This aluminium smelting town set at the head of a narrow and steep-sided fiord-like sea-loch is thus distinctly described in its name.

Kinloss (Grampian) Possibly 'head of the garden'. *Ceann* (Scottish Gaelic) 'head'; *lios* (Scottish Gaelic) 'garden'. The origin of the name remains a puzzle, as the village is at the 'head' of the almost enclosed FINDHORN Bay, and the River Lossie is not close by.

Kinross (Tayside) 'Head of the promontory'. *Ceann* (Scottish Gaelic) 'head'; *ros* (Scottish Gaelic) 'promontory'. This historic and former county town stands on a promontory that protrudes into Loch Leven, which lies to the east with its famous island castle associated with Mary Queen of Scots. The name of the town was recorded as *Kynros* in 1144.

Kinsale (Cork) 'Head of the sea'. *Ceann* (Irish Gaelic) 'head'; *saile* (Irish Gaelic genitive of *sal*) 'of the sea'. This name aptly describes the situation of this town south of CORK, lying at the high tidal watermark of the drowned river valley on which it stands. *Compare* KENMARE. **Kinsale Head** is the recent name of a nearby offshore natural gas field in the CELTIC SEA.

Kintail (Highland) 'Head of the sea-water'. *Ceann* (Scottish Gaelic) 'head'; *an t-saille* (Scottish Gaelic) 'of the briny, salt water'. This dramatic, mountainous area of the northwest Highlands, which includes the peaks known as the 'Five Sisters of Kintail', lies at the end of the long sea loch, Loch Duich.

Kintyre (Strathclyde) 'At the head of the land'. *Cinn* (Scottish Gaelic) 'at the head of'; *tire* (Scottish Gaelic) 'land'. This name so aptly describes this long peninsula, at the end of which is the Mull of Kintyre, a place-name that recently became popularised in song; *mull* (Scottish Gaelic) 'headland'. An early record of 807 indicates *Ciuntire*.

Kippen (Central) Place of 'the little stump'. *Ceap* (Scottish Gaelic) 'stump', 'block'; *-en* (diminutive suffix). This village sits up on an elevated stump of the GARGUNNOCK Hills overlooking Flanders Moss.

Kirby *see* **West Kirby**.

Kirk o' Shotts (Strathclyde) 'Church on the steep slopes'. *Kirk* (Scots) 'church'; *sceots* (Old English) 'steep slopes'. The derivation is very descriptive of this elevated village at the highest point on the so-called 'M8 corridor' in central Scotland. *See* SHOTTS.

Kirk Yetholm *see* **Yetholm**

Kirkcaldy (Fife) 'Fort on the hard hill'. *Caer* (Brythonic Celtic) 'fort'; *caled* (Brythonic Celtic) 'hard'; *din* (Brythonic Celtic) 'hill'. The fort here presumably was on the elevated site of the present 15th-century Ravenscraig Castle, above the town on what is in effect a post-glacial raised beach on the northshore of the Firth of FORTH. Records show: *Kircalathin* in 1150. It is pronounced 'Ker-coddy'.

Kirkby (Merseyside) 'Village with a church'. *Kirkju- by* (Old Scandinavian) 'church village'. Recorded as *Cherchebi* in the Domesday Book of 1086, the name of this town northeast of LIVERPOOL is common in the North and Midlands of England, where Norse and Danish influence was strongest. *See* other examples below.

Kirkby in Ashfield (Nottinghamshire) 'Church village in open land with ash trees'. *Kirkju-by* (Old Scandinavian) 'church village'; *aesc* (Old English) 'ash tree'; *feld* (Old English) 'open land'. This town, southwest of MANSFIELD, lies in the former district of Ashfield, which was added as a distinguishing affix to the basic name; it was recorded as *Chirchebi* in the Domesday Book of 1086.

Kirkby Lonsdale (Cumbria) 'Church village in the valley of the River Lune'. *Kirkju-by* (Old Scandinavian) 'church village'; *Lune* (Brythonic Celtic river name) 'healthy', 'pure'; *dalr* (Old Scandinavian) 'valley'. This small town, southeast of KENDAL, like the latter adds the distinguishing affix of the local valley name to the basic name; records show *Cherchebi* in 1086 (Domesday Book); *Kircabi Laurenesdale* 1090-7.

Kirkby Stephen (Cumbria) Probably 'the village with a church dedicated to St Stephen'. *Kirkju-by* (Old Scandinavian) 'church village'; *Stephanus* (Old English personal name) medieval abbot of St Mary's Abbey, YORK. The name of this small town, southeast of APPLEBY-IN-WESTMORLAND, was recorded as *Cherkaby Stephan* in about 1094.

Kirkcudbright (Dumfries and Galloway) 'Church of St Cuthbert'. *Kirk* (Scots, derived from the Old English *cirice*, or the Old Norse *kirkja*) 'church'; *Cuthbert* (Old English personal name) meaning 'famous-bright'; of 7th-century prior of LINDISFARNE and known missionary to these parts. The name of this former country town, southwest of CASTLE DOUGLAS, was recorded as *Kirkcutbrithe* in 1291. *See* STEWARTRY.

Kirkham (Lancashire) 'Village with a church'. *Cirice* replaced by *kirkja* (Old English influenced by Old Norse) 'church'; *ham* (Old English) 'village', 'farmstead'. The Scandinavian-influenced name of this small town, lying midway between BLACKPOOL and PRESTON, was recorded as *Chicheham* in the Domesday Book, and *Kyrkham* in 1094.

Kirkhope (Borders) 'Church in the valley'. *Kirk* (Scots, derived from Old Norse kirkja) 'church'; *hop* (Old Norse) 'shelter', 'valley'. This village lies in the valley of Ettrick Water, immediately southwest of ETTRICKBRIDGE. *See* HOBKIRK.

Kirkintilloch (Strathclyde) 'Fort at the head of the hillock'. *Caer* (Brythonic Celtic) 'fort'; *cinn* (Scottish Gaelic) 'at the head of'; *tulaich* (Scottish Gaelic) 'hillock'. The origin of the name lies in the existence here, northeast of GLASGOW, of a 2nd century AD Roman fort which was built as part of the ANTONINE WALL defences on a small hill in what is now the old part of the town. The name is recorded around 1200 as *Kirkintulach*.

Kirkoswal (Strathclyde) 'Church of St Oswald'. *Kirk* (Scots) 'church'; *Oswald* (Old English personal name) of the 7th-century missionary King Oswald of Northumbria, who had links with this part of ancient Strathclyde, southwest of MAYBOLE.

Kirkwall (Orkney) 'Church on the bay'. *Kirkja* (Old Norse) 'church'; *vagr* (Old Norse) 'bay'. This place, the main town of the islands, is situated at the head of a small sheltered bay, off the Wide Firth. The name was recorded in the *Orkneyinga Saga* of around 1225 as *Kirkiuvagr*, and later as *Kirkvaw* in a text of 1400.

Kirriemuir (Tayside) 'The great quarter'. *Creathramh* (Scottish Gaelic) a land measure that was a fourth of a *dabhach*:, 192 Scots acres: *mor* (Scottish Gaelic) 'great', 'big'. The name of this attractive small town, north of Dundee, the birthplace of J.M. Barrie of *Peter Pan* fame , was recorded as *Kerimor* in 1250. *Compare* ARROCHAR; HADDO.

Knapdale (Strathclyde) 'Hill and dale country'. *Knappr* (Old Norse) a protuberant, sharp-sided small hill; *dale* (Old Norse) 'dale', 'valley'. The name is an apt one for this northern part of the ARGYLL peninsula, where hills rise and fall in parallel folds and from high ground can look like a choppy sea.

Knaresborough (North Yorkshire) Probably Cenheard's fortified place'. *Cenheard* (Old English personal name); *burh* (Old English) 'fortified place', 'stronghold'. This town, lying in the gorge of the River Nidd immediately northeast of HARROGATE, is dominated by the ruins of a 14th-century castle on a rocky knoll, which was almost certainly the site of an earlier fort. Some authorities consider that an alternative derivation of, or at least an influence on, the first element may have been *cnearr* (Old English conjectural version of Middle English *knar*) 'rugged rock'. The name appears in the Domesday Book as *Chenaresburg* and in a document of 1130 as *Chenardesburg*.

Knighton (Powys) 'Servant's village'. *Cniht* (Old English) 'knight', 'servant'; *tun* (Old English) 'village'. This small 'border' town, lying on the Teme river halfway between LLANDRINDOD WELLS and LUDLOW, has a medieval name reflecting the feudal system of a baron having a group of personal followers, or servants, who were called knights. Early records show *Cnihtatune* 957; *Cnihtetun* 1108; *Cnigheton* 1218. The Welsh name is *Treyclo*, which derives from *Tref-y-clawdd*, meaning 'hamlet by the dyke', a clear reference to OFFA'S DYKE, which passes to the north of the town.

Knightsbridge (Greater London) 'Bridge of the soldiers or servants'. *Cniht* (Old English) 'baronial servant'- 'soldier, 'young man'; *brycg* (Old English) 'bridge'. The name of this famous thoroughfare and fashionable district of west-central LONDON probably originates from an early bridging point of the former Westbourne river. It was noted as *Cnihtebricge* in the mid-11th century. *Compare* BAYSWATER; KNIGHTON.

Knock (Mayo) Simply the 'hill'. *Cnoc* (Irish Gaelic) 'hill'. This small town east of CASTLEBAR has become an important pilgrimage site since it was alleged that the Virgin Mary manifested herself here on the 'hill' in 1879.

Knockmealdown Mountains (Waterford) 'Hill of the Maol Duin'. *Cnoc* (Irish Gaelic) 'hill'; *Mhaoldonn* (Irish Gaelic personal name) Moal Duin, a semi-legendary hero associated with the main mountain of this well-known range in southern Ireland. His own name means 'warrior of the fort'.

Knottingley (West Yorkshire) 'Woodland clearing of Cnotta's people'. *Cnotta* (Old English personal name); *inga* (Old English—genitive of *ingas*) 'people of'; *leah* (Old English) 'woodland clearing'. The name of this town on the River Aire, downstream and southeast of LEEDS, was recorded as *Notingeleia* in the 1086 Domesday Book.

Knotty Ash (Merseyside) Place of 'the knotty ash tree'. This district of LIVERPOOL, popularised in modern comedy, has a simple name that describes the village built here in the late 17th century.

Knoydart (Highland) 'Cnut's fiord'. *Cnut* (Old Norse personal name) of unknown connection; *art* (Scottish Gaelic corruption of Old Norse *fjordr*) 'sea loch'. This remote area of mountain wilderness is situated on the west coat of Scotland, between Loch NEVIS and Loch Hourn. Both these sea lochs are long, deep, fiord-like inlets that have names of uncertain meaning, although Celtic folklore has referred to them respectively as the lochs of 'Heaven' and 'Hell'. *See* NEVIS.

Knutsford (Cheshire) Probably 'Cnut's ford'. *Cnut* (Old English personal name); *ford* (Old English) 'river crossing'. The name of this small town, west of ALDERLEY EDGE, has been traditionally associated with the famous King Canute, or Cnut, but it is almost certain that another less important Anglo-Saxon is involved in this name, which was recorded as *Cunetesford* in the Domesday Book of 1086.

Kyle of Lochalsh (Highland) Place by 'the narrows of Loch Alsh'. *Caol* (Scottish Gaelic) 'narrows'; *loch* (Scottish Gaelic) 'arm of the sea'; *alsh* (Scottish Gaelic corrupted form of *aillse*) 'of the fairy'. This small town, the railhead and main ferry terminal for Skye, is situated at the narrow sea entrance into Loch Alsh, and opposite Kyleakin to which a new road bridge is shortly to be opened.

Kyleakin (Highland) Place by 'the straits of Haakon'. *Caol* (Scottish Gaelic) 'straits', 'narrows'; *Haakon* (Old Norse personal name) king of Norway, Greenland and Iceland, who reputedly sailed through this narrow stretch of the sea, which separates Skye from the Scottish mainland, after his defeat at the battle of Largs in 1263. Kyleakin is on Skye, and for long has been the island's main ferry port, a function that will come to an end with the opening of the Skye Bridge.

Kylesku (Highland) 'The narrow narrows'. *Caolas* (Scottish Gaelic) 'narrows', 'strait'; *cumhann* (Scottish Gaelic) 'narrow', 'thin'. This name, with an apparent tautology, aptly describes the very narrow sea entrance into the remote Loch Glencoul in the North West Highlands. This was formerly the place of a free and very short ferry crossing, but now the road passes overhead on a most spectacular, high bridge.

L

Lagan (Antrim/Down) 'Little hollow'. *Lag* (Irish Gaelic) 'hollow'; *-an* (Irish Gaelic diminutive suffix) 'little'. This river, which forms the boundary between the counties of ANTRIM and DOWN and flows northeastwards through BELFAST, takes its name from a little hollow presumably to be found somewhere near its source.

Lairg (Highland) 'The shank'. *Lairg* (Scottish Gaelic) 'shank', 'thigh'. Just why this particular descriptive name has been given to this remote but important road and rail junction remains a mystery. Any notion that the name of this nodal place may be directly connected to its location on the River Shin as it flows from Loch Shin is merely fanciful; the probable derivation of the latter being *sine* (Scottish Gaelic) 'of the storm'.

Lairig Ghru (Grampian/Highland) 'The gloomy pass'. *Lairig* (Scottish Gaelic) 'pass'; *ghru* (Scottish Gaelic) 'gloomy'. A descriptive name, most fitting, for this spectacular gash through the CAIRNGORMS, particularly at its forbidding boulder-strewn crest which reaches a height of 2750 ft (840m).

Lake District (Cumbria) The familiar name for this core of CUMBRIA, distinctively characterized by a compact, rugged mountainous area of deeply incised lakes that radiate like the spokes of a wheel, is a relatively recent descriptive term that has been used by way of promotion only since the late 18th century, when the natural beauty of the 'Lakes' was popularised by poets, writers, and artists, thereby opening up this region, earlier regarded as remote and bleak.

Lake of Menteith *see* **Menteith, Lake of**

Lambeth (Greater London) 'Landing place for lambs'.

Lamb (Old English) 'lamb'; *hyth* (Old English) 'landing place'. The name of this riverside LONDON borough, on the south bank of the THAMES, was recorded as *Lambhyth* in 1041. *Compare* ROTHERHITHE.

Lammermuir (Borders/Lothian) Possibly 'lambs' moor'. *Lombor*, *lambre* (Old English) 'lamb'; *muir* (Scots version of Old English *mor*) 'moorland'. The name fits well with sheep grazing, which is the main land use, past and present, of the Lammermuir Hills, which form most of this area. Indeed, there are individual hills within the range called Lamb Hill, Lammer Law, Wedder Law and Hog Law. In an early-9th-century document this upland area was named *Lombormore*, and in a later text as *Lambremor*.

Lampeter (Dyfed) 'Church of St Peter'. *Llan* (Welsh) 'church'; *Pedr* (Welsh) St Peter. This small market and university college town lying in the upper Teifi valley northeast of CARMARTHEN takes its name from its parish church dedication. Its full Welsh name, *Llanbedr Pont Steffan*, gives recognition to another aspect of the town's early situation, namely 'by the bridge of Stephen', the latter referring to someone who guarded the river crossing point.

Lanark (Strathclyde) 'The glade'. *Llanerc* (Brythonic Celtic) 'forest glade'. This historic market and former county town is located on a typical early forest clearing settlement site at the top of the steep east bank of the River CLYDE, some 50 miles (80 km) upstream from its estuary mouth. **New Lanark**, a model mill town set up by Robert Owen and David Dale in 1784, lies below Lanark on the river, near the Falls of Clyde, and was so named by way of contrast. The name is recorded as *Lannarc* 1188, *Lanerch* 1430.

Lancashire *see* **Lancaster**.

Lancaster (Lancashire) Place of 'the Roman station on the River Lune'. *Lune* (Brythonic Celtic river name) 'healthy', 'pure one'; *ceaster* (Old English) 'Roman fort'. The name of this city and county town on the River

Lune, north of PRESTON, was recorded as *Loncastre* in the Domesday Book of 1086. The present-day county name is a contracted form of the 14th-century rendering: *Lancastreshire*.

Lanchester (Durham) Place of 'the long Roman fort'. *Lang* (Old English) 'long'; *ceaster* (Old English) 'Roman station'. This small town, northwest of DURHAM, is on the site of the former Roman fort of *Longovicium*, and some authorities consider that the meaning of the first element may have been incorrectly translated from the latter Romano-British name, which itself probably derives from *longo-* (Brythonic Celtic conjectural root element) 'ship', referring to 'the place of the ship-fighters'. It was recorded as *Langescestr* in 1196.

Lancing (West Sussex) Settlement of 'Wlanc's people'. *Wlanc* (Old English personal name); *ingas* (Old English) 'people of'. This town east of WORTHING, officially **North** and **South Lancing**, was called *Lancinges* in 1086.

Land's End (Cornwall) Literally 'land's end'. *Land* (Old English) 'land'; *ende* (Old English) 'end'. The name of this well-known westernmost point of the English mainland is said to be a translation of *Pen an Wlas* (Old Cornish) for 'end of the land'. It was recorded as *the Londis end* in the 14th century. *See* PEMBROKE; PENWITH.

Langbank (Strathclyde) Presumably 'long bank'. *Lang* (Scots derived from Old English lang) 'long'; 'bank' (English). This simple name is apt for this straggling village on the raised south bank of the Firth of CLYDE.

Langdale (Cumbria) 'Long valley'. *Lang* (Old English) 'long'; *denu* replaced by *dalr* (Old English influenced by Old Norse) 'valley', 'dale'. This name associated with the rugged peaks west of GRASMERE, known as the 'Langdale Pikes', was recorded as *Langedene* around 1160.

Langholm (Dumfries and Galloway) 'Long water meadow'. *Lang* (Scots) 'long'; *holm* (Scots elided form of Old Norse *holmr*) 'water meadow', 'haugh'. Standing on a level strip of land by the meandering River Esk, upstream and north of CANOBIE, this name, recorded in 1376 as it is spelt now, well describes the situation of this Border woollen-manufacturing town.

Langley, Abbots and **Kings** (Hertfordshire) 'Long wood or clearing, on estates possessed early by abbots and kings'. *Lang* (Old English) 'long'; *leah* (Old English) 'wood', 'grove', 'woodland clearing'; *abbotes* (Old English manorial affix) 'abbots'; *cyninges* (Old English manorial affix) 'kings'. These two satellite towns, on opposite sides of the Grand Union Canal northwest of WATFORD, have the same common basic name, distinguished by respective affixes that indicate that the manor originally granted to the Abbots of St Albans, was subsequently split, with a portion falling to a royal holding. Records confirm: *Langalege c.*1060; *Langelai* 1086; *Abbotes Langele* 1263; *Kyngeslangeley* 1436.

Laois (Ireland) 'The lands of Lewy Leeshagh's people'. *Laeighis* (Irish Gaelic tribal and territorial name) Leesh: the descendants of Lughaidh Laeighseach and their lands. This part of the central lowlands of Ireland ultimately derives its name from Lughaidh Laeighseach, the semi-legendary 2nd-century ancestor of the O'Mores, who gave their tribal name *Laeighis* to this ancient territory, which was granted to him by the king of LEINSTER for helping to expel invading forces from MUNSTER. During the Anglo-Norman period the name became anglicised as Leix. Then in 1556, in honour of the Tudor policy of 'plantations', it was renamed Queen's County, and remained so until under Irish independence in 1921 it reverted to a Gaelic form of its old name, *Laois*, pronounced 'Leesh'. *See* OFFALY.

Larbert (Central) Possibly 'half wood'. *Lled* (Brythonic Celtic) 'half', 'part'; *pert* (Brythonic Celtic) 'wood'. Recorded as *Lethberth* 1195; *Larbert* 1251.

Largo (Fife) 'Steep place'. *Leargach* (Scottish Gaelic) 'steep slope'. This town, made famous as the birthplace of Alexander Selkirk ('the real Robinson Crusoe'), climbs up a hillside. It is actually divided into two parts: **Lower Largo** on the shore of the Firth of FORTH, and **Upper Largo** situated above on the post-glacial raised beach. It was recorded as *Largaugh* 1250; *Largaw* 1279; *Largo* 1595.

Largs (Strathclyde) 'Hillside'. *Learg* (Scottish Gaelic) 'hillside'. This resort town on the Firth of CLYDE sits on the shore under the immediate slopes of the RENFREWshire hills. The *s* ending of the name would appear to have been a later addition as part of the anglicization process. It was documented *Larghes* 1140.

Larne (Antrim) 'Lands of Lathair's people'. *Latharna* (Irish Gaelic tribal and territorial name) the lands of the people of Lathair. This major port of Northern Ireland, lying at the mouth of the Larne Lough, and strategically at the narrowest point of the North Channel separating Ireland from Britain, was named after the ancient lands held here by Lathair, the son of Hugony, the great legendary ruler of Ireland.

Lasswade (Lothian) Probably 'the ford by the meadow'. *Leas* (Old English) 'meadow'; *gewaed* (Old English) 'ford'. The village, southwest of DALKEITH, lies on the North Esk river. A record of 1150 shows the name as *Leswade*.

Lauder (Borders) This small town lies, southeast of EDINBURGH, on the Leader Water and presumably takes its name from that of this river, which could be derived; *lou* (Brythonic Celtic) 'wash'; *dobhar* (Brythonic Celtic) 'water'. Recorded as *Loueder* 1208; *Lawedir* 1250; *Loweder* 1298

Launceston (Cornwall) Probably 'estate near St Stephen's church'. *Lann* (Old Cornish) 'church'; *Stave* (Old Cornish conjectural personal name) Stephen; *tun* (Old English) 'estate', 'settlement'. The hybrid name of this inland town, northwest of PLYMOUTH, has proved difficult to derive satisfactorily; it was recorded as *Lanscavetone* in the 1086 Domesday Book.

Laurencekirk (Grampian) 'St Laurence's kirk'. This small market town, southwest of STONEHAVEN, was founded by Lord Gardenstone in 1770 and at first was named Kirkton of St Laurence, the latter being a reference to the patron saint of its church, St Laurence of CANTERBURY. Formerly Conveth.

Laurieston (Central) This small town to the east of FALKIRK was originally known as *Langtoune*, a name recorded in 1393, which still aptly describes its straggling form along the old EDINBURGH road. In 1774 it was briefly called *Merchistown* before being renamed after its owner, Sir Lawrence Dundas of Kerse, then taking the form LAURENCETON, before finally assuming its present-day rendering.

Laxey (Isle of Man) Place on the 'salmon river'. *Lax* (Old Norse) 'salmon'; *a* (Old Norse) 'river'. This small coastal resort northeast of DOUGLAS, dominated by 'Lady Isabella', the world's largest water wheel, takes the name of its river. *Compare* LAXFORD BRIDGE.

Laxford Bridge (Highland) 'Bridge by the salmon fiord'. *Lax* (Old Norse) 'salmon'; *fjord* (adaptation of Old Norse *fjordr*) 'sea loch'; 'bridge' (English). This much signposted place has no settlement, just a bridge at an important road junction in a remote part of the northwest Highlands. The 'place', and the river that flows under the bridge are named after the sea loch immediately to the west.

Leadhills (Strathclyde) Simply,' the place in the lead hills'. *Lead hills* (Middle English) reflects that this former mining village, near WANLOCKHEAD, was once an important site for the extraction of lead, as well as gold and silver.

Leamington Spa (Warwickshire) 'Farmstead on the River Leam'. *Leam* (Brythonic Celtic river name) 'elm river'; *ing* (Old English connective particle) 'associated with'; *tun* (Old English) 'farmstead'. The name of this town, south of COVENTRY, to which a *Royal* prefix as well as *Spa* were added in 1838, was noted as *Lamintone* in 1086.

Leatherhead (Surrey) Place of 'the grey-coloured ford'. *Led* (Brythonic Celtic) 'grey', 'pale': *rid* (Brythonic Celtic) 'ford'. This derivation was only recently established by a member of the English Place-Name Society, the name of this town on the River Mole, on the LONDON side of the North DOWNS, being previously interpreted as 'the public ford', from *leode* (Old English) 'people'; *rida* (Old English conjectural word) 'riding path' or 'ford'. It was recorded as *Leodridan* in about 880; and *Leddrede* 1195.

Lechlade (Gloucestershire) Probably 'the river crossing near the River Leach'. *Laec* (Old English river name root word) 'muddy', 'boggy'; *gelad* (Old English) 'river crossing'. This large village, north of Swindon, lies on the River THAMES near its source and close to where it is joined by the River Leach. Its name was documented as *Lecelade* in the Domesday Book of 1086.

Lecht, The (Grampian) 'The declivity'. *Leachd* (Scottish Gaelic) 'declivity', a downward hillslope as in a mountain pass. The derivation is certainly descriptive of this high pass in the CAIRNGORMS, where the old 18th-century military road (now a modern highway—the A939) rises to over 2000 ft (635m) and is frequently mentioned in the winter road reports as being 'blocked by snow'. In recent years a ski centre has been developed here.

Ledbury (Hereford and Worcester) Probably 'stronghold on the River Leadon'. *Leadon* (Brythonic Celtic river name) 'broad one'; *byrig* (Old English—dative of *burh*) 'fortified place'. This attractive town, east of HEREFORD, stands on a tributary of the River SEVERN, the River Leadon, from which it derives its name. It appears in the Domesday Book as *Liedeberge*, and in a text of 1140 as *Ledburia*.

Leeds (West Yorkshire) 'District on the River Aire'. *Ladenses* (Brythonic Celtic tribal district name) 'people living by a strongly flowing river'. The name of this great northern industrial city has its origins in an ancient name for a wider district here based on the River Aire, which was formerly known as the *Lat*, or something similar. Records show: *Loidis* c.730; *Ledes* 1086 (Domesday Book); *Leedes* c.1185

Leek (Staffordshire) Place at 'the brook'. *Loekr* (Old Scandinavian) 'brook', 'stream'. The simple name of this textile town, northeast of STOKE-ON-TRENT, was recorded as *Lec* in 1086; *Lech* in *c.*1100; *Leke* in 1247.

Lee-on-the-Solent (Hampshire) Place of 'the meadow by the SOLENT estuary'. *Leah* (Old English) 'clearing', 'meadow'. This residential town and coastal resort, west of GOSPORT, has a very common basic name to which the distinguishing affix was added only in the 19th century by way of a promotional tag. It was recorded simply as *Lie* in 1212. *Compare* LEIGH; LEIGH-ON-SEA.

Leicester (Leicestershire) 'Roman town of the Ligore people'. *Ligore* (probably Romano-British tribal name) unidentified ; *ceaster* (Old English) 'Roman town' or 'stronghold'. The name of this major East MIDLANDS city, like that of LEEDS, would appear to have its origins in an ancient tribal district name based on a local river, in this case probably a tributary of the River Soar, which may have been called the River *Legra*. Records show the name of the early settlement as: *Legorensis civitasis* 803; *Ligera ceaster* 917; *Ledecestre* 1086 (Domesday Book); *Legrecestra* 1130; *Leirchestre* 1205.

Leigh (Greater Manchester) Place of 'the meadow'. *Leah* (Old English) 'meadow', 'clearing', 'woodland'. The name of this town, in the coal-mining district west of SALFORD, is a single element commonly to be found as the ending of a place-name, especially those with origins as a woodland clearing. However, in this case it is more likely that the derivation of a 'meadow' would have been apt for this low-lying former marshland area. The names was recorded as *Legh* in 1276. *Compare* LEE-ON-SOLENT; LEIGH-ON-SEA.

Leigh-on-Sea (Essex) Place of 'the meadow by the sea'.

Leah (Old English) 'meadow'. The derivation of the basic name of this western district of SOUTHEND-ON-SEA is identical with those above for LEE-ON-THE-SOLENT and LEIGH. The distinguishing affix here is also a 19th-century addition directly associated with the railway-linked promotion of the place as a coastal resort. It was early recorded as *Leye* in 1254.

Leighton Buzzard (Bedfordshire) 'Leek or vegetable enclosure on the estate of the Busard family'. *Leac- tun* (Old English) 'leek farm', 'herb garden', 'vegetable enclosure'; *Busard* (later Anglo-Norman manorial affix). The name of this manufacturing town, west of DUNSTABLE, was recorded as simply as *Lestone* in the Domesday Book, and as *Letton Busard* in 1254.

Leinster (Ireland) This is the name of the ancient kingdom and historic province of east and southeast Ireland. It is named after the Lagin people (possibly meaning 'spear folk'), a Celtic tribe who, it is said, settled here in the 3rd century BC. The latter *ster* element is thought to be a combination of the Old Norse genitive *s* and the Irish Gaelic *tir* for 'land'.

Leiston (Suffolk) Probably 'farmstead near a beacon fire'. *Leg* (Old English) 'fire;' *tun* (Old English) 'farmstead'. The name of this small town, northeast of ALDEBURGH, could reflect its situation close to the sea, where a beacon could have been lit; ironically, today this coastal site is the home of the Sizewell nuclear power station. The name was documented *Leistuna* in the Domesday Book, and *Legestona* in 1168.

Leith (Lothian) Possibly 'moist place'. *Lleith* (Brythonic Celtic) 'moist'. This district and long-time port of EDINBURGH, which was an independent burgh until 1920, lies at the mouth of the Water of Leith on the Firth of FORTH, and hence its name may reflect this coastal situation. Some authorities consider more likely the alternative derivation: *liath* (Scottish Gaelic) 'grey'. Records show *Inverlet* 1145; *Leth* 1570.

Leith Hill (Surrey) 'The slope'. *Hlith* (Old English)

'slope', 'hillside'. This hill, on the North DOWNS southwest of DORKING, at 965 ft (294m) is the highest point in southeast England. The current tautological name was originally recorded as *La Lida* in 1168.

Leitrim (Ireland) Place of the 'grey ridge'. *Liath* (Irish Gaelic) 'grey'; *droim* (Irish Gaelic) 'ridge'. This relatively common Irish place name is given to this northwestern county from the village of Leitrim, near CARRICK-ON-SHANNON, where such a feature is evident. The modern Irish name is *Liatroim*.

Lennoxtown (Strathclyde) This small town to the north of GLASGOW, established in the 1780s with the introduction of calico printing, was named after the local family of dukes and earls of Lennox, who took their title in turn from the ancient territory of Lennox that encompassed the former county of DUMBARTONshire, much of STIRLINGshire, and parts of PERTHshire and RENFREWshire. The name *Lennox* was originally *Levenach* ('field of the Leven') and elided through *Levenax*.. It is probably derived as *leamhanach* (Scottish Gaelic) 'covered in elms'. *See* LEVEN.

Leominster (Hereford and Worcester) 'Church in the district of the streams'. *Leon* (Old English district name translated from Old Welsh *lian* or *lion*) 'at the streams'; *mynster* (Old English) 'church'. The name of this main service town for the surrounding agricultural area north of HEREFORD is a part translation of its Welsh form, *Llanllieni*, and reflects its location at the apex of a triangular district that fans out from here, bounded by the Lugg and Arrow rivers. It was documented as *Leomynster* in the 10th century.

Lerwick (Shetland) Place on 'the mud bay'. *Leir* (Old Norse) 'mud'; *vik* (Old Norse) 'bay'. As is to be expected, the name of the main town of SHETLAND is authentic Norse, but there was no town here until about 1600, many centuries after the end of the Viking era. Previously, the capital of these islands was SCALLOWAY.

Leslie (Fife) Possibly 'garden by the pool'. *Leas* (Scottish Gaelic) 'enclosure', 'garden'; *linn* (Scottish Gaelic) 'pool'. Alternatively, some authorities consider the equally probable derivation of *llys* (Brythonic Celtic) 'court'; *celyn* (Brythonic Celtic) 'holly'. The name of this old town, just west of GLENROTHES, was recorded in the late 12th century as *Lesslyn*.

Lesmahagow (Strathclyde) 'Church of Mahagow'. *Eaglais* (Scottish Gaelic corruption) 'church'; *Mahagow* (personal name corruption) of St Machute, also known as Mahago; or alternatively some authorities suggest that the saint commemorated here is Fechin, reduced to the affectionate form Mo-Fhegu ('my Fechin'). Records show *Lesmahagu* 1130; *Ecclesia Machuti* 1144; *Lesmachute* 1316. The name of this town, 30 miles (48 km) southeast of GLASGOW, is pronounced 'Lees-ma-hay-go'.

Letchworth (Hertfordshire) Probably 'place of the locked enclosure'. *Lycce* (Old English conjectural word) 'locked place'; *worth* (Old English) 'enclosure'. This town north of STEVENAGE, founded as the first planned English 'garden city' in 1903, takes the name of the original settlement here that was recorded as *Leceworde* in the Domesday Book of 1086.

Letterkeny (Donegal) 'Wet hillside of the O'Cannons'. *Leitir* (Irish Gaelic) 'wet hillside'; *Ceanainn* (Irish Gaelic personal name) of the local O'Cannon family. This main settlement in DONEGAL is located on the slopes of Gregory Hill above the River SWILLY.

Leuchars (Fife) Probably place of 'the rushes'. *Luachair* (Scottish Gaelic) 'rushes'. This village, with a modern military airfield, is situated in northeast Fife close to the estuary of the river Eden. It is pronounced 'Lookerrs'.

Leven (Fife) Probably, 'place of the elm river'. This town takes its name from the River Leven, which flows into the Firth of FORTH nearby. The pre-Celtic river name derives here, as in the case of the River Leven draining

Loch LOMOND, from *leamhain* (Scottish Gaelic) 'elm'. It is documented in a text of 1535 as *Levin. See* LENNOXTOWN.

Levenshulme (Greater Manchester) 'Leofwine's island'. *Leofwine* (Old English personal name); *holmr* (Old Norse) 'island' 'elevated drier land in a marshland'. The name of this southeastern district of MANCHESTER was documented as *Lewyneshulm* in 1246.

Lewes (East Sussex) Place of 'the tumuli'. *Hlaewes* (Old English plural of *hlaew*) 'burial mounds', 'tumuli'. The simple name of this county town, situated on the River Ouse in a major gap in the South DOWNS, upstream and north of NEWHAVEN, was recorded as *Laewes* in the mid-10th century, and *Lewes* in 1086.

Lewis (Western Isles) Apparently 'marshy land'. *Leoghuis* (Scottish Gaelic) 'marshiness'. This northern part of the largest Outer Hebridean island is a vast tract of mainly low-lying peat and bog with much surface water and a scatter of small lochs. It was recorded as: *Leodus* and *Lyodus* c.1100; *Liodhus* in the *Orkneyinga Saga* 1225; *Leoghuis* 1449.

Lewisham (Greater London) 'Leofsa's homestead'. *Leofsa* (Old English personal name) shortened form of *Leofsige*; *ham* (Old English) 'homestead', 'village'. Early records of the name of this southeastern LONDON borough are: *Liofshema* 862; *Leofsnhaema* 987; *Liofesham* 1060; *Leueseham* 1081; *Levesham* 1086 (Domesday Book).

Leyburn (North Yorkshire) Probably 'the shelter by the stream'. *Hleg* (Old English conjectural word) 'shelter'; *burna* (Old English) 'stream'. The name of this small market town, southwest of RICHMOND, was entered in the Domesday Book survey of 1086 as *Leborne*.

Leyland (Lancashire) Place of 'the fallow land'. *Laege* (Old English) 'fallow', 'untilled'; *land* (Old English) 'tract of ground'. This town, south of PRESTON, famous for the production of the buses and trucks that bear its name, appears as *Lailand* in 1086.

Leyton (Greater London) 'Farmstead on the River Lea'.

Lea (Brythonic Celtic river name) probably 'bright one' or reference to the river-god Lugus; *tun* (Old English) 'farmstead'. This district of the borough of WALTHAM FOREST was named *Lugetune* in a text of around 1050, and *Leintune* in the Domesday Book. *Compare* LUTON.

Leytonstone (Greater London) The neighbouring district to the northeast, has the same basic name derivation as LEYTON, but with the addition of a distinguishing affix, representing the site of a former Roman milestone here.

Lichfield (Staffordshire) 'Open land near the Licced forest'. *Licced* (Old English version of Brythonic Celtic *Letoceton*) 'grey wood'; *feld* (Old English) 'open land'. The name of this cathedral city, north of BIRMINGHAM, is based on an ancient Celtic local forest-district name that is represented in a 4th-century record of the nearby Roman station at Wall, known as *Letocetum*. The town itself was first noted as *Liccedfeld* in c.730, and later in 1130 as *Lichesfeld*.

Liffey (Dublin/Wicklow) The origin of the name of this well-known river, on which DUBLIN stands, remains obscure.

Lifford (Donegal) Place 'beside the water'. *Leifear* (Irish Gaelic) 'side of the water'. This 'border town' is located on the west side of the River FOYLE, directly opposite STRABANE in Northern Ireland. The *d* ending has been added in the anglicisation of the Irish name and by association with 'ford' at this important crossing point.

Lillingstone Dayrell and **Lovell** (Buckinghamshire). Estate of 'the boundary stone of Lytel's people', later possessed by the 'Dayrell' and 'Lovell' families. *Lytel* (Old English personal name); *inga* (Old English—genitive of *ingas*) 'people of'; *stan* (Old English) 'boundary stone'; *Dayrell* and *Lovell* (Anglo-Norman manorial affixes) the former represents D'Airelle (Normandy) and the latter derives: *lovel* (Old French) 'wolf cub'. The names of these twin villages, north of BUCKINGHAM, reflect the split ownership by incoming Norman families in the 12th century: *Lillingestan* 1086 (Domesday Book); *Litlingestan Daireli* 1167.

Limavady (Londonderry) Place of the 'dog's leap'. *Leim* (Irish Gaelic) 'a leap'; *an* (Irish Gaelic) 'of the'; *madadh* (Irish Gaelic) 'dog'. The name of this market town, midway between LONDONDERRY and COLERAINE, probably refers to the site of a nearby castle that overhangs a deep gorge in the River Roe valley and some legendary incident that took place there.

Limerick (Limerick) 'Bare land'. *Luimneach* (Irish Gaelic adaptation of *lom*, meaning 'bare') 'open, vacant, ungrassed land'. The name of the third city of the Republic of Ireland, and ultimately that of its surrounding county, refers to such 'bare land' that originally would have been found by the lower reaches of the River SHANNON. In the process of anglicisation of this Irish name the commonplace corruption of an interchange of *r* for *n* has taken place.

Lincoln (Lincolnshire) 'Roman colony by the pool'. *Lindo-* (Brythonic Celtic conjectural root element) 'pool', 'lake'; *colonia* (Latin) 'Roman colony for veteran legionaries'. The name of this historic cathedral city and county town has its origins in Roman times, with the establishment of their station of *Lindum* by the 'pool', there being one on the River Witham here. Early documentation shows: *Lindon* c.150; *Lindum colonia* c.650; *Lincolia* 1086 (Domesday Book). The county name was first recorded as *Lincolnescir* in 1016.

Lindisfarne (Northumberland) Probably 'island of travellers from Lindsey'. *Lindis* (Old English) old district name for North LINCOLNSHIRE; *faran* (Old English) 'travellers'; *eg* (Old English) 'island'. Thus the link with LINDSEY is made in the former and alternative name for HOLY ISLAND, noted as *Lindisfarnae c.*700.

Lindsey (Lincolnshire) 'Territory of the Lindenses'. *Lindis* (Old English territorial name) an ancient Anglo-Saxon kingdom based on the earlier Roman administrative unit centred on *Lindum* or LINCOLN; *eg* (Old

English) 'island'. The name of this former division of Lincolnshire reflects the virtual 'island' that existed here in the north of the county before the FENS besides the River Witham were drained. It was recorded as *Lindissae prouincia* in about 730; *Lindesse* in 838; and *Lindesi* in the Domesday Book of 1086. *See* HOLLAND; KESTEVEN.

Lingfield (Surrey) Probably 'open land of the people of the woodland clearing'. *Leah* (Old English) 'woodland clearing'; *ingas* (Old English) 'people of'; *feld* (Old English) 'open land'. The not-so-obvious derivation of the name of this large village, north of EAST GRINSTEAD, is however manifested in a late 9th-century text, which records it as *Leangafeld*.

Linlithgow (Lothian) Place by 'the lake in the moist hollow'. *Llyn* (Brythonic Celtic) 'lake'; *lleith* (Brythonic Celtic) 'moist'; *cau* (Brythonic Celtic) 'hollow'. This historic royal burgh, west of Edinburgh, takes its name from Linlithgow Loch, which lies in a post-glacial hollow immediately below the impressive ruins of its 12th-century palace. Recorded in 1147 as *Linlitcu*.

Linwood (Strathclyde) Hybrid name meaning 'wood by the pool'. *Llyn* (Brythonic Celtic) 'pool'; *wudu* (Old English) 'wood'. This suburb of PAISLEY, famous for its former car plant, presumably had originally been settled by a wooded pool of the Black Cart Water.

Liphook (Hampshire) Probably 'hook of land where the deer leap'. *Hliep* (Old English) 'deer leap'; *hoc* (Old English) 'corner', 'angle', 'hook of land'. The name of this small town, west of HASLEMERE, is very descriptive of its situation, even today; it was noted a *Leephook* in the 14th century, and *Liephok* in the 15th century.

Lisburn (Antrim) Possibly 'fort of the fairy palace'. *Lios* (Irish Gaelic) 'fort'; *na* (Irish Gaelic) 'of the'; *bhuidhne* (Irish Gaelic) 'fairy palace'. This derivation has been suggested by one authority to explain the new name of this 'plantation town' established just southwest of BELFAST in the 17th century. Previously the small settlement here was called Lisnagarvey, an anglicised version of both its original and current Irish name, *Lios na gCearrbhach*, which simply translates as the 'fort of the gamblers'. In earlier times, old forts amidst former thickets here would have been ideal sites for illegal gambling.

Lisdoonvarna (Clare) 'The gapped fort'. *Lios* (Irish Gaelic) 'fort'; *dun* (Irish Gaelic) 'fort'; *bearna* (Irish Gaelic) 'a gap'. This small town, northwest of ENNIS, has a name that refers to the large fort nearby. It is thought that the tautology at the beginning of the name has resulted in the same way that river names are often doubled up with a generic and a specific of the same meaning. The Irish current name is *Lios Duin Bhearna*.

Liskeard (Cornwall) Probably 'Kerwyd's hall'. *Lys* (Old Cornish) 'hall', 'court', 'palace'; *Kerwyd* (Old Cornish personal name) unidentified. The name of this town to the south of BODMIN Moor was recorded as *Lyscerruyt* in the 11th century and *Liscarret* in the Domesday Book.

Lismore (Strathclyde) Island of 'the big garden'. *Lios* (Scottish Gaelic) 'garden', 'enclosure'; *mor* (Scottish Gaelic) 'big'. The derivation here refers to the island in Loch Linnhe which was reputedly 'a fertile paradise' in the early days of the large monastic community set up here by St Moluag in the 6th century. *See* APPIN

Liss (Hampshire) Place of 'the court'. *Lis* (Brythonic Celtic conjectural word) 'court', 'palace'. The simple name of this large village, northeast of PETERSFIELD, was recorded as *Lis* in the Domesday Book of 1086.

Listowel (Kerry) 'Tuathal's fort'. *Lios* (Irish Gaelic) 'ring fort'; *Tuathail* (Irish Gaelic personal name) unidentified. This small market town, northeast of TRALEE, has a typical Irish ring fort, where a circular stronghold is contained inside a larger fortification.

Littleborough (Greater Manchester) Place of 'the litle fort'. *Lytel* (Old English) small; *burh* (Old English) 'fort', 'stronghold'. The name of this town, northeast of ROCHDALE, was recorded as *Littlebrough* only in 1577.

Littlehampton (West Sussex) 'The homestead' with a later comparative. *Lytel* (Old English) 'smaller'; *hamtun* (Old English) 'home farm', 'homestead'. The name of this seaside resort, west of WORTHING, was originally called 'Hampton', or *Hantone*, as recorded in the Domesday Book of 1086. Later it was prefixed by 'Little-', presumably to distinguish it from SOUTHAMPTON farther west along the south coast, which itself formerly had been simply 'Hampton'. A record of 1482 shows the name as *Lyttelhampton*.

Liverpool (Merseyside) Place of 'the muddy creek or pool'. *Lifer* (Old English) 'thick', 'muddy', 'coagulated water'; *pol* (Old English) 'pool', 'creek'. The name of this famous city and port, on the north side of the MERSEY estuary, does not derive from the mythical 'liver bird', but has its origins in a former tidal creek here around which the early settlement was founded. It was recorded as *Liuerpol* in 1190.

Liversedge (West Yorkshire) 'Leofhere's edge'. *Leofhere* (Old English personal name); *ecg* (Old English) 'edge'. The name aptly describes the location of this town on a low ridge above the River Calder, upstream and northwest of DEWSBURY. It appears in the Domesday book of 1086 as *Livresec*.

Livingston (Lothian) Place of 'Leving's village'. *Leving* (Old English personal name) an early Saxon landowner well established in these parts; *tun* (Old English) 'village'. Designated as a New Town in 1962, it lies west of EDINBURGH, and incorporates the old village, recorded as *Leuinistun* 1250; *Levyngestone* 1297

Lizard, The (Cornwall) Place of 'the court on a height'. *Lys* (Old Cornish) 'court'; *ard* (Old Cornish) 'height'. The name of this renowned peninsula and its headland, **Lizard Point**, the southernmost projection of the English mainland, refers to a medieval administration centre formerly sited here, at the village of **Lizard**; its entry in the Domesday Book was *Lisart*.

Llanberis (Gwynedd) 'Church of St Peris'. *Llan* (Welsh) 'church'; *Peris* (Welsh personal name) said to have been a cardinal sent as a missionary from Rome in the 6th century. This mountain valley resort at the foot of SNOWDON on its northern side commemorates St Peris in its name. Nearby is Llyn Peris.

Llandaff (South Glamorgan) 'Church on the Taff'. *Llan* (Welsh) 'church'; *Taf* (Brythonic Celtic river name) Taff. This district of CARDIFF, lying northwest of the city centre, refers to the cathedral church of St Teilo which sits on the west bank of the River Taff.

Llandeilo (Dyfed) 'Church of St Teilo'. *Llan* (Welsh) 'church'; *Teilo* (Welsh personal name) 6th-century bishop and saint who was a major figure in the early church in South Wales. This town, standing on the Tywi river upstream and east of CARMARTHEN, is named after the popular St Teilo, as are many other smaller places. By way of distinction, early records show the name as *Lanteliau Maur*, the latter element representing the modern Welsh *mawr*, meaning 'great'.

Llandovery (Dyfed) 'Church by the water'. *Llan* (Welsh) 'church'; *am* (Welsh) 'by the'; *dwfr* (Welsh) 'water'. This small town northeast and upstream of LLANDEILO lies at the centre of a catchment area for the upper Tywi river and has a name that aptly describes its situation. Llandovery is an anglicised rendering of its Welsh name, *Llanymddfri*, often abbreviated to *Llanddfri*. It was recorded as *Llanamdewri* in the 12th century.

Llandrindod Wells (Powys) 'Church of the Trinity spa'. *Llan* (Welsh) 'church'; *trindod* (Welsh) 'trinity'; *wells* (English derived from Old English *wella*) 'spa'. This small town in east-central Wales has a name that reflects both its ecclesiastical capital status and, by the 18th century addition of 'Wells', its development as a spa town tapping the nearby natural springs.

Llandudno (Gwynedd) 'Church of St Tudno'. *Llan* (Welsh) 'church'; *Tudno* (Welsh personal name) unidentified. This popular seaside resort, lying to the east of GREAT ORMES HEAD, has a name dedicated to a saint who may have been active here in the 6th century.

Llanelli (Dyfed) 'Church of St Elli'. *Llan* (Welsh) 'church'; *Elliw* (Welsh personal name) a female saint, said to be one of the granddaughters of the legendary Celtic prince, Brychan of BRECON. The name of this industrial town on the South Wales coast immediately west of the GOWER Peninsula, was until recently spelt as Llanelly. It has the difficult pronunciation for the English-speaking tongue of 'Hlanthly', where the initial *Ll* consonant has the sound of a voiceless *l*.

Llanfairfechan (Gwynedd) 'Little St Mary's church'. *Llan* (Welsh) 'church'; *Fair* (Welsh mutated form of *Mair*) Mary, i.e. the Virgin Mary; *bychan* (Welsh) 'little'. The name of this small coastal resort between BANGOR and CONWY is basically the common Welsh place name *Llanfair* with a specific differentiating addition.

Llanfairpwllgwyngyll (Gwynedd) This 'abbreviated' version, or the shorter postal address of *Llanfair P.G.*, represents the name of a village near MENAI BRIDGE on ANGLESEY, which is generally regarded as the longest place name in the British Isles. Contrived in the 19th century, the full name is *Llanfairpwllgwyngyll-gogerychwyrndrobwllllandysiliogogogoch*, meaning 'St Mary's church in the hollow of the white hazel near the fierce whirlpool and St Tysilio's church by the red cave'.

Llanfyllin (Powys) 'Church of St Myllin'. *Llan* (Welsh) 'church'; *Myllin* (Welsh personal name) unidentified. Little is known about the saint to whom dedication is made in the name of this small town northwest of WELSHPOOL.

Llangefni (Gwynedd) 'Church on the Cefni'. *Llan* (Welsh) 'church'; *Cefni* (Welsh river name possibly derived as genitive of *cefn*) 'of the ridge'. The name of this market town in the centre of ANGLESEY was recorded as *Llangevni* in 1254.

Llangollen (Clwyd) 'Church of St Collen'. *Llan* (Welsh) 'church'; *Collen* (Welsh personal name) said to have been a 7th-century abbot of GLASTONBURY before becoming an austere hermit. This mecca for tourists, set in the pastoral valley of the Welsh DEE and famous for its annual international *eisteddfod*—a folk festival of music, poetry and dance, was recorded in 1234 as having the name *Lancollien*.

Llanidloes (Powys) 'Church of St Idloes'. *Llan* (Welsh) 'church'; *Idloes* (Welsh personal name) a saint who is said to have been active here in the 7th century. This small market town in central Wales, east of ABERYSTWYTH, was recorded as *Lanidloes* in the 13th century and today is colloquially referred to by locals as 'Llani'.

Llanrwst (Gwynedd) 'Church of St Grwst'. *Llan* (Welsh) 'church'; *Grwst* (Welsh personal name) unidentified. Not much is known about the Celtic saint to whom dedication is made in the name of this small town north of BETWS-Y-COED in the Vale of CONWY. A 13th-century record shows the name as *Lhannruste*.

Llanwrtyd Wells (Powys) 'Church of St Gwrtud spa'. *Llan* (Welsh) 'church'; *Gwrtud* (Welsh personal name) unidentified; *wells* (English derived from Old English *wella*) 'spa'. This small 19th-century spa town southwest of BULITH WELLS has a duplex name, the basic element being originally that of an older nearby village.

Lleyn, The (Gwynedd) Possibly the 'land of the Lagin people'. This long peninsula that protrudes southwestwards from Snowdonia into the Irish Sea has a name of uncertain origin. Some authorities consider that it may derive from the name of the local Celtic tribe known to the Romans as *Lagenii*, with their own name possibly having a common root with the ancient *Lagin* people of LEINSTER, towards which this peninsula thrusts.

Loanhead (Lothian) 'At the top of the lane'. *Loan* (Scots) 'lane'; 'head' (English) 'at the top of'. This latter day coal-mining town just southeast of EDINBURGH by the attractive environs of the North Esk's glen was for long a summer retreat for inhabitants of the city. The original loan here would have been one that climbed up from the river. Recorded as *Loneheid* in 1618.

Lochaber (Highland) Probably 'area of the loch confluence'. *Loch* (Scottish Gaelic) 'sea loch', 'lake'; *aber* (Brythonic Celtic) 'confluence of'. In this area, centred on FORT WILLIAM, numerous major lochs converge into the Firth of LORNE: Loch Linnhe, Loch Leven; Loch Eil; Loch Lochy.

Lochcarron (Highland) Presumably village on 'the loch of the cairn'. *Loch* (Scottish Gaelic) 'sea loch'; *carron* (Scottish Gaelic genitive of *carn*) 'of the cairn'. This large village, northeast of KYLE OF LOCHALSH, lies on the north shore of Loch Carron.

Lochgelly (Fife) Place of 'the shining loch'. *Loch* (Scottish Gaelic) 'loch', 'lake'; *geal* (Scottish Gaelic) 'bright', 'shining'. This former coal-mining town just to the northeast of COWDENBEATH takes its name from the small loch to the southeast of it.

Lochgilphead (Strathclyde) 'Head of Loch Gilp'. 'Head' (English) 'at the top of'; *loch* (Scottish Gaelic) 'sea loch'; *gilp* or *gilb* (Scottish Gaelic) 'chisel'. This chief market town and administrative centre for Mid-ARGYLL is located at the head of a chisel-shaped nick out of Loch Fyne's otherwise long straight coastline.

Lochinver (Highland) Simply 'loch at the river mouth'. *Loch* (Scottish Gaelic) 'sea loch'; *inver* (Scottish Gaelic) 'river mouth'. This fishing port is at the mouth of the Abhainn na Clach Airigh is the main centre of ASSYNT.

Loch Lomond *see* **Lomond**.

Lochmaben (Dumfries and Galloway) Possibly place of the 'loch by the bare-topped hill'. *Loch* (Scottish Gaelic) 'loch', 'lake'; *maol* (Scottish Gaelic) 'bare top'; *beinn* (Scottish Gaelic) 'hill'. The derivation of the name of this village, west of LOCKERBIE, remains unattested as far as the second element is concerned.

Lochnagar (Grampian) 'Loch of the noise or laughter'.

Loch (Scottish Gaelic) 'loch', 'lake'; *na* (Scottish Gaelic) 'of the'; *gaire* (Scottish Gaelic) 'noise', 'laughter'. Strangely, this is in fact the name of a dramatic mountain whose towering cliffs rise to 3791 ft (1155 m). In recent times it has become familiar to millions through a children's story 'The Old Man of Lochnagar', written by Charles, Prince of Wales. Indeed, here we witness the strange sight of a loch 'running uphill', for the name of the lochan at the foot of the mountain has displaced the summit's original name. The latter was *Beinn nan Ciochan* (Scottish Gaelic) 'the mountain of the breasts', referring to the protruding granite tors on its corrie rim. Gradually, during the late 18th and the 19th centuries the process of transformation took place, and it was finally completed with the publication of Lord Byron's romantic poem on 'Dark Lochnagar', and the royal seal of approval given by Queen Victoria from her adjoining BARMORAL estate.

Loch Ness *see* **Ness**

Lockerbie (Dumfries and Galloway) Apparently 'Locard's village'. *Locard* (Old Scandinavian personal name—unattested); *by* (Old Scandinavian) 'village', 'farmstead'. It was recorded as *Lokardebi* in a document of 1306. In more recent times, the name of this market town to the east of DUMFRIES hit the headlines, when on 22 December 1988, a Pan American jumbo jet was blown up in mid-air overhead and the debris rained down here.

Loddon (Norfolk) Place on 'the muddy one'. *Lutna* (Brythonic Celtic river name) 'muddy'. This small town, northwest of BECCLES, lies on the River Chet, formerly called the Loddon, from which it derives its name. It was recorded as *Lodne* in 1043, and *Lotna* in 1086.

Lomond (Central; Fife; Strathclyde) Probably 'beacon'. *Laomuinn* (Brythonic Celtic) 'beacon'. This name almost certainly was applied to **Ben Lomond** (Central) and the twin **Lomond Hills** (Fife) in the sense that their prominent positions would have made them suitable as beacon hills. Thus, **Loch Lomond** (Central/Strathclyde), the largest and one of the best-known inland stretches of water in Britain, takes its name from the overlooking 'ben'. Apparently the 'loch' was in early times called Loch Leven. *See* LEVEN.

London (Greater London) The ancient name of the world-famous capital city of the UNITED KINGDOM remains obscure in origin and meaning. For a long time it was considered by many authorities to derive from a Brythonic Celtic root and reflect the personal name of a man called *Londinos*, but this possible explanation has now been discredited. The Romans established a fortified station by their lowest bridging point of the THAMES (near present-day Lombard Street) in the 1st century AD, and within 100 years they had established the impressive walled city of *Londinium* as the capital of the province of *Britannia*. Subsequent early records of its name include: *Londinion* c.150; *Lundenbyrig* 457; *Lundonia* c.730; *Lundenne* 839; *Lundenceaster* c.890; *Lundres* c.1175; *London* 1298. *See* GREATER LONDON.

Londonderry (Londonderry) The basic name of this major city of Northern Ireland has long been simply **Derry**. This derives as: *doire* (Irish Gaelic) 'oak wood'. Ancient records indicate that it was first suffixed as *Doire-Chalaich*, referring to the personal name of Calgach or Galgacus. In the 10th or 11th century it began to be called *Derry-Columcille*, in honour of St Columbkille, who founded a monastery here in 546. This name continued until the early 17th century when by decree of a charter granted by James I to a group of LONDON merchants the name Londonderry was imposed.

Long Eaton (Derbyshire) 'Extensive island farm'. *Lang* (Old English distinguishing affix) 'extensive'; *eg* (Old English) 'island'; *tun* (Old English) 'farm'. This now manufacturing town, southwest of NOTTINGHAM, lies on a virtual 'island' of land bounded by the meanders of the TRENT and Erewash rivers, and its name reflects this situation. It was recorded as *Aitone* in the Domesday Book of 1086, and by 1288 the comparative prefix had been added as *Long Eyton*, presumably to distinguish it from **Little Eaton**, a village 15 miles (24 km) to the northwest.

Longford (Longford) 'The fortress'. *Longphort* (Irish Gaelic) 'fortress'. This county town and its territory around it, in the centre of Ireland, take their name from the ancient fortress of the O'Ferral (or O'Farrel) family, which once dominated a site here but of which no trace remains. The modern Irish name is *An Longfort*.

Longformacus (Borders) Apparently 'church on the land of Maccus'. *Long* (Brythonic Celtic corrupted form of *lann*) 'church'; *fothir* (Brythonic Celtic) 'land', 'meadow'; *Maccus* (Irish-Scandinavian form of personal name *Magnus*) reputed to have lived in this remote part of the LAMMERMUIR.

Long Mynd, The (Shropshire) 'The long ridge-like hill'. *Lang* (Old English) 'long'; *mynydd* (Welsh) 'hill'. This distinctive ridge in the hilly 'Marches', west of CHURCH STRETTON, has a hybrid name that reflects its location close to the Welsh border. Records show: *Longameneda* in the 12th century; *Longemenyede* in 1275.

Longniddry (Lothian) 'Church of the new hamlet'. *Long* Brythonic Celtic corrupt form of *lann*) 'church'; *nuadh* (Brythonic Celtic) 'new'; *tref* (Brythonic Celtic) 'hamlet'. The name of this large village, northwest of HADDINGTON, was recorded as *Langnedre* in 1595.

Longridge (Lancashire) Place by 'the long ridge'. *Lang* (Old English) 'long'; *hrycg* (Old English) 'ridge'. This small town, northeast of PRESTON, is named after the nearby Longridge Fell, whose own derivation is aptly obvious. It was recorded as *Langrige* in 1199.

Longtown (Cumbria) 'Long farmstead or estate'. *Lang* (Old English) 'long'; *tun* (Old English) 'farm', 'estate'.

Recorded as *Longeton* in 1267, the name of this small town reflects its situation on lowlying land alongside an open stretch of the River Esk, north of CARLISLE. *Compare* LANGHOLM, 16 miles (25 km) north and upstream on the same river.

Looe, East and **West** (Cornwall) Place on 'the creek'. *Logh* (Old Cornish conjectural word related to Gaelic *loch* and Welsh *llwch*) 'inlet of water'. This coastal town, south of LISKEARD, takes its name from the river here, which in its lower reaches is a typical Cornish drowned river valley or creek that at its mouth divides this settlement into its two respective parts. It was documented as *Lo* in 1237.

Lorn(e) (Strathclyde) This area of the west coast of Scotland, centred on present-day OBAN, was named after Loarn, brother of Fergus of ULSTER, and one of the leaders of the 'Scots' invasion from Ireland in the late 5th century.

Lossiemouth (Grampian) Simply, 'mouth of the River Lossie'. Thus this town, north of ELGIN, takes its name from the river at the mouth of which it stands. The river name in turn is derived: *lus* (Scottish Gaelic) 'herbs', 'plants'. The otherwise modern English derivation of this name is an indication that the town was only developed in the late 17th century, when a harbour was built here.

Lostwithiel (Cornwall) 'At the tail end of the woodland district of Withiel'. *Lost* (Old Cornish) 'tail'; *gwydhyel* (Old Cornish) 'woodland'. This town at the head of the Fowey river estuary, southeast of BODMIN, takes its name from its situation on the edge of the wooded upland area that extends from the village of Withiel, some 8 miles (13 km) to the northwest. It was recorded as *Lostwetell* in 1194.

Lothian (Scotland) An ancient area, centred on present-day EDINBURGH, that is reputed to have been named after its historical founder, one Leudonus (Brythonic Celtic or pre-Celtic personal name) of uncertain origin.

Early records show: *Loonia* c.970; *Lothene* 1091; *Louthion* c.1200; *Laodinia* 1245. Currently it is the name of an administrative region, divided into four districts corresponding to former counties: Midlothian, East Lothian, West Lothian and the City of Edinburgh.

Loughborough (Leicestershire) 'Luhhede's stronghold'. *Luhhede* (Old English personal name; *burh* (Old English) 'stronghold', 'fortified house'. The name of this EAST MIDLANDS university and manufacturing town, situated midway between LEICESTER and NOTTINGHAM, was misrecorded as *Lucteburne* in the Domesday Book of 1086, but as *Lucteburga* in the 12th century.

Lough Conn *see* **Conn, Lough**.

Lough Corrib *see* **Corrib, Lough**.

Lough Derg *see* **Derg, Lough**.

Lough Erne *see* **Erne, Upper and Lower Lough**.

Lough Foyle *see* **Foyle, Lough**.

Lough Neagh *see* **Neagh, Lough**.

Lough Oughter *see* **Oughter, Lough**.

Loughrea (Galway) Place of the 'grey lake'. *Loch* (Irish Gaelic) 'lake': *riabhach* (Irish Gaelic) 'grey'. This small market town, northeast of GORT, takes its name from the Lough Rea immediately to the south. Its modern Irish name is *Baile Loch Riach*.

Lough Swilly *see* **Swilly, Lough**.

Loughton (Essex) 'Estate associated with a man called Luca'. *Luca* (Old English personal name); *ing* (Old English connective particle) 'associated with'; *tun* (Old English) 'estate', 'farmstead'. The name of this former village, and now satellite town by EPPING Forest on the northeastern fringe of the Greater LONDON conurbation, was recorded as *Lukintone* in 1062.

Louth (Lincolnshire) Place on 'the River Lud, or loud one'. *Lud* (Old English river name, derived from *hlud*) 'loud'. This agricultural servicing centre and food-processing town, south of GRIMSBY, takes its name directly from the river on which it sits east of the LINCOLNSHIRE WOLDS. It was noted as *Lude* in 1086.

Louth (Louth) The full meaning of the name of the Republic's most northeastern county remains uncertain. It is based on the small village of the same name to the southwest of DUNDALK. In current Irish this is *Lu*, but it represents the longer *Lugh-mhaigh*; of which only the second element, meaning 'plain' is evident.

Lowestoft (Suffolk) 'Hlothver's homestead'. *Hlothver* (Old Norse personal name); *toft* (Old Danish) 'homestead'. This coastal town by the Oulton Broad, south of GREAT YARMOUTH, has a name with an ending common to many villages in the former Danelaw of eastern and northern England. It was documented as *Lothu Wistoft* in 1086.

Loweswater (Cumbria) 'leafy lake'. *Lauf* (Old Norse) 'leaf'; *saer* (Old Norse) 'lake'; *waeter* (Old English) 'expanse of water'. This is one of the smaller lakes of the LAKE DISTRICT, lying northwest and above CRUMMOCK WATER. Its tautological name was recorded as *Lausewatre* in around 1200.

Lucan (Dublin) 'Place of elms'. *Leamhcan* (Irish Gaelic) 'elm place'. This small satellite town and former spa west of DUBLIN lies in the wide valley of the LIFFEY, once much wooded.

Luce (Dumfries and Galloway) 'Place of herbs or plants'. *Lus* (Scottish Gaelic) 'herbs', 'plants'.The name of this river, in the far southwest of the region, has given its name to the villages of **Glenluce** and **New Luce**, as well as **Luce Bay**. *See* LUSS.

Ludgershall (Wiltshire) Probably the place of 'a nook with a trapping spear'. *Lute-gar* (Old English) 'spear set as a trap for wild animals'; *halh* (Old English) 'nook', 'secluded corner of land'. The name of this army town on the edge of SALISBURY Plain, northwest of ANDOVER, was recorded as *Lutegaresheale* in 1015.

Ludlow (Shropshire) 'Hill by the rapid'. *Hlude* (Old English) 'rapid', 'loud water'; *hlaw* (Old English) 'hill'. The name of this town, south of SHREWSBURY, aptly describes its situation on a hill above the River Teme. It was recorded as *Ludelaue* in 1138.

Lulworth Cove (Dorset) 'Bay near Lulla's enclosure'. *Lulla* (Old English personal name); *worth* (Old English) 'enclosure'; *cofa* (Old English) 'sheltered bay'. This near-circular bay, east of WEYMOUTH, where the chalk cliffs end in dramatic arches and chasms of Purbeck and Portland stone, takes its name from the nearby villages of **East** and **West Lulworth**. The latter was recorded as *Lulvorde* in the Domesday book of 1086.

Lundy (Devon) 'Puffin island'. *Lundi* (Old Norse) 'puffin'; *ey* (Old Norse) 'island'. This isolated island, lying at the entrance to the BRISTOL Channel, some 11 miles (18 km) northwest of HARTLAND POINT, has a name that even today aptly reflects the large puffin colonies to be found here. It appears as *Lundey* in the *Orkneyinga Sagas* of around 1145.

Lurgan (Armagh) 'The little leg or shin'. *Lorg* (Irish Gaelic) 'leg', 'shin'; *-an* (Irish Gaelic diminutive suffix) 'little', 'low'. The sense here for this 17th-century 'plantation town', close to the southeastern corner of Lough NEAGH, is that of a low long shin-like hill.

Luss (Strathclyde) 'Place of herbs or plants'. *Lus* (Scottish Gaelic) 'herbs', 'plants'.The name of this picturesque former estate village, on the west shore of LOCH LOMOND, is aptly descriptive of this verdant spot. *See* LUCE.

Luton (Bedfordshire) 'Farmstead on the River Lea'. *Lea* (Brythonic Celtic river name); *tun* (Old English) 'farmstead'. This industrial town, northwest of LONDON, lies on the same river, and has a name of identical origin and meaning as LEYTON, although the reason for its different rendering remains unexplained. It was recorded as *Lygetun* in 792, and *Loitone* in the Domesday Book of 1086.

Lutterworth (Leicestershire) Probably 'enclosure on the bright, clean stream'. *Hlutre* (Old English conjectural river name derived from *hluttor*) 'clear', 'bright', 'clean one'; *worth* (Old English) 'enclosure'. This town, northeast of RUGBY, lies on the River Swift, and it is considered by many authorities that its name may have taken its first element from a possible former name of the river rather than being a personal name, as is the normal case with '-worth' ending places. Its entry in the Domesday Book is *Lutresurde*.

Lybster (Highland) 'Settlement in the lee'. *Hlee* (Old Norse) 'leeward'; *bol-stathr* (Old Norse) 'settlement'. This sheltered coastal village, southwest of WICK, is aptly named.

Lydd (Kent) Place 'at the slopes'. *Hlidum* (Old English—dative plural of *hlid*) 'slopes'. This town, located inland on the otherwise low-lying DUNGENESS peninsula, is on a slight slope behind the Denge Marsh here. Records show: *Hlidum* 774; *Hlide* c.1100.

Lydney (Gloucestershire) 'Lida's island'. *Lida-n* (Old English personal name—genitive form) 'sailor'; *eg* (Old English) 'island', 'river meadow'. This small town, at the southern edge of the FOREST OF DEAN, lies between two streams near to where they enter the SEVERN estuary, thus effectively on an 'island'. The name was noted as *Lidaneg* in 972, and *Lidenei* in 1086.

Lyme Regis (Dorset) 'Royal town on the River Lyme'. *Lim* (Brythonic Celtic river name) 'stream', or 'a flood'; *regis* (Latin affix) 'of the king'. This coastal resort, west of Bridport, takes its original basic name from the river at the mouth of which it stands. The regal affix was added in the late 13th century when it received a royal charter from Edward I in return for its surrender to the Crown. Records show: *Lim* 774; *Lime* 1086 (Domesday Book); *Lyme Regis* 1285.

Lymington (Hampshire) 'Farmstead on the River Limen'. *Limen* (Brythonic Celtic conjectural river name) 'elm' or 'marshy stream'; *tun* (Old English) 'farmstead'. This coastal resort and yachting centre, east of BOURNEMOUTH, takes its name from the river on which it stands, formerly the Limen. It was recorded as *Lentune* in 1086; *Limington* in 1186.

Lymm (Cheshire) Place of 'the noisy stream'. *Hlimme*

(Old English) 'noisy stream', 'torrent'. This town, east of WARRINGTON, stands on a small stream that drains into the MERSEY; it may have been called something like *Hlimme*. The name was entered in the Domesday Book as *Lime*.

Lyndhurst (Hampshire) 'Lime-tree-wooded hill'. *Lind* (Old English) 'lime tree'; *hyrst* (Old English) 'wooded hill'. This small town, north of LYMINGTON, lies at the centre of the NEW FOREST, and has an appropriately arboreal name that appears in the Domesday Book as *Linhest*.

Lynmouth (Devon) Place 'at the mouth of the River Lyn'. *Hlynn* (Old English river name) 'noisy one', 'torrent'; *mutha* (Old English) 'river mouth'. This small coastal town sits below the cliffs on which LYNTON stands. The meaning of its name rang all to true in 1952 when the town was struck by a torrential flood that violently swept away many buildings and bridges, causing much injury and loss of life. It was recorded as *Lymmouth* in 1330.

Lynton (Devon) 'Farmstead on the River Lyn'. *Hlynn* (Old English river name) 'noisy one', 'torrent'; *tun* (Old English) 'farmstead'. This elevated resort is situated on the cliffs at the seaward edge of EXMOOR, immediately above LYNMOUTH. It was entered in the Domesday Book in 1086 as *Lintone*.

Lytham St Anne's (Lancashire) Place 'at the slopes or dunes' + a place 'dedicated to St Anne'. *Hlithum* (Old English—dative plural of *hlid*) 'at the slopes'. The name of this seaside resort and residential town, south of BLACKPOOL, in fact represents two places that amalgamated in 1922. **St Anne's** is named after its dedicated church in the newly laid out town here at the end of the 19th century. **Lytham**, on the other hand, is much older, and its name was recorded as *Lindun* in the Domesday Book of 1086. *Compare* LYDD.

M

Mablethorpe (Lincolnshire) 'Malbert's outlying farm'. *Malbert* (Old French personal name of Old German origin); *thorp* (Old Danish) 'secondary settlement'. The name of this coastal resort, northwest of SKEGNESS, is recorded as *Malbertorp* in the Domesday Book of 1086.

Macclesfield (Cheshire) Probably 'Maccel's open land'. *Maccel* (Old English personal name); *feld* (Old English) 'open land'. The name of this textiles town, south of STOCKPORT, was noted as *Maclesfeld* in the Domesday Book of 1086.

Macduff (Grampian) This old BANFFshire fishing port was renamed in 1783 by James Duff, 2nd Earl of Fife, who redeveloped the settlement, previously known as *Down*. Macduff, as in the surname, simply means 'son of Duff; the black(-haired one)'.

Macgillycuddy's Reeks (Kerry) The romantic-sounding name of these mountains on the Iveragh Peninsula to the southwest of KILLARNEY apparently refers to the refuge that these 'reeks', or ridges, once provided to the Macgillycuddys, an ancient local tribal sept. By contrast, their Irish name is a simple but apt description: *Na Cruach Dubha* (Irish Gaelic) meaning 'the black rick-shaped peaks'. *See* CARRANTUOHILL.

Machrihanish (Strathclyde) Possibly 'plain of the high headland'. *Machair* (Scottish Gaelic) 'plain'; *ha* (Old Norse) 'high'; *nes* (Old Norse) 'headland'. Although it is assumed that the first element was added at a later date, the current name aptly describes the situation of this coastal village at the break of the slope between a large machair to the north and east, and the hilly Mull of KINTYRE to the south.

Machynlleth (Powys) 'Plain of Cynllaith'. *Mach* (Brythonic Celtic) 'plain'; *Cynllaith* (Welsh personal name) unidentified. This small market town northeast of ABERYSTWYTH lies on the broad River Dovey, or Dyfi, valley floor which represents the 'plain' here. A 13th-century record shows *Machenleyd*.

Maesteg (Mid Glamorgan) 'Fair field'. *Maes* (Welsh) 'open field'; *teg* (Welsh) 'fair'. This industrial town was a 19th-century 'green-field site' development, and it takes its name directly from its situation.

Maghera (Londonderry) Simply 'plain'. *Machaire* (Irish Gaelic) 'plain'. This small market town lies on the wide plain to the east of the Sperrin Mountains. The fuller meaning of its Irish name, *Machaire Ratha*, is 'plain of the fort'.

Magherafelt (Londonderry) 'Plain of Fiolta'. *Machaire* (Irish Gaelic) 'plain'; *Fiolta* (Irish Gaelic personal name) unidentified. The second element may have been added later to distinguish this settlement on the plain from MAGHERA, only 8 miles (12 km) to the north.

Maghull (Merseyside) 'Nook of mayweed'. *Maegthe* (Old English) 'mayweed'; *halh* (Old English) 'nook of land', 'secluded corner'. This town north of LIVERPOOL was named *Magele* in the Domesday Book, and recorded as *Maghal* in 1219.

Maida Vale (Greater London) This district of west-central LONDON, lying north of PADDINGTON, was developed in the 19th century and so named in commemoration of the British victory in 1806 over Napoleon's French army at the Battle of Maida in Calabria, Italy, and an allusion to a 'vale' as a stretch of WATLING STREET passes between so-called Maida Hill to the west and a rise up to St John's Wood on the other side.

Maidenhead (Berkshire) Maidens' landing place'. *Maegden* (Old English) 'maiden'; *hyth* (Old English) 'landing place'. This town, on the River THAMES west of SLOUGH, has a name that suggests that either the original landing place here was easy to negotiate or that it was a place particularly noted for the congregation of young women. It was recorded as *Maydehuth* in 1248, and *Maydenhith* in 1262.

Maidstone (Kent) 'Maidens' or the peoples' stone'. *Maegden*; *maegth* (Old English) 'maiden'; 'people', 'folk'; *stan* (Old English) 'assembly stone'. The name of this historic county town on the River MEDWAY was documented as *Maegthan stan* in the 10th century.

Mainland (Orkney; Shetland) Literally 'the main land'. *Megin* (Old Norse) main, chief; *land* (Old Norse) tract of land. self-explanatory name of Viking origin, applies to the largest, by far, and most important, of the islands of both the ORKNEY and SHETLAND archipelagoes.

Malahide (Dublin) Probably 'the hilltop of Ide'. *Mullach* (Irish Gaelic) 'hilltop', 'summit'. *Ide* (Irish Gaelic personal name) unidentified. This seaside town north of DUBLIN is situated by the Hill of Feltrim, once the seat of the ancient Fagan tribe. Its modern Irish name is *Mallach Ide*.

Malden (Greater London) 'Hill with a cross'. *Mael* (Old English) 'cross', 'crucifix'; *dun* (Old English) 'hill'. This district of KINGSTON UPON THAMES, and that of its northern neighbour, **New Malden**, which was developed in the 19th century, has a basic name whose meaning and origin is the same as for MALDON. It was recorded in the Domesday Book in 1086 as *Meldon*.

Maldon (Essex) 'Hill with a cross'. *Mael* (Old English) 'cross', 'crucifix'; *dun* (Old English) 'hill'. the name of this small town at the head of the Blackwater estuary, east of CHELMSFORD, appears in an early 10th-century text as *Maeldune*, and in the Domesday Book of 1086 as *Malduna*.

Malham Cove (North Yorkshire) 'Secluded cavern by the gravelly places'. *Malgun* (Old Scandinavian—dative of *malgi*) 'gravely place'; *cofa* (Old English) 'cavern'. The descriptive name of this spectacular natural amphitheatre of exposed limestone cliffs, east of

SETTLE, actually derives from the nearby village of **Malham**, which lies on the Millstone Grit that covers much of the northern PENNINES. It was recorded as *Malgun* in the 1086 Domesday Book.

Malin Head (Donegal) 'The headland brow'. *Malainn* (Irish Gaelic) 'brow of a head'. The name of this most northerly point of Ireland, familiar from the radio shipping forecasts, is thus most descriptively apt to its situation.

Mallaig (Highland) Possibly 'headland bay'. *Muli* (Old Norse) 'headland'; *aig* (Scottish Gaelic adaptation of Old Norse *vagr*) 'bay'. This significantly describes the location of this small fishing and ferry port, lying in a little bay on the otherwise sheer headland that rounds into Loch NEVIS. One commentator considers a more likely alternative in the derivation: *mol-aig* (Old Norse) 'shingle bay'. The corruption of *mol* to *mal* is attested in two place names in Yorkshire.

Mallow (Cork) 'Plain of the Allow'. *Magh* (Irish Gaelic) 'plain'; *Eala* (Irish Gaelic river name) 'Allow'. This market town northwest of CORK sits in the middle of a fertile valley of the River Blackwater, formerly the Eala or Allow. The current Irish name is *Mala*.

Malmesbury (Wiltshire) 'Maeldub's stronghold'. *Maeldub* (Irish Gaelic personal name) 7th-century abbot and founder of local monastic cell; *byrig* (Old English—dative form of *burh*) 'fortified place'. The name of this town, west of SWINDON, was early documented as *Maildufi urbs* in about 730, and as *Maldulfes burgh* around 890.

Malpas (Cheshire) Place by 'the difficult passage'. *Mal* (Old French) 'bad', 'difficult'; *pas* (Old French) 'pass', 'passage'. The name of this small town near the Welsh border, east of WREXHAM, was introduced here, as in other places, by the Anglo-Normans to signify a particularly muddy track or generally marshy terrain. It was recorded in a document of the early 12th century with the spelling exactly as now.

Maltby (South Yorkshire) 'Malti's farmstead'. *Malti* (Old Danish personal name; *by* (Old Danish) 'farmstead'. This town, in the coal-mining district east of ROTHERHAM, has name that is relatively common in this part of the former Danelaw; it was recorded as *Maltbi* in the Domesday Book of 1086.

Malton (North Yorkshire) 'Middle farm'. *Methal* (Old Scandinavian version of Old English *middel*) 'middle'; *tun* (Old English) 'farmstead'. This town, northeast of YORK, lies on the south side of the Vale of PICKERING, amidst fertile farmland. Records show: *Maltune* 1086 (Domesday Book); *Maaltun c.*1150

Malvern Hills (Hereford and Worcester) 'The bare hill'. *Moil* (Brythonic Celtic conjectural word related to Welsh *moel*) 'bare'; *brinn* (Brythonic Celtic conjectural word related to Welsh *bryn*) 'hill'. This distinctive, single, narrow range of rough hill land, southwest of WORCESTER, has given its name to several places established in its lee, including the town of **Great Malvern** and its northern district of **Malvern Link**, the villages of **Little Malvern**, **Malvern Wells**, and **West Malvern**, as well as the modern administrative district here that has adopted the title **Malvern Hills**. The original basic name was documented as *Maelfern* in 1030 and appears in the Domesday Book as *Malferna*.

Man, Isle of (British Isles) The name of this island, a British Crown Dependency in the middle of the Irish Sea, is reputed to be derived from its association with the ancient Irish Celtic god Manannan mac Lir. Its Roman name was *Monapia*, which, according to some authorities, is said to have common etymological roots with that other major island of the Irish Sea, namely ANGLESEY, which was called *Mona* by the Romans. Here the sense is of a 'mountain', which in this case is SNAEFELL. The Old Manx name is *Ellan Vannan*.

Manchester (Greater Manchester) Probably the place of 'the Roman fort on the breast-shaped hill'. *Mamm* (Brythonic Celtic conjectural word) 'breast'; *ceaster*

(Old English) 'Roman station.' It is widely recognised that this famous northern city had its beginnings as the Roman fort of *Mamucium*, and that the well-known adjective 'Mancunian' must have resulted from a miscopying of the Roman name, which itself clearly had Brythonic Celtic roots. Records show: *Mamucio* in the 4th century; *Mameceaster* in 923; *Mamecestre* in the Domesday Book of 1086, and *Manchestre* by 1330. **Greater Manchester** was created as a new metropolitan county in 1974, covering the surrounding, largely urban conurbation.

Mangotsfield (Avon) 'Mangod's open land'. *Mangod* (Old German personal name); *feld* (Old English) 'open land'. The name of this town, adjoining BRISTOL to the northeast, was recorded as *Manegodesfelle* in the Domesday Book of 1086.

Manningtree (Essex) Possibly 'the tree associated with a man called Manna'. *Manna* (Old English personal name); *ing* (Old English connective particle) 'associated with'; *treow* (Old English) 'tree'. Like the nearby towns of BRAINTREE and TIPTREE, the name of this small town, northeast of COLCHESTER, may well have represented an actual tree or a man-made cross that could have been a prominent marker of a meeting place. However, some authorities now favour the alternative derivation of the first element as: *manig* (Old English) 'many', thus giving the sense of the whole name as the place of 'many trees' (*contrast* AINTREE). It was noted as *Manitre* in 1274 and *Manyngtre* in the 14th century.

Manorhamilton (Leitrim) This 'plantation town' east of SLIGO, is so named after Sir Frederick Hamilton, who was granted large confiscated lands here by Charles I.

Mansfield (Nottinghamshire) 'open land by the River Maun'. *Maun* (Brythonic Celtic river name based on root word *mamm*) 'breast'; *feld* (Old English) 'open land'. This industrial town, north of NOTTINGHAM, takes its name from the river on which it stands, which in turn derives from a nearby breast-like hill that was formerly known as *Mammesheud*. The name of the original settlement was recorded in the Domesday Book as *Mamesfelde*.

Mansfield Woodhouse (Nottinghamshire) 'Woodland hamlet near Mansfield'. This town, lying immediately to the north of MANSFIELD, after which it acquires its first name, was established early as a separate settlement, probably by people from the former. What appears as a distinguishing affix is simply derived from *wudu* (Old English) 'wood'; *hus* (Old English) 'house', but a record of 1230 shows that originally it was named *Wodeshuse* and in a text of 1280 it had become *Mamesfeud Wodehus*.

March (Cambridgeshire) Place on 'the boundary'. *Mearc* (Old English—locative form) 'boundary'. This Fenland town, east of PETERBOROUGH, sits on the old course of the River Neme, which would have provided a good natural boundary in this otherwise ill-defined flat terrain; it has been suggested that this may have been the western delimitation of the former 'Eel District' centred on ELY. The Domesday Book names it *Merche*.

Margam (West Glamorgan) This southeastern district of PORT TALBOT, with its large steel works here on the Margam Burrows, has a name that is essentially that of Morgan, who gave his name to GLAMORGAN.

Margate (Kent) Probably the place of 'the sea gate'. *Mere* (Old English) 'sea'; *geat* (Old English) 'gate', 'gap'. The name of this Isle of THANET resort at the eastern end of the north KENT coast may reflect a gap in the cliffs here that allowed for access down to the sea. It was documented as *Meregate* in 1254. *Compare* nearby RAMSGATE and BROADSTAIRS.

Market Drayton (Shropshire) 'Farmstead by a place used for dragging or to or from which loads were dragged'. *Merket* (Middle English distinguishing affix—later addition) 'market'; *draeg* (Old English) 'portage'; *tun* (Old English) 'farmstead'. This important farming town, northeast of SHREWSBURY, lies on the

River Tern, where the 'dragging' would have taken place in one form or another. The Domesday Book names it simply *Draitune*.

Market Harborough (Leicestershire) 'Market place on the hill where oats are grown'. *Merket* (Middle English status affix—later addition) 'market place'; *haefera* (Old English conjectural word corresponding to Old Scandinavian *hafri*) 'oats'; *beorg* (Old English) 'hill'. This agricultural town, southeast of LEICESTER, has a truly agrarian name that was recorded simply as *Hauerberga* in the 12th century, *Haverberge* in 1237, but *Mercat Heburgh* by 1312. *Compare* HAVERHILL.

Markethill (Armagh) This small town southeast of ARMAGH has an English name that simply means what it says, a description echoed in its Irish name, *Cnoc an Mhargaidh*, although the elements are reversed.

Market Rasen (Lincolnshire) 'Market place by the plank bridge'. *Raesn* (Old English) 'plank'; *merket* (Middle English affix) 'market'. This market town northeast of Lincoln, simply *Resne* in 1086, was thus distinguished later from the nearby hamlets of **Middle** and **West Rasen**.

Market Weighton (Humberside) 'Farmstead by an earlier Romano-British settlement'. *Market* (Modern English—19th-century distinguishing affix) 'market place'; *wic* (Old English—early loan word from Latin *vicus*) 'Romano-British settlement'; *tun* (Old English) 'farmstead'. The name of this agricultural town, northwest of HULL, appears in the Domesday Book of 1086 simply as *Wicstun*.

Markinch (Fife) 'Water meadow of the horse'. *Marc* (Scottish Gaelic) 'horse'; *inch* (Scottish Gaelic elided from *innis*) 'water meadow', 'island'. This small town, to the east of GLENROTHES, was reputedly built originally on an island in a lake that has since been drained, was recorded as *Marcinche* around 1200.

Marlborough (Wiltshire) Possibly Maerle's or gentian hill'. *Maerle* (Old English personal name); *meargella*

(Old English) 'gentian'; *beorg* (Old English) 'hill'. The name of this small town and its famous public school, which lie on the upper River Kennet at the foot of the **Malborough Downs**, was recorded in the Domesday Book as *Merleberge*.

Marlow (Buckinghamshire) Place on the land of 'the former pool'. *Mere* (Old English) 'pool', 'lake'; *laf* (Old English) 'residual', 'that which has been left or remains'. This riverside town on the north bank of the THAMES, south of HIGH WYCOMBE, arose on a dried-out pool by the river. It was recorded as *Merelafan* in 1015 and as *Merlaue* in the Domesday Book of 1086.

Marple (Greater Manchester) Place of 'the boundary stream'. *Gemaere* (Old English) 'boundary'; *pyll* (Old English) 'stream', 'river pool'. This small town, east of STOCKPORT, lies on the River Goyt, which formerly formed the boundary between CHESHIRE and DERBYSHIRE here. Early records of its name show: *Merpel* 1248; *Merphull* 1285; *Merpil* 1288.

Marsden (West Yorkshire) 'Boundary valley'. *Mearc* (Old English) 'boundary'; *denu* (Old English) 'valley'. This small town, southwest of HUDDERSFIELD, is set in a deep valley immediately east of the PENNINE watershed, and as such formerly represented part of the historic border between 'red rose' LANCASHIRE and 'white rose' YORKSHIRE. The name was documented in a 12th-century text as *Marchesden*. *Compare* TODMORDEN.

Marske-by-the-Sea (Cleveland) Place at 'the marshes'. *Merscum* (Old English—dative plural of *mersc*) 'marshes'. The basic name of this residential satellite town and coastal resort, east of MIDDLESBROUGH, is clearly descriptive of its original situation, while the later affix was added partly to distinguish it from the village of **Marske** near RICHMOND, as well as being of promotional benefit. The spelling of the basic name also witnesses Scandinavian influences; it was recorded as *Mersc* in the Domesday Book, and *Merscum* in 1104-08.

Maryhill (Strathclyde) This northside suburb of GLASGOW was named in 1760 after the local landowner, Mary Hill of Gairbraid. This proves to be an exception to the many 'real hill' district names in the city.

Marylebone (Greater London) Place by 'St Mary's stream'. *Mary* (English version of Church Latin *Sancte Marie*, name of the Virgin Mary) named after dedication of local church; *le* (Old French) 'the'—17th-century intrusive affectation; *burna* (Old English) 'stream'. This north-central LONDON district takes its name from the former Tyburn stream, which was renamed St Mary's in the 15th century, and by popular etymology it became Mary-le-bone, still commonly misinterpreted as 'Mary-the-Good'. Records show: *Tiburne* 1086 (Domesday Book); *Maryburne* 1453; *Maryborne* 1490.

Maryport (Cumbria) This coastal town on the SOLWAY FIRTH is named after Mary, the wife of Humphrey Senhouse who developed a harbour here by the earlier village of *Ellnesfoote* in the 18th century for the export of coal. This was the former site of the Roman station of *Alauna*, which also derived its name from the River Ellen, at whose mouth Maryport stands. *See* BRIDGE OF ALLAN.

Masham (North Yorkshire) 'Maessa's homestead'. *Maessa* (Old English personal name); *ham* (Old English) 'homestead', 'village'. The name of this small town, northwest of RIPON, was recorded as *Massan* in the Domesday Book of 1086.

Matlock (Derbyshire) 'The oak-tree meeting place'. *Maethel* (Old English) 'assembly'; *ac* (Old English) 'oak tree'. The name of this 'Derbyshire Dales' resort and former spa is noted as *Meslach* in 1086; *Matlac* in 1196.

Mauchline (Strathclyde) 'Plain with a pool'. *Magh* (Scottish Gaelic) 'plain'; *linne* (Scottish Gaelic) 'pool'. This small town, much associated with Robert Burns, lies on a fertile plain between the River AYR and the Cessnock Water. Its name is pronounced 'Mochlin', with a hard *ch* as in loch.

Maybole (Strathclyde) Possibly 'plain of danger'. *Magh* (Scottish Gaelic) 'plain'; *baoghail* (Scottish Gaelic) 'danger'. Presumably the open terrain here south of AYR, on the traditional 'land route' between Scotland and Ireland, was considered as offering little cover in early times. It was recorded as *Mayboill* in 1275. *See* MORPETH.

Mayfair (Greater London) Place of the annual 'May fair'. This opulent district of LONDON's 'West End', renowned for its galleries, shopping arcades and luxury hotels, was, until it was built over in the 18th century, the site of a long-standing annual fair held here during the month of May.

Maynooth (Kildare) 'Nuadu's plain'. *Maigh* (Irish Gaelic) 'plain'; *Nuadu* (Irish Gaelic personal name) legendary ancestor of the peoples of LEINSTER. This town situated on the plain to the west of DUBLIN is rendered as *Maigh Nua* in modern Irish.

Mayo (Mayo) 'Plain of the yew tree'. *Maigh* (Irish Gaelic) 'plain'; *eo* (Irish Gaelic) 'yew tree'. The village after which the county was named lies to the southeast of CASTLEBAR. It was originally associated with a monastery established here in the 7th century by St Colman, who retired from LINDISFARNE, and a group of English monks. As such it was then called *Magheo-na-Saxan*, signifying its pedigree as 'Mayo of the Saxons'. Its Irish name today is simply *Maigh Eo*.

Mearns, The (Grampian) 'The stewardship'. *An mhaoirne* (Scottish Gaelic) an area administered by an officially appointed steward. The area of the Mearns covers a triangular fertile area south of STONEHAVEN, as far as the North Esk river, and east of the Highlands, corresponding to the eastern part of the former county of KINCARDINEshire. This is the setting for Lewis Grassic Gibbon's trilogy about local rural life, *A Scots Quair*.

Meath (Ireland) 'The middle'. *Mide* (Irish Gaelic) 'middle'. The name of this county of east-central Ireland has its origins in ancient times, when it assumed significance as the fifth province and encompassed a wider area that included the present-day county of WESTMEATH. Thus its name then reflected its location between the lands of LEINSTER to the south, Connacht (*see* CONNAUGHT) to the west, and ULSTER to the north. The county of Meath dates from the 12th century. The modern Irish name is *An Mi*.

Medway (Kent/Sussex) Probably 'mead way'. *Medu* (Brythonic Celtic) 'mead'; *wey* (obscure etymology) 'way'. This river, which flows northeastwards from the WEALD to the THAMES estuary, has a name that implies that its waters where mead-like on account of either their colour or sweetness. The three towns of CHATHAM, GILLINGHAM and ROCHESTER, situated at the river mouth, are often collectively referred to as the 'Medway Towns'. The name was recorded in the 8th century as *Medeuuaege*.

Meironnydd *see* **Merioneth**

Melbourne (Derbyshire) Probably 'mill stream'. *Myln* (Old English) 'mill'; *burna* (Old English) 'stream'. Recorded as *Mileburne* in the Domesday Book of 1086, this small estate town, south of DERBY, lent its name to the city of Melbourne, state capital of Victoria, Australia, by way of the 19th-century British prime minister, Lord Melbourne, who took his title from the original place.

Melksham (Wiltshire) Probably 'homestead or river enclosure where cows produced plenty of milk'. *Meoluc* (Old English) 'milk'; *ham*; *hamm* (Old English) 'homestead'; 'riverside pasture', 'water meadow'. The name of this town on the River Avon, downstream and south of CHIPPENHAM, was recorded as *Melchesham* in 1086.

Melrose (Borders) Place on the 'bare moor'. *Mailo* (Brythonic Celtic) 'bare'; *ros* (Brythonic Celtic) 'moor'. This could well have described the original situation of this small abbey town set above the River TWEED. It was recorded as *Mailros* in a document of *c*.700.

Meltham (West Yorkshire) Possibly 'homestead by the

mill stream'. *Mylen-gelaet* (Old English) 'mill stream'; *ham* (Old English) 'homestead'. Although this small town, lying at the foot of the PENNINES southwest of HUDDERSFIELD, was named as now in the Domesday Book entry, it is on the basis of a later record of 1316 that renders it as *Muletham*, that this derivation is postulated by some authorities.

Melton Mowbray (Leicestershire) 'Middle farm on the Moubray estate'. *Middel* (Old English, Scandinavianised to *methal*) 'middle'; *tun* (Old English) 'farmstead'; *Moubray* (later Anglo-Norman manorial affix). The name of this historic market town and hunting centre, northeast of LEICESTER, appears as simply *Medeltone* in the Domesday Book, while a record of 1284 shows it to be *Melton Moubray*, confirming the possession of the local estate in the early 12th century by Roger de Moubray, from Montbray in Normandy.

Menai Bridge (Gwynedd) This town at the ANGLESEY end of the famous Thomas Telford road bridge across the Menai Strait arose and took its name directly from both the latter when the bridge was opened in 1826. The basic name is believed to have its origins in the Welsh root element *men-*, meaning 'carrying', with reference to the swift current in the narrows here. The Welsh name for the original smaller settlement before the bridge was built describes situation: *Porthaethwy*, meaning the 'ferry of the Daethwy people'.

Mendip Hills (Somerset) Probably the upland district of 'hills and valleys'. *Monith* (Brythonic Celtic conjectural word—related to Welsh *mynydd*) 'hill'; *hop* (Old English) 'valley'. This range of limestone hills, south of BRISTOL, recorded as *Menedepe* in 1185 and *Menedup* in 1225, has a second element whose derivation still remains unsatisfactory..

Menteith, Lake of (Central) The celebrated name of Scotland's only so-called 'lake', at least the only natural one, is not what appears at first sight to be a simple translation. Situated to the east of ABERFOYLE, it significantly occupies low-lying land up against the Highland edge, and its peculiarly non-Scottish generic name is a corruption of *laicht* (Scottish Gaelic) 'low-lying land'. Menteith derives as *mynydd* (Brythonic Celtic) 'mountain land'; *Teith* (Celtic river name) hence the name of the ancient local lands of Menteith. Early maps show *Loch Monteith* on the *Laicht of Monteith*, and records: *Menetethe* 1185; *Mynynteth* 1234; *Monteath* 1724.

Merioneth (Wales) 'Seat of Meirion'. The former county, sometimes known as Merionethshire, and now represented by the Welsh name *Meirionnydd* as the southern district of GWYNEDD, refers to Meirion, the son or possibly grandson of the 5th-century chieftain Cunedda, whose own name gave rise to that of Gwynedd.

Mersea, East and **West** (Essex) Places on 'the island of the sea'. *Mere-s* (Old English—genitive ending) 'sea'; *eg* (Old English) 'island'. Situated south of COLCHESTER, this coastal village and town are respectively located at the eastern and western end of **Mersea Island**, from which they derive their basic name. Early records show their names as: *Meresig* 895 (Anglo-Saxon Chronicle); *Meresai* 1086 (Domesday Book); *Estmereseia* 1196; *Westmeresheye* 1238.

Mersey (Greater Manchester/Merseyside) 'Boundary river'. *Gemaere* (Old English) 'boundary'; *ea* (Old English) 'river'. This famous English river has long formed an important natural boundary line; first, between the ancient kingdoms of Mercia and Northumbria in the early centuries of Anglo-Saxon settlement, and subsequently between the Anglo-Norman counties of CHESHIRE and LANCASHIRE, until the creation of the straddling MERSEYSIDE in recent times. The river name was recorded in a document of 1002 as *Maerse*, and it appears in the Domesday Book of 1086 as *Merse*.

Merseyside (England) This is the name adopted by the new metropolitan county, centred on LIVERPOOL on the MERSEY, and set up under the major boundary reforms of 1974. Technically speaking, as an administrative unit, its name no longer exists, as the powers of this and all the other five metropolitan counties were transferred in 1986 to the individual boroughs and districts of each former authority. *See* GREATER MANCHESTER; SOUTH YORKSHIRE; WEST MIDLANDS; WEST YORKSHIRE; TYNE AND WEAR.

Merthyr Tydfil (Mid Glamorgan) The burial place of the 'martyr Tydfil'. *Merthyr* (Welsh) 'martyr'; *Tudful* (Welsh personal name) female saint who was the daughter of the 5th-century Welsh prince Brychan. The name of this large industrial town at the head of the Merthyr Vale is thus dedicated to where she was murdered by Saxon pagans.

Merton (Greater London) 'Farmstead by the pool'. *Mere* (Old English) 'pool', 'lake'; *tun* (Old English) 'farmstead'. The origins of the name of this southwestern LONDON borough probably lie in a 'pool' in the River Wandle here. It was recorded as *Mertone* in 967 and *Meretone* in the Domesday Book of 1086.

Methil (Fife) Probably 'boundary wood'. *Maid* (Brythonic Celtic) 'boundary'; *choille* (Scottish Gaelic) 'wood.' Alternatively, as one authority suggests, it may derive: *methal* (Old Scandinavian) 'middle', signifying its location 'in the middle of' the two older places of Buckhaven and LEVEN. A record of 1250 shows *Methkil*.

Mevagissey (Cornwall) Church of 'Mewa and Ida'. *Mewa* (Old Cornish personal name) unidentified saint; *ag* (Old Cornish—contraction of *hag*) 'and'; *Ida* (Old Cornish personal name—*d* replaced by *s*) unidentified saint. The unusual name of this popular small resort, on the coast south of ST AUSTELL, was documented as *Mevagisi* in 1410.

Mexborough (South Yorkshire) 'Meoc's or Miuk's stronghold'. *Meoc*; *Miuk* (Old Danish personal name); *burh* (Old English) 'fortified place'. The name of this industrial town in the coal-mining district northeast of ROTHERHAM was noted as *Mechesburg* in the Domesday Book of 1086.

Middlesbrough (Cleveland) 'The middlemost stronghold'. *Midlest* (Old English) 'middlemost'; *burh* (Old English) 'fortified place'. Recorded as *Midelesburc* in a document of about 1165, the name of this now large industrial town and port on the TEES estuary, is considered by local historians to signify its location midway between DURHAM and WHITBY, originally serving as a 'halfway house' for travellers between these religious centres.

Middlesex (England) Tribal territory of 'the Middle Saxons'. *Middel* (Old English) 'middle'; *Seaxe* (Old English tribal name) 'Saxon'. Recorded as *Middelseaxan* in 704 and *Midelsexe* in the Domesday Book of 1086, this name originally referred to the 'Middle Saxon kingdom' that lay between the East Saxons of ESSEX, the South Saxons of SUSSEX and the West Saxons of WESSEX, and covered not only all of present-day GREATER LONDON but also most of SURREY and part of HERTFORDSHIRE. Subsequently, the smaller Anglo-Norman county of Middlesex was created to the north and west of LONDON, but since its absorption into Greater London in 1965, the name has ceased to exist except for certain London postal districts and various county activities such as cricket.

Middleton (Greater Manchester) 'Middle farmstead or estate'. *Middel* (Old English) 'middle'; *tun* (Old English) 'farm', 'estate'. This very common English place-name represents here a town midway between MANCHESTER to the south and ROCHDALE to the north. It was documented as *Middelton* in 1194.

Middlewich (Cheshire) 'The middlemost saltworks'. *Midlest* (Old English) 'middlemost'; *wic* (Old English) 'saltworks'. This salt and chemicals town lies almost equidistant between NORTHWICH and NANTWICH on the CHESHIRE Plain, under which is a major rock-salt deposit. *Wic*, the loan word from the Latin *vicus*, is seen here in one of its specialised meanings, reflecting the economic and social importance of salt in early times.

Records show: *Wich* and *Mildestvic* 1086 (Domesday Book); *Middelwich* 1185; *Medius Vicus* 1240.

Mid Glamorgan *see* **Glamorgan**.

Midhurst (West Sussex) Place 'amid wooded hills'. *Midd* (Old English—preposition) 'amid'; *hyrst* (Old English) 'wooded hill'. Recorded in a document of 1186 as *Middeherst*, the name of this small town midway between CHICHESTER and HASLEMERE aptly describes the local wooded topography even today.

Midlands *see* **West Midlands**.

Midleton (Cork) This 'plantation town' was built 'midway' between CORL and YOUGHAL by William III's mistress, Elizabeth Villiers, who was granted lands here, confiscated from James II after the Battle of the BOYNE in 1690.

Midlothian *see* **Lothian**.

Midsomer Norton (Avon) 'The north village of the midsummer festival of St John the Baptist'. *Midsomer* (Old English) 'midsummer'; *north* (Old English) 'north'; *tun* (Old English) 'village'. The very common English basic name of this town, southwest of BATH, is prefixed by an unusual term that refers to the former annual midsummer festival held here in medieval times and now represented by the Midsomer Norton Fair. The name was recorded as *Midsomeres Norton* in 1248, and *Midsummernorton* in 1269. *Compare* MAYFAIR.

Milborne Port (Somerset) Place of 'the mill stream, later made a borough'. *Mylen-burna* (Old English) 'mill stream'; *port* (Old English status affix) 'borough'. This small town, northeast of SHERBORNE, was recorded as *Mylenburnan* around 880; as *Meleburne* in 1086, and *Milleburnport* in 1249 after it was declared a borough.

Mildenhall (Suffolk) Probably place at 'the middle nook of land'. *Middel* (Old English) 'middle'; *halh* (Old English) 'nook or corner of land'. The name of this town, northeast of NEWMARKET, still associated with the discovery here in 1942 of a hoard of Roman silver, since known as the 'Mildenhall Treasure', was recorded as *Mildenhale* in about 1050, and *Middelhala* in 1162.

Mildenhall (Wiltshire) 'Milda's nook'. *Milda-n* (Old English personal name—genitive form); *halh* (Old English) 'nook of land'. Although spelt the same as the above SUFFOLK town, the origin of the name of this village east of MARLBOROUGH is quite different, as records confirm: *Mildanhald c.*800; *Mildenhalle* 1086.

Mile End (Greater London) Place at 'the end of a mile'. *Mil* (Old English) 'mile'; *ende* (Old English) 'end'. The simple and not uncommon name of this district of TOWER HAMLETS in this case reflects its location, literally a mile northeast of the ALDGATE, on the old HARWICH road. Recorded as *La Mile End* in 1288, the 'Hamlet of Mile End' was expanded in the 17th century.

Milford Haven (Dyfed) 'Sand fiord harbour'. *Melr* (Old Norse) 'sand'; *fjordr* (Old Norse) 'sea inlet', 'fiord'; *haven* (English related to Old English *haefen*) 'harbour'. Like many places associated with Welsh coastal features, this town and major port for large oil tankers to the south of HAVERFORDWEST, takes the Scandinavian name given to the large estuary and natural harbour on which it stands. The last element was added later when probably the original meaning had been lost. Early records show: *Milverdicus portus* c.1190; *Melyford* 1425; *Mylford* 1450; *Millford Havon* 1593. The Welsh name is *Aberdaugleddau*, meaning 'mouth of the two Cleddau', which describes the town's situation where these two rivers combine to form the estuary.

Millom (Cumbria) Place at 'the mills'. *Mylnum* (Old English—dative plural of *myln*) 'mills'. The name of this small town north across the Duddon Sands from BARROW-IN-FURNESS was recorded as *Millum* in 1180.

Millport (Strathclyde) This resort and port on the island of Great CUMBRAE, in the Firth of CLYDE, is so named after the large grain mill that stood above the harbour when the town was originally developed in the early 19th century.

Milngavie (Strathclyde) Apparently the place of the 'windmill'. *Muilleann* (Scottish Gaelic) 'mill'; *gaoithe* (Scottish Gaelic) 'wind'. However, there is no evidence of a windmill having existed here, although there were many traditional water mills. Alternatively, the origin of the name of this small town to the north of GLASGOW may be derived: *Meal-na-gaoithe* (Scottish Gaelic) 'hill'-'of the'-'wind', reflecting its location at the foot of the open Mugdock Moor. The name is pronounced 'Mul-guy' or 'Mill-guy'.

Milton Keynes (Buckinghamshire) 'Middle farmstead on the Kaynes estate'. *Middel* (Old English) 'middle'; *tun* (Old English) 'farmstead;' *Kaynes* (later Anglo-Norman manorial affix) Lucas de Kaynes, from Cahagnes in Normandy, took possession of the estate here in 1221. This New Town, designated in 1967, was developed around the original manorial village to the northeast of BLETCHLEY. Early records show: *Middeltone* 1086 (Domesday Book); *Middeltone Kaynes* 1227.

Minch, The (Highland/Western Isles) Possibly the sea of the 'great headland(s)'. *Megin* (Old Norse) 'great'; *nes* (Old Norse) 'headland'. This notoriously stormy stretch of sea between the northwest mainland of SCOTLAND and the Outer HEBRIDES is almost certainly Scandinavian in origin. The cape in question could either be CAPE WRATH, or the Butt of LEWIS, or indeed both, with them acting as the two pillars of the entrance to the Viking domain of the Hebrides and western Scotland.

Minehead (Somerset) Probably the place by 'the headland hill'. *Monith* (Brythonic Celtic conjectural word—related to Welsh *mynydd*) 'hill'; *heafod* (Old English) 'headland'. Recorded as *Mynheafdon* in 1046 and as *Maneheve* in the Domesday Book, the name of this BRISTOL Channel resort, northwest of TAUNTON, aptly describes its situation. *Compare* MENDIP HILLS.

Mintlaw (Grampian) Presumably the place of 'the mint mound'. *Minte* (Old English) 'mint'; *hlaw* (Old English) 'mound'. However, the derivation remains uncertain, which is surprising for this, the largest of the BUCHAN villages, was founded west of PETERHEAD only in 1813 as part of major agricultural improvements taking place at that time.

Mirfield (West Yorkshire) 'Pleasant open land' or 'open land where festivities took place'. *Myrge* (Old English) 'merry', 'pleasant'; *feld* (Old English) 'open land'. the name of this industrial town, southwest of DEWSBURY, was noted as *Mirefeld* in the Domesday Book.

Missenden, Great and **Little** (Buckinghamshire) Probably 'valley where the marsh water plants grow'. *Mysse* (Old English conjectural word—possible derivative of *mos*) 'water arum', 'marsh plant'; *denu* (Old English) 'valley'. These two neighbouring villages in the CHILTERN valley of the River Misbourne, northeast of HIGH WYCOMBE, were named simply *Missdene* in the Domesday Book of 1086, before distinguishing affixes were added.

Mitcham (Greater London) 'Large homestead'. *Micel* (Old English) 'large'; *ham* (Old English) 'homestead'. The simple name of this district of MERTON was documented as *Michelham* in the Domesday Book of 1086.

Mitcheldean (Gloucestershire) Place at 'the valley', with later superlative meaning 'great'. *Micel* (Old English distinguishing affix) 'great'; *denu* (Old English) 'valley'. The aptly descriptive name of this small town on the northern fringe of the FOREST OF DEAN was recorded as simply *Dena* in 1220, but as *Muckeldine* in a document of 1224.

Mitchelstown (Cork) This market town, north of FERMOY, apparently is named after its 13th-century Welsh-Norman founder, Mitchel Condon. In modern Irish the town's name is a straight translation: *Baile Mhistealai*.

Moffat (Dumfries and Galloway) Possibly the place of the 'long plain'. *Magh* (Scottish Gaelic) 'plain'; *fada* (Scottish Gaelic) 'long'. The reference here is to Annandale, this small market town being near the head of this long fertile valley.

Moher, Cliffs of (Clare) 'Cliffs of the ruined fort'. *Mothar* (Irish Gaelic term used in the south of Ireland) 'ruin of a caher', 'rath' or 'fort'. These precipitous sandstone sea cliffs, almost 700 ft (200m) high and stretching for five miles (8 km) along the Atlantic coast west of Ennistymon, are named after such an old fort at Hag's Head, which is known as *Moher O'Ruan*.

Moidart (Highland) Place of the 'muddy fiord'. *Moda* (Old Norse) 'mud'; *art* (Scottish Gaelic adaptation of Old Norse *fjordr*) 'sea loch'. This area of the west Highlands, sandwiched between ARDNAMURCHAN to the south and MORAR to the north, takes its name from the shallow and muddy sea loch that penetrates its hilly terrain.

Mold (Clwyd) 'High hill'. *Mont* (Old French) 'hill'; *hault* (Old French) 'high'. The name of this county town to the northwest of WREXHAM has a Norman French origin in which the root words of its derivation have been merged and shortened to its present form. Early records show the progressive contraction: *Montem Altum* 1278; *Moald* 1284. Bailey Hill, to the northwest of the town, on which there has been successive fortification over the ages, is the 'high hill' here.

Monadhliath (Highland) 'Land of the grey mountains'. *Monadh* (Scottish Gaelic) 'mountain land'; *liath* (Scottish Gaelic) 'grey'. This appropriate description applies to the extensive mountain range of grey mica-schist rock, lying between upper SRATHSPEY and the GREAT GLEN. These mountains are also grey in the sense of dull and uninteresting. In the first element is the derivation of 'The Mounth', the old name for the east GRAMPIANS.

Monaghan (Monaghan) The place of 'little thickets'. *Muineachan* (Irish Gaelic adaptation of *muine* with the diminutive suffix *-an*) 'small shrubbery' or 'thicket'. This northern county of the Republic is so named after its county town, lying over the border from ARMAGH.

Monifieth (Tayside) 'Peat-bed of the bog'. *Moine* (Scottish Gaelic) 'peat bed'; *feithe* (Scottish Gaelic) 'bog'. This residential town situated on the Firth of TAY, at the east of the DUNDEE built-up area was largely developed in the 19th century on a previously worked peat moss close to the shore. It is recorded as *Munifeth* 1220.

Monklands (Strathclyde) Simply 'monk lands'. This administrative district east of GLASGOW and centred on the adjoining towns of AIRDRIE and COATBRIDGE takes its name from the former parishes of Old and New Monkland of this area. However, the origin of the name goes back to the 12th century when King Malcolm IV granted lands here to the monks of Newbattle Abbey near DALKEITH.

Monks Risborough *see* **Risborough, Monks** and **Princes**.

Monmouth (Gwent) 'Mouth of the Monnow'. This historic market town, northeast of NEWPORT, lies at the confluence of the Wye and Monnow rivers, and thus its name is derived. The Welsh name is *Trefynwy*, meaning 'homestead on the Mynwy', the latter being Welsh for the Monnow river. Monmouth gave its name to the former county of **Monmouthshire** (now GWENT), which officially was part of England for three centuries until 1830.

Montgomery (Powys) The former county town of the shire of the same name, but now a village to the south of WELSHPOOL, is named after Roger de Montgomery, a loyal henchman of William the Conqueror, who acquired lands here after 1066. The Welsh name is *Trefaldwyn*, after Baldwin de Boulers, a later Norman baron here.

Montrose (Tayside) 'The peat-moss of the promontory'. *Moine* (Scottish Gaelic) 'peat bed'; *ros* (Scottish Gaelic) 'promontory'. The derivation precisely describes this historic east coast town's situation on a lowlying peninsula at the entrance to the tidal Montrose Basin, east of BRECHIN. The *t* in the name would seem to have been added at some point. Records show: *Munros* c.1200; *Montrose* 1296; *Monros* 1322; *Montross* 1480.

Moorgate (Greater London) 'Gate by the moor'. *Mor* (Old English) 'moorland', 'marshland'; *geat* (Old English) 'gate'. This district of east central LONDON has a self-descriptive name that reflects the building of a late medieval postern gate in the city walls here, just northeast of The Guildhall, which gave access on to 'The Moor' lying outside to the north and what is now the district of **Moorfields**.

Morar (Highland) Place of the 'big water'. *Mor* (Scottish Gaelic) 'big'; *dhobhar* (Scottish Gaelic loan word from Brythonic Celtic) 'water'. This part of the west Highlands, between KNOYDART to the north and MOIDART to the south, takes its name from the large loch that lies east-west at the centre of area, dividing it into North and South Morar. This freshwater loch, connected to the sea by the shortest of rivers, is also big in the sense of its great depth—at over 1000 ft (300 m) below sea level it is the deepest inland water in Britain.

Moray (Grampian) 'Sea settlement'. *Mori* (Old Gaelic elements related to Brythonic Celtic: *mor-tref*='sea-home'). The current administrative district and former county takes its name from the much larger ancient province of Moray, which gave its name to the **Moray Firth**.

Morden (Greater London) 'Elevated land by the marshes'. *Mor* (Old English) 'marshland'; *dun* (Old English) 'hill', 'elevated land'. The descriptive name of this district of MERTON was recorded as *Mordune* in 969, and *Mordone* in the Domesday Book of 1086.

Morecambe (Lancashire) Place on 'the curved arm of the sea'. *Mori-* (Brythonic Celtic root element) 'sea'; *cambo-* (Brythonic Celtic root element) 'curved'. This seaside resort, northwest of LANCASTER, takes its name from the bay on which it stands, whose own name was the result of an 18th-century revival of the old Celtic name *Morikambe*, first recorded by Ptolemy in about

150 AD. Prior to 1870, the town was known as *Poulton-le-Sands*.

Morningside (Lothian) The origin of the name of this pleasant residential EDINBURGH suburb, developed mainly in the 19th century, remains a mystery. It has been suggested that it simply reflected the movement of wealthier citizens to the sunny southern 'morning side' of town.

Morpeth (Northumberland) Apparently 'murder path'. *Morth* (Old English) 'murder'; *paeth* (Old English) 'path'. Recorded as *Morthpath* in about 1200, the somewhat unusual name of this market town, north of NEWCASTLE UPON TYNE, probably reflects a sense of prevailing danger, which was based on some early tragic event that took place on the Great North Road that passes by here. *Compare* MAYBOLE.

Mortlake (Greater London) Either 'Morta's or salmon stream'. *Morta* (Old English personal name); *mort* (Old English) 'young salmon'; *lacu* (Old English) 'stream'. Noted as *Mortelege* in 1086, the name of this riverside district of the borough of RICHMOND may refer to early descriptions of Beverley Brook, which flows through Richmond Park to enter the THAMES here.

Morvern (Strathclyde) 'Land of the sea gap'. *Mor* (Old Gaelic) 'sea'; *bhearn* (Scottish Gaelic) 'gap'. This is a triangular peninsula on the west Highland coast, lying south of ARDNAMURCHAN and bounded by the Sound of MULL and Loch Linnhe. The 'sea gap' is possibly Loch Sunart, a long fiord that penetrates along the north of this area, virtually cutting it off.

Mossley (Greater Manchester) 'Woodland clearing by a moss or peat bog'. *Mos* (Old English) or *mosi* (Old Scandinavian) 'mossy land'; *leah* (Old English) 'woodland clearing'. The name of this town in the valley of the River Tame, northeast of MANCHESTER, probably reflects the topographic conditions of the original settlement here. It was noted as *Mosslegh* in 1319.

Moss Side (Greater Manchester) Place at 'the edge of

the moss or marsh'. *Mos* (Old English) 'moss', 'peat bog'; *side* (Old English) 'edge', 'fringe', 'side'. This district of south MANCHESTER, developed in the late 19th century as a typical 'Coronation Street' area of working-class red-brick terraced houses, underwent major demolition in the 1960s and 1970s in favour of high-rise blocks. Although today often synonymous with urban deprivation and drug-related violence, its fairly common name originally described quite a different scene. It was recorded in 1530 as *Mossyde*.

Mostrim *see* **Edgeworthstown**.

Motherwell (Strathclyde) Simply 'Mother's well'. This former steel-making town in the CLYDE Valley to the southeast of GLASGOW takes its name from an ancient well dedicated to the Virgin Mary, the site of which is today marked by a plaque in Ladywell Road.

Mountain Ash (Mid Glamorgan) This South Wales town in the coal-mining district southeast of ABERDARE has a relatively modern English name that it acquired in the 19th century at the time of its industrial expansion. It is said to have been taken from the name of a local inn, whose own name may have referred to the common alternative for a rowan tree. The Welsh name of this settlement is *Aberpennar*, which describes its location at the confluence of the Penardd and Cynon rivers.

Mountmellick (Laois) 'Bogland of the water-meadows'. *Mointeach* (Irish Gaelic) 'bogland'; *miliuc* (Irish Gaelic) 'land near a river'. A descriptive name that is apt for this small market town in a boggy part of central Ireland.

Mourne Mountains (Down) This well-known range in the southwest of Northern Ireland is called *Beanna Boirche* in Irish, an ancient name that refers to 'the peaks of Boirche', claimed to be a 3rd-century royal shepherd of the ULSTER cattle. However, their English name is of a later origin, deriving from that of the Mughdhorna tribe who settled this area in the mid 12th century.

Mousehole (Cornwall) Place of a large 'mousehole' sea-cliff cavern. *Mus* (Old English) 'mouse'; *hol* (Old English) 'hole'. Pronounced 'Mowzell', this figuratively speaking straightforward name applies to the picturesque old fishing village on the coast south of PENZANCE. It was documented as *Musehole* in 1284.

Moville (Donegal) 'Plain of the ancient tree'. *Maigh* (Irish Gaelic) 'plain'; *bile* (Irish Gaelic) 'sacred' or 'historic tree'. This small market town and former transatlantic port of call on the west shore of Lough FOYLE has currently the Irish name of *Maigh Bhile*.

Much Wenlock *see* **Wenlock Edge**.

Muck (Highland) 'Pig island'. *Muc* (Scottish Gaelic) 'pig'. It is presumed that pigs once were kept here rather than the name describing a local feature of this small Inner Hebridean island.

Muckle Flugga (Shetland) 'Great cliffs'. *Mikill* (Old Norse) 'great', 'big'; *flugga* (Old Norse) 'cliffs'. Commonly held to be the most northerly piece of land of Britain, this is the outermost and highest of a group of sharp rocks or skerries protruding from the sea, just off the great cliffs of Herma Ness on the island of UNST. *See* OUT STACK.

Muine Bheag (Carlow) 'Little grove'. *Muine* (Irish Gaelic) 'grove', 'shrubbery'; *beag* (Irish Gaelic) 'small', 'little'. This small market town south of CARLOW was formerly called Bagenalstown, named after the English Bagenal family, who lived and developed the town here from the 16th century. The current Irish name of *Muine Bheag* is pronounced, roughly, 'Moneybeg'.

Muir of Ord (Highland) 'The moor of the rounded hill'. *Muir* (Scots version of Old English *mor*) 'moor'; 'of' (English); *ord* (Scottish Gaelic) 'rounded hill'. This linguistic mix describes well this important market town for the BLACK ISLE.

Mull (Strathclyde) Probably island of the 'headland'. Muli (Old Norse) 'headland'. Other suggestions have been made including: *maol* (Scottish Gaelic) 'bare summit'; *meuilach* (Scottish Gaelic) 'favoured one'. Thus the origin and meaning name of the third largest of the HEBRIDES remains in doubt.

Mullingar (Westmeath) 'The anticlockwise mill'. *Muileann* (Irish Gaelic) 'mill'; *cearr* (Irish Gaelic) 'wrong way'. This county town, lying at the centre of WESTMEATH, has a current Irish name of this meaning, namely *An Muileann gCearr*.

Mullion (Cornwall) Place of 'the church of St Melan'. This large village, south of HELSTON, lies just inland of the spectacular and secluded **Mullion Cove**, infamous in the past for smuggling. It was recorded as *Sancti Melani* in 1262 and *Seynt Melan* in 1284.

Mull of Kintyre *see* **Kintyre**

Munster (Ireland) 'Land of the Mumu people'. *Mumhan* (Irish Gaelic tribal name) Mumu people; *s* (Old Norse genitive); *tir* (Irish Gaelic) 'land', 'territory'. This ancient kingdom and historic province lay in the south of Ireland, including all lands southwest of a line running roughly from WATERFORD Harbour to the south side of GALWAY Bay. *See* CONNAUGHT, LEINSTER, MEATH and ULSTER.

Murrayfield (Lothian) This western suburb of EDINBURGH, which is the home of Scotland's national rugby ground, was named after an 18th-century local landowner and advocate, Archibald Murray.

Musselburgh (Lothian) Simply 'mussel town'. *Musle* (Old English) 'mussel'; *burh* (Old English) 'town'. This ancient burgh on the Firth of FORTH, immediately to the east of EDINBURGH, has been famous for its mussels for over 800 years. Its name was documented in 1100 as *Musleburge*.

Muswell Hill (Greater London) Hill of the 'mossy spring'. *Meos* (Old English) 'moss'; *wella* (Old English) 'spring', 'well'; *hyll* (Old English—later addition) 'hill'. This district of HARINGEY, famous as the second home of the 1862 international exhibition-built Alexandra Palace, which became the world's first television transmitting station in 1936, had a ancient well dedicated to St Mary, the site of which is still commemorated today in Muswell Road. Records of its name show: *Mosewella* 1152-60; *Muswell* 1535; *Mussell Hill* 1631. *Compare* MOTHERWELL.

N

Naas (Kildare) 'The assembly place'. *Nas* (Irish Gaelic) 'assembly place'. This county town of KILDARE, lying a little southwest of DUBLIN, was the ancient seat of the kings of LEINSTER until the 10th century, and as such was then an important meeting place for the great assemblies of state. In modern Irish its name is simply *An Nas*.

Nailsea (Avon) 'Naegel's island'. *Naegel* (Old English personal name); *eg* (Old English) 'island of elevated drier land'. This small town, southwest of BRISTOL, is on raised ground in this otherwise low-lying terrain here; its name was documented as *Nailsi* in 1196.

Nailsworth (Gloucestershire) 'Naegel's enclosure'. *Naegel* (Old English personal name); *worth* (Old English) 'enclosure'. The name of this small COTSWOLDS town, south of STROUD, has the same personal name although not necessarily the same man as in NAILSEA; it was recorded as *Naillleswurd*, also in 1196.

Nairn (Highland) This resort and former county town on the MORAY Firth, northeast of INVERNESS, takes its name from the river at whose mouth it stands. The meaning of this pre-Celtic river name is thought to be something to do with 'submerging' or 'penetrating'. The town's location was further reflected in early records of its name showing the 'inver' prefix: *Ilvernarran c.*1200; *Inernarn* 1283; *Narne* 1583.

Nantwich (Cheshire) Place of 'the famous saltworks'. *Named* (Middle English - later distinguishing affix) 'renowned', 'famous': *wic* (Old English) 'special premises'—'saltworks'. Originally simply *Wich*, as recorded in the Domesday Book in 1086, and later *Nametwihc*, as in a document of 1196, the name of this town situated southwest of CREWE, attests to its former role as a major centre of the salt industry. *See* DROITWICH; MIDDLEWICH; NORTHWICH.

Narberth (Dyfed) Place 'by the bushes'. *Yn* (Welsh) 'in' or 'by'; *ar* (Welsh) 'the'; *perth* (Welsh) 'bush', 'hedge'. Thus the anglicised name of this small market town east of HAVERFORDWEST is simply derived by the commonplace dropping of the initial *y* of the first word, and the consonant change from *p* to *b* in the last. The Welsh name, *Arberth*, is further abbreviated. *Compare* PERTH.

Naseby (Northamptonshire) 'Hnaef's stronghold'. *Hnaef* (Old English personal name); *byrig* (Old English—dative of *burh*, later replaced by Old Danish *by*) 'fortified place' substituted by 'village'. The name of this village, southwest of MARKET HARBOROUGH, is famous for the nearby site of the decisive victory for the Parliamentarian forces in 1645 during the Civil War; it was *Navesberie* in the Domesday Book of 1086, but by 1167 its recorded form had changed to *Nauesbi*.

Navan (Meath) 'The cave'. *Uaimh* (Irish Gaelic) 'cave'. This county town of MEATH, located at its centre, at the confluence of the BOYNE and Blackwater rivers, has an English name that is a corruption of its still commonly used Irish alternative name, *An Uaimh*, both alluding to a cave or grotto that originally would have been found by the rivers here.

Neagh, Lough (Antrim/Armagh/Londonderry/Tyrone) 'The lake of Eochy'. *Loch* (Irish Gaelic) 'lake'; *nEchach* (Irish Gaelic personal name) Eochy or Eochaid, the legendary king of MUNSTER who is said to have been drowned here in the 1st century at the time of an eruption beneath the lake. This, the largest area of inland water in the BRITISH ISLES, was recorded as Lough Eaugh on maps of the 16th and 17th centuries, and the initial *N* is a mere grammatical inflection deriving from its Irish root name.

Neasden (Greater London) 'Nose-shaped hill'. *Ness* (Middle English) 'nose'; *dun* (Old English) 'hill'. The name of this district of the borough of BRENT in northwest LONDON was noted as *Neosdune* in about 1000.

Neath (West Glamorgan) This metal-industries town northeast of SWANSEA lies on the River Neath, from which it takes its name. The river name, which is *Nedd* in modern Welsh, is of ancient Celtic origin and may mean 'shining one'. The Welsh name for the town is *Castell-nedd*, after the old Roman fort of *Nidum* here.

Needham Market (Suffolk) 'Homestead of the needy'. *Ned* (Old English) 'poverty'; *ham* (Old English) 'homestead'. Recorded as *Nedham* in the 13th century, this town southeast of STOWMARKET had become *Nedeham Markett* by 1511.

Needles, The (Isle of Wight) Place of 'the sharp rock pillars'. *Naedl* (Old English) 'needle', 'pillar', 'obelisk'. This is the aptly descriptive name given to the western tip of the island, where a central east-west ridge of vertically upturned white chalk ends dramatically in an exposed line of huge pointed sea stacks that extend out into the English Channel. A document of around 1400 refers to this notable physical feature as *Les nedeles del Isle de Wight*.

Nelson (Lancashire) The name of this 19th-century cotton textile town to the north of BURNLEY was taken from a local inn, called the 'Lord Nelson', which like many other public houses and places had been so named in commemoration of the admiral's famous victory at the Battle of Trafalgar in 1805. *Compare* WATERLOOVILLE.

Nenagh (Tipperary) The place of 'the fair'. *Aenach* (Irish Gaelic) 'a fair'. The initial *N* is a contraction for the Irish definite article *an* , as incorporated in its current Gaelic rendering, An tAnonach. This market town, northwest of LIMERICK, has long been a gathering point of one kind or another, its famous horse fairs of the past having been replaced today by its regular cattle market.

Ness (Highland) The celebrated **Loch Ness** (of 'Mon-ster' fame), which stretches for some 24 miles (38 km) down the GREAT GLEN, takes its name from the short River Ness that flows from it towards INVERNESS, and out to the North sea via the MORAY Firth. This pre-Celtic river name, which was *nesta* in an earlier form, means 'roaring' or 'rushing'. *See* INVERNESS.

Neston (Cheshire) 'Headland farmstead'. *Naess* (Old English) 'headland'; *tun* (Old English) 'farmstead'. This small town, together with the absorbed settlement of **Little Neston** and the neighbouring village of **Ness**, are all located near the DEE estuary at the western neck of the WIRRAL, and it is considered by some authorities that their names are a relic of *Ness*, which may have once been the name applied to the whole peninsula. Alternatively, there is a short ridge nearby that may be the local reference here. The Domesday Book record of 1086 shows *Nestone*.

Nevis (Highland) The origin of the name of Britain's highest mountain, **Ben Nevis** (4409 ft/1344m), is misted over by time as much as its top often is by cloud. Many authorities consider that it takes its name from the **River Nevis** in **Glen Nevis** skirting the mountain below, and the most favoured derivation is: *beinn* (Scottish Gaelic) 'mountain'; *nimheis* (Old Gaelic) 'venomous'. Many other unattested interpretations have been made, including: 'the awesome', 'the sky-high', 'the peak in the clouds', 'the Heaven'; the latter also applying to **Loch Nevis**, to the west. *See* KNOYDART.

New Abbey (Dumfries and Galloway) This small town, near the mouth of the River Nith, is so named after the Cistercian abbey founded here in 1273 by a Lady Devorgilla, who is buried in front of the high altar with the heart of her dead husband. The latter is the basis of the romantic name 'Sweetheart Abbey', now commonly given to the its ruins.

New Alresford *see* **Alresford**.

Newark-on-Trent (Nottinghamshire) Place of 'the new fortifications'. *Niwe* (Old English) 'new'; *weorc* (Old

English) 'works', 'buildings', 'fortifications'. This town on the River TRENT, upstream and northeast of NOTTINGHAM, derives its name by way of comparison with the former Roman station of *Margidunum*, which although some 10 miles (16 km) away was in early medieval times referred to as *Aldewerke*. The Newark here was recorded as *Niweweorce* in the late 11th century, and the distinguishing affix was added later.

Newbiggin-by-the-Sea (Northumberland) Place of 'the new buildings'. *Niwe* (Old English) 'new'; *bigging* (Middle English) 'building'. The basic name of this fishing port and coastal resort, east of ASHINGTON, is common in the north of England and Scotland, and simply denotes new building on an earlier occupied site. In this case the earliest record of 1187 shows the name as *Niwebiginga*; the distinguishing affix being added later.

Newbridge *see* **Droichead Nua**.

New Brighton (Merseyside) This coastal district of WALLASEY, occupying the northern tip of the WIRRAL peninsula, was founded as a resort in 1845, taking its name from the then very fashionable SUSSEX seaside town.

Newburgh (Fife) Simply 'new town'. *Neowe* (Old English) 'new'; *burh* (Old English) 'town'. However, it is one of the oldest 'new' towns in Scotland, having received its *Novus burgus* charter in 1266.

Newburn (Tyne and Wear) Place of 'the new stream'. *Niwe* (Old English) 'new'; *burna* (Old English) 'stream'. This industrial suburb on the north bank of the River TYNE, west of NEWCASTLE UPON TYNE, has a simple name that indicates the change in the course of a local stream. It was recorded as *Neuburna* in about 1125.

Newbury (Berkshire) 'New market town'. *Niwe* (Old English) 'new'; *byrig* (Old English—dative of *burh*) 'fortified place', but here with a later sense of a market town. The name of this historic market town, located at an ancient crossroads of major north-south and east-west routes, was noted as *Neuberie* c.1080.

Newcastle (Down) The self-explanatory name of this coastal resort, lying in the shadow of SLIEVE DONARD of the MOURNE MOUNTAINS, stems from a 16th-century castle that was built here in this then new 'plantation town'.

Newcastle Emlyn (Dyfed) This small market town, east and upstream on the River Teifi from CARDIGAN, is so called on account of the 'new castle' built here in the 13th century. The distinguishing second element was the name of the local district in medieval times, and it is derived directly from the Welsh *am glyn*, which literally means 'round the valley'. The Welsh name, *Castellnewydd Emlyn*, has precisely the same meaning.

Newcastle upon Tyne (Tyne and Wear) Place of 'the new castle above and by the River Tyne'. *Niwe* (Old English) 'new'; *castel* (Old English) 'castle'; *upp-an* (Old English—related to Old Saxon *up-an*) 'above and by'; *Tyne* (Brythonic Celtic river name) simply 'river'. The name of this famous city in northeast England refers to the building, in the late 11th century, of a 'new' Anglo-Norman castle here on the steep north bank of the River TYNE, at a strategic bridging point that had been formerly guarded by the Roman fort of *Pons Aelii*, which meant 'Hadrian's Bridge'. The current name was first recorded in a Latin text of 1130 as *Novum Castellum*.

Newcastle West (Limerick) This market town to the east of LISTOWEL derives its name from the large, mainly 15th-century Desmond castle here. The locative element of 'West' is a latterday addition to distinguish this town from others in the east that have this fairly common name.

Newcastle-under-Lyme (Staffordshire) Place of 'the new castle in the elm-tree region'. *Niwe* (Old English) 'new'; *castel* (Old English) 'castle'; *under* (Old English—related to Old Saxon *undar*) 'near'; *Lyme* (Brythonic Celtic district name) 'place of elms'. The basic name of this industrial town, adjoining STOKE-ON-TRENT to the west, denotes the then 'new' Anglo-Norman castle built here in the 12th century. The distinguishing affix makes reference, as in ASHTON-UNDER-LYNE, to the extensive elm forest that once existed near here. The complete name is recorded in a Latin text of 1173: *Novum castellum subtus Lymam*.

New Forest (Hampshire) Literally 'the new forest'. *Niwe* (Old English) 'new'; *forest* (Old French from Medieval Latin *forestis*) 'large, heavily wooded area'. This extensive area of woodland and heath, to the south and west of SOUTHAMPTON, was created as a 'new' royal hunting preserve by William the Conqueror in the 1070s. Its entry in the Domesday Book of 1086 appears as *Nova Foresta*.

New Galloway (Dumfries and Galloway) This small Royal burgh, at the head of Loch Ken, had its charter granted by King Charles I in 1629 to Sir John Gordon. Its name, first recorded as The New Town of Galloway in 1682, is a reference to the fact that the Gordon family already owned other properties in GALLOWAY.

Newham (Greater London) The name of this east-central LONDON borough was devised and adopted in 1965 upon the amalgamation of the two existing towns of East and West Ham, under the provisions of the London Government Act of 1963. Although originally intended to be rendered as two separate words, the coalesced form has prevailed. *See* GREATER LONDON; WEST HAM.

Newhaven (East Sussex) Place of 'the new harbour'. *Niwe* (Old English) 'new'; *haefen* (Old English) 'harbour'. The name of this busy Channel port, southeast of BRIGHTON, refers to the 16th-century development of a 'new harbour' here at the site of the former settlement of *Mechingas*, as part of the efforts of a local landowner to drain the marshland in the valley of the River Ouse, at the mouth of which the town is situated. A record of 1587 shows *Newehaven*.

New Lanark *see* **Lanark**

Newlyn (Cornwall) Probably 'the pool for a fleet of boats'. *Lu* (Old Cornish) 'host', 'army', 'fleet of boats'; *lynn* (Old Cornish) 'pool', 'harbour'. The name of this former fishing port, now a southern suburb of PENZANCE, was recorded as *Lulyn* in 1290, and it is considered by some authorities that it has assumed its current form by a process of association.

New Malden *see* **Malden**.

Newmarket (Suffolk) 'New' settlement with a 'market'. *Niwe* (Old English rendered by Latin *novum*) 'new'; *market* (Middle English rendered by Latin *forum*) 'market place'. This town, northeast of CAMBRIDGE, famous as the home of the National Stud and headquarters of British horse racing, has a name like NEWBURY in that the implication here is of an entirely new establishment rather than a new for old market place. A record of 1200 shows *Novum Forum*.

Newport (Gwent; Isle of Wight) 'New market town/port'. *Niwe* (Old English) 'new'; *port* (Old English) 'gate', that comes to represent a market town. These two notable examples of this common place-name, one the GWENT county town near the mouth of the River Usk, the other the chief town of the ISLE OF WIGHT at the head of the Medina river estuary, exemplify its double meaning of being both a new 'market town' and 'port' in the literal sense. Often it is the former meaning that is the origin of the name, especially where such names occur inland. *See* NEWPORT-ON-TAY; NEWPORT PAGNELL.

Newport-on-Tay (Fife) This town on the south side of the Firth of TAY, directly across from DUNDEE, was established as a 'new' port in medieval times with ferry connections until the advent of the late 19th-century rail bridge and the road bridge in 1966.

Newport Pagnell (Buckinghamshire) 'New town with market rights, later incorporated into the Paynel manor'. *Niwe* (Old English) 'new'; *port* (Old English) 'town with market'; *Paynel* (later Anglo-Norman manorial affix) Fulc Paynel, 12th-century lord of the manor. The name of this town, north of MILTON KEYNES, was recorded as simply *Neuport* in the Domesday Book of 1086, but *Neuport Paynelle* in 1220.

New Quay (Dyfed) This small resort on the coast of CARDIGAN Bay southwest of ABERAERON was so named in 1835 with the construction of a 'new quay' at the harbour here, which was a catalyst for development of the town. Its Welsh name, *Ceinewydd*, has the same meaning.

Newquay (Devon) Place of 'the new quay'. *Niew* (Old English) 'new'; *key* (Middle English) 'quay'. This seaside resort and renowned surfing centre, north of TRURO, acquired its present name in the 15th century when a new harbour wall and quay were built here on behalf of the Bishop of Exeter; it appeared as *Newe Kaye* in 1602.

New Romney *see* **Romney, New** and **Old**.

New Ross (Wexford) This 12th-century Anglo-Norman town and inland port on the River Barrow acquired its name by way of distinction from the nearby village of the now-called Old Ross that originally had the Irish name *An Sean Ros*, meaning 'the old wood'.

Newry (Down) Apparently 'the yew tree at the end of the strand'. *Iubhar-ceann-traigh* (Irish Gaelic) 'yew tree'-'at the head of'-'the strand'. This ancient, rather than 'new', name was later shortened to *Iubhar* but with the initial *N* of the abbreviated definite article prefixed, and the *y* added to give its present form. Traditionally the name of this port inland from CARLINGFORD Lough, is said to be associated with a yew tree planted at the head of the lough by St Patrick in the 6th century when he founded a monastery here. The tree and monastery were both later burned down.

New Scone *see* **Scone**

Newtonabbey (Antrim) This large mainly residential town lying on the west shore of BELFAST Lough, north of the city boundary, has a name that originates only from 1958. It was the creation of the new suburban district authority that had arisen from the expansion and coalescing of seven former villages, thus forming a 'new town'. The latter 'abbey' element is taken from one of the constituent settlements, namely Whiteabbey.

Newton Abbot (Devon) 'New farm of the abbey'. *Niwe* (Old English) 'new'; *tun* (Old English) 'farm'; *abeie* (Old French—distinguishing monastic affix) 12th-century possession by Torre Abbey. This market town, north-west of TORQUAY, has the commonest English basic name. Records show: *Nyweton c.*1195; *Nyweton Abbatis* 1270.

Newton Aycliffe (Durham) This post-war New Town, north of DARLINGTON, is one of the earliest, having been designated in 1947. As such it adopted the common placename form of 'Newton' for its own obvious reasons, attaching it as a prefix to the name of the existing village of **Aycliffe**, which is now incorporated as a southern suburb of the town. Recorded as *Aclea* in about 1085, the original meaning of the latter is 'oak wood or clearing', being derived: *ac* (Old English) 'oak tree'; *leah* (Old English) 'wood', 'woodland clearing'.

Newtongrange (Lothian) This former coal-mining town south of DALKEITH was so called in contradistinction to the older grange of the nearby Newbattle Abbey, namely Prestongrange near PRESTONPANS.

Newton-le-Willows (Merseyside) 'New farmstead by the willow trees'. *Niwe* (Old English) 'new'; *tun* (Old English) 'farmstead'; *le* (Old French definite article remaining after loss of preposition) 'by the'; *welig* (Old English) 'willow tree'. Recorded in the Domesday Book as simply *Neweton*, this town in the coal-mining district east of ST HELENS, subsequently became *Neuton Macreffeld*, as documented in 1257, before adopting the alternative of its present distinguishing affix. *See* ASHTON-IN-MAKERFIELD.

Newtonmore (Highland) 'New town on the moor'. This holiday village in upper STRATHSPEY was virtually a late-19th-century creation of the PERTH to INVERNESS railway and the tourist trade it brought. It is situated where the valley floor gives way to moorland.

Newton St Boswells *see* **St Boswells**

Newton Stewart (Dumfries and Galloway) This 'new town', on the right bank of the River Cree close to its discharge into WIGTOWN Bay, was established in 1671 by William Stewart, third son of the 2nd Earl of GALLOWAY, who obtained a burgh charter from King Charles II.

Newtownards (Down) Although on the site of a ruined 13th-century Dominican priory, this town and its name stem from its creation as a 17th-century 'plantation town'. The last element is simply the locative suffix distinguishing this 'new town' as being the one set up on the ARDS PENINSULA, a little way inland from the head of CARLINGFORD Lough. In Irish it is *Baile Nua na hArda*.

Newtownstewart (Tyrone) Another 'plantation town' of the 17th century, situated midway between OMAGH and STRABANE, and named after its founder, William Stewart, who was confirmed in lands here by Charles I.

New Tredegar (Mid Glamorgan) This mid-19th-century industrial town in the Rhymney Valley is named after the landowner of the time, Lord Tredegar. The 'New' prefix was included to distinguish this place from TREDEGAR, which had been established in the next valley east only a few years earlier.

Neyland (Dyfed) Place 'at the island'. *Atten* (Middle English abbreviated to the initial *N*) 'at the'; *eg-land* (Old English) 'island'. This small town and former port on a virtual island-peninsula east of MILFORD HAVEN, was at the turn of the century known as *New Milford*.

Nigg (Highland) Place on 'the bay'. *An uig* (Scottish Gaelic adaptation of the Old Norse *vik*) 'bay'. This village, which has greatly expanded in recent times as an oil rig construction centre, is situated on the tautologic **Nigg Bay** in the northern part of the CROMARTY Firth.

Nithsdale (Dumfries and Galloway) The River 'Nith's dale'. This administrative district centred on Dumfries is named after the River Nith, which derives from *Nedd* (*Neath* in Wales; *Nidd* in England) meaning 'glistening'.

Norfolk (England) Territory of 'the northern folk' of the East Angles. *North* (Old English) 'north', 'northern'; *folc* (Old English) 'folk', 'people'. The relatively self-explanatory contracted name of this northernmost county of EAST ANGLIA was recorded as *Nordfolc* in the Domesday Book of 1086. *Compare* SUFFOLK.

Normanton (West Yorkshire) 'Farmstead of the Norsemen or Norwegian Vikings'. *Northman* (Old English) 'Viking from Norway', 'Norseman'; *tun* (Old English) 'farmstead'. This fairly common name in the north of England applies here to a coal-mining town northeast of WAKEFIELD. It appears as *Normantone* in the Domesday Book.

Northallerton (North Yorkshire) 'Aelfhere's farm'. *Aelfhere* (Old English personal name); *tun* (Old English) 'farmstead'. This town, south of DARLINGTON, was noted as *Aluretune* in the Domesday Book, and with the 'north' affix added later, it became *North Alverton* by 1293.

Northam (Devon) Simply 'northern homestead'. *North* (Old English) 'northern'; *ham* (Old English) 'homestead'. This small town, north of BIDEFORD, was recorded in the Domesday Book exactly as now. It is not known what settlement represented the 'Southam' in the normal process of contradistinction.

Northampton (Northamptonshire) 'Northern home farm'. *North* (Old English—distinguishing affix) 'northern'; *ham-tun* (Old English) 'home farm', 'homestead'. Recorded as simply *Hamtun* in 917, the name of this county town on the River Nene, 60 miles (96 km) northwest of LONDON, had by 1065 been prefixed by 'north' to distinguish it from SOUTHAMPTON. Documentation of the corresponding county name also manifests the same change: *Hamtunscir* 1011; *Northhamtunscir* 1114. The widely used abbreviation for the latter is 'Northants', the basis for this name form being exactly the same as 'Hants' is short for HAMPSHIRE.

North Berwick (Lothian) North 'barley farmstead'. *Bere* (Old English) 'barley'; *wic* (Old English) 'farmstead'. This coastal resort on the Firth of FORTH is set amidst the rich barley fields of East LOTHIAN and thus its name is very descriptive. However, the first locative element may suggest that this name was transferred here from BERWICK-UPON-TWEED, presumably at an early date. It was recorded as *Northberwyk* in 1250. Mysteriously, there is a reference in a text of 1187 to the border town as *Suth Berwyc*. *See* BERWICK-UPON-TWEED.

North Downs *see* **Downs, The**.

Northern Ireland (Ireland) The official name of the 'constituent region' of the UNITED KINGDOM occupying the northeastern part of Ireland, and constitutionally separated from the rest of Ireland when the latter became independent in 1921. It is commonly referred to as 'Ulster', or even as 'the Province', but it contains only six of the nine counties that made up the former province of ULSTER. *Compare* REPUBLIC OF IRELAND.

Northfleet (Kent) 'Northern' place at 'the stream'. *North* (Old English—distinguishing affix) 'northern'; *fleot* (Old English) 'stream'. Recorded as *Flyote* in the 10th century, this now industrial town that originally arose on a creek off the THAMES, immediately upstream of GRAVESEND, was later documented as *Norflvet* in the Domesday Book, in contradistinction to the nearby village of Southfleet.

North Lancing *see* **Lancing**.

Northolt (Greater London) 'Northern nooks of land'. *North* (Old English) 'northern'; *healum* (Old English—dative plural of *halh*) 'nooks', 'secluded corners of land'. This district of EALING, whose name is well known for its military airport, is the 'northern' counterpart to SOUTHALL. Its name was noted as *Northealum* in a 10th-century text.

North Queensferry *see* **Queensferry, North** and **South.**

North Ronaldsay *see* **Ronaldsay, North.**

North Shields *see* **Shields, North** and **South**.

North Tidworth *see* **Tidworth, North** and **South**.

North Uist *see* **Uist, North** and **South.**

Northumberland (England) Territory of the peoples living 'north of the Humber'. *Northhymbre* (Old English tribal name) Anglo-Saxon peoples who settled in northern England and southeastern Scotland from the 6th century; *land* (Old English) 'district'. The early kingdom of *Northumbria*, as it is more commonly known, was a much larger territory than the present county of Northumberland, which as part of the new Anglo-Norman administration, dates from the early 12th century. The name was recorded as *Northhymbre* in 867, *Northhymbraland* in 895, and *Norhumberland* in 1130.

North Walsham (Norfolk) 'Walh's homestead'. *North* (Old English—distinguishing affix) 'northern'; *Walh* (Old English personal name); *ham* (Old English) 'homestead', 'village'. The name of this market town, north of NORWICH, was noted in a text of 1044-47 as *Northwalsham* in contradistinction to the village of South Walsham, 12 miles (20 km) to the southeast.

Northwich (Cheshire) 'Northern saltworks'. *North* (Old English) 'northern'; *wic* (Old English) 'saltworks'. The aptly descriptive name of the northernmost of the CHESHIRE saltworking towns was recorded as *Norwich* in the Domesday Book of 1086. *See* MIDDLEWICH; NANTWICH.

North Yorkshire *see* **Yorkshire**.

Norton (North Yorkshire) 'Northern farmstead'. *North* (Old English) 'northern'; *tun* (Old English) 'farmstead', 'village'. Recorded as *Nortone* in the Domesday Book, this town on the south bank of the River Derwent, opposite MALTON, has the very common English placename that implies that it was 'a farmstead that was north of another'. In this case, the 'southern' counterpart settlement could have been the village of Full Sutton, *Sudtone* in the Domesday Book, that is 10 miles (16 km) to the south, or Sutton upon Derwent, also *Sudtone* in 1086, 16 miles (25 km) southwards and downstream on the common river.

Norwich (Norfolk) 'North port or harbour town'. *North* (Old English) 'north'; *wic* (Old English) 'specialised place', in this case 'harbour town'. This county town and cathedral city, although well inland, has since early times been an important tidal river port at the confluence of the Are and Wensum rivers. It was regarded as the 'northern' counterpart of the harbour town of IPSWICH, which lies 40 miles (64 km) due south. It was documented as *Northwic* around 930 and appears in the Domesday Book of 1086 as *Noruic*.

Noss (Shetland) 'The nose'. *Nos* (Old Norse) 'nose'. This small uninhabited island, lying just off the far east side of BRESSAY from LERWICK, is aptly named. Its green sward rises to a high snout in the spectacular cliffs of the Noup of Noss—the archetypal 'bird city'.

Nottingham (Nottinghamshire) 'Homestead of Snot's people'. *Snot* (Old English personal name); *inga* (Old English—genitive of *ingas*) 'people of'; *ham* (Old English) 'homestead'. The name of this county town and major East MIDLANDS city was recorded as *Snotengaham* in 862; *Snotingaham* in 922; *Snotingeham* in 1086; and *Notingham* 1087-1100, showing that the dropping of the initial *S-* was due to Norman influence. The county name, **Nottinghamshire**, was originally recorded as *Snotingahamscir* in 1016, and appears in the Domesday Book as *Snotingehamscyre*.

Notting Hill (Greater London) Probably 'hill of the Knotting family'. *Knotting* (Old English personal name) possible early landowner—a surname that derives from Knotting in Bedfordshire; *hyll* (Old English) 'hill'. The name of this west LONDON district, nowadays associated with its colourful annual street carnival, was recorded as *Knottynghull* in 1356.

Nuneaton (Warwickshire) 'Riverside farmstead of the nuns'. *Nunne* (Old English—later prefix) 'nun'; *ea* (Old English) 'river'; *tun* (Old English) 'farmstead'. Recorded as simply *Etone* in the Domesday Book of 1086, the name of this industrial town, north of COVENTRY, became *Nonne Eton* as in a text of 1247, with reference to a Benedictine nunnery that was founded here in the 12th century. *Compare* ETON.

O

Oadby (Leicestershire) Probably 'Authi's farmstead'. *Authi* or *Outhi* (Old Danish personal name); *by* (Old Danish) 'farmstead', 'village'. The name of this original Danelaw settlement, now a town adjoining LEICESTER to the southeast, is documented as: *Oldebi* 1086 (Domesday Book); *Outheby* 1199; *Oudeby* 1204.

Oakengates (Shropshire) 'The gap where oak trees grow'. *Acen* (Old English) 'oak trees'; *geat* (Old English) 'gate', 'gap'. The name of this town, which now forms part of TELFORD New Town, was noted in 1535 as *Lee Okynyate*.

Oakham (Leicestershire) Either 'Oca's or Occa's homestead or meadow'. *Oca* or *Occa* (Old English personal name); *ham* or *hamm* (Old English) 'homestead' or 'riverside pasture'. The latter derivation would appear the more likely for this former county town of RUTLAND, situated between two streams west of Rutland Water. It was recorded as *Ocham* in 1167, and *Ocheham* in the 1086 Domesday Book.

Oban (Strathclyde) Place of 'the little bay'. *Ob* (Scottish Gaelic) 'bay'; *-an* (Scottish Gaelic diminutive suffix) 'little'. This west Highland port, railhead and resort lies on a small sheltered bay off the Sound of Kerrera, which is off the wider Firth of LORN. Indeed, its name derives from the fuller Gaelic version: *An t- Oban Lartharnach*, which means 'the little bay of Lorn'.

Ochill Hills (Central/Tayside) 'High hills'. *Uchel* (Brythonic Celtic) 'high'; 'hills' (English) 'upland area'. The 'Ochills', as they are colloquially known, stretch some 25 miles (40 km) from STIRLING to PERTH, and rise steeply to over 2000 ft (600 m), and as such not only appear to be but are the highest of the upland areas of central Scotland. The earliest references are to *Cind Ochil* in AD700; *Sliab Nochel* 850; *Oychellis* 1461.

Offaly (Ireland) 'Lands of Ui Failghe people'. *Ui Failghe* (Irish Gaelic tribal and territorial name) corrupted to Offaly: the descendants of Ros Failghe and their lands. The name of this county at the centre of Ireland ultimately derives from Ros Failghe, the semi-legendary eldest son of Cahirmore, the 2nd-century king of Ireland. The present county was established in 1556 under the name of King's County, after King Philip II of Spain, who was married to the Tudor Queen Mary of England and Ireland. This name remained until Irish independence in 1921, when the territory's ancient name was reinstituted. *Uibh Fhaili* is the current Irish name for the county. *Compare* LAOIS.

Offa's Dyke (England/Wales) This is the English name for the immense system of earthworks extending over 140 miles (250 km) from PRESTATYN on the North Wales coast to the SEVERN estuary near CHEPSTOW, built at the command of King Offa, an 8th-century ruler of Mercia, who wished to consolidate the frontier between Saxon and Welsh territory along this visible boundary line. The modern English word 'dyke' is derived from the Old English *dic*, which can mean a ditch as well as an embankment, and in this sense is an appropriate description of this spectacular construction which included a deep ditch dug on the Welsh side and above this an earthwork barrier that rose up to 20 ft (6 m), the overall structure being over 70 ft (22 m) wide in places. Its Welsh name is *Clawdd Offa*.

Okehampton (Devon) 'Farmstead on the River Okement'. *Okement* (Brythonic Celtic river name) 'swift one'; *tun* (Old English) 'farmstead'. This town takes its name from the river whose east and west branches meet here on the northern slopes of DARTMOOR. Records show: *Ocmundtun* c.970; *Ochenemitona* 1086 (Domesday Book).

Oldham (Greater Manchester) Place of 'the old promontory'. *Ald* (Old English) 'old'; *holm* (late Old English from Old Norse *holmr*) 'promontory'. Recorded late as *Aldholm* in 1226-28, the name of this town northeast of MANCHESTER reflects its location on a spur of land, a feature emphasised in the northern district of the town known as **Oldham Edge**.

Old Kilpatrick (Strathclyde) Old place of 'St Patrick's church'. *Cill* (Scottish Gaelic) 'church'; *Padraig* (Scottish Gaelic personal name) Patrick, patron saint of Ireland (AD387-458) who, according to tradition, was born here. This village is situated on the north bank of the River CLYDE, 10 miles (16 km) downstream from GLASGOW, at the western end of both the ANTONINE WALL and the FORTH and CLYDE Canal. Formerly known simply as Kilpatrick, the parish was split in 1649, since when it was prefixed first by 'West', and latterly by 'Old'. The Kilpatrick Hills rise immediately behind the village.

Oldmeldrum (Grampian) Possibly old 'bare-topped ridge'. *Maol* (Scottish Gaelic) 'bare-topped'; *druim* (Scottish Gaelic) 'ridge'. This small rural town lies in undulating country to the northeast of ABERDEEN. The 'Old' was added later when the former parish was split.

Old Sarum *see* **Salisbury**.

Old Scone *see* **Scone.**

Old Trafford (Greater Manchester) The name of this southern dockland district of SALFORD, better known today for it famous cricket and football grounds, is a Normanised form of STRETFORD, the neighbouring town. *See* the latter for derivation of the original name.

Olney (Buckinghamshire) 'Olla's island'. *Olla-n* (Old English personal name—genitive form); *eg* (Old English) 'island'. This small town lies in a pronounced river bend of the Great Ouse, which would have given rise to the 'island-like' situation. Records show: *Ollanege* in 979 and *Olnei* in the Domesday Book of 1086.

Omagh (Tyrone) Possibly just means the place on the

'plain'. *Maigh* (Irish Gaelic) 'plain'. Certainly this simple description suits this market town at the centre of a plain lying southwest of the Sperrin Mountains. The origin of the initial *O* remains a mystery. The name was recorded in the 15th century as *Oghmaigh* and its current Irish form is *An Omaigh*.

Ongar *see* **Chipping Ongar**.

Orkney (Scotland) Possibly 'the Boar tribe's islands'. *Orc* (pre-Celtic root mentioned in Latin texts of 320BC) 'boar', 'pig' or 'whale'; assimilated into Old Norse as *Orkn-ey*, meaning 'seal island(s)'. This ancient name of uncertain derivation was recorded by the Romans in the 1st century AD as *Orcades*, which may have evolved from the contemporary record of a cape *Orcas* (probably Dunnet Head) as being the extremity of Britain.

Ormskirk (Lancashire) 'Ormr's church'. *Ormr* (Old Norse personal name); *kirkja* (Old Norse replacement for Old English *cirice*) 'church'. The name of this town, north of LIVERPOOL, was documented as *Ormeschirche* in about 1196 and *Ormeskierk* in 1203.

Oronsay (Strathclyde) 'St Oran's isle'. *Oran* (Irish Gaelic personal name) 6th-century Irish monk; *ey* (Old Norse) 'island'. This small island, separated from COLONSAY to the north by a narrow tidal strand, was where, traditionally, Columba first landed with Oran.

Orpington (Greater London) 'Estate associated with a man called Orped'. *Orped* (Old English personal name); *ing* (Old English connective particle) 'associated with'; *tun* (Old English) 'estate', 'farmstead'. The name of this residential suburb on the southeast edge of LONDON, well known for the famous Liberal by-election victory here in 1962, was recorded as *Orpedingtun* in 1032.

Orrel (Greater Manchester) Probably 'hill where ore is dug'. *Ora* (Old English) 'ore'; *hyll* (Old English) 'hill'. The name of this town in the coal-mining area to the west of WIGAN reflects possible early ore extraction here; records show *Horhill* 1202; *Orhille* 1206.

Orwell (Suffolk) the origin and meaning of the name of

this tidal estuary, which extends southeast from IPSWICH, remain uncertain.

Ossett (West Yorkshire) 'Osla's fold' or 'a fold frequented by blackbirds'. *Osla* (Old English personal name) or *osle* (Old English) 'blackbird'; *geset* (Old English) 'fold', 'stable'. The name of this industrial town, west of WAKEFIELD, was *Osleset* in 1086.

Oswaldtwistle (Lancashire) 'Oswald's river-fork land'. *Oswald* (Old English personal name) unidentified; *twisla* (Old English) 'river confluence', 'fork of a river'. The name of this textile town, immediately southwest of ACCRINGTON, was noted as *Oswaldestwisel* in 1246.

Oswestry (Shropshire) 'Oswald's tree'. *Oswald* (Old English personal name) possibly St Oswald, 7th-century king of Northumbria; *treow* (Old English) 'tree', 'cross', 'meeting place marker'. The name of this town, northwest of SHREWSBURY near the Welsh border, was recorded as *Osewaldstreu* in 1190, and *Oswaldestre* in 1272.

Otley (West Yorkshire) 'Otta's clearing'. *Otta-n* (Old English personal name—genitive form); *leah* (Old English) 'woodland clearing'. The name of this town, northwest of LEEDS, was recorded as *Ottanlege* in about 972, and *Otelai* in the Domesday Book of 1086.

Ottery St Mary (Devon) Place by 'the otter river, with church dedicated to St Mary'. *Otter* (Old English river name, derived from *oter+ea*) 'otter stream'; *Sancte Marie* (Medieval church Latin—distinguishing affix). This town, east of EXETER, is named after the river by which it is located, and its name was recorded as simply *Otri* in the Domesday Book of 1086, and *Otery Sancte Marie* in 1242.

Oughter, Lough (Cavan) 'Upper lake'. *Loch* (Irish Gaelic) 'lake'; *uachter* (Irish Gaelic) 'upper'. This lake to the west of CAVAN on the River Erne is 'upper' in relation to Lough ERNE, the later being downstream.

Oughterard (Galway) Place of the 'upper height'. *Uachter* (Irish Gaelic) 'upper'; *ard* (Irish Gaelic) 'height'.

The name of this village and angling centre lying to the southwest of Lough CORRIB conveys its location at the beginning of the higher land rising to the hills of CONNEMARA in the west.

Oundle (Northamptonshire) Settlement of 'the Undalas tribe'. *Undalas* (Old English tribal name) 'those without a share', or 'those given the land left over'. This town, southwest of PETERBOROUGH, was recorded as *Undolum* in the early 8th century, and *Undele* in 1086.

Out Skerries (Shetland) 'Far out islets'. *Ut* (Old Norse) 'far out', 'farthermost'; *sker* (Old Norse) 'small', often 'sharp, rock' or 'island'. This triangular shaped group of islands, some no more than rocks but with the two largest linked by a bridge and inhabited, represents the easternmost part of the Shetland archipelago; they lie 5 miles (8 km) out from WHALSAY.

Out Stack (Shetland) 'Far out rock'. *Ut* (Old Norse) 'far out', 'farthermost'; *stakkr* (Old Norse) 'steep-sided', often 'conical, detached rock'. This solitary outlying rock, just under half a mile (800m) northeast of MUCKLE FLUGGA, is the most northerly point of the BRITISH ISLES.

Oxford (Oxfordshire) 'Ford used by oxen'. *Oxna* (Old English—genitive plural of *oxa*) 'oxen'; *ford* (Old English) 'river crossing place'. The name of this famous university city on the River THAMES simply means what it says and was noted as *Oxnaforda* in the Anglo-Saxon Chronicle of 912. The surrounding county of **Oxfordshire** was first named *Oxnafordscir* around 1010.

Ox Mountains (Sligo) In English this name means simply what it says, 'mountains of the oxen'. However, the Irish name for this range is *Sliabh Ghamh*, meaning the 'mountains of the storms', revealing that the English name has been derived mistakenly as a translation of *Sliabh Dhamh*.

Oxshott (Surrey) 'Ocga's corner of land'. *Ocga* (Old English personal name); *sceat* (Old English) 'corner or projecting piece of land'. The name of this residential suburb at the southwestern fringe of the GREATER LONDON conurbation, just south of ESHER, was noted as *Okesseta* in 1179.

Oxted (Surrey) 'Place of the oak trees'. *Ac* (Old English) 'oak tree'; *stede* (Old English) 'place'. The derivation of the name of this town on the south slope of the North DOWNS, east of REIGATE, is manifested in its entry as *Acstede* in the Domesday Book of 1086.

P

Paddington (Greater London) 'Estate associated with a man called Padda'. *Padda* (Old English personal name); *ing* (Old English connective particle) 'associated with'; *tun* (Old English) 'estate', 'farmstead'. The name of this west-central LONDON district, well known for its railway terminus for lines from the west, was recorded as *Padintun* in 959, and *Paddington* in 998.

Paddock Wood (Kent) 'The small enclosure'. *Pearroc* Old English) 'paddock'; *wudu* (Old English—later addition) 'wood'. This small town, east of TONBRIDGE, has a name that means exactly what it says, as recorded in its old name form of *Parrock* in 1279.

Padstow (Cornwall) 'St Petroc's holy place'. *Saint Petroc* (Old Cornish personal name) local patron saint; *stow* (Old English) 'holy place', 'church'. The name of this resort and port on the River Camel estuary, downstream and northwest of WADEBRIDGE, was documented as *Sancte Petroces stow* in 981, *Petrokestowe* in 1297, *Padristowe* in 1351, and *Padstou* in 1361.

Paignton (Devon) 'Estate associated with a man called Paega'. *Paega* (Old English personal name); *ing* (Old English connective particle) 'associated with'; *tun* (Old English) 'estate', 'farmstead'. The name of this coastal resort, immediately southwest of TORQUAY, was recorded as *Peintone* in the Domesday Book of 1086.

Paisley (Strathclyde) Possibly place of the 'church'. *Baisleac* (Old Irish Gaelic elided from Latin *basilica*, in turn from Greek *baslikos*) 'church', 'king's house'. There are many other unattested derivations for the name of this large manufacturing town just west of GLASGOW, but the above origin is the most likely given the many

Irish Celtic Christian connections here, including the 7th-century St Mirin. Recorded as *Paisleth* 1158.

Pangbourne (Berkshire) 'Stream of Paega's people'. *Paega* (Old English personal name); *inga* (Old English—genitive of *ingas*) 'people of'; *burna* (Old English) 'stream'. Noted as *Pangeborne* in the Domesday Book, the derivation of the name of this small town, immediately northwest and upstream on the River THAMES from READING, is more clearly manifested in an earlier record of 844 in which the name appears as *Pegingaburnan*.

Papa Stour (Shetland) 'Great priest island'. *Pap* (Old Norse) 'priest'; *ey* (Old Norse) 'island'; *storr* (Old Norse) 'great'. The comparative here distinguishes this island from all the other many Old Norse 'priest islands'.

Partick (Strathclyde) 'Bushy place'. *Perth* (Brythonic Celtic-Pictish) 'thicket'. This inner suburb of GLASGOW lies on the north bank of the CLYDE, which in pre-urban times may well have been a bushy place. Early records show: *Perdyec* 1136; *Pertheck* 1158; *Perthik* 1362.

Passage West (Cork) The name of this former naval dockyard town immediately to the southeast of CORK is a simple expression of its location on the main western but narrow tidal passage of the Cork Harbour estuary, which is split by the presence of Great Island, on which COBH stands. Its locative second element also serves to distinguish it from the village of **Passage East**, on the eastern side of the River Suir estuary, some 60 miles (100 km) to the northeast.

Patna (Strathclyde) This name was transferred from the city in India to this former mining village, southeast of Ayr, on its establishment in 1810 by the local landowner, Provost William Faulkner, who apparently had lived and made his fortune in the Indian Patna.

Peacehaven (East Sussex) This resort and residential satellite town built during World War I, just west of NEWHAVEN, acquired its name in a 1916-17 competition.

Peak District (Derbyshire/Staffordshire/Cheshire) This popular upland area, which lies between MANCHESTER, SHEFFIELD and ASHBOURNE in DERBYSHIRE, has an aptly obvious name, deriving from *peac* (Old English) 'a peak' or 'a pointed hill'. It probably once applied to a single peak, but has been used of a more extensive area since early times, being recorded as simply *Pec* in the Domesday Book, but in an even earlier 7th-century reference as *Pecsaetna lond*, meaning 'land of the peak dwellers'. *See* KINDER SCOUT.

Peebles (Borders) Place of 'sheilings'. *Pebyll* (Brythonic Celtic) 'sheilings', temporary huts, tents. This small market town and resort on the upper TWEED lies in a sheep-grazing area, and this may have been a favoured summer pasture in the past. *See* GALASHIELS.

Peel (Isle of Man) 'The palisade'. *Pel* (Middle English) 'a fortified enclosure', a fence of stakes for defensive purposes, represented by the modern English word 'pale'. This resort on the west side of the island thus takes its name from the presence of the medieval castle on St Patrick's Isle, now connected by a breakwater to the harbour. It also was known by the alternative name Holmtown, meaning 'island town'. The Old Manx name *Port-na-Hinsey*, meaning 'port of the island', also refers to the latter.

Pembroke (Dyfed) 'End of the land'. *Penn* (Brythonic Celtic) 'end'; *bro* (Brythonic Celtic) 'land'. This town located on the southwesternmost peninsula of WALES has a name that reflects the sense of geographical extremity. Comparable situations are to be found in the more obvious Cornish LAND'S END but also Finistère and Finisterre on the northwest corners of France and Spain respectively. Records show: *Pennbro* c.1150; *Pembroch* 1180; *Pembrok* 1350; *Pembroke* 1450. The modern Welsh version is *Penfro*. Pemroke gave its name to the former county of **Pembrokeshire**.

Penarth (South Glamorgan) Place of the 'headland hill'. *Pen* (Welsh) 'head'; *garth* (Welsh) 'hill'. This South

Wales resort and port on the coast between CARDIFF and BARRY was developed, like them, in the 19th century to export coal and takes its name from the promontory, Penarth Head, on which it is situated.

Pencaitland (Lothian) Possibly 'head of the wood enclosure'. *Penn* (Brythonic Celtic) 'head', 'top of'; *coed* (Brythonic Celtic) 'wood'; *lann* (Brythonic Celtic) 'enclosure'. This description of a pastoral place enclosed by woods is apt even today for this village, southeast of EDINBURGH.

Pendlebury (Greater Manchester) 'Manor by the hill called Penn'. *Penn* (Brythonic Celtic conjectural hill name); *hyll* (Old English) 'hill'; *byrig* (Old English dative of *burh*) 'manor', 'fortified dwelling'. The name of this town, northwest of MANCHESTER, was noted in a text of 1202 as *Penelbiri*.

Penge (Greater London) Place of 'the chief wood'. *Penn* (Brythonic Celtic conjectural word) 'head', 'chief'; *coed* (Brythonic Celtic) 'wood'. The name of this district of BROMLEY was recorded as *Penceat* in 1067.

Penicuik (Lothian) 'Hill of the cuckoo'. *Penn* (Brythonic Celtic) 'hill'; *y* Brythonic Celtic) 'the'; *cog* (Brythonic Celtic) 'cuckoo'. This small town lies south of EDINBURGH on the lower wooded slopes of the PENTLAND HILLS, frequented by cuckoos. Recorded as *Penicok* in 1250.

Penistone (South Yorkshire) Probably 'a farmstead by a hill called Penning'. *Penn* (Brythonic Celtic conjectural word) 'hill'; *ing* (Old English connective particle) 'by the'; *tun* (Old English) 'farmstead'. Although today there is no nearby hill known as Penning or similar, this town is situated on quite high ground west of BARNSLEY. It was recorded as *Pengestone* in the Domesday Book, and *Peningeston* in 1199.

Penmaenmawr (Gwynedd) 'Great stony head'. *Pen* (Welsh) 'head'; *maen* (Welsh) 'stone'; *mawr* (Welsh) 'big', 'great'. This North Wales coastal resort between LLANFAIRFECHAN and CONWY takes its name from

Penmaen Mawr, a large headland with a bare rock face that plunges sheer into Conwy Bay west of the town and that provided a fearful hazard for travellers until the shore road was tunnelled through in this century.

Pennan (Grampian) 'Headland water'. *Pen* (Brythonic Celtic) 'headland', 'hill'; *an* (Brythonic Celtic) 'water', 'stream'. Normally such a name would indicate a place 'at the head of a stream', but here, in this small BANFFshire coastal village made famous in the film *Local Hero*, the local burn flows into the sea off a steep headland, beneath which nestle the former fishermen's cottages.

Pennines (England) The name of this major range of hills, which forms the high backbone of northern England extending from the PEAK DISTRICT to the CHEVIOT HILLS, was somewhat surprisingly first recorded only in the 18th century. Whether an ancient name or modern invention, its origin and meaning remain obscure, but it is very likely that it is based on *penn-* (Brythonic Celtic conjectural root element) meaning 'hill' or 'head', or even both, in the sense of being 'the chief hills'.

Penrith (Cumbria) 'Ford by a hill'. *Penn* (Brythonic Celtic-Cumbric conjectural root word) 'hill'; *rid* (Brythonic Celtic-Cumbric conjectural root word) 'ford'. The descriptive name of this market town, southeast of CARLISLE, probably refers to a ancient crossing point of the River Eamont two miles (3 km) upstream at Brougham, which was once guarded by the Roman fort of *Brocavum*. The name was spelt as now in a document of around 1100.

Penryn (Cornwall) Place on 'the promontory'. *Pen-ryn* (Old Cornish conjectural word) 'headland', 'promontory'. This town, northwest of FALMOUTH, has a name that aptly describes its location on a small promontory at the head of the Penryn river estuary; it was rendered exactly as now in a record of 1236.

Pentland Firth (Highland/Orkney) 'Sea of Pictland'.

Pettr (Old Norse) 'Picts'; *land* (Old Norse) 'land'; *firth* (Scottish gaelic adaptation of Old Norse *fjordr*) 'sea inlet' or 'passage'. This notoriously rough stretch of sea between the north CAITHNESS coast and the ORKNEY Islands has a name understandably given to it by the Vikings.

Pentland Hills (Lothian) 'Hill-land'. *Penn* (Brythonic Celtic) 'hill'; *land* (Old English) 'tract of land'. Thus the name of these hills to the south of EDINBURGH have quite a different origin from that of the PENTLAND FIRTH. The Celtic root is attested in many other local names with the *penn* prefix: PENICULK, PENCAITLAND etc.

Penwith (Cornwall) 'Far end' district. *Pen* (Old Cornish conjectural word) 'head', 'end'; *wid* (Old Cornish related to Old Breton root element uuid) 'far'. This Old Cornish name for LAND'S END applies to the extreme peninsular district, west of the PENZANCE-ST IVES axis, that is a remote area of rough topography with many prehistoric remains and the ruins of former tin mines. It was recorded as *Penwid* in 1186.

Penzance (Cornwall) Place of 'the holy headland'. *Pen* (Old Cornish) 'headland'; *sans* (Old Cornish) 'holy'. Recorded as *Pensans* in 1284, the name of this resort and port, which is the southwesternmost town in England, refers to the former chapel of St Marys on a headland here. *Compare* HOLYHEAD.

Perranporth (Cornwall) 'St Piran's port'. *Peran* (Old Cornish personal name) St Piran; *porth* (Old Cornish) 'port', 'harbour', 'cove'. The name of this coastal resort southwest of NEWQUAY was originally *Porth Perane*.

Pershore (Hereford and Worcester) Place of 'the osier slope'. *Persc* (Old English) 'osier', 'twig'; *ora* (Old English) 'slope', 'bank'. The name of this small town northwest of EVESHAM was noted as *Perscoran* in 972.

Perth (Tayside) Place of the 'thicket'. *Perth* (Brythonic Celtic) 'bush', 'thicket'. It was recorded as *Perth* in 1150. However this ancient royal burgh and early medieval capital of Scotland was for several hundred years known as *St Johnstoun* after the building of the St John's Kirk in the 12th century.

Peterborough (Cambridgeshire) 'St Peter's town'. *Peter* (Middle English based on Old French *Piers*) saint's name from dedication of former abbey; *burh* (Old English) 'town'. This industrial and cathedral city, northwest of CAMBRIDGE, is on the site of the former Anglo-Saxon 7th-century monastic settlement of *Medeshamstede*, destroyed by the Danes in the 9th century but rebuilt as a Benedictine foundation in the mid-10th century. The new 'town' was simply called just that by its entry as *Burg* in the Domesday Book, and it was only in 1333 that its current form was recorded as *Petreburgh*.

Peterculter (Grampian) 'Corner land of St Peter'. *Cuil* (Scottish Gaelic) 'corner'; *tir* (Scottish Gaelic) 'land'. The first element, dedicated to its church, was added later to distinguish this satellite residential area of ABERDEEN from the nearby village of Maryculter.

Peterhead (Grampian) 'St Peter's headland'. This major fishing port was founded only in 1593, taking its name from the large St Peter's Kirk built here in 1132 on the headland near to the mouth of the Ugie Water, and hence in the former parish of Inverugie.

Peterlee (Durham) This New Town, designated in 1948 on the DURHAM coalfield, midway between SUNDERLAND and HARTLEPOOL, is named in commemoration of the popular local miner and trade union leader, Peter Lee, who died in 1935.

Petersfield (Hampshire) Probably place at 'the open land with a church of St Peter'. *Peter* (Middle English based on Old French Piers) saint's name from dedication of church; *feld* (Old English) 'open land'. First recorded as *Peteresfeld* in 1182, this small town, northeast of PORTSMOUTH, was established by the Anglo-Normans.

Petworth (West Sussex) 'Peota's enclosure'. *Peota* (Old English personal name); *worth* (Old English) 'enclosure'. The name of this historic small town, east of MIDHURST, appears in the Domesday Book of 1086 as *Peteorde*.

Pevensey (East Sussex) Place by 'Pefen's river'. *Pefen* (Old English personal name); *ea* (Old English) 'river'. This large village and the nearby seaside resort of **Pevensey Bay**, northeast of EASTBOURNE, are near the site of the former Roman fort of **Anderita.** The current name was first recorded as **Pefenesea** in 947.

Pewsey (Wiltshire) 'Pefe's island'. *Pefe* (Old English personal name); *eg* (Old English) 'island'. Recorded as *Pefesigge* c.880, the name of this small town in the Vale of Pewsey reflects its riverside situation.

Phoenix Park (Dublin) The name of this very large park (five times bigger than LONDON's Hyde Park) to the west of DUBLIN city centre has nothing to do with the legendary Arabian firebird but owes its origin to a semantic error on the part of the English who misdocumented at face value the sound of *Fionn Uisg* (Irish Gaelic meaning 'clear water'), the name of a local spring here.

Pickering (North Yorkshire) Probably settlement of a ancient tribe called 'Piceringas'. *Picer* (Old English personal name); *ingas* (Old English) 'people of'. Appearing as the entry *Picheringa* in the Domesday Book, the origin of the name of this market town for the Vale of Pickering, west of SCARBOROUGH, remains uncertain.

Piddletrenthide (Dorset) 'Thirty hides farm on the River Piddle'. *Pidele* (Old English river name) 'marshy one'; *trente* (Old French) 'thirty'; *hid* (Old English) 'hide'. The name of this village, north of DORCHESTER, was originally recorded as *Uppidelen* in 966, indicating its location on the upper River Piddle. In a document of 1212 it appeared as *Pidele Trenthydes*, the second part of this hybrid name denoting the amount of land required for a family to live on as being that capable of supporting thirty head of cattle, referred to here as 'hides'.

Pitlochry (Tayside) 'Piece of land by the stones'. *Pett* (Brythonic Celtic-Pictish) 'portion' or 'piece of land'; *cloichreach* (Scottish Gaelic) 'stones'. This Highland resort, made popular with Queen Victoria's approval, has a name with a distinctive Pictish prefix. The 'stones' referred to here were almost certainly stepping stones across the River Tummel by which the town stands.

Pittenweem (Fife) 'Place of the cave'. *Pett* (Bythonic Celtic-Pictish) 'piece of land', 'place'; *na* (Scottish Gaelic) 'of the'; *h-uamha* (Scottish Gaelic) 'cave'. This East Neuk fishing port on the Firth of FORTH has a cave, near the harbour, said to be associated with St Fillan. Recorded in 1150 as *Petnaweem*

Plymouth (Devon) Place at 'the mouth of the River Plym'. *Plym* (Old English river name—back formation of **Plympton**) 'river of the plum-tree farm'; *mutha* (Old English) 'river mouth'. Previously called *Sutton*, this historic maritime city and naval port on the Tamar estuary off the western approaches of the English Channel, became known by its current name only in the 13th century, as a record of 1235 shows it as *Plummuth*.

Pocklington (Humberside) 'Estate associated with a man called Pocela'. *Pocela* (Old English personal name); *ing* (Old English connective particle) 'associated with'; *tun* (Old English) 'estate', 'farmstead'. This small agricultural town, northwest of MARKET WEIGHTON, was recorded as *Poclinton* in the Domesday Book of 1086.

Pollok (Strathclyde) 'Little pool'. *Poll* (Brythonic Celtic) 'pool'; *-oc* (Brythonic Celtic diminutive suffix) 'little'. This southwestern district of GLASGOW, near the confluence of the Levern and White Cart Waters, is an area where there would have been many pools. The name also occurs in the adjoining districts of Pollokshaws and Pollokshields.

Polperro (Cornwall) Probably 'Pyra's harbour'. *Porth* (Old Cornish changed to *pol-* by dissimilation) 'harbour'; *Pyra* (Old Cornish personal name) unidentified. Noted as *Portpira* in 1303, the second element of the name of this popular resort and former fishing port southwest of LOOE may also be an old name for the river here.

Pontefract (West Yorkshire) Place of 'the broken bridge'. *Pons* (Latin) 'bridge'; *fractus* (Latin) 'broken'. Situated southeast of LEEDS, the name of this town, well known for its special liquorice sweets or 'Pumfret cakes', was recorded as *Fracti-pontis* (genitive) 1069; *Pontefracto* (dative) 1100-1102; *Pontfreit* (Norman French adaptation) 1177. The pronunciation is 'Pontifrakt', locally as 'Pumfrit'.

Ponteland (Northumberland) 'Cultivated land by the River Pont'. *Pont* (Brythonic Celtic river name) 'valley'; *ea-land* (Old English) 'riverside land'. The name of this small satellite town, northwest of NEWCASTLE UPON TYNE, was documented as *Punteland* in 1203.

Pontycymer (West Glamorgan) 'Bridge at the confluence'. *Pont* (Welsh) 'bridge'; *y* (Welsh) 'the'; *cymer* (Welsh) 'confluence'. This coal-mining town north of BRIDGEND has a simple name thus describing its location at the confluence of two rivers, by a bridge.

Pontypool (Gwent) 'Bridge by the pool'. *Pont* (Welsh) 'bridge'; *y* (Welsh) 'the'; *pool* (English) 'pool'. This town north of CWMBRAN has a linguistically hybrid name, part Welsh, part English. The Welsh name, *Pont-y-pwl*, gives the full back-translation. This name is quite recent, with a 17th-century record showing *Pont y Poole*.

Pontypridd (Mid Glamorgan) 'Bridge of the earth-house'. *Pont* (Welsh) 'bridge'; *y* (Welsh) 'the'; *ty* (Welsh) 'house'; *pridd* (Welsh) 'earth'. This town, northwest of CARDIFF, lies at the confluence of the RHONNDA and Taff rivers, where once there must have been such a house by the bridge. The *ty*, or 'house' element, was later dropped as these two letters were already represented. For a time after 1755, when a new bridge was built here, the town was called Newbridge, but it eventually reverted to its former name.

Poole (Dorset) Place at 'the pool'. *Pol* (Old English) 'pool', 'creek'. Recorded as *Pole* in 1183, the simple name of this ferry port, west of BOURNEMOUTH, aptly describes its location on the natural **Poole Harbour**, a large, almost enclosed, sea inlet.

Portadown (Armagh) 'Landing place of the little fort'. *Port* (Irish Gaelic) 'landing place'; *an* (Irish Gaelic) 'of the'; *dun-ain* (Irish Gaelic diminutive of *dun*) 'little fort'. This ancient town lies at a strategic crossing point on the River Bann southwest of LURGAN.

Portarlington (Laois) The name of this 'plantation town', northeast of PORT LAOISE, derives from that of Lord Arlington (Sir Henry Bennet) who was granted land here in the 17th century.

Port Bannatyne (Strathclyde) This resort on the east coast of BUTE takes its name from the Bannatyne family who established their seat at the nearby Kames Castle in the 13th century.

Port Charlotte (Strathclyde) This coastal settlement in southwest ISLAY is named after Lady Charlotte, the mother of W. F. Campbell who founded the village in 1828. *See* PORT ELLEN.

Portchester (Hampshire) 'Roman fort by the harbour'. *Port* (Old English) 'harbour'; *ceaster* (Old English) 'Roman station'. This town, on the northern shore of PORTSMOUTH Harbour, built on the site of the Roman fort of *Portus Ardaoni*, was noted as *Porteceaster* in about 960.

Port Ellen (Strathclyde) This, the main port of ISLAY, situated at the south end of the island, is named after Lady Ellenor, wife of the Gaelic scholar W.F. Campbell who founded the small town in 1821. *See* PORT CHARLOTTE.

Port Erin (Isle of Man) 'Port of Ireland'. *Port* (Old Manx) 'port, harbour'; *Erin* (Old Manx and English adaptation of Irish Gaelic *Eirinn*) poetic name for Ireland.

Thus the name of this small port at the southwest end of the island commemorates its strong links with Ireland, towards which it faces.

Port Glasgow (Strathclyde) This Lower CLYDE industrial town was developed east of GREENOCK in the 1660s with the aim of becoming the main port for GLASGOW; later dredging of the River CLYDE put paid to the plan.

Porthcawl (Mid Galmorgan) 'Kale harbour'. *Porth* (Welsh) 'harbour'; *cawl* (Welsh) 'sea kale'. This seaside resort west of BRIDGEND was probably in early times a favoured place for the collection of this edible seaweed.

Porthmadog (Gwynedd) 'Madocks' port'. This resort on the Glaslyn river estuary at the head of TREMADOC BAY is a fabricated Welsh name of early 19th-century origin, referring to the harbour constructed here in 1821 by William Alexander Madocks, MP, for the export of the slate quarried near BLAENAU FFESTINIOG. It is the terminus for the former narrow-gauge mineral railway that has been revived as a popular tourist attraction. Until recently the more anglicised form of Portmadoc was used.

Portishead (Avon) 'Harbour by the ridge'. *Port* (Old English) 'harbour'; *heafod* (Old English) 'ridge', 'headland'. The aptly descriptive name of this satellite town, west of BRISTOL, where there is a natural harbour by a ridge of hills along the SEVERN estuary, was recorded as *Portesheve* in 1086 and *Portesheved* in 1200.

Portknockie (Grampian) 'Harbour by the little hill'. *Port* (Scottish Gaelic) 'harbour'; *cnoc* (Scottish Gaelic) 'rounded hill'; *-ie* (colloquial diminutive) 'little'. An apt name for this small fishing port founded in 1677 on a hilly promotory on the west side of Cullen Bay.

Portland, Isle of (Dorset) 'Estate by the harbour'. *Port* (Old English) 'harbour'; *land* (Old English) 'estate', 'land'. This 'beak-like' peninsula, which protrudes into the English Channel south of WEYMOUTH and **Portland Harbour**, ending at the aptly named **Portland**

Bill (*bile* - Old English for 'beak') was noted as simply *Port* in 837 and as the entry *Porland insula* in the Domesday Book.

Port Laoise (Laois) 'Fort of Leeshagh's people'. *Port* (Irish Gaelic) 'fort'; *Laeighis* (Irish Gaelic tribal and territorial name) lands of Leeshagh's people. The latter has the same derivation as LAOIS itself. Also between 1556 and 1921 this county town of Laois was known as Maryborough, after Queen Mary, just as the county was Queen's County.

Portmeirion (Gwynedd) This small 'Italianate fantasy village', built on a headland west of PORTHMADOG by the architect Clough Williams-Ellis in the 1920s, has a modern fabricated name, with 'port' reflecting its coastal site, which includes a mock harbour, and 'meirion' denoting its location in the then county of MERIONETH.

Portobello (Lothian) The romantic sounding name of this seaside district of EDINBURGH and former independent burgh until amalgamated in 1896, is the result of a transfer from the name of a house built here by a sailor who had seen action at the battle of Puerto Bello in Panama in 1739. The name thus derives: (Spanish) 'fine harbour', which is somewhat inappropriate here, as there is none.

Portpatrick (Dumfries and Galloway) 'Harbour of St Patrick'. *Port* (Scottish Gaelic) 'harbour'; Padraig (Scottish Gaelic personal name) patron saint of Ireland, dedicated in a chapel in this coastal resort on the west side of the RHINNS OF GALLOWAY. An apt name for this former main port for the short crossing to Ireland.

Portree (Highland) 'Harbour of the slope'. *Port* (Scottish Gaelic) 'harbour'; *ruigheadh* (Scottish Gaelic) 'of the slope'. This derivation aptly describes the main town and port on SKYE. The second element is often mistakenly thought to derive as *righ* (Scottish Gaelic) 'king', related to a royal visit here by James V in 1540.

Portrush (Antrim) Simply 'harbour of the headland'. *Port* (Irish Gaelic) 'port', 'harbour'; *ros* (Irish Gaelic) 'headland'. This seaside resort beside Ramore Head, north of COLERAINE, is thus aptly described.

Portsea Island (Hampshire) 'Harbour island'. *Port* (Old English) 'harbour'; *eg* (Old English) 'island'. Recorded as *Portesig* in 982, this now tautological name applies to the island largely occupied by PORTSMOUTH, and separated from the mainland only by the narrow Port Creek, which itself has been mainly built over by the elevated M27 motorway.

Portslade-by-Sea (East Sussex) 'Harbour by the river crossing'. *Port* (Old English) 'harbour'; *gelad* (Old English) 'river crossing'. The name of this resort west of BRIGHTON refers directly to its situation on a creek of the River Adur behind the shore. It was recorded as *Porteslage* in the Domesday Book, and *Portes Ladda* in about 1095. The distinguishing affix was added later, distinguishing it from the original centre and now suburb that lies further inland.

Portsmouth (Hampshire) 'Port at the mouth of the harbour. *Port* (Old English) 'port'; *mutha* (Old English) 'harbour mouth'. This major ferry port and naval base lies on PORTSEA ISLAND by the narrow entrance to **Portsmouth Harbour**. Its name was recorded as *Portesmuthan* in the late 9th century.

Portsoy (Grampian) 'Harbour of the warrior'. *Port* (Scottish Gaelic) 'harbour'; *saoi* (Scottish Gaelic) 'warrior'. This well-preserved historic port on the MORAY Firth is a place of great antiquity, but there is no clue as to who might be the 'warrior' in its name.

Portstewart (Londonderry) This resort to the west of PORTRUSH on the north coast of Ireland, is named after the Stewart family who were local landowners in the mid-18th century when the town was first developed. Its Irish name, *Port Stiobhaird*, has the same meaning.

Port St Mary (Isle of Man) This small resort and former fishing port, at the south end of the island just east of PORT ERIN, has a simple name referring to the harbour here as well as the dedication of its parish church.

Port Sunlight (Merseyside) This model 'industrial village' built on the WIRRAL shore of the MERSEY estuary in the late 19th century by William Lever, was somewhat unusually called after the brand name of a soap product produced here by his company, rather than the other way round, as in the case of BOURNVILLE.

Port Talbot (West Glamorgan) This major steelmaking town and port, east of SWANSEA, is named after the Talbot family of MARGAM Abbey, who as local landowners built docks and founded the new industrial settlement here in 1836.

Port William (Dumfries and Galloway) This small seaport and resort situated on LUCE Bay southwest of WIGTOWN takes its name from Sir William Maxwell of Monrieth, who established the town here in 1770.

Potters Bar (Hertfordshire) 'Potter's forest gate'. *Potter* (Middle English personal name); *barre* (Middle English from Old French *barre*) 'bar', 'gate'. The name of this town, in the for mer heavily wooded area north of BARNET, was recorded as *Potterys Barre* in 1509.

Potton (Bedfordshire) 'Farmstead where pots are made'. *Pott* (Old English) 'pot'; *tun* (Old English) 'farm'. The name of this small town, in the brick-making area northeast of BIGGLESWADE, was noted as *Pottun c.*960.

Poulton-le-Fylde (Lancashire) 'Farmstead by the pool'. *Pol* (Old English) 'pool', 'creek'; *tun* (Old English) 'farm'; *le* (Old French definite article remaining after loss of preposition) 'on the'; *Flyde* (Old English distinguishing affix derived from *gefilde*) 'plain'. Recorded as *Poltun* in the Domesday Book of 1086, the first element of the name of this town, lying immediately north of BLACKPOOL, may be a reference to the same 'pool' that gave the second part of the latter name. The later addition of the affix was in contradistinction with Poulton-le-Sands, the former name for MORECAMBE.

Powys (Wales) Apparently 'provincial land'. *Pagensis* (Latin adjective of *pagus*) 'province', 'open region'. According to one authority, the name of this modern county, formed out of former BRECONshire, MONTGOMERYshire and RADNORshire, which is also that of the ancient kingdom of east-central Wales between the 6th and 9th centuries, implies 'an open tract of upland' that was not as well protected as the areas to the north and south, where valleys and hills afforded better shelter. The reality of this situation was probably significant in the early demise of the ancient Powys kingdom, which suffered from constant Mercian raids across the line of OFFA'S DYKE.

Poynton (Cheshire) 'Estate associated with a man called Pun'. *Pun* (Old English personal name) unidentified; *ing* (Old English connective particle) 'associated with'; *tun* (Old English) 'estate', 'farmsted'. The name of this small town, south of STOCKPORT, was recorded as *Poninton* in 1248.

Prescot (Merseyside) Place of 'the priests' cottage or parsonage'. *Preost* (Old English) 'priest'; *cot* (Old English) 'cottage', 'specialised dwelling'. It is thought that the name of this town lying between LIVERPOOL and ST HELENS reflects an early attachment to the church at nearby ECCLESTON; it was documented as *Prestecota* in 1178. *Compare* PRESTATYN; PRESTON; PRESTONPANS; PRESTWICH; PRESTWICK.

Prestatyn (Clwyd) 'Priests' village'. *Preosta* (Old English) 'priests'; *tyn* (Welsh corruption of Old English *tun*) 'village'. Thus this North Wales seaside resort, which developed east of RHYL in the 19th century, has a name that is a 'Welshified' version of the English PRESTON. Although this was the site of an ancient castle of the POWYS princes, the origin of the 'priests' connection is unclear; there may be some link with the cathedral at ST ASAPH to the southwest.

Preston (Lancashire) Place of 'the priests' farmstead'. *Preost* (Old English) 'priest'; *tun* (Old English) 'farmstead'. This large industrial town, at the head of the Ribble river estuary, has a name that like that of PRESCOT, probably indicating an endowment for priests serving nearby but not necessarily here. it was recorded in the Domesday Book as *Prestune*.

Prestonpans (Lothian) 'Priests' village by the pans'. *Preost* (Old English) 'priest'; *tun* (Old English) 'village'; *-pans* (Middle English suffix) refers to salt-panning here on the Firth of FORTH by monks of Newbattle Abbey from the 13th century. Recorded as *Saltprestoun* 1587.

Prestwich (Greater Manchester) Place of 'the priests' outlying farm or parsonage'. *Preost* (Old English) 'priest'; *wic* (Old English) 'outlying farm', 'specialised dwelling'. The name of this textiles town, northwest of MANCHESTER, was in 1194 as now. *Compare* PRESTWICK.

Prestwick (Strathclyde) 'Priests' settlement'. *Preost* (Old English) 'priest'; *wic* (Old English) 'settlement'. This resort town on the AYRshire coast, well known for its airport, was presumably, like Prestongrange near PRESTONPANS, an 'outlying farm' for a religious house elsewhere. The name was recorded as *Prestwic* in a document of 1170. *Compare* PRESTWICH.

Princes Risborough *see* **Risborough, Monks** and **Princes**.

Princetown (Devon) This remote and bleak town, standing at 1400 ft (427m) on central DARTMOOR east of TAVISTOCK, arose in the early 19th century beside a prison originally built to accommodate French prisoners taken in the Napoleonic Wars. It is named after the Prince Regent, later to become King George IV, who gave land here from the estates of the Duchy of CORNWALL.

Pruhoe (Northumberland) 'Pruda's hill spur'. *Pruda* (Old English personal name); *hoh* (Old English) 'hill spur'. This small industrial town with its 12th-century Anglo-Norman castle on the elevated south bank of the River TYNE, upstream and west of BLAYDON, was named *Prudho* in a document of 1173.

Puddletown (Dorset) 'Farmstead by the River Piddle'. *Pidele* (Old English river name) 'marshy one'; *tun* (Old English) 'farmstead'. The name of this village, northeast of DORCHESTER, misleadingly appears as *Pitretone* in the Domesday Book but was correctly recorded as *Pideltone* in 1212 before assuming its current form, possibly out of a sense of propriety. *See* PIDDLETRENTHIDE; TOLPUDDLE

Pudsey (West Yorkshire) Probably 'Pudoc's island land'. *Pudoc* (Old English personal name) unidentified; *eg* (Old English) 'island', 'elevated drier land in a marsh'. The name of this industrial town, lying midway between LEEDS and BRADFORD, was recorded as *Podechesaie* in the Domesday Book of 1086.

Puffin Island (Gwynedd) This small island, lying off the easternmost point of ANGLESEY, has a name that denotes its fame as a seabird sanctuary, but today its colonies of puffins are sadly on the decline. It is alternatively called Priestholm, deriving from *preost* (Old English) 'priest'; *holmr* (Old Norse) 'island'. This refers to the 6th-century monastery founded here by St Seriol, whose name is commemorated in the Welsh name of the island, *Ynys Seiriol*.

Pulborough (West Sussex) 'The pool by the mound'. *Pol* (Old English) 'pool'; *beorg* (Old English) 'mound', 'hillock'. Recorded as *Poleberge* in the Domesday Book of 1086, this small town on the River Arun, upstream and north of ARUNDEL, is aptly named, with the 'pool' almost certainly represented by a bend in the meandering river here, and the 'mound' being the hillock on which much of the old town is situated.

Purbeck, Isle of (Dorset) 'Bittern beak-shaped place'. *Pur* (Old English) 'bittern', 'snipe'; *bic* (Old English conjectural word) 'beak-like', 'pointed'. This peninsula, south of POOLE Harbour, derives its name from the long pointed ridge of the **Purbeck Hills**, which runs across the centre of the district. The earliest spelling is *Purbcinga* in a text of 948; the name is combined with *ingas* (Old English) 'dwellers in'. *Compare* PORTLAND, Isle of.

Purfleet (Essex) 'Purta's creek'. *Purta* (Old English personal name); *fleot* (Old English) 'creek', 'inlet'. This riverside industrial locality on the north bank of the THAMES, immediately west of the DARTFORD Tunnel and Bridge, has a name recorded as *Purteflyete* in 1285, which reflects is situation by the mouth of the Mar Dyke tributary river.

Purley (Greater London) 'Pear-tree wood or clearing'. *Pirige* (Old English) 'pear tree'; *leah* (Old English) 'wood' or 'woodland clearing'. The name of this former SURREY town and now district of the borough of CROYDON was recorded as *Pirlee* in 1200.

Putney (Greater London) 'Putta's landing place'. *Putta-n* (Old English personal name—genitive form); *hyth* (Old English) 'landing place'. This riverside district of WANDSWORTH on the south side of the THAMES has a name, well known today for its rowing activities, that was misrecorded as *Putelei* in the Domesday Book of 1086, but the original derivation of which is more recognisably documented as *Puttenhuthe* in 1279.

Pwllheli (Gwynedd) 'Pool of salt water'. *Pwll* (Welsh) 'pool;' *heli* (Welsh) 'brine'. The name of this small town and port on the south coast of The LLEYN peninsula reflects its siting beside a small circular sea inlet almost enclosed by surrounding sand dunes and spits. The name is pronounced 'Pool-thelly'.

Q

Quantock Hills (Somerset) Probably hills of 'the wooded edge'. *Canto-* (Brythonic Celtic root element) 'edge', 'rim'; *wudu* (Old English) 'wood'. The name of this range of hills, extending northwest from TAUNTON to the BRISTOL Channel coast near WATCHET, was recorded as *Cantucuudu* in 682.

Queenborough (Kent) 'Borough named in honour of Queen Philippa of Hainault, wife of Edward III'. *Cwen* (Old English) 'queen'; *burh* (Old English) 'borough'. This industrial complex at the western end of the Isle of SHEPPEY was granted its royal charter in 1367, shortly after Queen Philippa died. It was documented as *Queneburgh* in 1376.

Queensbury (West Yorkshire) The name of this town, north of HALIFAX, was confirmed as a act of royal acclaim taken in a vote at a public meeting in 1863. It had previously been known as *Queen's Head*, named after a local inn.

Queensferry (Clwyd) This industrial town on the south bank of the River Dee just to the southeast of CONNAH'S QUAY has clearly been an important river-crossing point for a long time. It took its present name in 1837 on the accession of Queen Victoria; previously it had been known as Kingsferry. However, the town does not appear to have had any direct association with a particular monarch, so it may have been so titled simply as a mark of some past royalist enthusiasm; a village called Mancot Royal lies immediately to the south. *Compare* QUEENSFERRY, NORTH and SOUTH.

Queensferry, North and South (Fife and Lothian)

Queensferry

Both these towns, on respective sides of the Firth of FORTH and lying underneath the famous latter-day rail and road bridges, have a basic name that commemorates Queen Margaret, wife of King Malcolm Canmore of Scotland, who regularly crossed the mile-wide estuary here in the 11th century en route between EDINBURGH and her royal residence in DUNFERMLINE. A ferry plied between the two towns for hundreds of years until the opening of the Forth Road Bridge in 1964.

R

Raasay (Highland) 'Roe-deer ridge island'. *Rar* (Old Norse) 'roe deer'; *ass* (Old Norse) 'ridge'; *ey* (Old Norse) 'island'. This derivation is very descriptive of this long 'ridge-tent' shaped island lying off the east coast of SKYE; roe deer are still found here.

Radcliffe (Greater Manchester; Nottinghamshire) Place of 'the red cliff or bank'. *Read* (Old English) 'red'; *clif* (Old English) 'cliff', 'bank'. This straightforward name aptly describes the situation of both these towns, the former by a red sandstone cliff overlooking the River Irwell southwest of BURY, and the other, officially called **Radcliffe on Trent**, sitting on a slope of red soils down to the river, east of NOTTINGHAM. Respective Domesday Book entries are: *Radecliue*; *Radeclive*.

Radnor (Powys) Place of the 'red slopes'. *Read* (Old English) 'red'; *ofer* (Old English) 'slope', 'bank'. The name of the former shire and presently that of the central district of POWYS in eastern Wales reflects the predominating colour of the hill slopes and banks here, which are underlaid with Old Red Sandstone bedrock. An 11th-century Domesday Book entry shows *Raddrenore*.

Radstock (Avon) 'Place or farm by the road'. *Rad* (Old English) 'road'; *stoc* (Old English) 'place', 'outlying farmstead'. The name of this small town at the centre of a minor coalfield district, southwest of BATH, was recorded as simply *Stoche* in the Domesday Book of 1086, but a document of 1221 notes it as *Radestok*, giving due recognition to its location on the FOSSE WAY.

Rainford (Merseyside) Probably 'Regna's ford'. *Regna* (Old English personal name—short form in *Regn-*) e.g. *Regengar*; *Regnheah*; *Regnhere*; *ford* (Old English) 'river crossing'. The name of this small town, north-west of St Helens, was recorded as *Raineford* in 1198.

Rainham (Greater London; Kent) Probably 'homestead of the Roegingas'. *Roegingas* (Old English tribal name) of uncertain meaning; *ham* (Old English) 'homestead'. This derivation almost certainly applies in the case of the Kent settlement, which has become an eastern suburb of the Medway Towns; it was recorded as *Roegingaham* in 811. However, the name of the former Essex town, now a district of the borough of Havering, may have derived from *Regna-* as it appears in the Domesday Book as *Renaham*.

Ramsbottom (Greater Manchester) 'Ram's or wild-garlic valley'. *Ramm* (Old English) 'ram'; *hramsa* (Old English) 'wild garlic'; *bothm* (Old English) 'valley'. The name of this textiles town, north of Bury, was inconclusively documented as *Romesbothum* in 1324.

Ramsey (Cambridgeshire) Probably 'wild-garlic island'. *Hramsa* (Old English) 'wild garlic'; *eg* (Old English) 'island', 'drier elevated land in marshes'. The name of this small Fenland town, southeast of Peterborough, has the same meaning as the Welsh Ramsey but a different root origin; it was recorded as *Hramesege* in about 1000. Many attendant village names emphasise the derivation: **Ramsey Forty Foot**; **Ramsey Heights**; **Ramsey Mereside**; **Ramsey St Marys**.

Ramsey (Isle of Man; Dyfed) 'Wild garlic river/island'. *Hramsa* (Old Norse) 'wild garlic'; *a* (Old Norse) 'river'; *ey* (Old Norse) 'island'. The name of both these places is Scandinavian in origin, with the first element an identical reference to the local vegetation. The second element of the small town in the north of the Isle of Man indicates the presence of the 'river' on which it stands, while in the latter case the literal description is of the 'island' off the far west coast of Wales. The Welsh name of this island is *Ynys Dewi*, meaning 'St David's island', a recognition of its proximity to the famous town of St David's.

Ramsgate (Kent) 'Hraefn's gap'. *Hraefn* (Old English personal name); *geat* (Old English) 'gate', 'gap'. This popular coastal resort and 'cross-Channel' ferry port, at the extreme eastern tip of the county, has a name that refers to a gap in the cliffs leading down to the sea here. It was recorded as *Remmesgate* in 1275. *Compare* MARGATE; BROADSTAIRS.

Randalstown (Antrim) This small 'plantation town', located just north of Lough NEAGH, takes its name from Randal MacDonell, first Marquis of Antrim, to whose wife lands here were granted by Charles II in 1683. It had previously been known as Mainwater, after the name of the local stream, and as Ironworks, on account of a former forge. Its Irish name, *Baile Raghnaill*, means the same as its current English name.

Rannoch (Highland, Strathclyde, Tayside) 'Bracken'. *Raineach* (Scottish Gaelic) 'bracken fern'. This name, apart from being the name of an extensive historic region of the Highlands, forms part of several places in it: **Rannoch Moor**, **Rannoch Forest**, **Loch Rannoch**, etc. The original meaning probably only applied to the area around Loch Rannoch.

Rathlin Island (Antrim) The name of this island lying off the north coast of NORTHERN IRELAND has an ancient but uncertain origin. It was recorded as *Rikini* by the renowned 2nd-century Roman geographer, Ptolemy. One authority considers it may derive from a Brythonic Celtic root word, similar to the modern Welsh *rhygnu*, meaning 'to scrape or rub', this being a reference to the island's manifestly eroded terrain.

Ráth Luirc (Cork) 'Lorc's fort'. *Rath* (Irish Gaelic) 'circular fort'; *Luirc* (Irish Gaelic personal name—genitive case) Lorc. This small town, to the south of LIMERICK, is simply called An Ráth in Irish. Between the mid-17th century and 1921 it had the name Charleville, given to it by the royalist Earls of CORK in honour of Charles II.

Rathmines (Dublin) 'De Moenes fort'. *Rath* (Irish Gaelic) 'circular fort'; *De Moenes* (Anglo-Norman personal name) of a family who were 14th-century landowners of this area, which is now a southern suburb of DUBLIN. Its Irish name, *Ráth Maonais*, means the same.

Rathmullan (Donegal) 'Maolán's fort'. *Rath* (Irish Gaelic) 'fort'; *Maoláin* (Irish Gaelic personal name) unidentified. The Irish name of his small town on the western shore of Lough SWILLY is *Rath Maoláin*.

Raunds (Northamptonshire) Place at 'the boundaries or edges'. *Randan* (Old English plural of *rand*) 'boundaries', 'borders', 'edges'. Recorded as *Randan* in about 980, this town, southeast of KETTERING, lies near the point where the county boundaries of NORTHAMPTONSHIRE, BEDFORDSHIRE, and the former HUNTINGDONSHIRE, all met.

Ravenglass (Cumbria) 'Glas's share'. *Rann* (Old Gaelic related to Irish Gaelic *rann*) 'part share of land'; *Glas* (Old Gaelic personal name) meaning 'green'. This village on the Esk river estuary, southeast of SEASCALE, lies on the site of the former Roman fort of *Glannoventa*, but appears to have ultimately derived its name from Gaelic connections across the Irish Sea. The name was recorded as *Rengles* in about 1180.

Rawtenstall (Lancashire) Place of 'the rough cow pasture'. *Ruh* (Old English) 'rough'; *tun-stall* (Old English) 'farm site', specifically 'high cow pasture'. The name of this textiles town set in an elevated location in the Irwell valley , southwest of BURNLEY, was documented as *Routonstall* in a text of 1324.

Rayleigh (Essex) Place of 'the doe clearing'. *Raege* (Old English) 'doe deer'; *leah* (Old English) 'woodland clearing'. The name of this town, northwest of SOUTHEND-ON-SEA, was noted in the Domesday Book of 1086 as *Ragheleia*.

Reading (Berkshire) Settlement of 'Reada's people'. *Reada* (Old English personal name) meaning 'red one'; *ingas* (Old English) 'people of'. The name of this county and university town, west of LONDON, was recorded as *Readingum* around 900, and appears in the Domesday Book as *Reddinges*.

Redbridge (Greater London) This former ESSEX town, now a borough of northeast LONDON, is named after a 'red bridge' that crossed the River RODING between Wanstead and Ilford. The name was first recorded as *Red Bridge* in 1777.

Redcar (Cleveland) Place of 'the reedy marsh'. *Hreod* (Old English) 'reed'; *kjarr* (Old Norse) 'marsh'. Recorded as *Redker* in about 1170, this North Sea resort, well known for its racecourse, is situated on low-lying coastal land immediately northwest of the significantly named town of MARSKE-BY-THE SEA.

Redditch (Hereford and Worcester) Probably place of 'the reedy ditch'. *Hreod* (Old English) 'reed'; *dic* (Old English) 'ditch'. Alternatively, some authorities favour the derivation of the first element to be *read* (Old English) 'red'. Records show the name of this town, southwest of BIRMINGHAM, as *Rubeo Fossato* (Latin) *c.*1200; *la Rededich* (Norman French) 1247.

Redruth (Cornwall) Place of the 'red ford'. *Rid* (Old Cornish) 'red'; *rudh* (Old Cornish) 'ford'. The name of this market town and former tin-mining centre, west of TRURO, was documented as *Ridruthe* in 1259.

Reigate (Surrey) Place of 'the doe gate'. *Raege* (Old English) 'doe deer'; *geat* (Old English) 'gate', 'gap'. Noted as *Reigata* around 1170, the name of this town north of CRAWLEY probably refers to an old deer-park entrance.

Renfrew (Strathclyde) 'Point of the torrent'. *Rhyn* (Brythonic Celtic) 'point'; *frwd* (Brythonic Celtic) 'torrent'. For this town located west of GLASGOW the derivation means the point at which the CLYDE is joined by both the White and Black Cart rivers, thus creating a torrent at their confluence. Records show: *Renifry* 1128; *Reinfrew* 1158; *Renfrew* 1160.

Renton (Strathclyde) This early industrial town, lying in the Vale of Leven to the north of DUMBARTON, was named in 1782 by its founder, Jean Telfer Smollett (sister of Tobias Smollett), after her daughter-in-law, Cecilia Renton.

Repton (Derbyshire) 'The hill of the Hrype tribe'. *Hrype* (tribal name of obscure etymology); *dun* (Old English) 'hill'. The name of this small town and its public school, southwest of DERBY, in part reflects its situation on a southern slope above the River TRENT; it was recorded as *Hrypadun* in 730-40, and *Rapendune* in the Domesday Book of 1086. *See* RIPON.

Republic of Ireland (Ireland) The official name of the state comprising the 26 counties of 'Southern Ireland', as it is commonly known. Formerly called the Irish Free State on independence in 1921 till 1937, and by the Irish name *Eire* from 1937 to 1949. See IRELAND.

Retford (Nottinghamshire) Place of 'the red ford'. *Read* (Old English) 'red'; *ford* (Old English) 'river crossing'. Often referred to as **East Retford**, in contradistinction to the small village of **West Retford** just across the River Idle, the name of this town, east of WORKSOP, was documented as *Redforde* in the Domesday Book of 1086, and originally may have indicated exposed red bedrock or soil at the ford here.

Rhondda (Mid Glamorgan) This 19th-century coal-mining and steel-making town lies northwest of PONTYPRIDD in the famous Great Rhondda valley, or *Rhondda Fawr* in its Welsh name. As one might expect, the town takes its name from the Rhondda river, which means 'noisy one', deriving from the Welsh *rhoddni*, with middle consonant changes. Recent local administrative changes have erased this famous name from the map.

Rhosllanerchrugog (Clwyd) 'Moor of the heather glade'. *Rhos* (Welsh) 'moor'; *llannerch* (Welsh) 'glade', 'clearing'; *grugog* (Welsh adjective of *grug*) 'heather'. This self-descriptive Welsh name applies to the colliery township to the southwest of WREXHAM.

Rhuddlan (Clwyd) Place of the 'red banks'. *Rhudd* (Welsh) 'red'; *glan* (Welsh) 'bank'. Although today this small village has virtually been swallowed up as a southern suburb of RHYL, it is a place of great antiquity, which is manifest in many old buildings, particularly the ruins of Edward I's mighty castle. Its name reflects the red-coloured soil on the banks of the River CLWYD here, which would have been noted in early times when this was the lowest place on the river that could be forded. Recorded in 1036 as *Rudelan*.

Rhum *see* **Rum**

Rhyl (Clywd) 'The hill'. *Yr* (Welsh) 'the'; *hyll* (Old English) 'hill'. This North Wales coastal resort, which developed in the early Victorian era, has an old name that is a linguistic hybrid with a meaning that does not accord to the normal description of a 'hill'. The land does however gradually slope southwards from the shore. A mid-14th century record shows *Ryhull*.

Rhymney (Mid Glamorgan) 'The auger'. *Rhwmp-ni* (Welsh) 'auger', 'borer'. This South Wales coal-mining and industrial town east of MERTHR TYDFIL lies at the head of the Rhymney Valley and takes its name from the river of the same name. In Welsh, it is *Rhymni*.

Ribchester (Lancashire) Place of 'the Roman fort on the River Ribble'. *Ribble* (Old English river name from *ripel*) 'tearing one'; *ceaster* (Old English) 'Roman station'. This village on the River Ribble, upstream and northeast of PRESTON, is on the site of the former Roman fort of *Bremetenacum Veteranorum*. It appears in the Domesday Book as *Ribelcastre*.

Richmond (Greater London; North Yorkshire) Place of 'the strong hill'. *Riche* (Old French) 'strong'; *mont* (Old French) 'hill'. Recorded as *Richemund* around 1110, the renowned northern castellated market-town, situated southwest of DARLINGTON, clearly reveals its Anglo-Norman origin. The LONDON borough bearing this name, and centred on the famous **Richmond Park**, was an area previously known as *Sheen*, which Henry VII had renamed after the northern town in the 15th century; it was noted as *Richemount* in 1502.

Rickmansworth (Hertfordshire) 'Ricmaer's enclosure'. *Ricmaer* (Old English personal name); *worth* (Old

English) 'enclosure'. The name of this town, northwest of LONDON, was noted as *Prichemareworde* in the Domesday Book, and as *Richemaresworthe* in about 1180.

Rievaulx (North Yorkshire) Place at 'the valley of the River Rye'. *Rye* (Brythonic Celtic river name—probably cognate with Latin *rivus*) 'stream'; *val* (Old French) 'valley'. The name of this village north of YORK, famous for the majestic ruins of its 12th-13th-century Cistercian abbey, was documented in 1157 as *Rievalle*, manifesting a strong Anglo-Norman influence and translation of a possible earlier *Ryedale*. It is correctly pronounced 'Revo' but locally as 'Riverz'. *Compare* JERVAULX ABBEY.

Ringwood (Hampshire) Probably place of 'the boundary wood'. *Rimuc* (Old English conjectural word) 'boundary'; *wudu* (Old English) 'wood'. Recorded as *Rimucwuda* in 955, this town, to the southwest of SOUTHAMPTON, reflects its location on the western edge of the NEW FOREST.

Rinns of Galloway (Dumfries and Galloway) The land of 'the promontories'. *Roinn* (Scottish Gaelic) 'point', 'promontory'. This long hammer-head-shaped peninsula in the far southwest of Scotland is qualified by Galloway as the specific locative. The Rinns of ISLAY is another notable example of the use of this name form.

Ripley (Derbyshire) Place of 'the strip-shaped clearing'. *Ripel* (Old English) 'strip'; *leah* (Old English) 'woodland clearing'. The relatively common name of this town, in the coal-mining district north of DERBY, was recorded as *Ripelei* in the Domesday Book of 1086.

Ripon (North Yorkshire) Place in the territory of 'the Hrype tribe'. *Hrypum* (dative plural of *Hrype*—old tribal name of obscure etymology). The name of this small town with its renowned cathedral was recorded as *Hyrpis* in the early 8th century, and *Ripum* in the Domesday Book of 1086. *Compare* REPTON.

Risborough, Monks and **Princes** (Buckinghamshire) Places by 'the hill where brushwood grows'. *Hrisen*

(Old English) 'growing with brushwood'; *beorg* (Old English) 'hill'. Lying at the foot of the CHILTERN HILLS south of AYLESBURY, the town of Princes Risborough and its attendant village was first recorded as *Hrisanbyrge* in 903 and later as *Risenberge* in the Domesday Book. Distinguishing manorial affixes were added in the 14th century, indicating possession by the Black Prince and monks of CANTERBURY respectively.

Risca (Gwent) 'The bank'. *Rhisga* (Welsh) 'bank'. The name of this heavy-industry town northwest of NEWPORT aptly describes the rising or banking ground on which it stands above the Ebbw River.

Rishton (Lancashire) 'Farmstead where rushes grow'. *Risc* (Old English) 'rushes'; *tun* (Old English) 'farmstead'. This small textiles town, northeast of BLACKBURN, was recorded as *Riston* in about 1205.

Robin Hood's Bay (North Yorkshire) This coastal resort is located on the bay of the same name, southeast of WHITBY. The name first appeared as *Robin Hoode Baye* in 1532, representing one of several places that have so commemorated the renowned legendary folk hero and outlaw, whose adventures were popularised in ballards.

Roby (Merseyside) 'Farmstead or village by a boundary-mark'. *Ra* (Old Norse) 'boundary', 'landmark'; *by* (Old Norse) 'farmstead', 'village'. This town, immediately east of LIVERPOOL, was questionably noted as *Rabil* in the Domesday Book of 1086, but is recorded in 1185 as *Rabi*.

Rochdale (Greater Manchester) 'Valley of the River Roch'. *Rache* (Old English river name, back-formation from *Recedham*—former name of settlement here); *dalr* (Old Norse) 'valley'. The name of this industrial town, on the River Roch northeast of MANCHESTER, was originally called something like *Recedham*, as recorded in the Domesday Book of 1086; meaning 'homestead by the hall', it derived from *reced* (Old English) 'building', 'hall'; *ham* (Old English) 'homestead'. Later, around 1195, it was documented as *Rachedal*.

Rochester (Kent) 'Roman station called Hrofi'. *Hrofi* (Brythonic Celtic name contracted form of *Durobrivis*—the Roman name of the fort here); *ceaster* (Old English) 'Roman fort or town'. The name of this ancient city and port on the River MEDWAY, now part of the 'Medway Towns' conurbation, was recorded as *Hrofaescaestir* in 731, and *Rovecestre* in the Domesday Book of 1086.

Rochford (Essex) 'Ford of the hunting dog'. *Raecc* (Old English) 'hunting dog'; *ford* (Old English) 'river crossing'. This town north of SOUTHEND-ON-SEA was recorded as *Rochefort* in the Domesday Book of 1086.

Rockall (Western Isles) Apparently 'bald island in a rough sea'. *Rok* (Old Norse) 'stormy sea'; *kollr* (Old Norse) 'bald head'. This derivation, as suggested by one authority, aptly describes the small, uninhabited and remote island that rises to only 63 ft (19 m) above sea level and lies some 186 miles (300 km) west of ST KILDA.

Rodings, The (Essex) Settlements of 'Hrotha's people'. *Hrotha* (Old English personal name); *ingas* (Old English) 'people of'. This is the general name for the area between CHELMSFORD and BISHOP'S STORTFORD, which is centred on the River Roding, after which eight local villages have been named **Roding**, each with the addition of their respective distinguishing affixes: **Abbess**; **Aythorpe**; **Beauchamp**; **Berners**; **High**; **Leaden**; **Margaret**; and **White**.

Romford (Greater London) Place of 'the broad ford'. *Rum* (Old English) 'broad', 'wide'; *ford* (Old English) 'river crossing'. This former ESSEX town, now a district of the borough of HAVERING, was recorded as *Romfort* in 1177. The River Rom here has a back- formation name.

Romiley (Greater Manchester) 'Spacious woodland clearing'. *Rum* (Old English) 'broad', 'spacious'; *leah* (Old English) 'clearing'. The name of this town, east of STOCKPORT, was documented in the 1086 Domesday Book as *Rumelie*.

Romney (Kent) 'Place of the broad river'. *Rum* (Old

English) 'broad'; *ea* (Old English) 'river'. This low-lying area, west of the coast near DYMCHURCH, known today as the **Romney Marsh**, is well drained but presumably once had a 'broad river' running through it. At the southern edge of this area, the town of **New Romney** (one of the original five Cinque Ports) and the village of **Old Romney** derive their basic name from this former marshland feature.

Romsey (Hampshire) 'Rum's island'. *Rum* (Old English personal name); *eg* (Old English) 'island' or 'elevated drier land in marsh'. The original settlement of this town, northwest of SOUTHAMPTON, probably grew up on the raised ground above the River Test, where a 10th-century abbey was founded. Its name was noted as *Rummaesig* in about 970, and *Romesy* in the Domesday Book of 1086.

Rona (Highland) 'Rough rocky island'. *Hraun* (Old Norse) 'rough', 'rocky'; *ey* (Old Norse) 'island'. Such a derivation aptly describes this small, uninhabited island lying to the north of RAASAY, with a terrain mainly of exposed ancient Lewisian gneiss bedrock. It is sometimes referred to as **South Rona** to distinguish it from **North Rona**, a small, isolated, rocky islet in the Atlantic Ocean, 45 miles (72 km) northwest of CAPE WRATH.

Ronaldsay, North (Orkney) Apparently 'Ringan's isle'. *Ringan* (Old Norse personal name) of unknown origin; *ey* (Old Norse) 'island'. This island, the most northerly and one of the smallest in the ORKNEY archipelago, is farthest from South Ronaldsay, with which it appears to share a basic name element only by coincidence.

Ronaldsay, South (Orkney) 'Rognvaldr's isle'. *Rognvaldr* (Old Norse personal name) equivalent to *Ranald* (Scottish Gaelic) or *Ronald* (Scots); *ey* (Old Norse) 'island'. South Ronaldsay is connected to Burray, which is in turn joined on to the MAINLAND of ORKNEY by the Churchill Barrier, a causeway built as a World War II defence of SCAPA FLOW

Roscommon (Roscommon) 'St Coman's wood'. *Ros* (Irish Gaelic) 'wood'; *Comain* (Irish Gaelic personal name) an 8th-century monk who established a religious foundation here in this county town, that in turn gave its name to the county. The Irish name is *Ros Comain*.

Roscrea (Tipperary) 'Cré's wood'. *Ros* (Irish Gaelic) 'wood'; *Cré* (Irish Gaelic personal name) unidentified. The association of someone called Cré with this market town north of THULES remains obscure.

Rosemarkie (Highland) 'Promontory of the horse'. *Ros* (Scottish Gaelic) 'promontory'; *marc* (Scottish Gaelic) 'horse'. This BLACK ISLE village lies to the north of a long promontory known as Chanonry Point, which juts into the MORAY Firth; the town south of the same point is FORTROSE.

Roslin (Lothian) Apparently 'unploughable land by the pool'. *Ros* (Scottish Gaelic elided form of *riasg*) 'stubborn land with dirk grass', 'unploughable moor'; *linn* (Scottish Gaelic) 'pool'. This former mining village lies on the north bank of the deeply incised North Esk river, upstream of PENICUIK and close to the 14th-century Rosslyn Castle and its collegiate chapel of 1446. The name was recorded as *Roskelyn* in 1240.

Ross (Highland) According to one authority 'moorland'. *Ros* (Scottish Gaelic elided form of *riasg*) 'moor'. The other meanings of *ros*:, 'headland' and 'wood', it has been suggested, might equally be appropriate here. This ancient territorial name has been incorporated into the administrative district and former county of **Ross and Cromarty**, or ROSS-SHIRE, also split geographically into **Wester Ross** and **Easter Ross**.

Rossendale, Forest of (Lancashire) The name of this high moorland region to the south of BURNLEY, bounded by the valleys of the Irwell and Calder rivers, has an origin and meaning that remains uncertain. It is considered by some authorities that, like the Scottish region of ROSS, the roots of the first element may lie in an ancient Celtic word that conveys the sense of 'moorland', while the latter part represents the 'dales'. Records show: *Rocendal* 1241; *Rossendale* 1292; *Roscindale* 1296.

Rosslare (Wexford) 'Middle headland'. *Ros* (Irish Gaelic) 'headland'; *lair* (Irish Gaelic) 'middle'. This popular seaside resort and ferry port takes its name from the *Ros Lair*, the middle headland here that lies between Raven Point to the north and Greenore Point to the south.

Ross-on-Wye (Hereford and Worcester) Place on 'the hill spur above the River Wye'. *Rhos* (Welsh) 'hill spur'; *an* (Old English) 'beside', 'above'; *Wye* (pre-English river name—distinguishing affix) 'the mover'. This market town situated on a steep hill above the River Wye, upstream and northeast of MONMOUTH, is close enough to Wales to have a name of Welsh origin, the full modern translation of which is *Rossan-ar-Wy*. The entry in the Domesday Book of 1086 was simply *Rosse*.

Rosyth (Fife) Possibly 'headland of the arrows'. *Ros* (Scottish Gaelic) 'headland'; *saighead* (Scottish Gaelic) 'arrow'. The original association of the latter is unclear, but apt for the large naval dockyard now here on the Firth of FORTH, west of INVERKEITHING.

Rotherham (South Yorkshire) 'Homestead on the River Rother'. *Rother* (Brythonic Celtic river name derived from the root words *ro* + *dubro*) 'chief river'; *ham* (Old English) 'homestead'. The name of this industrial town, at the river confluence of the Rother and Don northeast of SHEFFIELD, was recorded as *Rodreham* in the Domesday Book of 1086.

Rotherhithe (Greater London) 'Landing place for cattle'. *Hryther* (Old English) 'cattle', 'oxen'; *hyth* (Old English) 'landing place'. This riverside district of SOUTHWARK, renowned as the site of the first tunnel under the THAMES and the former Surrey Docks, has an appropriate water transport name, recorded as *Rederheia* in a document of about 1105.

Rothes (Grampian) Place of the 'fortified dwelling'. *Rath* (Scottish Gaelic) 'fortified dwelling'. This small town, situated southeast of ELGIN, is the site of a 13th-century castle, and perhaps earlier fortification.

Rothesay (Strathclyde) 'Rudri' island'. *Rudri* or *Ruari* (Scottish Gaelic personal name) for Roderick Macdonald who was granted BUTE in the 13th century; *ey* (Old Norse) 'island'. Thus this chief town and port of BUTE took an early name of the latter.

Rothwell (Northamptonshire) 'Spring by a clearing'. *Roth* (Old English conjectural word) 'clearing'; *wella* (Old English) 'spring'. The 1086 Domesday Book entry for this small town northwest of KETTERING is *Rodewelle*.

Rottingdean (East Sussex) Probably 'the valley of Rota's people'. *Rota* (Old English personal name); *inga* (Old English—genitive of *ingas*) 'people of'; *denu* (Old English) 'valley'. This coastal town just east of BRIGHTON lies under the slopes of the South DOWNS in a hinterland where the significance of the local 'valley' has resulted in many like-named settlements: Bevendean; Ovingdean; Saltdean; Woodingdean. This name appears in the Domesday Book of 1086 as *Rotingedene*.

Rousay (Orkney) 'Hrolfr's island'. *Hrolfr* (Old Norse personal name—adaptation of Old German *Hrodulf*) 'renown-wolf'; *ey* (Old Norse) 'island'. The name of this island ORKNEY, north of MAINLAND, was documented in 1260 as *Hrolfsey*.

Roxburgh (Borders) 'Hroc's fortified dwelling'. *Hroc* (Old English personal name) 'rook'; *burh* (Old English) 'fortified dwelling', 'castle'. This once great Royal Burgh is now a mere village with but a vestigal mound of the former castle. Recorded as *Rokisburc* in 1127.

Royal Leamington Spa *see* **Leamington Spa**.

Royal Tunbridge Wells *see* **Tunbridge Wells**.

Royston (Hertfordshire) Place of 'Rohesia's cross'. *Crux* (Medieval Latin) 'cross'; *Roaisie* (Medieval Latin personal name) 'woman called Rohesia'; *tun* (Old English—later addition) 'village'. This small town, at the intersection of the ancient ICKNIELD Way and the Roman ERMINE STREET, southwest of CAMBRIDGE, was originally called *Crux Roaisie* in a document of 1184, and referred to a stone cross erected at this important 'crossing' in medieval times. Later records show the transition of the name to its current form: *Crux Roheis* 1209-19; *Croyroys* 1262; *Reyston* 1280; *Roiston* 1286.

Royston (South Yorkshire) 'Hror's farmstead'. *Hror* (Old English personal name); *tun* (Old English) 'farmstead', 'village'. The name of this town, in the coal-mining district to the north of BARNSLEY, was recorded as *Rorestone* in the Domesday Book of 1086.

Royton (Greater Manchester) 'Rye farm'. *Ryge* (old English) 'rye'; *tun* (Old English) 'farmstead'. The simple name of this textiles town, north of OLDHAM, was noted as *Ritton* in 1226. *Compare* RUYTON; RYTON.

Rugby (Warwickshire) 'Hroca's stronghold'. *Hroca* (Old English personal name); *byrig* (Old English—dative of *burh*, later replaced by Old Danish *by*) 'fortified place'. The name of this town, east of COVENTRY, with its famed school noted as the birthplace of rugby football, was recorded as *Rocheberie* in 1086, and *Rokebi* in 1200.

Rugeley (Staffordshire) 'Clearing on or near a ridge'. *Hrycg* (Old English) 'ridge'; *leah* (Old English) 'woodland clearing'. Recorded as *Rugelie* in the Domesday Book, the name of this town, southeast of STAFFORD in the coal-mining district close to the northeastern edge of CANNOCK CHASE, would have aptly described its original situation.

Ruislip (Greater London) 'Rushy leaping place'. *Rysc* (Old English) 'rush'; *hlyp* (Old English) 'leap'. The name of this district of HILLINGDON, at the western end of the LONDON conurbation, probably refers to a ancient crossing point of the local River Pinn that was passable only by leaping over a stretch thick with rushes. It appears in the 1086 Domesday Book as *Rislepe*.

Rum (Highland) 'Roomy island'. *Rom* (Old Norse) 'roomy', 'wide', 'large'; *ey* (Old Norse) 'island', the latter having been dropped. Some prefer *ruim* (Scottish Gaelic) to derive the same meaning of spaciousness. The *h* in the

Rhum alternative spelling was inserted by its early-20th-century owner, Sir George Bullough, a wealthy Lancashire textile magnate. Recorded as *Ruim* in 677.

Runcorn (Cheshire) Place of 'the wide creek'. *Rum* (Old English) 'wide', 'broad'; *cofa* (Old English) 'creek', 'bay'. Designated as a New Town in 1964, it lies on the site of the original settlement here on the south shore of the MERSEY estuary at a point where the latter significantly widens as a result of the River Weaver entering it on the southwestern side of the town. It was recorded as *Rumcofan* in a text of around 1000.

Runnymede (Surrey) 'Council island-meadow'. *Run* (Old English) 'council', 'secret'; *eg* (Old English) 'island'; *maed* (Old English) 'meadow'. This broad meadow, beside the River THAMES near WINDSOR, was so named as it was already a meeting place for royal gatherings and other assemblies long before the famous negotiations that took place here in 1215 between King John and his barons, leading to the sealing of the Magna Carta. The name was recorded as *Ronimede* in that year.

Rushden (Northamptonshire) 'Valley where rushes grow'. *Ryscen* (Old English) 'rushy'; *denu* (Old English) 'valley'. Recorded as *Riseden* in the Domesday Book of 1086, the relatively common name of this footwear-manufacturing town east of WELLINGBOROUGH reflects its location by the low-lying wide valley of the River Nene.

Rutherglen (Strathclyde) Place in the 'red valley'. *Ruadh* (Scottish Gaelic) 'red'; *gleann* (Scottish Gaelic) 'glen', 'valley'. This industrial town is situated southeast of GLASGOW in the CLYDE valley where reddish coloured soils are to be found.

Ruthin (Clwyd) 'The red fort'. *Rhudd* (Welsh) 'red'; *din* (Welsh) 'fort'. This historic and attractive market town in the upper Vale of CLWYD takes its name from either the castle of Edward I, built here in the late 13th century of red sandstone, or a similar red-coloured earlier fort on this commanding ridge site.

Rutland (Leicestershire) 'Rota's estate'. *Rota* (Old English personal name) *land* (Old English) 'estate'. Recorded as *Roteland* in about 1060, the name of this southeastern district of LEICESTERSHIRE, centred on OAKHAM, was the smallest county in BRITAIN from the 13th century until the major local authority reorganisation of 1974.

Ruyton-XI-Towns (Shropshire) 'Rye farm'. *Ryge* (Old English) 'rye'; *tun* (Old English) 'farmstead'. This large village, northwest of SHREWSBURY, is so named with its unusual distinguishing affix on account of the parish here formerly being composed of eleven townships. It was recorded simply as *Ruitone* in the Domesday Book of 1086. *See* ROYTON; RYTON.

Rydal Water (Cumbria) 'Rye valley lake'. *Ryge* (Old English) 'rye'; *dael* (Old English) 'valley'; *waeter* (Old English) 'expanse of water', 'lake'. This lake in the centre of the LAKE DISTRICT between AMBLESIDE and GRASMERE, is one of its smallest. It was formerly known as *Routhmere*, as indicated in a 13th-century document, while the present name first appeared only in 1576, along with that of the nearby village of **Rydal**, well known for its connections with William Wordsworth, the famous Lakeland poet, who lived here between 1817 and 1850.

Ryde (Isle of Wight) Place of 'the small stream'. *Rith* (Old English—in local dialect 'ride') 'small stream'. The name of this coastal resort, on the northeast side of the island, was recorded as *La Ride* in 1257.

Rye (East Sussex) Place 'at the island'. *Atter* (Middle English) 'at the'; *ieg* (Old English) 'island', 'drier land in a marshland'. This town, one of the original five Cinque Ports, now lies 2 miles (3 km) inland, midway between HASTINGS and NEW ROMNEY. The name has come about with the initial *R* being taken from *atter* and added to a smoothed *ie* to give *atte Rie*, and eventually just the modified latter part, recorded as *Ria* in 1130.

Ryton (Tyne and Wear) 'Rye farm'. *Ryge* (Old English) 'rye'; *tun* (Old English) 'farmstead'. The name of this former coal-mining town on the southside of the River TYNE, west of NEWCASTLE UPON TYNE, was recorded as *Ritona* in 1183. *See* ROYTON; RUYTON-XI-TOWNS.

S

Saffron Walden (Essex) 'Valley of the Britons—where saffron was extensively grown'. *Safron* (Middle English—later distinguishing affix) 'saffron'; *wala* (Old English—genitive plural of *walh*) Britons; *denu* (Old English) 'valley'. The name of this historic town, located between CAMBRIDGE and BISHOP'S STORTFORD, was recorded as simply *Waledana* in the Domesday Book of 1086, but noted as *Saffornewalden* in a text of 1582. *See* WALES.

St Agnes (Cornwall) Either of two places in the county: one a village near **St Agnes Head**, southwest of PERRANPORTH, that takes its names from the dedication of the local parish church, recorded as *Sancta Agnes* in 1327; the other, the fourth largest of the ISLES OF SCILLY, apparently has a bogus self-styled 'saintly' name, that locally is known simply as 'Agnes', and in Cornish is *Ag Innis*, probably deriving as *enys* (Old Cornish) 'island'.

St Albans (Hertfordshire) 'Holy place of Saint Alban'. First recorded in its present form as *Aeccelesia santi Albani* in 792, later in 1007 as *Sancte Albanes stow*, and entered in the Domesday Book of 1086 as *Villa Sancti Albani*, the name of this well-known ancient town and cathedral city northwest of LONDON is in commemoration of St Alban who was martyred here in 209. The 8th-century Benedictine abbey, now part of the cathedral, was founded on the site of his execution. Formerly this was the Roman station of *Verulamium*, a name of uncertain Celtic origin and meaning. Subsequently, as documented in the Venerable Bede's '*Historia Ecclesiastica*' of 730, it had two alternative early English names, both incorporating the 'ceaster' ending as reference to the town's previous Roman fortification status, namely: *Verlamaceastir* and *Waeclingaceastir*, with the latter deriving its first element from the Waeclingas tribe who gave their name to WATLING STREET, which runs through here.

St Andrews (Fife) This historic university town and internationally famous home of golf is named after its cathedral, built in 1160 and first called *Kilrule* ('the church of St Regulus'). According to legend it was St Regulus who brought the relics of St Andrew here, not only causing his dedication to this town but also his adoption as the patron saint of Scotland.

St Asaph (Clwyd) This village and its small cathedral situated on the River Elwy to the south of RHYL, take their name from St Asaph, the 6th-century pupil of St Kentigern, later to become a bishop active in these parts. The Welsh name is *Llanelwy*, meaning 'church on the Elwy'.

St Austell (Cornwall) Church of 'St Austol'. This market town and centre for the Cornish china-clay industry, northest of TRURO, takes the name of the local 6th-century monk and saint. It was recorded as *ecclesia de Austol* in the mid 12th century.

St Bees Head (Cumbria) 'The headland of St Bega'. This prominent headland of red sandstone cliffs, protruding into the Irish Sea as the most westerly point of CUMBRIA, together with the nearby village of **St Bees** with its former 12th-century priory, has a name dedicated to a 7th-century virgin saint said to be of Irish descent. The village name when first recorded in 1125 was *Cherchebi*, derived from *kirkju-by* (Old Norse) 'church village', to which the saint's name was added briefly before the original name was dropped to become *Sancte Bege* in a text of 1291. *See* KENDAL.

St Boswells (Borders) This small town, in the Tweed valley, is named after St Boisil, the 7th-century abbot of MELROSE and friend of St Cuthbert. Nearby is **Newtown St Boswells**, the administrative headquarters for BORDERS region.

St Brides Bay (Dyfed) This large bite out of the southwest coast of Wales takes its name from the small village of St Brides near its southern end. St Bride is more often known as St Brigid of Ireland, the 6th-century abbess of KILDARE, to whom many places in both Wales and Ireland are dedicated.

St David's (Dyfed) This village with its cathedral, situated on the westernmost peninsula of Wales, are dedicated to the patron saint of the principality. In Welsh its name is *Tyddewi*, literally meaning 'house of David'.

St Helens (Merseyside) Lying to the northeast of LIVERPOOL, this industrial town famous for the manufacture of glass, was founded only in the 17th century, with its name referring to the earlier dedication of a chapel to St Helen here, as recorded in a document of 1522.

St Helier (Channel Islands) The name of the capital and main port of JERSEY, which developed from the 16th century, commemorates the island's first saint, a 6th-century Belgian monk who settled here.

St Ives (Cambridgeshire; Cornwall) Both these towns have names of dedication to saints: for the former small agricultural centre on the Great Ouse river, east of HUNTINGDON, it was a St Ivo whose relics where discovered here in the 10th century; and in the case of the Cornish resort and port, north of PENZANCE, was St Ya, a female saint about whom little is known. Respective records show: *Sancto Ivo de Slepe* 1110 (the former affix is derived from the Old English *slaep*, meaning 'slippery place'); *Sancta Ya* 1284.

St Just (Cornwall) Officially known as **St Just in Penwith**, this town to the north of LAND'S END, is the westernmost in England. Its name probably derives from Justus (Latin), an obscure Breton saint and martyr. A record of 1334 refers to *Sancti Justi in Penwithe*. *See* PENWITH.

St Kilda (Western Isles) 'Islands of shields'. The origin of the name of this remote group of rugged islands, lying 35 miles (56 km) northwest of NORTH UIST, does not derive from an association with a St Kilda—no saint of this name has ever existed. According to some authorities, its current name came about by the misreading of its Old Norse name *Skildar*, and by the simple 'crossing of a *t*', a phantom saint was created. The Old Norse name means 'like shields', an apt description of the sharp precipitous cliffs of these islands. The main island of the group is Hirta, another Old Norse name, derived as *hjorth-ey*: 'herd island'.

St Martin's (Cornwall) The third largest of the ISLES OF SCILLY, and most northerly of the five inhabited islands has a name that is dedicated to St Martin of Tours, who conducted much early missionary work in outlying places.

St Mary's (Cornwall) The largest and most populated of the ISLES OF SCILLY is named after the dedication of its parish church to the Virgin Mary as its patron saint.

St Mawes (Cornwall) This coastal town, on the eastern side of the entrance to the Carrick Roads estuary, opposite FALMOUTH, is named after the patron saint of its church, St Maudyth, an obscure Celtic monk with Breton connections. The name was noted as *Sanctus Maudetus* in 1284.

St Monans (Fife) This small East Neuk fishing port on the Firth of FORTH is apparently named after St Monans, the 6th-century bishop of Clonfert in Ireland, to whom its 13th-century Auld Kirk is dedicated. This place name is sometimes spelt as **St Monance**.

St Neots (Cambridgeshire) This town on the Great Ouse river, upstream and southwest of HUNTINGDON, arose around a 10th-century monastery founded here to commemorate the Cornish saint, Neot, whose relics were brought here from the village of **St Neot**, near LISKEARD. A text of 1132 records the name as *S'Neod*.

St Peter Port (Channel Islands) The capital and chief port of GUERNSEY takes the first part of its name from the dedication of its 12th-century church. The 'Port' element was presumably added to emphasize the town's important seaport trading and former fishing activities. The historic association of seafaring folk and strong religious tradition is renowned and manifests itself in many other place names. *See* PORTMARNOCK; PORTPATRICK; PORT ST MARY.

Salcombe (Devon) 'Salt valley'. *Saelt* (Old English) 'salt'; *cumb* (Old English) 'valley'. The name of this resort, on the western side of the entrance to the Kingsbridge Estuary, may be a direct reference to the latter, a ria, or steep-sided river valley drowned by the sea, which is a common topographical feature along the south coast of DEVON and CORNWALL. On the other hand, it may have indicated a place where salt was made, as at BUDLEIGH SALTERTON, further up the coast. The name was noted as *Saltecumbe* in 1244.

Sale (Greater Manchester) Place at 'the sallow tree'. *Sale* (Old English—dative form of *salh*) 'sallow tree', a small willow tree. The name of this former CHESHIRE town, now a residential satellite for MANCHESTER, was recorded in 1205 exactly as now. Its situation on the River MERSEY would have been ideal for willow trees.

Salford (Greater Manchester) 'Ford where sallow trees grow'. *Salh* (Old English) 'sallow tree'; *ford* (Old English) 'river crossing'. This large industrial town, with the former dockland terminal of the ship canal serving MANCHESTER, lying on the River Irwell east of the city centre of the latter, was in pre-urban times, like SALE, an area conducive to willow growth. Its name is noted in the Domesday Book exactly as now.

Salisbury (Wiltshire) 'Stronghold at Sorvio'. *Sorvio-* (Brythonic Celtic root element) of uncertain meaning; *byrig* (Old English—dative form of *burh*) 'fortified place'. Situated on the River Avon, which flows southwards from the nearby **Salisbury Plain**, the name of this ancient site of settlement has had a complex development. The Roman name for their station here was *Sorviodunum*, the second half of the name being based on *dunos* (Brythonic Celtic element), which refers directly to their fort, which was located 2 miles (3 km) to the north at OLD SARUM, itself renowned for its huge Iron Age earthworks and camp. The early Saxon settlers substituted the two parts of the Roman name with their own *searu* + *byrig* (Old English) 'armour-stronghold', which gave the entry of *Sarisberie* in the Domesday Book. It was from a contracted form of the latinised version of this word, *Sarisburiensis*, that the 'Sarum' in Old Sarum is derived. Finally, under Anglo-Norman influence the first *r* was replaced by *l* by a process of phonetic dissimilation during the 13th century, at the time of the building of its majestic cathedral. It was recorded in 1227 as *Salesbury*. Today, the term 'New Sarum' is sometimes used to describe the modern city ,which otherwise is locally pronounced 'Salsbury'.

Salop *see* **Shropshire.**

Saltash (Cornwall) Originally place at 'the ash tree'. *Salt* (Old English prefix) 'salt'; *aesc* (Old English) 'ash tree'. This town at the western end of the Tamar estuary bridge, opposite west of PLYMOUTH, was simply *Aysh* in 1284; but *Saltesh* in 1337, after saltworks set up here.

Saltburn-by-the-Sea (Cleveland) Place by 'the salt stream'. *Salt* (Old English) 'salt'; *burna* (Old English) 'stream'. This coastal resort, east of MIDDLESBROUGH, has a basic name, like that of SALCOMBE, which probably refers not only to the salty river here, but also to the former presence of salt pans by the stream. The name was documented as *Saltburnam* around 1185; the distinguishing affix was added later, largely by way of a promotional enticement.

Saltcoats (Strathclyde) Place of the 'salt sheds'. *Salt* (English) 'saline extraction by panning'; *cotes* (Middle English) 'cottages', 'huts'. The name of this town and resort on the Firth of CLYDE derives from the salt-works established here in the 16th century by James V.

Sandbach (Cheshire) 'Sandy stream in a valley'. *Sand* (Old English) 'sand'; *baec* (Old English) 'stream in a valley'. The name of this small town, northeast of CREWE, was recorded as *Sandbec* in the Domesday Book of 1086.

Sandhurst (Berkshire) 'Sandy wooded hill'. *Sand* (Old English) 'sand'; *hyrst* (Old English) 'wooded hill'. Recorded as *Sandherst* in 1175, the name of this town, with its well-known Royal Military Academy, aptly describes the local wooded hill topography, underlain with 'Bagshot Sands' bedrock.

Sandown (Isle of Wight) Probably the place of 'the sandy enclosure or river meadow'. *Sand* (Old English) 'sandy'; *hamm* (Old English) 'river pasture' or 'enclosure in a river bend'. The name of this coastal resort, northeast of SHANKLIN, has a misleading name that may refer to the upper reaches of the River Yar. Early records document: *Sande* 1086 (Domesday Book); *Sandham* 1271.

Sandringham (Norfolk) 'The sandy part of Dersingham'. *Sand* (Old English prefix) 'sandy'; *Deorsige* (Old English personal name); *inga* (Old English—genitive form of *ingas*) 'people of'; *ham* (Old English) 'homestead'. This aptly descriptive name of the well-known estate-village with its royal residence, northeast of KING'S LYNN, refers comparatively to the neighbouring village of Dersingham just to the north, as indicated in the Domesday Book entry of *Sandersincham*.

Sandwell (West Midlands) 'Sandy spring'. *Sand* (Old English) 'sand'; *wella* (Old English) 'spring'. The name of this administrative district, between BIRMINGHAM and DUDLEY, was noted as *Saundwell* in the 13th century.

Sandwich (Kent) 'Sandy harbour'. *Sand* (Old English) 'sand'; *wic* (Old English) 'harbour'. Recorded as *Sandwic* in 993, this resort east of CANTERBURY, one of the original Cinque Ports, which, like RYE, is now set inland from the sea because of a changing coastline.

Sandy (Bedfordshire) 'Sandy island'. *Sand* (Old English) 'sand'; *eg* (Old English) 'island', 'area of elevated drier ground'. Documented as *Sandeia* in the Domesday Book of 1086, the name of this town, east of BEDFORD, aptly denotes its location on raised sandy land above the valley floor of the River Ivel.

Sankey, Great and **Little** (Cheshire) The basic name of these former LANCASHIRE villages, now western suburbs of WARRINGTON, that lie beside the Sankey Brook Navigation, which in 1755 was the first canal to be cut in England, is named after the Sankey Brook, a Brythonic Celtic river name of obscure origin and meaning.

Sanquhar (Dumfries and Galloway) Place of the 'old fort'. *Sean* (Scottish Gaelic) 'old'; *chathair* (Scottish Gaelic) 'fort'. An ancient earthwork known as the Devil's Dyke is found here. Recorded as *Sanchar* 1150.

Sark (Channel Islands) Tentatively 'the shirt'. *Serkr* (Old Norse) 'shirt'. The forth largest of the island group possibly derives its name from Scandinavian origin, on account of its supposed shape, which is remarkably convincing from a southwesterly viewpoint. It certainly was commonplace for the keen power of Viking observation to make such deductions, and translate them into placenames, especially for islands and coastal features as seen from a seaborne perspective.

Sawbridgeworth (Hertfordshire) 'Saebeorht's enclosure'. *Saebeorht* (Old English personal name); *worth* (Old English) 'enclosure'. Recorded in the Domesday Book of 1086 as *Sabrixteworde*, and *Sabrichteworda* in 1130, the name of this town, just north of HARLOW, manifests Anglo-Norman influences in its transcription to the current form.

Saxmundham (Suffolk) 'Seaxmund's homestead'. *Seaxmund* (Old English personal name) meaning 'protector of the Saxons'; *ham* (Old English) 'homestead'. This small town, inland and northwest of ALDEBURGH, has a very obviously Anglo-Saxon name that appears as the slightly 'softer' *Sasmundesham* in Domesday

Book of 1086, but had assumed its present form in a document of 1213.

Scafell Pike (Cumbria) 'The peak of the hill with a summer pasture'. *Skali* (Old Norse) 'sheiling', 'temporary hut'; *fjall* (Old Norse) 'fell', 'hill'; *pic* (Old English) 'pointed peak'. Situated in the centre of the LAKE DISTRICT, this mountain, which is the highest point in England at 3206 ft (977m) above sea level, has a name that reflects the practice of transhumance. *See* AMBLESIDE. **Sca Fell** is a separate mountain close by.

Scalloway (Shetland) 'Bay of the huts'. *Skali* (Old Norse) 'huts'; *vagr* (Old Norse) 'bay'. This port and second settlement of SHETLAND, 6 miles (10 km) west of LERWICK, derives its name from the temporary huts or booths the Viking people erected here by the bay when attending the annual 'Lawting', or open assembly, held at nearby Tingwall. Scalloway remained Shetland's capital until the early 1600s. *See* DINGWALL.

Scapa Flow (Orkney) Probably 'Sea-flood bay of the boat isthmus'. *Skalpr* (Old Norse) 'boat'; *eith* (Old Norse) 'isthmus'; *floa* (Old Norse) 'flood'. This vast, almost circular bay is surrounded by a chain of islands, which in parts resembles an isthmus but for very narrow channels through which boats could pass and the incoming tide flooded. It was used as a major naval base in both World Wars.

Scarborough (North Yorkshire) 'Skarthi's stronghold'. *Skarthi* (Old Norse personal name) nickname meaning 'hare-lipped'; *burh* (Old English) 'fortified place'. According to Kormak's Saga, this North Sea fishing port and resort, south of WHITBY, was founded as *Scarthaborg* in about 965 by a Viking called Thorgils Skarthi. Subsequent records show: *Scardeburc* 1158; *Escardeburg* c.1160;

Schiehallion (Tayside) 'Fairy hill of the Caledonians'. *Sidh* (Scottish Gaelic) 'fairy hill'; *chaillean* (Scottish Gaelic) 'Caledonians'. This conspicuously striking isolated mountain, of seemingly near perfect conical shape, maintains a certain mystical quality.

Scilly Isles (Cornwall) Lying 28 miles (45 km) southwest of LAND'S END, this group of some 140 islands, the five largest of which are inhabited, has a basic collective name whose origin and meaning remain obscure. Records show: *Sylinancim* (Latin) *c.*400; *Sully c.*1168; *Insula Suilli c.*1200; *Insula de Scilly* 1345.

Scone (Tayside) Place of the 'mound'. *Sgonn* (Scottish Gaelic) 'mound', 'lump'. The reference here is to the Mote Hill, an ancient ritual site of Scottish kings. It was recorded as Sgoinde in 1020. In the early 19th century the name of this small village became **Old Scone**, to distinguish it from the then developing residential town of **New Scone** immediately to the east.

Scotch Corner (North Yorkshire) This well-known road junction and service centre on the Great North Road (formerly the Roman *Dere Street* and now the A1), northeast of RICHMOND, is so called because the main route to southwest Scotland (the A66) branches off here, following the line of another Roman road to cross the PENNINES by the high pass over BOWES MOOR.

Scotland (Britain) 'Land of the Scots'. A country occupying the northern part of Great BRITAIN, and an independent nation until 1707. The original Scots were Celtic invaders from northern IRELAND who in the 5th and 6th centuries settled in the southwest of what was then *Caledonia* or *Pictavia*, the Latin names given earlier by the Romans. By the mid-9th century the name *Scotia* had replaced the latter. The original meaning of Scot-land is unknown. In Scottish Gaelic the name is *Alba*.

Scunthorpe (Humberside) 'Skuma's outlying settlement'. *Skuma* (Old Danish personal name); *thorp* (Old Danish) 'outlying farmstead or hamlet'. This 19th-century iron and steel-making town, east of DONCASTER, takes the name of the small outlying settlement that originated here in the times of the Danelaw. The Scandinavian name had already been 'softened' by Norman influences when recorded in the 1086 Domesday Book as *Escumetorp*.

Seaford (East Sussex) 'Ford by the sea'. *Sae* (Old English) 'sea'; *ford* (Old English) 'river crossing'. Recorded as *Saford* around 1150, the straightforward name of this coastal resort and residential town, southeast of NEWHAVEN, reflects the fact that until a major development of the latter port in the 16th century diverted the River Ouse, there was a ford across its old mouth here.

Seaham (Durham) 'Homestead by the sea'. *Sae* (Old English) 'sea'; *ham* (Old English) 'homestead'. This 19th-century coal port, south of SUNDERLAND, has a simple original name, recorded in a document of about 1050 as *Saeham*.

Seascale (Cumbria) 'Sheilings by the sea'. *Saer* (Old Norse) 'sea'; *skali* (Old Norse) 'temporary huts'; 'sheilings'. The name of this small town and coastal resort, southeast of ST BEES HEAD, was recorded as *Sescales* around 1165. *Compare* SCALLOWAY.

Seaton (Devon) 'Farmstead by the sea'. *Sae* (Old English) 'sea'; *tun* (Old English) 'farmstead', 'village'. Noted in a document of 1244 as *Seton*, this simple and common English placename applies here to the small coastal resort at the mouth of the River Axe, downstream and southwest of AXMINSTER.

Seaton Carew (Cleveland) 'Farmstead by the sea, later possession of Carou manor'. *Sae* (Old English) 'sea'; *tun* (Old English) 'farmstead'; *Carew* (distinguishing manorial affix) family name of Peter Carou, who held the estate here from the late 12th century. The name of this coastal locality, south of HARTLEPOOL, was recorded simply as *Setona* in the 12th century, but as *Seton Carrowe* in 1345.

Sedbergh (Cumbria) Place by 'the flat-topped hill'. *Setberg* (Old Norse) 'flat-topped hill'. Recorded as *Sedberge* in the Domesday Book of 1086, the name of this small town on the slopes of such a hill in lower Garsdale, east of KENDAL, is similar to a form commonplace in Norway and Iceland.

Selborne (Hampshire) Place on 'the stream of the sallow-tree copse'. *Sele* (Old English conjectural derivative of *salh*) 'copse of sallow trees'; *burna* (Old English) 'stream'. This village, southeast of ALTON, renowned as the setting of Gilbert White's celebrated 'Natural History of Selborne', takes the original name of the Oakhanger Stream here. It was recorded as *Seleborne* in a document of 903. *Compare* SELBY.

Selby (North Yorkshire) 'Village by a copse of sallow trees'. *Sele* (Old English conjectural derivative of *salh*) 'sallow-tree copse'; *by* (Old Danish—possible replacement of earlier Old English *-tun* ending) 'farmstead', 'village'. The name of this town on the river Ouse, downstream and south of YORK, was recorded as *Seleby* in about 1030.

Selkirk (Borders) 'Church by the hall'. *Sele* (Old English) 'hall', 'manor house'; *circe* (Old English) 'church'. This woollen-manufacturing town on the Yarrow Water, southwest of GALASHIELS, was recorded as *Selechirche* in 1124.

Sellafield (Cumbria) Probably 'land by the willow-tree mound'. *Selja* (Old Norse) 'willow tree'; *haugr* (Old Norse) 'mound'; *feld* (Old English) 'open land'. Recorded as *Sellofeld* in 1576, the aptly descriptive name of this former small settlement, on the River Calder close to the Cumbrian coast northwest of SEASCALE, has more recently taken on a very modern significance as the name of the Atomic Energy Authority's major research centre, which was formerly known as *Windscale* and included the *Calder Hall* atomic power station, whose reactors were the first in the world to generate electricity on a commercial scale.

Selsey (West Sussex) 'Seal island'. *Seolh* (Old English) 'seal'; *eg* (Old English) 'island'. This seaside resort and residential town, south of CHICHESTER, occupies the 'beak-like' promontory culminating in **Selsey Bill**, which in early times would have been virtually cut off by a stream running across the low-lying hinterland. It is assumed that the shore here was once frequented by seals. The name was noted as *Seolessiae* in 715. *Selsey Bill* was not documented until the 18th century. *Compare* PORTLAND BILL.

Sennen (Cornwall) This village, immediately east of LAND'S END, and the nearby former fishing port of **Sennen Cove** are named after St Senan, the patron saint of the local parish church. Little is known of him or her, except that there may have been a Breton connection. The basic name of these places was documented as the parish of *Sancta Senana* in 1327.

Sevenoaks (Kent) Place by 'seven oak trees'. *Seofon* (Old English) 'seven'; *ac* (Old English) 'oak tree'. Recorded as *Sevenac* in about 1200, the name of this residential town to the south of the North DOWNS, west of MAIDSTONE, reflects the legendary magic of the number 'seven'. Here, tradition is maintained with civic preservation of seven oaks planted in recent times, despite the temporary loss of six in the 1987 hurricane.

Seven Sisters (East Sussex) This is the relatively recent name given to the seven white chalk cliffs, representing the dramatic end of the South DOWNS, west of BEACHY HEAD. A record of 1588 refers to this famous coastal feature as *the Seven Cliffes*.

Severn (England/Wales) This, the longest river in Britain, rising in central Wales and flowing some 220 miles (350 km) to its estuary and eventually the BRISTOL Channel, has an ancient pre-Celtic name of uncertain origin. It was recorded by the Romans as *Sabrina*, and later as *Saefern* in 863, and *Saverna* in the Domesday Book of the late 11th century. In Welsh it is *Hafren*.

Shaftesbury (Dorset) Probably 'Sceaft's stronghold'. *Sceaft* (Old English personal name) unidentified; *byrig* (Old English—dative form of *burh*) 'fortified place'. The name of this town, situated on a steep escarpment overlooking Blackmoor Vale, northeast of YEOVIL, was recorded as *Sceaftesburi* in 877.

Shankill (Antrim) Place of the 'old church'. *Sean* (Irish Gaelic) 'old'; *cill* (Irish Gaelic) 'church'. A 19th-century western suburb of BELFAST whose name has become familiar because of the recent 'troubles'. Its simple name probably stems from an old church that was the centre of a pre-urban settlement here.

Shanklin (Isle of Wight) Place of 'the hill with a cup'. *Scenc* (Old English) 'cup'; *hlinc* (Old English) 'hill', 'ridge'. The real sense of the name of this resort on SANDOWN Bay is the waterfall at Shanklin Chine, with water tumbling down as if flowing out of a cup. The name appears in the 1086 Domesday Book as *Sencliz*.

Shannon (Ireland) Probably, 'the old one'. This, the longest river in the BRITISH ISLES, flowing 240 miles (386 km) from its source in CAVAN, forms part of the boundaries of ten other counties before discharging into the Atlantic Ocean. Its ancient name derives from a root word similar to the Irish Gaelic *sean*, meaning the 'old' one; the personification of some life-giving water god perhaps. The 2nd-century Roman geographer Ptolemy recorded the river's name as *Senos*.

Shap (Cumbria) 'Heap of stones'. *Heap* (Old English) 'heap'. Named as *Hep* in *c*.1190, this small town, south of PENRITH, refers to an ancient stone circle, near **Shap Summit**, which is well known to road and rail travellers as the highest point on the main 'west-coast' route.

Sheerness (Kent) Place of 'the bright headland'. *Scir* (Old English) 'bright', 'clear'; *naess* (Old English) 'headland'. The name of this resort and port, on a promontory at the northeast end of the Isle of SHEPPEY, was recorded as *Shernesse* in 1221.

Sheffield (South Yorkshire) 'Open land by the River Sheaf'. *Sheaf* (Old English river name based on *sceath*) 'boundary' or 'dividing one'; *feld* (Old English) 'open land'. Documented as *Scafeld* in the Domesday Book of 1086, this famous steel-product-making city, east of the High Peak District, takes its name from the River Sheaf that joins the River Don here, previously forming the boundary between Derbyshire and the former West Riding of Yorkshire. *Compare* Mersey.

Sheppey, Isle of (Kent) 'Sheep island'. *Sceap* (Old English) 'sheep'; *eg* (Old English) 'island'. This low-lying island off, but close to, the north coast of the county, east of the Medway, has long been ideal grazing for sheep. The name was recorded as *Scepieg* around 700, and appears as *Scape* in the Domesday Book. *Compare* Fair Isle.

Shepton Mallet (Somerset) 'Sheep farm, later possession of Malet manor'. *Sceap* (Old English) 'sheep'; *tun* (Old English) 'farmstead'; *Malet* (later Anglo-Norman distinguishing manorial affix) of the family of Robert Malet from Normandy, who held the estate here in the early 12th century. The common basic name of this town at the eastern end of the Mendip Hills, to the south of Bristol, was recorded as *Sepetone* in the Domesday Book of 1086, but as *Sheopton Malet* in 1226-28.

Sherborne (Dorset) Place by 'the clear stream'. *Scir* (Old English) 'bright', 'clear'; *burna* (Old English) 'stream'. This historic agricultural market centre on the River Yeo, downstream and east of Yeovil, is presumably named after a description or even a former name of this river, as alluded to in a text of 864 that records it as *aet Scireburnan*.

Sheringham (Norfolk) 'Homestead of Scira's people'. *Scira* (Old English personal name); *inga* (Old English—genitive of *ingas*) 'people of'; *ham* (Old English) 'homestead'. This coastal resort, west of Cromer, was recorded in the Domesday Book as *Silingeham*, showing early Anglo-Norman influences in softening the pronunciation, but by 1242 a record indicated a reversion of the name to nearer its original form as *Scheringham*.

Sherwood Forest (Nottingham) 'Shire wood' *Scir* (Old English) 'shire', 'district'; *wudu* (Old English) 'wood', 'forest'. This ancient royal forest, famous for its associations with the folk hero Robin Hood, formerly covered an extensive area for about 20 miles (32 km) north of NOTTINGHAM, of which sizeable areas remain. Recorded in 955 as *Scirwudu*, the name implies that this important stretch of woodland had the distinctive status of 'belonging to the Shire'.

Shetland (Scotland) 'Hilt land'. *Hjalt* (Old Norse) 'hilt of a sword' or 'dagger'; *land* (Old Norse) 'land'. The reference here is to the sword-shaped outline of these islands as appreciated by the early Viking navigators. While the first *l* was dropped, the initial *Hj* was mutated to the now common *Sh*, and in some areas by the Gaelic mutation to *Z*, giving the alternative spelling of *Zetland*.

Shields, North and South (Tyne and Wear) Places of 'the temporary sheds or huts'. *Scheles* (Middle English) 'sheds or huts temporarily used', in this case by fishermen. These twin towns, which sit respectively on the north and south banks of the River TYNE at its mouth, were strategically placed as bases for early offshore fishing here. Records show their names as *Chelis* 1268 (North Shields); *Scheles* 1235 (South Shields).

Shifnal (Shropshire) 'Scuffa's nook'. *Scuffa-n* (Old English personal name—genitive form) unidentified; *halh* (Old English) 'nook', 'corner of land'. The name of this small town, east of TELFORD, was recorded as *Scuffanhalch* in a document of 644.

Shildon (Durham) Place of 'the shelf-hill'. *Scelf* (Old English) 'shelf'; *dun* (Old English) 'hill'. The aptly descriptive name of this town, in the hilly former coal-mining district to the southeast of BISHOP AUCKLAND, was recorded as *Sciluedon* in a document of 1214.

Shipley (West Yorkshire) Place of 'the clearing where sheep are kept'. *Sceap* (Old English) 'sheep'; *leah* (Old English) 'woodland clearing'. The relatively common name of this industrial town on the River Aire, north of BRADFORD, appears in the Domesday Book as *Scipeleia*.

Shoreditch (Greater London) Probably 'the ditch by, or draining, a slope'. *Scora* (Old English conjectural word) 'slope'; *dic* (Old English) 'ditch'. Noted as *Soredich* in about 1148, the origin of the well-known name of this district of HACKNEY remains uncertain.

Shoreham-by-Sea (West Sussex) 'Homestead by a slope'. *Scora* (Old English conjectural word) 'slope', 'bank'; *ham* (Old English) 'homestead'. The name of this container port, west of BRIGHTON, takes its name from the original settlement situated slightly inland by the slopes of the South DOWNS; recorded as *Sorham* in 1073, this is the district now called **Old Shoreham**. For a time the coastal extension was known as 'New Shoreham', being documented as *Noua Sorham* in 1235, the current promotional and distinguishing affix being applied only in the 19th century.

Shotton (Clwyd) The name of this steel-making town located on the south bank of the River DEE between CONNAH'S QUAY and QUEENSFERRY has several possible derivations, but without substantiation by historical records all remain conjectural: *Scot* + *tun* (Old English) 'Scots' village'; *Scot* + *dun* (Old English) 'Scots' hill'; *Sceot* + *tun* (Old English) 'farmstead by the steep slope'.

Shotts (Strathclyde) Place of 'steep slopes'. *Sceots* (Scottish Gaelic) 'steep slopes'. This former mining town lies on a high undulating plateau that forms part of the watershed between the FORTH and CLYDE river basins. *See* KIRK O' SHOTTS.

Shrewsbury (Shropshire) 'Fortified place of the scrubland'. *Scrobb* (Old English conjectural word) 'scrubland'; *byrig* (Old English—dative form of *burh*) 'stronghold'. The name of this county town has evolved over the centuries as records show: *Scobbesbyrig* 1016; *Sciropesberie* 1086 (Domesday Book); *Salopesberia* 1094; *Shrobesbury* 1327; *Schroysbury* 1387; *Schrevisbery* 1461; *Shrewsbury* 1485. From this transition it can be seen how the preferred pronunciation is still 'Shrowsbury'.

Shropshire (England) This name of the western MIDLANDS county, near to the Welsh border, is a contraction of an old version of SHREWSBURY, with the addition of *scir* (Old English) 'district'. It was first recorded as *Scrobbesbyrigscir* in 1006. The alternative county name **Salop** is an abbreviation of the 'softened' Anglo-Norman version, noted as *Salopescira* in 1094.

Sidlaw Hills (Tayside) Possibly 'hills of seats'. *Suidhe* (Scottish Gaelic) 'seat'; *hlaw* (Old English) 'hill'. This range of hills, extending northeastwards from PERTH to FORFAR, has a ridgy regularity apart from several notable flat-topped summits which may have prompted the 'seat' description.

Sidmouth (Devon) Place 'at the mouth of the River Sid'. *Sid* (Old English river name based on sid) 'broad one'; *mutha* (Old English) 'river mouth'. The simple name of this coastal resort, south of HONITON, was recorded as *Sedemutha* in the Domesday Book of 1086.

Silloth (Cumbria) 'Barn by the sea'. *Sae* or *saer* (Old English or Old Norse) 'sea'; *hlatha* (Old Norse) 'barn'. The name of this small resort and port, on the SOLWAY FIRTH west of WIGTON, appears in a document of 1299 as *Selathe*.

Silverstone (Northamptonshire) 'Saewulf's or Sigewulf's farmstead'. *Saewulf*; *Sigewulf* (Old English personal name); *tun* (Old English) 'farmstead'. The name of this village, southwest of NORTHAMPTON, internationally famous for the nearby British Grand Prix motor racing circuit, was recorded as *Sulueston* in 942, and as *Silvestone* in the Domesday Book of 1086.

Sittingbourne (Kent) 'Stream of the slope-dwellers'. *Side* (Old English) 'slope'; *inga* (Old English—dative of *ingas*) 'people of'; *burna* (Old English) 'stream'. This industrial town, east of the MEDWAY Towns, lies on the lower northern slope of the North DOWNS before reaching the flat coastal lowlands opposite the Isle of SHEPPEY. The name was documented as *Sidingeburn* in 1200.

Sixmilecross (Tyrone) The curious name of this TYRONE village would appear to have a similar origin to that of the not so far away FIVEMILETOWN. This place stands at the 'crossroads' six miles equidistant from OMAGH and Ballygawley, and also between Fintona and Pomeroy.

Sizewell (Suffolk) 'Sigehere's spring'. *Sigehere* (Old English personal name); *wella* (Old English) 'spring'. The name of this coastal locality east of LEISTON, well known today as the site of a large nuclear power station, was noted in 1240 as *Syreswell*.

Skara Brae (Orkney) 'Bank by the shore'. *Skari* (Old Norse) 'shore'; *brae* (Scots) 'bank'. This aptly describes the situation of this remarkable Neolithic settlement (3100–2450BC) which was well preserved by the high bank of sand behind the shore at Skaill Bay, on the west coast of MAINLAND, that covered it until excavation in 1850.

Skegness (Lincolnshire) Skeggi's promontory'. *Skeggi* (Old Norse personal name); *nes* (Old Scandinavian) 'promontory' 'headland'. Alternatively the name of this popular East Coast seaside resort, just north of The WASH, is considered by some authorities to derive from *skegg* + *nes* (Old Scandinavian) 'beard-shaped headland'. A 12th-century record has it as *Sceggenesse*.

Skelligs, The (Kerry) 'The splinters'. *Na Scealaga* (Irish Gaelic) 'splinters'. The name of three remote rocky islands off the extreme southwest of Ireland, which is very descriptive of their exposed sharp slates. On Skellig Michael (re Archangel) is a 7th-century cell.

Skelmersdale (Lancashire) 'Skjaldmarr's valley'. *Skjaldmarr* (Old Norse personal name) unidentified; *dalr* (Old Norse) 'dale', 'valley'. The name of this New Town, designated in 1961, and the former mining village, west of WIGAN, takes its form from the name of the original Scandinavian settlement here, recorded in the 1086 Domesday Book as *Schelmeresdale*.

Skerries (Dublin) The place of the 'sea rocks'. *Sceir* (Irish Gaelic) 'sea rocks', 'reefs'. This seaside resort to the north of DUBLIN is named after the group of small rocks lying just offshore here. *Na Sceiri* is the Irish name of this place. *Compare* OUT SKERRIES.

Skipton (North Yorkshire) 'Sheep farm'. *Scip* (Old English modified with Scandinavian *sk-*) 'sheep'; *tun* (Old English) 'farmstead'. The name of this historic sheep-market town in Airedale, northwest of BRADFORD, appears in the Domesday Book of 1086 as *Scipton*.

Skokholm (Dyfed) 'Block island'. *Stokkr* (Old Norse) 'log'; *holmr* (Old Norse) 'island'. This small island off the extreme southwest of Wales, like most islands in the Irish Sea, has a name of Scandinavian origin, which reflects its truncated shape as seen by Viking sailors. Thus it is similar in derivation to Sweden's Stockholm.

Skomer (Dyfed) 'Split island'. *Skalm* (Old Norse) 'split'; *ey* (Old Norse) 'island'. This slightly larger island than its neighbour SKOKHOLM, lies off the far southwest coast of WALES and also has a name describing its outline shape, which manifests a narrow isthmus near its eastern end that all but splits the island in two.

Skye (Highland) 'Winged Isle'. *Sgiathach* (Scottish Gaelic) 'winged'. This is a very obvious reference to the shape of this, the largest of the Inner HEBRIDES, with it many splayed peninsulas.

Sleaford (Lincolnshire) 'Ford over the River Slea'. *Slea* (Old English river-name derived from root element *slim*) 'slimy or muddy one'; *ford* (Old English) 'river crossing'. The relatively straightforward name of this agricultural services and food-processing town, northeast of GRANTHAM, was noted as *Slioford* in 852.

Sleat (Highland) 'The plain'. *Sletta* (Scottish Gaelic) 'plain'. This southwestern peninsula of SKYE, the land of the MacDonalds, can, in contrast to much of the rest of the island, be regarded as a fertile plain.

Slieve Donard (Down) 'Donart's mountain'. *Sliabh* (Irish Gaelic) 'mountain'; *Domhanghart* (Irish Gaelic personal name) Donard. This is the highest peak in the MOURNE MOUNTAINS, and consequently in NORTHERN IRE-

LAND, and is named after Domhanghart (anglicised to Donard), son of the king of Ulidia, and disciple of St Columba, who built his church on the mountain's summit.

Sligo (Sligo) 'Shelly place'. *Sligeach* (Irish Gaelic adaptation of *slige*, a shell) 'shelly'. The name of this cathedral and county town, and the county too, derive from the 'shelly' nature of the river bed here on the west coast of IRELAND.

Slough (Berkshire) Place of 'the muddy hollow'. *Sloh* (Old English) 'slough', 'miry place'. The name of this large 20th-century industrial town just west of the GREATER LONDON conurbation, reflects the original nature of its well-watered, low-lying site on the north side of the meandering River THAMES; it was documented as simply *Slo* in 1195.

Smoo Cave (Highland) 'The hiding place'. *Smuga* (Old Norse) 'hiding place'. This vast sea cavern discreetly cut into the cliffs near DURNESS is aptly named.

Snaefell (Isle of Man) Simply 'snow mountain'. *Snaer* (Old Norse) 'snow'; *fjall* (Old Norse) 'mountain'. The island's highest peak, rising to 2036 ft (621 m) is often snow-covered in the winter. *Compare* SNOWDON.

Snodland (Kent) 'Cultivated land associated with a man called Snodd'. *Snodd* (Old English personal name); *ing* (Old English connective particle) 'associated with'; *land* (Old English) 'agricultural land, newly cultivated'. This now industrial locality on the west bank of the River MEDWAY, south of ROCHESTER, was originally noted as *Snoddingland* in a document of 838.

Snowdon (Gwynedd) 'Snow-capped mountain'. *Snaw* (Old English) 'snow'; *dun* (Old English) 'hill'. This aptly descriptive name reflects the frequent winter appearance of Wales's highest mountain, which rises to 3560 ft (1085 m). Early records show: *Snawdune* 1095; *Mons Snaudunus* 1145; *Snauduna* 1235; *Snauwdon* 1461. Its Welsh name is *Yr Wyddfa*, meaning 'the cairn place'. The relatively modern name for the area around the mountain, now a major

National Park, is *Snowdonia*; the Welsh equivalent of this being the evocative name of *Eryri*, 'the abode of eagles'.

Soho (Greater London) Noted first in 1632, the name of this famous, or infamous, colourful and cosmopolitan district of WESTMINSTER is said to originate from the traditional huntsman's cry, 'So-Ho!', used in pre-urban days when hares thrived on the open land here.

Solent, The (Hampshire) The familiar name of the busy sea channel that separates the ISLE OF WIGHT from the mainland is thought to derive from an ancient Brythonic Celtic root, but its origin and meaning are uncertain. Records show: *Soluente c.*730 (Venerable Bede's *Historia Ecclesiastica*); *Solente c.*890; *Solentan* 948.

Solway Firth (Dumfries and Galloway/Cumbria) 'Fiord of the pillar ford'. *Sul* (Old Norse) 'pillar'; *vath* (Old Norse) 'ford'; *fjordr* (Old Norse) 'fiord', 'firth', 'estuary'. Apparently, the 'pillar' is the legendary LOCHMABEN Stone, a large granite boulder that marked the Scottish end of the ford across the inlet narrows. It was recorded as *Sulewad* in a document of 1229.

Somerset (England) District of 'the settlers around Somerton'. *Somer* (Old English contraction of the settlement name Somerton); *saete* (Old English) 'settlers', 'dwellers'. The name of this county in southwest England first applied to a more restricted area around SOMERTON, being recorded as *Sumaersaeton* in the Anglo-Saxon Chronicle of 1015. When the county as we know it today was formalised under Anglo-Norman rule, its name included the '-shire' ending as appears in the form *Sumersetescir*, as documented in a text of 1122.

Somerton (Somerset) 'Summer farmstead'. *Sumor* (Old English) 'summer'; *tun* (Old English) 'farmstead', 'dwelling'. This small market town, northwest of YEOVIL, has a name that, like AMBLESIDE or SCAFELL, implies the local farming practice of transhumance, but here the condition restricting the land to 'summer-only pasture' would be poor drainage rather than altitude. The name of this settlement was noted in the Domesday Book of 1086 as *Sumertone*.

Sompting (West Sussex) Settlement of 'the marsh dwellers'. *Sumpt* (Old English conjectural word) 'swamp', 'marsh'; *ingas* (Old English) 'people of', 'dwellers of'. Recorded as *Suntinga* in 956 and as the Anglo-Norman-influenced form of *Sultinges* in the Domesday Book of 1086, the name of this residential town, northeast of WORTHING, reflects the probable condition of this low-lying site, which in early times would have been subject to flooding by the nearby sea waters of the English Channel.

Southall (Greater London) 'Southern nook(s) of land'. *Suth* (Old English) 'south', 'southern'; *halh* (Old English) 'nook', 'corner of land'. This district of the borough of EALING has a name that represents the southern counterpart to that of NORTHOLT. it was recorded as *Suhaull* in 1198.

Southampton (Hampshire) 'Riverside farmstead', with later 'southern' prefix . *Suth* (Old English distinguishing affix) 'southern'; *hamm* (Old English) 'riverside land'; *tun* (Old English) 'farmstead'. Recorded in the early 9th century as just *Hamtun*, the former name of this present-day major port and city aptly described the site of the original settlement on a promontory between the Itchen and Test rivers. It was from this name form that the county name HAMPSHIRE was derived. Later, in the 10th century, the 'South' element was added in contradistinction with the other large 'Hampton', which was to become NORTHAMPTON, despite the considerable distance between these two counterparts. A document dated 962 records the name as *Suthhamtun*.

Southborough (Kent) 'Southern borough' of Tonbridge. *Suth* (Old English) 'southern'; *burh* (Old English) 'town' or 'manor'. The virtually self-explanatory name of this town, adjoining TUNBRIDGE WELLS to the north, in fact refers to its origin as an early southern manor in contrast to TONBRIDGE, just to the north. It was recorded as *la South Burgh in Tonbrigge* in 1450.

South Downs *see* **Downs, North** and **South**.

Southend-on-Sea (Essex) 'South end' of Prittlewell parish, 'by the sea'. *South* + *ende* (Middle English) 'southern part'. The basic name of this well-known 19th-century seaside town was originally a mere locational description for the southern part of the former parish here; it was referred to in a text of 1481 as *Sowthende*. The 'on-Sea' distinguishing and promotional affix was added later to attract rail-borne visitors.

South Glamorgan *see* **Glamorgan**.

South Lancing *see* **Lancing**

South Molton (Devon) Probably 'farmstead by the bare-hill'. *Mol-* (Brythonic Celtic conjectural root element related to Welsh *moel*) 'bare hill'; *tun* (Old English) 'farmstead'. Recorded as *Sudmoltone* in the Domesday Book, the basic name of this small market town, southeast of BARNSTAPLE, has added the 'South' affix at an early stage to distinguish it from North Molton, a village nearby to the north.

Southport (Merseyside) This popular seaside resort, north of LIVERPOOL, was developed in the late 18th century, and its artificially created name was first associated with the place in 1798.

South Queensferry *see* **Queensferry, North and South**.

South Ronaldsay *see* **Ronaldsay, South**.

Southsea (Hampshire) This residential town and coastal resort, at the south tip of PORTSEA Island, takes its self-explanatory name from Southsea Castle, built in 1540 at the command of Henry VIII to guard the entrance to PORTSMOUTH Harbour, which was home to an important section of his navy.

South Shields *see* **Shields, North** and **South**.

South Uist *see* **Uist, North and South**.

Southwark (Greater London) 'Southern defensive work'. *Suth* (Old English) 'southern'; *geweorc* (Old English) 'fortifications'. This historic borough, with its own cathedral, originally formed an outpost of the City of LONDON on the south side of the THAMES. Its name was recorded as *Suthgeweork* in 1023, and appears in the Domesday Book as *Sudwerca*. Earlier, in the 10th century, a text made reference to the place as *Suthringa Geweorche*, meaning 'fort of the men of SURREY'.

Southwell (Nottinghamshire) Place of the southern spring'. *Suth* (Old English) 'southern'; *wella* (Old English) 'spring'. The name of this town, with its fine minster church to the west of NEWARK-ON-TRENT, is in contradistinction to the nearby village of Norwell. The actual spring is the Lady Well at the church. The name was recorded in a document of 958 as *aet Suthwellan*.

Southwick (West Sussex) 'Southern farm'. *Suth* (old English) 'southern'; *wic* (Old English) 'outlying farmstead or dairy farm'. The name of this town, which is now part of the densely populated coastal strip west of BRIGHTON, was recorded as *Sudewic* in 1073.

Southwold (Suffolk) 'South forest'. *Suth* (Old English) 'south', 'southern'; *wald* (Old English) 'forest'. Entered in the Domesday Book record of 1086 as *Sudwolda*, the name of this small coastal town, east of HALESWORTH, reflects the former heavily wooded nature of this sandy area, remnants of which can still seen in several forests to the south.

South Yorkshire *see* **Yorkshire**.

Sowerby Bridge (West Yorkshire) 'Muddy place'. *Saurr* (Old Norse) 'mud', 'dirt'; *by* (Old Danish) 'village', 'place'; *brycg* (Old English) 'bridge'. This textiles town, southwest across the River Calder from HALIFAX, takes its basic name from the village of **Sowerby**, just upstream, which was recorded as *Sorebi* in the Domesday Book, while the town name was first noted as *Soureby Brygge* in 1478, suggesting the later building of a bridge over the river here.

Spalding (Lincolnshire) Settlement of 'the descendants of Spaldas'. *Spaldas* (obscure tribal name possibly related to continental place of origin called *Spald*) unidentified; *ingas* (Old English) 'people of'. This renowned bulb-growing centre, in the middle of the LINCOLNSHIRE FENS known as the district of HOLLAND, has a name with a first root element common to several other places in eastern ENGLAND: **Spalding Moor**; **Spaldington**; **Spaldwick**; **Spalford**. Records show: *Spallinge* 1086 (Domesday Book); *Spaldingis* c.1115.

Spennymoor (Durham) Probably 'the moor with a fence'. *Spenning* (Old English or Old Scandinavian conjectural word) 'fence', 'hedge'; *mor* (Old English) 'moor'. The name of this industrial town, northeast of BISHOP AUCKLAND, was noted as *Spendingmor* in about 1336.

Spithead (Hampshire) Roadstead off 'the headland of the pointed sandbank'. *Spitu* (Old English) 'elongated strip of sand projecting from the shore'; *heafod* (Old English) 'headland'. This famous stretch of water, regarded as a suitably sheltered anchorage for royal naval reviews in recent centuries, lies off the entrance to PORTSMOUTH Harbour, with an actual sandbank, formerly known as **Spit Sand**, now built over as part of GOSPORT. The name was first evident in 1673.

Spurn Head (Humberside) 'Hfran's spur-shaped gravel-bank headland'. *Hfran* (Old Scandinavian personal name) meaning 'raven'; *eyrr* (Old Scandinavian) 'gravel bank'; *spurn* (Middle English related to Old English *spurnan* 'to kick') 'spur', 'projecting strip of land'; *head* (Middle English related to Old English *heafod*) 'headland'. This distinctive headland at the end of a long spit of land on the north side of the entrance to the HUMBER estuary was recorded in 1399 as *Ravenserepourne*, which was contracted first to *Ravenspurn* in the 15th century and eventually to the current form with the addition of the later generic.

Staffa (Strathclyde) 'Pillar island'. *Stafr* (Old Norse) 'staff', 'rod', 'pillar'; *ey* (Old Norse) 'island'. This clearly describes the famous vertical columns of basaltic rock found on this small uninhabited island lying to the west of MULL. *See* FINGAL'S CAVE.

Stafford (Staffordshire) 'Ford by a landing place'. *Staeth* (Old English) 'landing place'; *ford* (Old English) 'river crossing'. This, the county town of STAFFORDSHIRE, lies on the River Sow, a tributary of the River TRENT, 5 miles (8 km) west of the confluence with the latter; its name was recorded as *Staefford* in 913. The name of the surrounding county was documented in 1016 as *Staeffordscir*, showing the addition of *scir* (Old English) 'district'.

Staines (Surrey) Place of 'the stone'. *Stan* (Old English) 'stone'. The name of this town on the River THAMES, south of HEATHROW airport, was first recorded as the singular *Stane* in the early 11th century, but by the time of the Domesday Book survey had acquired a plural *s*, as *Stanes*. It is said to refer to a former milestone on the Roman road that passed through here.

Stalybridge (Greater Manchester) 'Bridge at the wood where staves are got'. *Staef* (Old English) 'stave'; *leah* (Old English) 'wood' or 'woodland clearing'; *bridge* (later Modern English addition) 'bridge'. Originally the name of this town on the River Tame, east of MANCHESTER, was simply *Stavelay*, as recorded in 1282, but later expansion across the river resulted in the present name form being used in 1637. *Compare* STAVELEY.

Stamford (Lincolnshire) Place of 'the stone ford'. *Stan* (Old English) 'stone'; *ford* (Old English) 'river crossing'. The name of this ancient town, at an important crossing point of the Roman ERMINE STREET (later to become the Great North Road or A1) over the River Welland, almost certainly refers to the former ford here being paved with stones for ease of passage. It was recorded as *Steanford* in 922, and as *Stanford* in the Domesday Book of 1086.

Stamford Bridge (Humberside) Place of 'the bridge by the stone ford'. The name of this village, on the River Derwent northeast of YORK, famous as the site of King Harold of England's victory over King Harald Hardrada of Norway in 1066, has a basic origin and derivation identical with that of STAMFORD in LINCOLNSHIRE, even to being the place of a Roman road crossing. The ford here was replaced by an early bridge, as evident in a document of about 1075 that shows the name as *Stanfordbrycg*.

Stanford-le-Hope (Essex) 'Stone ford in the bay'. *Stan* (Old English) 'stone'; *ford* (Old English) 'river crossing'; *le* (Old French—definite article after loss of preposition) 'in the'; *hop* (Old English distinguishing affix) 'bay'. This town southwest of BASILDON lies on a small stream near the River THAMES at a point where the latter makes a wide bend, known as Lower Hope Reach. The name of this settlement in 1068 was recorded simply as *Stanford*, but in a document of 1361 the full version of *Stanford in the Hope* was evidenced.

Stanley (Durham) Place of 'the stony clearing'. *Stan* (Old English) 'stone'; *leah* (Old English) 'woodland clearing'. This former coal-mining town, west of CHESTER-LE-STREET, has a name that is relatively common in the Midlands and the north of England. It was recorded in 1287 with a spelling exactly as now.

Stansted (Essex) 'Stony place'. *Stan* (Old English) 'stone'; *stede* (Old English) 'place'. The name of this village, northeast of BISHOP'S STORTFORD, now well known for the nearby location of LONDON's third international airport, was recorded in the Domesday Book as *Stanesteda*. In order to distinguish this fairly common name, a manorial affix of the family of Richard de Munifichet was often incorporated to read *Stansted Mountfichet*, as in a text of around 1290.

Stapleford (Nottinghamshire) 'Ford marked by a post'. *Stapol* (Old English) 'post', 'pillar'; *ford* (Old English) 'river crossing'. The fairly common name of this town on the River Erewash, southwest of NOTTINGHAM, which appears in the Domesday Book as now, signifies a need to alert or direct travellers using this ford.

Staveley (Derbyshire) Place at 'the wood where staves are got'. *Staef* (Old English) 'stave'; *leah* (Old English) 'wood' or 'woodland clearing'. The name of this industrial town, northeast of CHESTERFIELD, was noted as *Stavelie* in the Domesday Book. *Compare* STALYBRIDGE.

Stenhousemuir (Central) 'Moorland by the stone house'. *Stan* (Old English) 'stone'; *hus* (Old English) 'house'; *mor* (Old English) 'moor'. The meaning in this order rather than the other way round, i.e. of the 'stone house on the moor', is clearly the case as the final element was added only in the 17th century. The name of the town, just northwest of FALKIRK was recorded in 1200 as *Stan House* and in 1601 as *Stenhous*.

Stepney (Greater London) Stybba's landing place'. *Stybba-n* (Old English personal name—genitive form); *hyth* (Old English) 'landing place'. The name of this riverside district of east LONDON was noted around 1000 as *Stybbanhythe*.

Stevenage (Hertfordshire) Either place at 'the strong gate or oak'. *Stith-an* (Old English—dative) 'strong', 'robust'; *haecce* or *aec* (Old English—dative) 'gate'; or 'oak tree'. The name of this New Town, designated in 1946 northwest of HERTFORD, stems from that of an earlier settlement here, recorded in about 1060 as *Stithenaece*.

Stewartry (Dumfries and Galloway) The contemporary name of the administrative district set up in 1975 records the former judicial stewardship by the earls of Douglas over the 'Stewarty of KIRKCUDBRIGHT. *See* MEARNS, THE.

Steyning (West Sussex) Either settlement of 'Stan's people' or 'dwellers at a stony place'. *Stan* (Old English) personal name or 'stone'; *ingas* (Old English) 'people of', 'dwellers'. The name of this small town on the northside of the South DOWNS, northwest up the Adur Valley from SHOREHAM-BY-SEA, was recorded as

Staeningum around 880, and it appears in the Domesday Book of 1086 as *Staninges*.

Stirling (Central) Possibly 'land enclosure by the stream'. *Sruth* (Scottish Gaelic) 'stream'; *lann* (Scottish Gaelic) 'land enclosure'. This would be apt for the site of this historic town with its castle rock enclosed in a loop of the River FORTH, apparently formerly called the Sruth. However, its meaning thus remains uncertain. It was recorded as *Strivlin* 1124; *Estriuelin* c.1250; *Striviling* 1445; *Sterling* 1470.

Stockport (Greater Manchester) 'Market place at an outlying settlement'. *Stoc* (Old English) 'secondary place'; *port* (Old English) 'market'. The name of this industrial town, located on the southeast side of MANCHESTER, where the Goyt and Tame rivers meet to form the River MERSEY, appeared in a text of around 1170 as *Stokeport*.

Stocksbridge (South Yorkshire) 'Bridge made of tree trunks'. *Stocc* (Old English) 'stock', 'tree trunks'; *brycg* (Old English) 'bridge'. Although not on record before 1841, the name of this 19th-century steel-making town, in the Little Don Valley northwest of SHEFFIELD, almost certainly has an identical origin and meaning to the more common 'Stockbridge' form.

Stockton-on-Tees (Cleveland) 'Farmstead at an outlying hamlet'. *Stoc* (Old English) 'secondary settlement'; *tun* (Old English) 'farmstead'. Recorded as simply *Stocton* in 1196, the relatively common basic name of this historic market and industrial town, west of MIDDLESBROUGH, has later added the distinguishing affix to indicate its location on the River TEES.

Stoke-on-Trent (Staffordshire) Place of 'the secondary settlement'. *Stoc* (Old English) 'outlying farmstead or hamlet'. This well-known city in the 'Potteries' district, northwest of STAFFORD, lies on the River TRENT, as its distinguishing affix indicates. The current name applies not only to the original settlement, noted as *Stoche* in the Domesday Book, but collectively to all of the so-called 'Five Towns' here.

Stone (Staffordshire) Place at 'the stone or stones'. *Stan* (Old English) 'stone'. The name of this town on the River TRENT north of STAFFORD means exactly what it says, although the particular significance or sense of the name is unclear; it was recorded as *Stanes* in a document of 1187.

Stonehaven (Grampian) Possibly 'stony landing place'. *Stan* (Old English) 'stone'; *hyth* (Old English) 'landing place'. Recorded in documents as *Stanehyve* 1587, *Steanhyve* 1629, which would suggest that the above derivation is more probable for this Scottish east coast fishing port, to the south of ABERDEEN, than the more literal Old Norse *steinn* + *hofn*.

Stonehenge (Wiltshire) Place of 'the stone hanging'. *Stan* (Old English) 'stone'; *hengen* (Old English) 'hanging'; 'gibbet'. The name of this famous Neolithic-Bronze Age earthwork and major stone circle on SALISBURY Plain has the sense of 'stones that are hung up', with particular reference to the distinctive construction here of lintel stones 'hung' over two upright pillars. Alternatively, as is suggested by one authority, the name may simply be a fanciful description of the ancient site's resemblance to gallows as erected in open places in the past. The name was first recorded as *Stanenges* around 1130.

Stormont (Down) Probably 'projecting hill'. *Starr* (Irish Gaelic) 'projection'; *muineach* (Irish Gaelic) 'hill', 'ridge'. This eastern suburb of BELFAST is the site of the huge neo-classical Parliament House, seat of the former NORTHERN IRELAND Government, which with the rest of the district does sit on what could be regarded as a 'projecting hill' to the north.

Stornaway (Western Isles) 'Rudder Bay'. *Stjorn* (Old Norse) 'rudder', 'steering'; *vagr* (Old Norse) 'bay'. The exact sense of this description remains uncertain, but the protruding Eye Peninsula, seen on approach to the bay on which this' the main town and port of LEWIS stands, does have a very 'rudder-like' outline. Such seafaring Viking morphological descriptions are common in these parts. Recorded as *Steornaway* in 1549.

Storrington (West Sussex) Probably 'the farmstead visited by storks'. *Storc* (Old English) 'stork'; *tun* (Old English) 'farmstead'. The name of this small town on the northern slope of the South Downs, northeast of Arundel, was recorded as *Storgetune* in the Domesday Book of 1086 and *Storkinton* in 1185.

Stourbridge (West Midlands) 'Bridge over the River Stour'. *Stour* (Brythonic Celtic river-name) probably meaning 'strong one'; *brycg* (Old English) 'bridge'. The name of this industrial town on the River Stour, west of Birmingham, was recorded as *Sturbrug* in a document of 1255.

Stourport-on-Severn (Hereford and Worcester) This town southwest of Kidderminster has a relatively late and self-explanatory name that reflects its development as an inland port in the 18th century at the confluence of the Stour and Severn rivers, and the opening of the Staffordshire and Worcestershire Canal through here.

Stowmarket (Suffolk) 'Holy place, assembly place and later market place'. *Stow* (Old English) 'important place with holy and administrative functions'; *merket* (Middle English) 'market place'. This modern-day market and industrial town on the River Gipping, upstream and northwest of Ipswich, reveals the nature of its successive status in the early records of its name: *ecclesia de Stou* 1086 (Domesday Book); *forum de la Stowe* 1253; *Stowmarket* 1268.

Stow-on-the-Wold (Gloucestershire) 'Holy place', later 'on the upland woodland clearing'. *Stow* (Old English) 'holy place'; *wald* (Old English) 'high ground cleared of forest'. This small Cotswold town, on the Fosse Way northwest of Cirencester was originally the holy place of St Edward, its name recorded in 1107 as *Edwardestowe*. Later it became *Stowe*, as noted in 1221.

Strabane (Tyrone) 'White riverside land'. *Srath* (Irish Gaelic) 'river holm' or 'haugh'; *ban* (Irish Gaelic) 'white', 'light-coloured'. This large market 'border town' lies on the east bank of the River FOYLE and the origin of its current anglicised name is more clearly manifest in its Irish form, *An Srath Ban*.

Strangeways (Greater Manchester) Place by 'the strong current'. *Strang* (Old English) 'strong'; *gewaesc* (Old English) 'washing', 'torrent of water'. This district of MANCHESTER, whose name is well known because of the prison here, lies on a strip of land between two streams to the north of the city centre; the name was originally recorded as *Strangwas* in 1322. *Compare* RENFREW.

Strangford Lough (Down) 'Violent fiord'. *Strangr* (Old Norse) 'strong', 'violent'; *fjordr* (Old Norse) 'fiord', 'sea inlet'; *loch* (Irish Gaelic) 'sea inlet', 'lake'. This notable indentation of the Irish Sea derives its name from the description of the powerful current that builds up on the tide at its narrow entrance. The tautology of the duplicated feature generic presumably was created later when the original meaning had been lost. The alternative Irish name is *Loch Cuan*, meaning 'haven lake', the focus being contrasted to that highlighted by the Vikings seaward approach.

Stranraer (Dumfries and Galloway) Place of the 'fat peninsula'. *Sron* (Scottish Gaelic) 'peninsula'; *reamhar* (Scottish Gaelic) 'fat', 'thick'. This description is clearly a comparative reference to this ferry port's location at the foot of the thicker of the two arms of the RINNS OF GALLOWAY.

Stratford-upon-Avon (Warwickshire) 'Ford on a Roman road, over the River Avon'. *Straet* (Old English based on Latin *via strata*) 'Roman road'; *ford* (Old English) 'river crossing'. The name of this town south-west of WARWICK, well known as the birthplace of William Shakespeare, was recorded as *Stretfordae* in about 700, and appears in the Domesday Book as

Stradforde. For the meaning of the distinguishing affix *see* AVON.

Strathaven (Strathclyde) 'Wide valley of the Avon'. *Srath* (Scottish Gaelic) 'wide valley'; *avon* (Scottish Gaelic elided form of *abhainn*) 'river'. The river flowing through this small town south of HAMILTON is the tautologous Avon Water. The town name is pronounced 'Strayvn'.

Strathclyde (Scotland) 'Wide valley of the cleanser'. *Srath* (Scottish Gaelic) 'wide valley'; *Clyde* (Brythonic Celtic river name) 'cleansing one'. This, the largest local authority area in Britain, encompasses the whole of the huge River CLYDE basin and also large parts of the Highlands that bound its penetrating firth and long sea lochs. The current region, established in 1975, takes as its name that of the ancient even larger kingdom of Strathclyde which existed here over 1000 years ago. *See* DUMBARTON.

Strathmore (Tayside) 'The great wide valley'. *Srath* (Scottish Gaelic) 'wide valley'; *mor* (Scottish Gaelic) 'big', 'great'. In its fullest sense this name refers to the far-stretching band of low country that skirts the entire length of the Highland frontier, with successive ranges of parallel uplands of the Central Lowlands on the other side (LENNOX, OCHILS, SIDLAWS). But it is more commonly regarded as consisting only of what is flanked by the SIDLAW HILLS.

Strathpeffer (Highland) 'Wide valley of the radiant one'. *Srath* (Scottish Gaelic) 'wide valley'; *pevr* (Brythonic Celtic-Pictish root word) 'radiant one'. Although there is no river, this small town southwest of DINGWALL was developed in the 19th century as a spa resort, there being mineral springs and many signs of early habitation here.

Strathspey (Grampian/Highland) 'Wide valley of the Spey'. The meaning of the river name is unknown.

Stratton (Cornwall) 'Village in the valley of the River Neet'. *Stras* (Old Cornish) 'valley'; *Neet* (Celtic river name) uncertain origin and meaning; *tun* (Old English) 'village'. Recorded as *Straetneat* in *c*.880, and *Stratone* in 1086, this town adjoining BUDE to the west has a name usually associated with a Roman road.

Street (Somerset) Place on 'a Roman road'. *Straet* (Old English based on Latin *via strata*) 'Roman paved way or road'. This leatherindustries town, to the west of GLASTONBURY, has a straightforward name that reflects its location on the old Roman road that connected Ilchester and the Bristol Channel coast. It was documented as *Stret* in 725.

Stretford (Greater Manchester) Place by 'a ford on a Roman road'. *Straet* (Old English based on Latin *via strata*) 'Roman road'; *ford* (Old English) 'river crossing'. This town southwest of MANCHESTER lies on the River MERSEY at the point crossed by the old Roman road from CHESTER. Recorded in 1212, exactly as now, its name is clearly a variant of STRATFORD.

Stromness (Orkney) 'The headland of the current'. *Straumr* (Old Norse) 'sea current'; *nes* (Old Norse) 'headland'. This aptly describes the most notable aspects of the situation of this fishing port and second town of these islands. The headland at the end of the settlement rounds on to the Sound of HOY and in the full face of the Atlantic swell very strong tidal currents ('roost' or Old Norse *rost*) 'race past'. Records show it as *Straumness* in 1150. It is little surprise that an earlier alternative name was *Hamnavoe*, meaning 'harbour on the bay'. *Compare* HAMNAVOE (Shetland).

Strontian (Highland) 'Promontory of the beacon'. *Sron* (Scottish Gaelic) 'promontory'; *teine* (Scottish Gaelic) 'beacon'. The mineral strontium, first discovered near here in 1790, is named after this Loch Sunart village.

Stroud (Gloucestershire) 'Marshy land overgrown with brushwood'. *Strod* (Old English) derivation as given above. Lying on the River Frome, such conditions could once have been prevalent in the valley floor here. The name was recorded as *La Strode* in 1200.

Sturminster Newton (Dorset) 'Church on the River Stour' and 'New farmstead or village'. *Stour* (Brythonic Celtic river name) probably meaning 'strong one'; *mynster* (Old English) 'large church'; *niwe* (Old English) 'new'; *tun* (Old English) 'farmstead'. This small town on the River Stour, upstream and northwest of BLANFORD FORUM, has a composite name of the two original places that developed separately on opposite banks of the river. Records show: *at Stoure Nywetone* 968; *Newentone* 1086; *Sturminstr Nyweton* 1291.

Sudbury (Suffolk) 'Southern fortified place'. *Suth* (Old English) 'southern'; *byrig* (Old English—dative form of *burh*) 'stronghold'. This town on the River Stour, northwest of COLCHESTER, was the birthplace of the artist Gainsborough, and is probably twinned with BURY ST EDMUNDS as its northern counterpart, some 12 miles (20 km) to the north. The name was recorded as *Suthbyrig* in *c*.995, and *Sutberia* in 1086.

Suffolk (England) Territory of 'the southern folk' of the East Angles. *Suth* (Old English) 'south', 'southern'; *folc* (Old English) 'folk', 'peoples'. This relatively self-explanatory contracted name of the present-day middle county of EAST ANGLIA as such represents the southern counterpart to NORFOLK. It was recorded as *Suthfolchi* in 895, and as *Sudfulc* in 1086.

Sullom Voe (Shetland) 'The gannets' fiord'. *Sulan* (Old Norse) 'gannets'; *vagr* (Old Norse) 'sea inlet'. This sheltered inlet, on northern MAINLAND, has given its name to a major North Sea oil terminal that was built here in the 1970s.

Sumburgh (Shetland) Probably 'Swyn's stronghold'. *Swyn* (Old Norse personal name) unidentified; *borg* (Old Norse) 'fort', 'stronghold'. The name of this famous southern headland of SHETLAND, and of the busy airport nearby, was recorded as *Swynbrocht* in 1506.

Summer Isles (Highland) These uninhabited islands off the coast of Wester Ross are so called because they were used by crofters for summer grazing.

Sunbury (Surrey) 'Sunna's stronghold'. *Sunna-n* (Old English personal name—genitive form); *byrig* (Old English—dative form of *burh*) 'stronghold', 'fortified place'. This town, often referred to as **Sunbury-on-Thames**, is located on the north bank of the said river, downstream and east of STAINES. The name was documented as *Sunnanbyrg* in 960, and as *Sunnanberie* in the Domesday Book of 1086.

Sunderland (Tyne and Wear) 'Sundered or detached part of the estate'. *Sundor-land* (Old English) 'separated land', i.e. apart from the main estate. The name of this large industrial city and port at the mouth of the River Wear, southeast of NEWCASTLE UPON TYNE, was recorded as now, in a document of 1168.

Surbiton (Greater London) 'Southern outlying grange'. *Suth* (Old English) 'south', 'southern'; *bere-tun* (Old English) literally 'barley farm', later to assume sense of 'outlying grange'. The name of this district of KINGSTON-UPON-THAMES reflects that this settlement was the southern counterpart to Norbiton, both being farms or granges dependent on the former royal manor of Kingston. It was noted as *Suberton* in a text of 1179.

Surrey (England) 'Southerly district'. *Suther* (Old English) 'southerly'; *ge* (Old English conjectural word) 'district'. The name of this 'Home County', to the south of LONDON, originally described the district inhabited by the Saxons of the middle THAMES valley, who settled south of area of the 'Middle Saxons', which was to become MIDDLESEX. It was first recorded as *Suthrige* in 722, and as *Sudrie* in the Domesday Book of 1086.

Sussex (England) Territory of 'the South Saxons'. *Suth* (Old English) 'south'; *Seaxe* (Old English tribal name) 'Saxon'. Recorded originally as *Suth Seaxe* in 722, the current application of the name since 1974 applies to two separate counties in southern ENGLAND, namely: **East Sussex** and **West Sussex**

Sutherland (Highland) 'Southern territory'. *Suthr* (Old Norse) 'south'; *land* (Old Norse) 'territory'. This present-day administrative district and former county takes its name from the original Viking settlers viewpoint, namely that this was their 'southern territory' comparative to their possession of the ORKNEY and SHETLAND isles. For the same reason the HEBRIDES were known to the Norsemen as *Suthreyar*, 'southern islands'.

Sutton (Greater London). 'Southern farm'. *Suth* (Old English) 'southern'; *tun* (Old English) 'farmstead'. This former SURREY town, now a district and a borough in the south of the GREATER LONDON conurbation, has a very common name, which is apparently twinned with ACTON as its northern counterpart. It appears in the Domesday Book as *Sudtone*.

Sutton Coldfield (West Midlands) 'Southern farm on open land where charcoal is produced'. *Suth* (Old English) 'southern'; *tun* (Old English) 'farmstead'; *col* (Old English) 'charcoal'; *feld* (Old English) 'open land'. Recorded first as simply *Sutone* in the Domesday Book, the common basic name of this town to the northeast of BIRMINGHAM was later distinguished by the addition of its descriptive affix to become *Sutton Colefeld* in a text of 1289.

Swanage (Dorset) Possibly 'dairy farm of the herdsmen' or 'the swannery'. *Swan* (Old English) 'herdsman'; 'swan'; *wic* (Old English) 'specialised premises', 'dairy farm'. The name of this coastal resort, on the Isle of PURBECK, was recorded as *Swanawic* in 877, and appears as *Swanwic* in the Domesday Book of 1086.

Swansea (West Glamorgan) 'Sweyn's sea' place. *Sveinn* (Old Danish personal name) Danish Viking who invaded England and Wales several times in the early 11th century, and meaning 'servant'; *saer* (Old Norse) 'sea'. The name of Wales's second city, situated on Swansea Bay at the mouth of the River Tawe, originates from early Scandinavian settlement here. It was recorded in 1188 as *Sweynsei*. The Welsh name, *Abertawe*, refers to the town's location.

Swilly, Lough (Donegal) This long sea inlet down the west side of the INISHOWEN peninsula takes the name of the river flowing into it, which in turn is derived from: *suil* (Irish Gaelic) 'eye'. It is considered by one authority that the sense here is of a 'bubbling river', thus one 'full of eyes'. The Irish name of the lough is *Loch Suili*.

Swindon (Wiltshire) 'Hill where pigs are kept'. *Swin* (Old English) 'swine', 'pig'; *dun* (Old English) 'down', 'hill'. This recently much expanded industrial town, north of MARLBOROUGH, was developed in the 19th century as the major engineering workshop for the Great Western Railway and has a name whose origin is far removed from the contemporary scene. Old Swindon, as the original centre is now called, is on a noticeable hill. The name was entered in the Domesday Book as *Svindune*.

Swindon (Greater Manchester) 'Pig farm'. *Swin* (Old English) 'swine', 'pig'; *tun* (Old English) 'farmstead'. The name of this industrial town, northwest of SALFORD, was noted as *Suinton* in a document of 1258.

Swiss Cottage (Greater London) The unusual name of this district of CAMDEN, well known to Londoners as that of an Underground station on the Jubilee Line, has its origin in an early 19th-century inn here, known as the Swiss Tavern, and later renamed Swiss Cottage.

Symbister (Shetland) The full meaning of the name of this prosperous fishing port and main settlement on WHALSAY remains obscure. The first part may be an Old Norse personal name, while the second element is the mutation of the Old Norse *bol-stathr* to *bister*, a common ending form in the Northern Isles, indicating a 'peasant farmer's steading'.

T

Tadcaster (North Yorkshire) 'Tata's Roman station'. *Tata* (Old English personal name); *ceaster* (Old English) 'Roman fort'. The name of this small town, southwest of YORK, declares itself to be the site of a former Roman settlement, in this case the camp of *Calcaria*; it was recorded in the Domesday Book as *Tatecastre*.

Tain (Highland) This small and ancient royal burgh, on the south shore of the DORNOCH Firth, probably has a pre-Celtic river name as the origin of its own. It stands at the mouth of a short river called the Tain Water. Like other similar names from the same root (e.g. Teign in Devon, or Tyne in Northumberland and Lothian) the meaning appears to be 'river' or 'water'. Also, the modern Gaelic *tain* means 'water'. However, some authorities consider the stream here to be so insignificant that they look for other derivations. It is recorded as: *Tene* 1227; *Tayne* 1375; *Thane* 1483.

Tamworth (Staffordshire) 'Enclosure on the River Tame'. *Tame* (Brythonic Celtic or pre-Celtic river name related to Taff, Tamar, Tavy, Teme and THAMES) 'dark one'; *worthig* (Old English replaced by *worth*) 'enclosure'. The name of this town, northeast of BIRMINGHAM, was noted as *Tamouuorthig* in 781, and later as *Tamuuorde* in the Domesday Book of 1086.

Tara (Meath) Traditionally 'the elevated assembly place'. *Teamhair* (Irish Gaelic) 'elevated place commanding an extensive view', 'assembly hill'. Situated southeast of NAVAN, this celebrated site of ancient royal power in Ireland does have a hilltop that may have been such a special place of assembly. However, recent reseach has linked the name with that of the earth goddess Temair, the 'dark one'. *See* THAMES.

Tarbert (Strathclyde; Western Isles) 'Place of the isthmus'. *Tairbeart* (Scottish Gaelic) 'isthmus', 'portage point'. Both, Tarbert in ARGYLL, south of Lochgilphead whose isthmus situation separates KNAPDALE and KINTYRE; and Tarbert (Tairbeart in Gaelic) whose natural 'land bridge' connects North and South Harris, reflects the ancient practice of portage, the crossing of boats and contents across narrow necks of land is made significant in the many places of this name or similar (eg. Tarbat, Tarbet).

Taunton (Somerset) 'Farmstead or village on the River Tone'. *Tone* (Brythonic Celtic river name based on the root element *tan-*) possibly 'roaring one'; *tun* (Old English) 'farmstead', 'village'. The name of this county town, situated in the wide valley of the River Tone south of the QUANTOCK HILLS, was recorded as *Tantun* in 737, and as *Tantone* in the Domesday Book of 1086.

Tavistock (Devon) 'Outlying settlement by the River Tavy'. *Tavy* (Brythonic Celtic river name possibly related to Taff, Tamar, Tame, Teme, Thame and THAMES) 'dark one'; *stoc* (Old English) 'outlying farmstead or hamlet'. The name of this market town, on the western fringe of DARTMOOR, was documented as *Tauistoce* in 981, and appears in the Domesday Book as *Tavestoc*.

Tay (Central/Tayside) This is Scotland's longest river, which flows 120 miles (192km) mainly eastwards through Loch Tay and on into the North Sea by way of the Firth of Tay. The name possibly derives from a Brythonic Celtic root *Tausos*, meaning 'silent one' or 'strong one'.

Tayport (Fife) This small town lies on the southern side of the Firth of TAY, opposite BROUGHTY FERRY, with which it had long-serving ferry links prior to the rail and road bridges being built nearby in the last 120 years. The current name dates only from 1888; before then this port was successively called: *Scotscraig*; *South Ferry*; *Portincraig*; *Port-on-Craig*; and *South Craig*, all these names having a reference either to its ferry across the TAY or to the crag on which the town is situated.

Tees (Cleveland/Cumbria) 'The boiling, surging one'. *Tees* (Brythonic Celtic river name related to Welsh *tes* and Irish Gaelic *teas*, both meaning 'heat') 'boiling, surging water'. This aptly named river rises on the eastern slopes of Cross Fell, the highest hill in the PENNINES, and flows with noticable force over many waterfalls and rapids southeasterly to MIDDLESBROUGH, where it enters a tidal estuary before reaching the North Sea, south of HARTLEPOOL. The basic name is incorporated in: **Tees Bay**; **Teesdale**; **Tees Mouth**; **Teesport**; **Teesside**.

Teignmouth (Devon) Place at 'the mouth of the River Teign'. *Teign* (Brythonic Celtic river name) simply 'stream'; *mutha* (Old English) 'river mouth'. The name of this holiday resort, on the coast southwest of DAWLISH, was recorded as *Tengemutha* in 1044.

Templemore (Tipperary) 'The great church'. *Teampall* (Irish Gaelic adopted from Latin *templum*) 'church', usually applied to those post-12th century; *mor* (Irish Gaelic) 'great'. Also in the case of this market town to the north of THULES, its name ties in with the Knights Templar who had a foundation here near to the original 'great church'. The Irish name is *An Teampall Mor*.

Tempo (Fermanagh) 'The right-hand-turn'. This village northeast of ENNISKILLEN has a name that is a shortened version of its full Irish name, *An t-Iompodh-deisiol*, literally translating as 'the turning right-handed'. This is considered to refer to the ancient custom of always turning towards the sun in worship.

Tenbury Wells (Hereford and Worcester) 'Stronghold on the River Teme', with later 'spa status'. *Teme* (Brythonic Celtic river name related to Taff, Tamar,

Tame, Tavy, Teme, THAME and THAMES) 'dark one'; *byrig* (Old English—dative of *burh*) 'fortified place'. This small town, northeast of LEOMINSTER, was noted as *Temedebyrig* in the 11th century, and it was only in the mid-19th century that the 'Wells' promotioal affix was added on the discovery of saline springs here.

Tenby (Dyfed) 'Little Fortress'. *Din* (Old Welsh) 'fortress'; *bych* (Old Welsh) 'little'. This seaside resort, on CAMARTHEN Bay east of PEMBROKE, has a name of identical derivation to DENBIGH, but modified by Scandinavian influences. The 'fort' was on Castle Hill, the site of the later 13th-century castle. The current Welsh name, *Dinbych-y-pysgod*, is of similar meaning but has the suffix 'by the fish'.

Tenterden (Kent) 'The swine pasture of the Thanet dwellers'. *Thanet* (Brythonic Celtic territorial name) see derivation below; *ware* (Old English) 'dwellers'; *denn* (Old English) 'woodland-clearing pasture', especially for pigs. Recorded as *Tentwardene* in 1179, the name of this small rustic town, southwest of ASHFORD, has its origins in providing outlying farm land to the ancient peoples from the Isle of THANET to the northeast.

Tetbury (Gloucestershire) 'Tette's stronghold'. *Tetta-n* (Old English personal name—genitive form) Tette was a sister of King Ine of WESSEX and an abbess of WIMBORNE in the 7th century; *byrig* (Old English—dative of *burh*) 'fortified place'. Recorded as *Tettan monasterium* in a Latin text of 681, this town northwest of MALMESBURY clearly was the site of an important early settlement. Later records show: *Tettanbyrg c.*900; *Teteberie* 1086 (Domesday Book).

Tewkesbury (Gloucestershire) 'Teodec's stronghold'. *Teodec* (Old English personal name); *byrig* (Old English—dative of *burh*) 'fortified place'. The name of this town with its famed abbey church, at the confluence of the Avon and SEVERN rivers, northwest of CHELTENHAM, was recorded as *Teodechesberie* in 1086.

Thame (Oxfordshire) Probably the place on 'the dark river'. *Thame* (Brythonic Celtic river name related to the group that includes: Taff; Tamar; Tame; Tavy; Teme and THAMES) possibly meaning 'dark one'. This small town, southwest of AYLESBURY, is simply named after the river on which it stands, downstream and northwest of the CHILTERN HILLS. Pronounced with a silent *h*, it was recorded as *Tamu* in 675, and as *Tame* in 975 (Anglo-Saxon Chronicle) and in 1086 (Domesday Book).

Thames (England) Simply 'the river' or 'the dark one'. *Teme-* (Brythonic Celtic root element—for large group of related river names) 'river', 'dark'. This famous river, which flows east from its source in the COTSWOLDS near CIRENCESTER, through OXFORDSHIRE, where a section of it is known as the Isis, on to a tidal stretch in Britain's capital city, and out into the North Sea by way of a deeply indented estuary, has a name of ancient origin, which is still the subject of much debate and research. Records show: *Tamesis* 51 BC; *Tamesa c.* AD 115; *Temis* 683; *Temes* 843.

Thamesdown (Wiltshire) This is a modern name created in 1974 for the new administrative district in the northeast of the county, centred on SWINDON; it reflects both the upper River THAMES that forms its northern boundary and the downland found here.

Thamesmead (Greater London) This is also a recently fabricated name that applies to the riverside residential 'new town' founded in 1967 to the northwest of the ERITH Marshes on the southern bank of the THAMES opposite DAGENHAM. The use of the archaic and poetic word 'mead', based on *maed* (Old English) 'meadow', was clearly a deliberate promotional word choice.

Thanet, Isle of (Kent) Probably 'the bright island'. *Tan-* (Brythonic Celtic conjectural root element) 'fire', 'bright', with possible reference to a beacon. This easternmost peninsula was an island in Roman times; it was recorded as *Tanatus* then, and as *Tanet* in 1086.

Thatcham (Berkshire) Probaby the place of 'the thatched homestead'. *Thaec* (Old English) 'thatch'; *ham* (Old English) 'homestead'. Alternatively, the second element of the name of this satellite suburb, in the Kennet valley to the east of NEWBURY, could have been represented by *hamm* (Old English) 'riverside land', implying that this location may have been a source of thatching materials. Records show: *Thaecham c.*954; *Taceham* 1086 (Domesday Book). *Compare* THAXTED

Thaxted (Essex) 'Place where thatch is got'. *Thaec* (Old English) 'thatch'; *stede* (Old English) 'place'. The name of this small town, southeast of SAFFRON WALDEN, appears as *Tachesteda* in the Domesday Book. *Compare* THATCHAM.

Thetford (Norfolk) Place of 'the people's ford'. *Theod* (Old English) 'people', 'public'; *ford* (Old English) 'river crossing'. The name of this town, located at an important crossing of the Little Ouse river by the main route between NEWMARKET and NORWICH, was recorded as *Theodford* in a document of 870.

Thirlmere (Cumbria) The origin and meaning of the name of this northern lake of the LAKE DISTRICT, that now acts as a reservoir for MANCHESTER's water supply, remains a mystery as its earliest record as *Thyrlcmere* in 1574 is too late for a sound etymology.

Thirsk (North Yorkshire) Place of 'the marsh'. *Thresk* (Old Scandinavian conjectural word related to Old Swedish *thraesk*) 'marshland', 'fen'. Recorded as *Tresch* in the Domesday Book, the name of this town on the low-lying Vale of YORK, west of the HAMBLETON HILLS may have described the former fen-like topography here.

Thornaby-on-Tees (Cleveland) 'Thormoth's farmstead or village'. *Thormoth* (Old Danish personal name); *by* (Old Danish) 'farmstead', 'village'. The name of this part of the TEESSIDE urban area, once known as South Stockton, it being across the river from STOCKTON-ON-TEES, was originally recorded as *Tormozbi* in 1086.

Thornbury (Avon) 'Fortified place where thorn trees grow'. *Thorn* (Old English) 'thorn tree or bush'; *byrig* (Old English -dative of *burh*) 'stronghold'. Recorded as *Thornbyrig* in 896 and softened by Anglo-Norman influences to *Turneberie* in the Domesday Book of 1086, the name of this small town, north of BRISTOL, with its imposing unfinished Tudor castle, presumably refers to a much earlier fortification here.

Thorne (South Yorkshire) Place of 'the thorn bushes'. *Thorn* (Old English) 'thorn tree or bush'. This town, northeast of DONCASTER, has a straightforward name that was documented as *Torne* in the Domesday Book, the Anglo-Normans having difficulty with the *th* sound. Significantly, the low-lying fenland to the north of the town is referred to as the **Thorne Waste or Moors**.

Thorney Island (West Sussex) 'Thorn-tree island'. *Thorn* (Old English) 'thorn tree or bush'; *eg* (Old English) 'island'. Like PORTSEA and HAYLING ISLANDS to the west, this penisular-like projection of land into CHICHESTER Harbour, joined to the mainland only by narrow causeways and bridges, must originally have been overgrown with thorn bushes. The name of the island's village, **West Thorney**, was noted as *Tornei* in the Domesday Book.

Thules (Tipperary) 'The stronghold'. *Dur* (Irish Gaelic) 'hard'; *lios* (Irish Gaelic) 'fort'. This market town north of CASHEL has a name which is an English corruption of its Irish name Durlas. The place was essentially founded as a fortified Anglo-Norman town and as such assumed much strategic importance in medieval times.

Thundersley (Essex) 'Wood or clearing dedicated to the heathen god Thunor'. *Thunor* (Old English sacred name) Thor/Donar—Nordic/Teuton god of thunder; *leah* (Old English) 'wood' or 'woodland clearing'. The name of this town, east of BASILDON, has an identical derivation to the SURREY village of **Thursley**. The Domesday Book entry of the former is *Thunreslea* while *Thoresle* is noted in 1292 for the latter. *Compare* WEDNESBURY.

Thurrock, Little and **West** (Essex) 'Place where filthy water collects'. *Thurruc* (Old English) 'bilge'. These former villages, now part of GRAYS THURROCK, take their basic name from a stretch of marshland west of TILBURY, to which this apt name originally referred.

Thursley *see* **Thundersley**.

Thurso (Highland) Place of the 'bull's river'. *Thjor-s* (Old Norse) 'bull's'; *a* (Old Norse) 'river'. This market town on the north CAITHNESS coast thus is named after the river at the mouth of which it stands. It was recorded as *Thorsa* in a document of 1152.

Tidworth, North and **South** (Wiltshire/Hampshire) 'Tuda's enclosure'. *Tuda* (Old English personal name); *worth* (Old English) 'enclosure'. This army town on the eastern edge of the SALISBURY Plain military training grounds, is actually two separate settlements coalesed into one that now straddles the county boundary formed by the River Bourne here. The Domesday Book entries are *Todeworde* and *Todeorde* respectively.

Tighnabruaich (Strathclyde) 'House of the bank'. *Tigh* (Scottish Gaelic) 'house'; *na* (Scottish Gaelic) 'of the'; *bruaich* (Scottish Gaelic) 'bank'. This small resort, developed in the 19th century, is situated where originally a solitary house stood on the high ground overlooking the western arm of the Kyles of BUTE.

Tilbury (Essex) 'Tila's stronghold'. *Tila* (Old English personal name) meaning 'useful one'; *byrig* (Old English—dative of *burh*) 'fortified place'. The name of this industrial town and major THAMES container port was originally recorded as *Tilaburg* in 731, and later 'softened' by Anglo-Norman influences to give *Tiliberia*, as entered in the Domesday Book of 1086.

Tillicoultry (Central) 'Hillock in the back land'. *Tulach* (Scottish Gaelic) 'hillock'; *cul* (Scottish Gaelic) 'back'; *tir* (Scottish Gaelic) 'land'. This former coal-mining town lies at the base of the OCHIL HILLS, and as such its name aptly describes its situation.

Tintagel (Cornwall) Probably 'fort by a narrow neck of land'. *Din* (Old Cornish conjectural word) 'fort'; *tagell* (Old Cornish conjectural word) 'constriction', 'neck'. Recorded as *Tintagol* around 1137, the name of this village, on the rocky coast northwest of CAMELFORD, describes the dramatic situation of the ruined castle here, on a site steeped in the Arthurian legend.

Tintern (Gwent) 'Chief's stronghold'. *Dinas* (Old Welsh) 'stronghold', 'fort'; *teyrn* (Old Welsh) 'chieftain', 'monarch'. This small village, set in the gorge of the Wye valley and dominated by the famous ruins of a 12th-century Cistercian abbey, has an ancient Brythonic Celtic name, which early records show as both *Dindyrn* and *Tindyrn*.

Tipperary (Tipperary) 'The well of Ara'. *Tipra* or *tobar* (Irish Gaelic) 'well'; *Arann* (Irish Gaelic river and local territorial name) 'ridge-backed'. The latter is the river on which this county town stands and the well that also gave name to the county used to be in Main Street but is now closed up.

Tiptree (Essex) Probably 'Tippa's tree'. *Tippa* (Old English personal name); *treow* (Old English) 'tree'. The name of this small town, southwest of COLCHESTER, like other '-tree' ending placenames, could have referred to an actual specific tree or a man-made cross, the significance of which may have been as a boundary marker or a place of public assembly. The name here was noted as *Typpetre* in 1225.

Tiree (Strathclyde) Possibly 'land of corn'. *Tir* (Scottish Gaelic) 'land'; *eadha* (Scottish Gaelic) 'corn'. This low-lying, relatively fertile island was formerly renowned for its high productivity of grain crops, and is in stark contrast to its neighbour, the rugged rocky Isle of COLL. Alternatively, some authorities consider the second element may be derived from a personal name, but this remains unattested.

Tiverton (Devon) 'Farm at the double ford'. *Twi-fyrde* (Old English conjectural compound word) 'double ford'; *tun* (Old English) 'farmstead'. This manufacturing and market town, north of EXETER, lies upstream on the River Exe where it is joined by a major tributary. Records show: *Twyfyrde* 880-85; *Tovretona* 1086.

Tobermory (Strathclyde) Place of St 'Mary's well'. *Tobar* (Scottish Gaelic) 'well'; *Moire* (Scottish Gaelic) 'Mary'. This resort and main town on the Island of MULL, developed in the 18th century by the British Fisheries Society, is named after a well dedicated to the Virgin Mary, and to be found nearby in an old ruined chapel.

Todmorden (West Yorkshire) Probably 'Totta's boundary valley'. *Totta* (Old English personal name); *maere* (Old English) 'boundary'; *denu* (Old English) 'valley'. This small industr ial valley town, on the River Calder, upstream and west of HALIFAX, lies near the PENNINE watershed that forms part of the historic boundary between the 'white rose' county of YORKSHIRE and the 'red rose' county of LANCASHIRE. The name was recorded as *Tottemerden* in 1246. *Compare* MARSDEN.

Tolpuddle (Dorset) 'Tola's estate on the River Puddle'. *Tola* (Old English personal name) widow of Urc, royal bodyguard of Edward the Confessor; *Pidele* (Old English river name) 'marshy one'. The name of this village, northeast of DORCHESTER, was made famous by the Tolpuddle Martyrs, agricultural workers who went on strike for their rights and were deported to Australia in 1834. It was originally recorded in the Domesday Book as simply *Pidele*, and later in 1210 as *Tollepidele*, the prefix in recognition of Tola's gift of her lands here to ABBOTSBURY Abbey around 1050. *See* PIDDLETRENTHIDE; PUDDLETOWN.

Tomintoul (Grampian) 'Little hill of the barn'. *Tom* (Scottish Gaelic) 'hillock', 'mound'; *an t-sabhail* (Scottish Gaelic) 'of the barn'. This village, northwest of THE LECHT, stands at an elevation of 1100 ft (340 m) on a small plateau, and is one of several places in the central Highlands with the prefix *tom* in their name.

Tonbridge (Kent) Probably 'bridge of the manor'. *Tun*

(Old English) 'manor', 'estate'; *brycg* (Old English) 'bridge'. The name of this industrial and residential town on the middle reaches of the MEDWAY could have had the original sense of a bridge connecting two parts of an early estate here that were separated by the river. *Tonbrige* is the Domesday Book entry. *Compare* TUNBRIDGE WELLS.

Torbay (Devon) This is a modern name, that applies both to an urban conglomeration that was formed in 1968 by the amalgamation of TORQUAY, PAIGNTON and BRIXHAM, and to a more extensive administrative district, created in 1974 and centred on the latter. Both are named after the semi-circular sea inlet here, called **Tor Bay**, which itself is derived from the hill known as Torre, which also gave rise to TORQUAY.

Torquay (Devon) 'The quay' at a place called 'Torre'. *Torre* (Old English place name derived from *torr*) 'the rocky hill'; *keye* (Middle English based on Old French *kai*) 'wharf'. This fashionable coastal resort at the heart of DEVON's so-called 'Riviera', has its origins in late medieval times when the monks from Torre Abbey (itself named after the hill here) built a quay nearby on the northern shore of TOR BAY. Although *Torre* is recorded as such in the Domesday Book, Torquay was first noted only in 1591, as *Torrekay*.

Torridon (Highland) This spectacular area of rugged mountains, of an ancient red sandstone to which its name has been given, has no satisfactory toponymical explanation. One authority has suggested its name might be derived as: *torr* (Scottish Gaelic) 'hill(s)'; *Aidan* (personal name) of a famous 7th-century Irish saint.

Torrington, Great and **Little** (Devon) 'Farm by the River Torridge'. *Torridge* (Brythonic Celtic river name related to Welsh *terig*) 'rough one'; *tun* (Old English) 'farmstead'. The hilltop town, officially known as Great Torrington, and its attendant village, distinguished as Little Torrington, derive their basic name from the River Torridge, beside which they are situated, upstream and southeast of BIDEFORD. The Domesday Book entry of 1086 shows the name as *Toritona*.

Tory Island (Donegal) 'Place of tors'. *Tor* (Irish Gaelic) 'tower'. This small island off northwest Ireland abounds in tower-like rocks. It is *Toraigh* in Irish.

Totnes (Devon) 'Totta's promontory'. *Totta* (Old English personal name); *naess* (Old English) 'headland'. The name of this town, situated on a small promontory at the head of the deeply indented tidal estuary of the River Dart, was recorded as *Totanaes* in a document of about 1000.

Tottenham (Greater London) 'Totta's homestead or village'. *Totta-n* (Old English personal name—genitive form); *ham* (Old English) 'homestead', 'village'. The name of this north LONDON district of HARINGEY was recorded in the Domesday Book of 1086 as *Toteham* and in a document of 1265 as *Totenham*.

Totton (Hampshire) 'Farmstead associated with a man called Tota'. *Tota* (Old English personal name); *ing* (Old English connective particle) 'associated with'; *tun* (Old English) 'farmstead', 'estate'. The name of this town at the head of the Test estuary, west of SOUTHAMPTON, appears as *Totintone* in the Domesday Book of 1086.

Towcester (Northamptonshire) 'Roman fort on the River Tove'. *Tove* (Old English river name) 'slow one'; *ceaster* (Old English) 'Roman station'. This small town, southwest of NORTHAMPTON, had its origins as the Roman settlement of *Lactodurum*, which was established here in the 1st century AD to guard the crossing of the River Tove by WATLING STREET.

Tower Hamlets (Greater London) This name of the LONDON borough that was formed in 1964 by the amalgamation of the former boroughs of BETNAL GREEN, Poplar, and STEPNEY was adopted on the basis of the same name that had been used as a general term since the 16th century to describe collectively many earlier East End 'hamlets under the jurisdiction of the Tower of London'. *See* MILE END.

Tow Law (Durham) Probably the place of 'the lookout mound'. *Tot* (Old English conjectural word) 'lookout'; *hlaw* (Old English) 'mound', 'hillock'. This small 19th-century coal-mining and industrial town is situated in a foothill district on the eastern side of the PENNINES, midway between BISHOP AUCKLAND and CONSETT. The name was noted as *Tollawe* in 1423.

Town Yetholm *see* **Yetholm.**

Toxteth (Merseyside) 'Toki's landing place'. *Toki* (Old Norse personal name); *stoth* (Old Norse) 'landing place'. This former dockland district, south of the city centre of LIVERPOOL, has an apt name in recognition of its waterfront location on the northern shore of the MERSEY estuary, where other Viking settlements were established; *see* AINTREE; CROSBY; KIRKBY; ROBY. It was recorded as *Stochestede* in the Domesday Book of 1086, and as *Tokestath* in a document of 1212.

Tralee (Kerry) 'The strand of the Lee'. *Traigh* (Irish Gaelic) 'strand'; *Li* (Irish Gaelic river name) Lee. This, the county and largest town of KERRY, has a name that describes its situation, the strand being the seashore at the mouth of the short River Lee, most of which has been covered over. Its Irish name is *Tra Li*.

Tranent (Lothian) Apparently 'village by the valley'. *Tref* (Brythonic Celtic) 'settlement'; *nant* (Brythonic Celtic) 'valley'. This former enlarged coal-mining village sits on a ridge of rising ground above the valley of the River Esk, east of MUSSELBURGH. Recorded as *Traunent* 1147.

Tranmere (Merseyside) 'Sandbank frequented by cranes'. *Trani* (Old Norse) 'crane', 'heron-like wading bird'; *melr* (Old Norse) 'sandbank'. This coastal district, south of the town centre of BIRKENHEAD, refers to former sands here; it was recorded as *Tranemor* in a text of 1260.

Trawsfynydd (Gwynedd) Place 'across the mountain'. *Traws* (Welsh) 'cross', 'transverse'; *mynydd* (Welsh) 'mountain'. This remote, elevated village, and now home of a first-generation nuclear power station, lies on the eastern side of the large earlier 20th-century man-made lake bearing the same name, the origins of which reflect its mountainous situation. *Compare* TROSSACHS.

Tredegar (Gwent) This 19th-century coal-mining town at the head of the Sirhowy Valley of South Wales was named after the local landowner, Lord Tredegar, whose own title comes from the family seat at Tredegar Park, near NEWPORT. *See* NEW TREDEGAR.

Trefaldwyn *see* **Montgomery**

Trefriw (Gwynedd) 'Homestead on the hill slope'. *Tref* (Welsh) 'homestead', 'village'; *rhiw* (Welsh) 'hill slope'. This village, just northwest of LLANRWST, has a name that aptly describes its situation on the steep slopes that rise up on the western side of the Vale of CONWY.

Trefynwy *see* **Monmouth**

Tregaron (Dyfed) 'Village of Caron'. *Tref* (Welsh) 'village'; *Caron* (Welsh personal name). This small town northeast of LAMPETER is named after an early saint to whom the local parish church is dedicated

Tremadoc Bay (Gwynedd) This northern sweep of CARDIGAN Bay, which washes the south side of the LLEYN Peninsula, takes the name of the village of Tremadoc here, founded by William Madocks, in the early 19th century, shortly after he had established the nearby PORTHMADOG. The more correct Welsh rendering of this name would be *Tremadog*.

Trent (England) 'The trespasser, or one liable to flooding'. *Tri* (Brythonic Celtic prefix) 'across', 'through'; *sento* (Brythonic Celtic root element) 'path'. This major English river, which rises in the hills of north STAFFORDSHIRE, flows initially southwards to round the DERBYSHIRE Dales and completely changes direction before joining the Ouse to form the HUMBER. It was first recorded in Roman times as *Trisantona*; of which its current name is a contracted version that hides the original sense of a river that frequently flooded 'across its path' or over its banks. Its name appears as an distinguishing affix for many places along its course.

Tresco (Cornwall) 'Elder-tree farm'. *Tre* (Old Cornish) 'farmstead'; *scaw* (Old Cornish) 'elder tree'. The name of this, the second largest of the Isles of SCILLY, was originally that of an individual farm on the island, recorded as *Trescau* in a document of 1305.

Trim (Meath) 'Town of the ford of the elder trees'. *Baile* (Irish Gaelic) 'town'; *ath* (Irish Gaelic) 'ford'; *trom* (Irish Gaelic) 'elder tree'. The English name of this historic Anglo-Norman town, upstream on the BOYNE from NAVAN, is in fact the final word of its Irish name, *Baile Atha Troim*.

Tring (Hertfordshire) Place by 'the tree-covered hillside'. *Treow* (Old English) 'tree'; *hangra* (Old English) 'wooded hillside or slope'. The name aptly describes the situation of this town amongst the wooded slopes at the northeastern end of the CHILTERN HILLS. The misleading Domesday Book entry is *Treunge*, but a later record of 1199 shows *Trehangr*.

Troon (Strathclyde) Place of the 'headland'. *Trwyn* (Brythonic Celtic) 'headland', 'point'. Alternatively, this name has been derived by some as: *an t-sron* (Scottish Gaelic) 'nose', 'point'. Either way, the name is most apt as this resort and port, on the Firth of CLYDE, is built around a distinct promontory. Recorded as *le Trune* in 1464.

Trossachs, The (Central) Apparently 'the cross-hills'. *Na Trosaichean* (Scottish Gaelic) 'the cross-hills'. As a reference to the transverse wooded ridges between Loch Achray and Loch Katrine, which have given name to this renowned beautiful area of the Highlands near the town of CALLANDER, the late 18th-century derivation is apt. It is said to have been transferred and translated into Gaelic from the Welsh place-name, TRAWSFYNYDD.

Trowbridge (Wiltshire) Place of 'the tree-trunk bridge'. *Treow* (Old English) 'tree'; *brycg* (Old English) 'bridge'.

The name of this county town, southeast of BATH, probably refers to an early bridge made of tree trunks laid across the River Bliss here. It was misrecorded in the Domesday Book as *Straburg*, but appears as *Trobrigge* in a later text of 1184.

Trumpington (Cambridgeshire) 'Farmstead associated with a man called Trump'. *Trump* (Old English personal name); *ing* (Old English connective particle) 'associated with'; *tun* (Old English) 'farmstead'. The name of this former village, now a southern suburb of CAMBRIDGE, was recorded as *Trumpintone* in a text of around 1050.

Truro (Cornwall) The name of this county town, at the head of the deeply indented tidal estuary of the River Truro north of FALMOUTH, remains a mystery; the first element is probably based on *tri* (Old Cornish conjectural word) meaning 'three', but the all-important second part is obscure. The name was documented as *Triueru* in around 1173.

Tuam (Galway) 'Burial mound'. *Tuaim* (Irish Gaelic) 'burial mound' or 'tumulus'. The original Irish name of this small market town northeast of GALWAY was *Tuaim an Da Ghualainn*, 'burial mound of the two shoulders', referring to its shape.

Tullamore (Offaly) Place of the 'big hill'. *Tulach* (Irish Gaelic) 'hill'; *mor* (Irish Gaelic) 'big'. The Irish name of this 18th-century county town in central Ireland is *Tulach Mhor*.

Tullow (Carlow) Simply 'the hill'. *Tulach* (Irish Gaelic) 'little hill'. Although the topography around this small market town to the east of CARLOW is not particularly hilly, this name could refer to any of a number of small eminences

Tunbridge Wells (Kent) 'Springs near Tonbridge'. This residential town was developed during the reign of James I of England, when medicinal springs were discovered here. It took is main name from the town of TONBRIDGE, 4 miles (6 km) to the north. Officially, it is known as **Royal Tunbridge Wells**, having, like Royal LEAMINGTON SPA, been granted the use of the regal prefix, in this case later by Edward VII.

Tunstall (Staffordshire) Place on 'the site of a farm'. *Tun-stall* (Old English conjectural combination) 'site of a farm', 'a farmstead'. The relatively common name of this urban locality, one of the constituent 'Five Towns' of STOKE-ON-TRENT, was recorded in a document of 1212 as *Tunstal*.

Turriff (Grampian) Possibly 'hill of anguish'. *Torr* (Scottish Gaelic) 'hill'; *bruid* (Scottish Gaelic) 'anguish' or 'a stab'. This is a name in which the second element may have changed, and as such its exact derivation remains uncertain. Records show: *Turbruad* in the *Book of Deer* *c.*1000; *Turrech* 1300; *Turreff* 1500.

Tweed (Borders/Northumberland) 'The strong one'. This famous salmon river, which rises at Tweed Well north of MOFFAT and basically flows eastwards to enter the North Sea at BERWICK-ON-TWEED, has a name that is probably the same as its tributary, the Teviot, in being derived from the Brythonic Celtic root element *teu*, which in turn is thought to be related to the Sanskrit *tavas*, meaning 'surging' or 'powerful'. The name was recorded in an early text of around AD700 as *Tuuide*.

Twelve Pins, The (Galway) 'The Twelve peaks'. A remarkable group of mountains in CONNEMARA whose name more corectly should have been anglicised as 'The Twelve Bens'. In Irish, their name is *Na Beanna Beola*, 'the peaks of Beola', an old Firbolg chief.

Twickenham (Greater London) Either 'Twicca's riverside land' or 'riverside land at the river fork'. *Twicca-n* (Old English personal name—genitive form) unidentified; *twicce* (Old English conjectural word) 'river fork', 'confluence'; *hamm* (Old English) 'riverside land'. This district of RICHMOND, famous as the home of England's national rugby stadium, is situated on the north bank of the THAMES where it meanders through southwest LONDON. As such, either of the two given derivations would be appropriate, the latter being based on the confluence of the River Crane here. A record of 793 shows the name as *Tuicanhamme*.

Tyldesley (Greater Manchester) 'Tilwald's clearing'. *Tildwald* (Old English personal name); *leah* (Old English) 'woodland clearing'. The name of this town southwest of BOLTON was noted as *Tildesleia c.*1210.

Tyne (Cumbria/Northumberland/Tyne and Wear; Lothian) Simply, 'the river' or 'the water'. *Ti-* (Brythonic Celtic root element) 'to flow'. The well-known river of northeast England has two branches, the **North Tyne**, rising in the KIELDER FOREST, and the **South Tyne**, from **Tynehead Fell**, join near HEXHAM to flow eastwards by NEWCASTLE UPON TYNE to enter the North Sea at TYNEMOUTH; it was recorded as: *Tina c.*150; *Tinus c.*730; *Tine* 875. The Scottish **Tyne** drains off the north slopes of the Moorfoot Hills and flows northeastwards, through HADDINGTON, reaching the North Sea at Tyninghame, just north of DUNBAR.

Tyne and Wear (England) This metropolitan county, formed in 1974 to provide administration for the urban conurbation extending basically from NEWCASTLE UPON TYNE to SUNDERLAND, and centred on the lower reaches of the TYNE and the WEAR, takes its name from these rivers.

Tynemouth (Tyne and Wear) Place at 'the mouth of the River Tyne'. *Tyne* (Brythonic Celtic river name) 'the river'; *mutha* (Old English) 'river mouth'. The self-explanatory name of this town and 19th-century resort on the North Sea coast describes a place of antiquity, it having developed on the site of a 7th-century monastery and an 11th-century priory. The name is documented in a record of about 1121 as *Tinanmuthe*.

Tyneside (Tyne and Wear) This often used general term for the urban conurbation on either side of the lower TYNE has since been incorporated into the official names of the two administrative districts of **North Tyneside** and **South Tyneside**, on respective banks of the river.

Tynwald Hill (Isle of Man) 'The parliament mound'. *Thing* (Old Norse) 'assembly'; *vollr* (Old Norse) 'field'; *hill* (English) 'mound'. This is the name of the famous artificial mound at St John's, east of PEEL, where in accordance with ancient Norse custom, the Manx Parliament, known as the Tynwald, holds its annual 'stadmot' or 'estate-meet', at which new laws are promulgated in open assembly. This Scandinavian name has similarly derived counterparts in DINGWALL (Highland); Tingwall (Shetland); Tinwald (Dumfries and Galloway)

Tyrone (Northern Ireland) 'Eoghan's land'. *Tir* (Irish Gaelic) 'land'; *Eoghain* (Irish Gaelic personal name) Eoghan or Owen; the semi-legendary 4th-century ruler of this northern part of Ireland that then covered a more extensive area including the present-day county of LONDONDERRY as well as TYRONE. *See* INISHOWEN

Tywyn (Gwynedd) Place on the 'seashore'. *Tywyn* (Welsh) 'seashore', 'strand'. This resort with its former slate-exporting harbour and terminus of the famous narrow-gauge Talyllyn Railway developed in the latter part of the 19th century and has a name that reflects its open strand location on the shore of CARDIGAN Bay, west of MACHYNLLETH. It was recorded as *Thewyn* in the mid 13th century.

U

Uckfield (East Sussex) 'Ucca's open land'. *Ucca* (Old English personal name); *feld* (Old English) 'open land'. The name of this small town, northest of LEWES, was recorded as *Uckefeld* in a document of 1220.

Uddingston (Strathclyde) 'Oda's people's farmstead'. *Od-ingas* (Old English personal family name) 'Oda's people's'; *tun* (Old English) 'farmstead'. Curiously, an early form of the name of this town, southeast of GLASGOW, is recorded in 1296 as *Odistoun*, just 'Oda's farmstead'.

Uig (Highland) Simply 'bay'. *Vik* (Old Norse) bay. This village in northwest SKYE is the island's main port for onward ferry crossings to the WESTERN ISLES, and lies on the only really sheltered deep-water bay on this part of its coast. *Compare* VOE, WICK.

Uist, North and South (Western Isles) 'An abode'. *I-vist* (Old Norse) 'in-dwelling'. The latter is the literal meaning traditionally ascribed to the basic name of these two Outer Hebridean islands, separated by the intervening BENBECULA. This was recorded in 1282 as *Iuist*.

Ullapool (Highland) 'Olaf's settlement'. *Olaf* (Old Norse personal name); *bol* (Old Norse mutated form of *bol-stathr*) 'settlement'. The name of this major west Highland fishing and ferry port, developed in 1788 by the British Fisheries Society to encourage the herring industry, was earlier recorded in 1610 as *Ullabill*.

Ullswater (Cumbria) 'Ulfr's lake'. *Ulfr* (Old Norse personal name); *waeter* (Old English) 'expanse of water', 'lake'. This is the second largest, and most northeasterly, lake in the LAKE DISTRICT, situated southwest of PENRITH. The name was documented as *Ulueswater* in a text of 1235.

Ulster (Ireland) 'Lands of the Uladh people'. *Uladh* (Old Irish tribal name); *s* (Old Norse genitive) possessive; *tir* (Irish Gaelic) 'land'. This ancient kingdom, and one of four historic provinces, occupied an area that was equivalent to all six of the present counties of NORTHERN IRELAND, plus CAVAN, DONEGAL and MONAGHAN. The name *Uladztir* was recorded by the early Norse settlers. *See* CONNAUGHT, LEINSTER and MUNSTER.

Ulverston (Cumbria) 'Wulfhere's farmstead'. *Wulfhere* (Old English personal name) meaning 'wolf-army'; *tun* (Old English) 'farmstead', 'estate'. The loss of the initial *W* is due to Scandinavian influence. The name appears as *Ulurestun* in the Domesday Book of 1086.

United Kingdom (British Isles) This is the familiar shortened version, also often abbreviated to U.K., of the full constitutional name for the sovereign state that is the United Kingdom of Great Britain and Northern Ireland. Established originally in 1801 as a union of GREAT BRITAIN and IRELAND, its name changed to the present description in 1921 when the Irish Free State was declared independent, with the 26 counties of Southern Ireland leaving the union. The constituent countries of the U.K. are: ENGLAND; SCOTLAND; WALES; and NORTHERN IRELAND.

Unst (Shetland) 'Eagles' nest'. *Orn* (Old Norse) eagle; *nyst* (Old Norse) 'nest'. This, the most northerly of Shetland's main islands, is still the famed home of many rare birds. Its name was recorded in a document of around 1200 as *Ornyst*.

Up Holland (Lancashire) Place by 'the upper hill-spur land'. *Upp* (Old English) 'up', 'upper'; *hoh* (Old English) 'hill spur'; *land* (Old English) 'land'. The unusual name of this urban area, between ORELL and SKELMERSDALE, aptly reflects its topographical situation. It was recorded in the Domesday Book as simply *Hoiland*.

Upminster (Greater London) Place of 'the higher church'. *Upp* (Old English) 'upper', 'higher'; *mynster* (Old English) 'church'. The name of this former ESSEX town, now a district of HAVERING at the extreme east of LONDON, was noted as *Upmunstra* in the Domesday Book.

Uppingham (Leicestershire) 'Homestead of the hill dwellers'. *Yppe* (Old English—derivative of *upp*) 'hill'; *inga* (Old English—genitive of *ingas*) 'dwellers of'; *ham* (Old English) 'homestead', 'village'. The name of this former RUTLAND small town, with its public school, situated to the south of Oakham, possibly refers to a prominent hillock just west of the town; it was documented as *Yppingeham* in 1067.

Urmston (Greater Manchester) 'Urm's farmstead'. *Urm* (Old Danish personal name related to Old Norse *ormr*) meaning 'snake'; *tun* (Old English) 'farmstead'. The name of this town, southwest of MANCHESTER, was recorded as *Wermeston* in 1194.

Usk (Gwent) This small market town, to the north and upstream of NEWPORT, takes its name from the River Usk on which it stands. The river name here is thought by some authorities to mean 'fish waters', deriving from an ancient Celtic root word that is reflected in the Latin *piscis*. Using the same basis, the Romans called the river *Isca*, after which they named their fort downstream at CAERLEON.

Uttoxeter (Staffordshire) Probably 'Wuttuc's heath'. *Wuttuc* (Old English personal name) unidentified; *haeddre* (Old English conjectural word) 'heath'. The name of this market town, northeast of STAFFORD, appears in the Domesday Book as *Wotocheshede*, and its current form has evolved by association with such names as the former Roman towns of EXETER and WROXETER.

Uxbridge (Greater London) Place of 'the bridge of the Wixan' tribe. *Wixan* (Old English tribal name); *brycg* (Old English) 'bridge'. This former MIDDLESEX town,

Uxbridge

now a district of HILLINGDON, at the far western edge of the LONDON conurbation, has a name originally recorded as *Wixebrug* in around 1145, then the initial *W* was dropped to give *Uxebregg* as noted in 1200.

V

Vale of White Horse (Oxfordshire) This name is that given to the valley of the River Ock, north of the BERKSHIRE Downs, specifically referring to White Horse Hill west of WANTAGE, where a prehistoric figure of a giant horse has been cut into the chalk. The name was recorded as *The Vale of Whithorse* in a document of 1368. The name has recently been adopted as that of the local administrative district.

Valentia Island (Kerry) 'Estuary of the island' *Beal* (Irish Gaelic) 'estuary'; *inse* (Irish Gaelic) 'island'. This island, lying just off the northwestern side of the Iveragh peninsula, derives its name from the narrow sound between. The current Irish name for this island is *Dairbhre*, meaning 'a place producing oaks'.

Vatersay (Western Isles) 'Glove's island'. *Vottr-s* (Old Norse) 'glove's'; *ey* (Old Norse) 'island'. This small inhabited island to the south of BARRA, with which it has very recently been linked by a causeway, has a rather strange first element in its name, and according to one commentator the possessive form may suggest that 'Glove' was a nickname for someone who always wore a pair of them.

Vauxhall (Greater London) Place of 'Faukes's manor'. *Faukes* (Old French personal name) Faukes de Bréauté, 13th-century Anglo-Norman nobleman; *hall* (Old English) 'manor house', 'hall'. This THAMES riverside district of LAMBETH was recorded as *Faukeshale* in 1279.

Ventor (Isle of Wight) Probably farm of 'Vinter'. *Vinter* (Old English manorial name) based on Anglo-Norman le Vyntener family. This resort and residential town, southwest of SHANKLIN, was recorded as *Vinter* in 1617.

Previously the settlement here had been called Holeway.

Virginia Water (Surrey) This residential district, south-west of STAINES, takes its name from a large artificial lake built here by the Duke of Cumberland in 1748, and was recorded as such a year later.

Voe (Shetland) Simply 'Bay'. *Vagr* (Old Norse) 'bay'. Several SHETLAND MAINLAND settlements at the head of deeply indented bays, firths, fjords or voes take the peculiarly local latter form for such sheltered coastal sites. *Compare* UIG.

W

Wadebridge (Cornwall) Place of 'the bridge by the ford'. *Gewaede* (Old English) 'ford'; *brycg* (Old English) 'bridge'. Originally known simply as *Wade*, as documented in 1258, this town at the head of the Camel river estuary was clearly the site of an important fording point that subsequently was bridged sometime in the 15th century, as evidenced by the name *Wadebrygge* recorded in 1478.

Wakefield (West Yorkshire) 'Open land where the wake or annual festival was held'. *Wacu* (Old English conjectural word) 'wake'; *feld* (Old English) 'open land'. The name of this county town and cathedral city on the River Calder, south of LEEDS, has a direct association with the custom of annual holiday festivals, the tradition of which is still evident in the north of England, where many towns have their 'Wakes Week'. The name appears in the Domesday Book as *Wachefeld*.

Wales (Britain) 'The land of strangers'. *Walas* (Old English plural of *walh*) 'strangers', 'foreigners' generally; Britons, Celts specifically. The principality, as it later became known after medieval English conquest, was originally viewed by the early Anglo-Saxons as the land of peoples ethnically different from themselves, i.e. the ancient Britons. Indeed, in the Anglo-Saxon Chronicles of 1055 it was referred to as *Brytland*, 'land of the Britons'. Other early records show the development of the current name: *Wealum* 922; *Wealan* 1046; *Walonia* 1160. It is considered by some that a similar Germanic root word is the basis of other comparable European names that have the same sense: e.g. Wallons (Belgium); Wallis (Switzerland); Walachia (Romania).

Compare CORNWALL. The Welsh name for Wales is *Cymru*, meaning 'land of our fellows', and it was from this ancient Celtic root that the medieval Latin name *Cambria* arose.

Walkerburn (Borders) 'Wauker's stream'. *Wauker* (Scots elided from Old English *walcere*) 'fuller of cloth'; *burna* (Old English) 'stream'. This small town on the River TWEED, EAST OF Inverleithen has long been associated with the woollen trade.

Wallasey (Merseyside) 'Island of the Welsh'. *Wala* (Old English—genitive plural of *walh*) 'foreigners', 'Britons', 'Welshmen'; *eg* (Old English) 'island'; *ey* (Middle English—later addition of explanatory generic) 'island'. The name of this industrial town and resort, at the northern end of the WIRRAL peninsula, originally applied to a larger area of the low-lying land here that at high tide was effectively an island. Entered in the Domesday Book as simply *Walea*, a later record of 1351 shows the name as *Waleyesegh*, indicating a tautological duplication of the second element.

Wallingford (Oxfordshire) 'Ford of Wealh's people'. *Wealh* (Old English personal name—probably related to *walh*) implying 'a Briton'; *inga* (Old English—genitive of *ingas*) 'people of'; *ford* (Old English) 'river crossing'. This town on the River THAMES (or ISIS), downstream and southeast of OXFORD, noted today for its annual regatta, has a name first recorded in 821 as *Waelingford*, and later as *Walingeford* in 1086.

Wallsend (Tyne and Wear) Place at 'the end of Hadrian's Wall'. *Wall* (Old English) 'wall', 'dyke', 'dividing structure'; *ende* (Old English) 'end', 'termination'. The self-explanatory name of this industrial town on the north bank of the River TYNE, east of NEWCASTLE UPON TYNE, marks the site of the eastern Roman end-fort of *Segedunum* on the famous HADRIAN'S WALL. This was one of many such 'wall' names that were given to places along its extent, including: **Walbottle**; **Wall**; **Wall Houses**; **Wall Town**; **Walwick**.

Walmer (Kent) 'Pool of the Britons'. *Wala* (Old English—genitive plural of *walh*) 'Britons'; *mere* (Old English) 'pool', 'lake'. This now southern suburb of DEAL, presumably arose as a settlement beside a former pool here, which was frequented by Britons as opposed to the new Anglo-Saxon settlers who gave it its name, which was first recorded as *Wealemere* in 1087.

Walney, Isle of (Cumbria) Probably 'killer-whale island'. *Vogn* (Old Norse) 'grampus', 'killer whale'; *ey* (Old Norse) 'island'. The name of this long narrow island, lying off BARROW-IN-FURNESS, may have been so called by Viking sailors acknowledging its blunt snout and humpback shape. It was recorded as *Wagneia* in 1127. *Compare* WHALSAY. *See* CANNA.

Walsall (West Midlands) 'Walh's nook'. *Walh* (Old English personal name or an ethnic tag) meaning 'Briton'; *halh* (Old English) 'nook', 'corner of land', 'little valley'. The name of this industrial town, northwest of BIRMINGHAM, was recorded as *Waleshale* in a document of 1163. *Compare* WALLINGFORD.

Walsingham, Great and **Little** (Norfolk) 'Homestead of Waels's people'. *Waels* (Old English personal name); *inga* (Old English—genitive of *ingas*) 'people of'; *ham* (Old English) 'homestead'. The basic name of these two villages on opposite banks of the River Stiffkey, north of FAKENHAM, was noted as *Walsingaham* in about 1035.

Waltham Abbey (Essex) 'Homestead in or by a forest'. *Wald* (Old English) 'forest'; *ham* (Old English) 'homestead'; *abeie* (Old French form of Church Latin *abbatia*—later affix) 12th-century Abbey of Holy Cross and St Lawrence. This town on the east side of the Lea Valley, opposite CHESHUNT, has a basic name that lends itself to several place-names in this area. Recorded in the Domesday Book as simply *Waltham*, it then became *Waltham Sancti Laurentii*, as in a text of 1291, confirming the dedication of the abbey built here by Henry II. *Compare* WALTHAMSTOW.

Waltham Forest (Greater London) This north LONDON borough, lying to the east of the River Lea and extending from the south end of EPPING Forest to HACKNEY Marshes, was created in 1965 from an amalgamation of CHINGFORD, LEYTON and WALTHAMSTOW, and takes its adopted name, somewhat artificially, from that of the latter place.

Walthamstow (Greater London) 'Wilcume's holy place'. *Wilcume* (Old English personal name) early local Saxon queen and abbess; *stow* (Old English) 'holy place'. This former ESSEX town, now a southern district of the borough of WALTHAM FOREST, at first sight appears to have a name related to WALTHAM ABBEY and its many attendant places in the region to the north. However, as indicated in the derivation given here, its origin and meaning are quite different, and the current spelling of the name has evolved by association with that of its neighbour. It was documented as *Wilcumestouue* in 1067.

Walton-le-Dale (Lancashire) 'Farmstead of the Britons'. *Wala* (Old English—genitive plural of *walh*) 'Britons'; *tun* (Old English) 'farmstead', 'village'; *le* (Norman French definite article remaining after loss of preposition) 'in the'; *dalr* (Old Norse) valley. This now suburb of PRESTON, lying in Ribblesdale, has a common name noted as: *Waletune* 1086; *Walton in La Dale* 1304.

Walton-on-Thames (Surrey) 'Farmstead or village of Britons'. The derivation of the basic name here is as given above for WALTON-LE-DALE, but this residential town, southwest of LONDON on the north bank of the THAMES, appropriately has added a distinguishing affix denoting its riverside location. Early records show: *Waletone* in the Domesday Book of 1086; *Waleton* in 1190; and *Waleton super Thamis* in 1279.

Walton on the Naze (Essex) 'Farmstead or village of the Britons'. Again the etymology of the basic name is the same as the above two examples, although in some instances the name Walton can mean 'village by the wood', deriving from *wald* not *walh*. The distinguishing affix here refers to the situation of this coastal resort by The Naze, a prominent headland (Old English *naess*) northeast of CLACTON-ON-SEA.

Wandsworth (Greater London) 'Waendel's enclosure'. *Waendel* (Old English personal name); *worth* (Old English) 'enclosure'. This LONDON borough on the south side of the THAMES is centred on one of its tributaries, the River Wandle, whose own name is a back-formation of the early settlement name, recorded as *Wendlesuurthe* in 1067, and *Wandelesorde* in the Domesday Book of 1086. *Compare* WELLINGBOROUGH.

Wanlockhead (Dumfries and Galloway) Place of the 'white flat stone'. *Gwyn* (Brythonic Celtic) 'white'; *llech* (Brythonic Celtic) 'flat stone'. The third element, *head* (Middle English) 'at the top of', was added at a later date. This mining village, at 1380 ft (425 m) up in the Lowther Hills (the highest village in Scotland), has, like its near neighbour LEADHILLS, been involved in mineral extraction, especially gold and silver, since the 16th century. It could be that the derivation of its name really means such a precious metal ore.

Wansdyke (Hampshire/Wiltshire/Avon) 'Woden's dyke'. *Woden* (Old English sacred name) the foremost Anglo-Saxon heathen god, of war—counterpart of Nordic Odin; *dic* (Old English) 'dike', 'ditch'. This ancient earthwork, possibly constructed for defensive purposes, ran along the downland of south-central England from ANDOVER to PORTISHEAD, although much of it is now obliterated. Its name, which was recorded as *Wodnes dic* in a document of 903, suggests that it may have been originally regarded as having actually been built by Woden, or at least created in his honour, or with his 'omnipotent blessing'. *Compare* WEDNESBURY.

Wantage (Oxfordshire) Place at 'the intermittent or waning stream'. *Wantage* (Old English river name derived from *wanian*, 'to wane' + *ing*) 'the diminishing one'. This downland town, on the south side of the VALE OF WHITE HORSE, famous as the birthplace of King Alfred the Great, stands on the River Wantage, from which it takes its name. Intermittent flow of surface river water is a characteristic condition of streams on permeable chalk downs, as here. It was first recorded as *Waneting* in a document of around 880, and as *Wanetinz* in the Domesday Book of 1086.

Wapping (Greater London) Probably settlement of 'Waeppa's people'. *Waeppa* (Old English personal name) unidentified; *ingas* (Old English) 'people of'. The name of this riverside district of central LONDON, on the north bank of the River THAMES immediately east of 'The Tower', was recorded as *Wapping* in about 1220, and as *Wappinges* in 1231.

Ware (Hertfordshire) Place of 'the weir'. *Waer* (Old English) 'weir'. The name of this small town on the River Lea, downstream and just northeast of HERTFORD, was recorded as *Waras* in the Domesday Book of 1086; as *Wares* in 1173, and as *Ware* in 1254.

Wareham (Dorset) 'Homestead by the weir'. *Waer* (Old English) 'weir'; *ham* (Old English) 'homestead'. This town is situated on the low-lying flood plain between the Frome and Piddle rivers just before they flow into POOLE Harbour; a very likely place for a weir. The name was noted as *Werham* in a document of 784.

Warlingham (Surrey) 'Homestead of Waerla's people'. *Waerla* (Old English personal name) unidentified; *inga* (Old English—genitive of *ingas*) 'people of'; *ham* (Old English) 'homestead'. The name of this valley town on the northern side of the North DOWNS, just south of CROYDON, was recorded as *Warlyngham* in a document of 1144.

Warminster (Wiltshire) Place of 'the church on the River Were'. *Were* (Old English river name based on *worian*) 'wandering one'; *mynster* (Old English) 'large church'. The name of this town, at the western edge of SALISBURY Plain, was recorded as *Worgemynster* in the early 10th century, and as *Werminister* in a document of around 1115.

Warrenpoint (Down) Apparently 'the point of warrens'. This 19th-century town on the north side of CARLINGFORD Lough, just southeast of NEWRY, has an English name that is said to derive from a former extensive rabbit warren here, although there is no real point or headland.

Warrington (Cheshire) 'Farm by the weir'. *Waering* (Old English conjectural word related to *waer*) 'weir'; *tun* (Old English) 'farmstead'. This large industrial town, on the flood plain of the meandering River MERSEY southwest of MANCHESTER, would, like WAREHAM, have been an appropriate place for a weir. its name appears in the Domesday Book as *Walingtune*, the *r* having been replaced by the *l*, a common feature of Anglo-Norman transcription.

Warsop (Nottinghamshire) 'Waer's enclosed valley'. *Waer* (Old English personal name) unidentified; *hop* (Old English) 'small enclosed valley'. The name of this small town was documented as *Wareshope* in the Domesday Book of 1086..

Warwick (Warwickshire) 'Dwellings by the weir'. *Waering* (Old English conjectural word related to *waer*) 'weir'; *wic* (Old English) 'dwellings'. The name of this historic county town, with its 14th-century castle commanding its situation on the River Avon, was recorded as *Waericwicum* in 1001, which had been shortened to *Warwic* by the time of its entry in the Domesday Book. The county name, **Warwickshire**, was first documented in 1016 as *Waerincwicscir*.

Wash, The (Lincolnshire/Norfolk) Inlet of 'the sandbanks washed by the sea'. *Waesc* (Old English) 'tidal sandbanks'. This wide and shallow North Sea inlet that penetrates the low-lying FENS was, according to a document of around 1545, originally called *The Wasshes*, specific reference being to two fordable tidal sandbanks.

Washington (Tyne and Wear) 'Estate associated with a man called Wassa'. *Wassa* (Old English personal name) unidentified; *ing* (Old English connective particle) 'associated with'; *tun* (Old English) 'estate', 'farmstead'. This New Town, designated in 1964, to the west of SUNDERLAND, has adopted the name of an early settlement here, recorded as *Wassyntona* in 1183.

Wast Water (Cumbria) 'The lake in Wasdale'. *Vatn* (Old Norse) 'lake'; *dalr* (Old Norse) 'dale', 'valley'; *waeter* (Old English) 'lake'. This lake, to the southwest of SCAFELL PIKE in the LAKE DISTRICT, lies in the steep-sided Wasdale, also called Wastdale, which is 'the valley of Wastwater', the lake having at one time been simply *Vatn*. Probably the name is a shortened form of a tautologous 'Wasdale-water'. It was recorded as *Wassewater* in 1294.

Watchet (Somerset) Probably the place of 'the lower wood' or place 'under the wood.' *Gwa* (Brythonic Celtic conjectural root element) 'under'; *ceto* (Brythonic Celtic root element) 'wood'. The name of this small town with a harbour on BRIDGEWATER Bay was noted: *Waeced* in 918; *Waecet* in 962; *Wacet* in 1086; and *Wechet* in 1243.

Waterford (Waterford) Place of 'the wether fiord'. *Vethr* (Old Norse) 'wether', 'ram'; *fjordr* (Old Norse) 'sea inlet'. The name of this city, port and county in southeast Ireland is not, as might be expected, anything to do with 'fording the water' of the River Suir, at the mouth of which the town stands. In common with most of the names of the main inlets of the 'Viking' east coast of Ireland, the origin of Waterford is Old Norse. This was the 9th-century Viking settlement where wethers, or castrated rams, were loaded on to boats. The Old Norse rendering was *Vadrefjord*. The Irish name is *Port Lairge*, 'port of the haunch', indicating the shape of the river estuary here.

Waterlooville (Hampshire) This 19th-century town, northeast and inland from PORTSMOUTH, like several places in Britain, commemorates the famous victory at the Battle of Waterloo in 1815. In this case, the basic first element was apparently taken from the name of an inn here, called the *Heroes of Waterloo*, while the '-ville' ending was added as a fashionable contemporary tag ascribed to new town developments like this. *Compare* BOURNVILLE; COALVILLE.

Watford (Hertfordshire) Place of 'the ford used by hunters'. *Wath* (Old English) 'hunting'; *ford* (Old English) 'river crossing'. The name of this well-known manufacturing town, on the River Colne just northwest of the LONDON conurbation, was documented as *Watford* in about 945, and noted as *Wathford* in a text of 1190.

Watford Gap (Northamptonshire) Possibly 'the ford in the pass.' This location northeast of DAVENTRY, familiar to motorists on the M1 motorway as the name of a service area, is nonetheless commonly confused with the HERTFORDSHIRE town of WATFORD, in as much as the geographical sense of the popular expression 'north of Watford' is often unwittingly transposed farther north to here. The descriptive term 'gap', has real significance here, where in addition to Britain's first motorway, the Roman WATLING STREET (now the A5), the Grand Union Canal, and the main 'London, Midland and Scottish' rail route all pass literally within feet of each other as they funnel through this natural break in a limestone escarpment known as the Northamptonshire Uplands. In this case, the basic name is taken from the small village of Watford, immediately east of the Gap, and is probably identical in origin and meaning to its southern counterpart. But it has also been suggested by one authority that the latter name may have been based on *vath* (Old Scandinavian) meaning 'ford', to which an explanatory *ford* (Old English) was added. This village name was recorded in the Domesday Book exactly as it is now.

Watling Street (England) 'Roman road associated with the Waeclingas tribe'. *Waeclingas* (Old English tribal name) 'Waecel's people'; *straet* (Old English) 'Roman road'. The name of this major Roman military road, which ran from DOVER to WROXETER (basically the route of the current A2 and A5), was derived as was then the custom, from the name of a local tribal territory en route, in this case the Waeclingas from around ST ALBANS, which was itself formerly called *Waeclingaceaster*. The name may have originally only applied to the stretch from LONDON to ST ALBANS, but has since been transposed to several other Roman roads. This name was recorded as *Waetlingastraet* in 880, and as *Waeclingastraet* in the early 10th century.

Watlington (Oxfordshire) Probably 'village associated with a man called Waecel'. *Waecel* (Old English personal name based on *wacol* meaning 'watchful') unidentified; *ing* (Old English connective particle) 'associated with'; *tun* (Old English) 'farmstead', 'village', 'estate'. The name of this small town, southeast of OXFORD, was recorded as *Waeclinctun* in a document of 880. *Compare* WATLING STREET.

Waverley (Surrey) Probably 'clearing by the swampy ground'. *Waefre* (Old English) 'spongy', 'unstable'; *leah* (Old Eng lish) 'woodland clearing'. This modern administrative district, in the southwest of the county, takes its name from **Waverley Abbey**, the oldest Cistercian house in England, the ruins of which remain on a low-lying, possibly once marshy, woodland clearing site by the River Wey, to the southeast of FARNHAM. It is said that the abbey here inspired Sir Walter Scott to adopt *Waverley* as the title of his first novel, a name that now collectively refers to all his novels, and through this association has been transposed to his native Scotland to be used for such places as the main Waverley Station and the more recent Waverley Market Shopping Centre, both in EDINBURGH. The original abbey name was noted as *Wauerleia* in 1147.

Weald, The (Hampshire/Kent/Surrey/East and West Sussex) The upland 'forest region'. *Weald* (Old English—Kentish dialect form of *wald*) 'woodland', 'forest'. The name of this region of southeast England, which assumes a distinctly oval-shaped tract of undulating wooded low hills bounded by the inward-facing scarps of the North and South DOWNS, was noted in the dative plural form of *Waldum* in 1185, and as *Wald* in 1235. *Compare* WOLDS, The.

Wear (Durham/Tyne and Wear) 'The water'. The name of this river, which flows generally eastwards from **Wearhead** in the PENNINES near ALSTON to enter the North Sea at SUNDERLAND, has an ancient pre-Celtic root that simply means 'water'. *See* TYNE AND WEAR.

Wednesbury (West Midlands) 'Stronghold associated with the heathen god Woden'. *Woden* (Old English sacred name) the foremost Anglo-Saxon heathen god, of war—counterpart to Nordic Odin; *byrig* (Old English—dative form of *burh*) 'fortified place'. Recorded as *Wadnesberie* in the Domesday Book of 1086, the name of this former STAFFORDSHIRE town, now a district of WEST BROMWICH, implies either that originally it was regarded as a place created by the great pagan deity or one given his protection. *Compare* WANSDYKE; WEDNESFIELD. *See* THUNDERSLEY.

Wednesfield (West Midlands) 'Woden's open land'. *Woden* (Old English sacred name) Anglo-Saxon heathen god; *feld* (Old English) 'open land'. This also former STAFFORDSHIRE town, now a district of WOLVERHAMPTON, only 4 miles (6 km) northwest of WEDNESBURY, has a name with a clearly similar origin and sense as the latter. It was documented as *Wodnesfeld* in 996.

Wellingborough (Northamptonshire) 'Stronghold of Waendel's people'. *Waendel* (Old English personal name) unidentified; *inga* (Old English—genitive of *ingas*) 'people of'; *burh* (Old English) 'fortified place'. The name of this town, in the iron-ore mining district northeast of NORTHAMPTON, was recorded in the Domesday Book as *Wedlingeberie* but as *Wendlingburch* in 1178. Compare WANDSWORTH; WENSLEYDALE.

Wellington (Shropshire; Somerset) Probably 'farmstead associated with a man called Weola'. *Weola* (Old English personal name) unidentified; *ing* (Old English connective particle) 'associated with'; *tun* (Old English) 'farmstead', 'estate'. This fairly common English placename applies here to a town that is now part of TELFORD New Town, and to a small manufacturing centre just southwest of TAUNTON. Respective records for these places show: *Walitone* 1086 (Domesday Book), and *Weolingtun* 904.

Wells (Somerset) Place of 'the springs'. *Wella* (Old English) 'springs', 'wells'. This famous small cathedral city, below the southern slopes of the MENDIP HILLS to the south of BRISTOL, has long been known for its natural springs. Its simple name was noted as *Willan* in about 1050 and as *Welle* in the Domesday Book.

Wells-next-the-Sea (Norfolk) Place of 'the springs'. *Wella* (Old English) 'springs', 'wells'. The name of this small commercial port and yachting centre on the coast north of FAKENHAM is identical in origin and meaning to that of WELLS, the SOMERSET cathedral city, but for its relatively recent distinguishing and clearly promotional affix. It was originally recorded as *Guelle* in the Domesday Book, showing Anglo-Norman influence, and later in 1291 as *Wellis*.

Welshpool (Powys) This market town located to the west of SHREWSBURY has a self-descriptive name that refers to a 'pool' at the confluence here of the Lledin Brook with the River SEVERN. The geographical possessive prefix was added to emphasise the location of the town, which is just on the 'Welsh' side of the border with England. The Welsh name is *Y Trallwng*, which simply means 'the pool'.

Welwyn Garden City (Hertfordshire) Place at 'the willow trees'. *Weligum* (Old English—dative plural of *welig*) 'willow trees'. The basic name of this New Town, designated in 1948, to the south of STEVENAGE, was taken from the old, small town of **Welwyn**, which it now adjoins to the north; it was originally documented as *Welingum* in about 945. The 'Garden City' affix represents an early 20th-century new town planning concept imported from the United States and brought to fruition here at a place with an appropriately arboreal name.

Wem (Shropshire) 'Dirty or muddy place'. *Wamm* (Old English) 'stain', 'filth'. Recorded as *Weme* in the Domesday Book, the name of this small town situated on the River Roden in a low-lying district north of SHREWSBURY originally would have been a 'marshy place', and hence the sense of filth likely to spoil.

Wembley (Greater London) 'Wemba's clearing'. *Wemba* (Old English personal name) unidentified; *leah* (Old English) 'woodland clearing'. Noted in 825 as *Wembalea*, the name of this district in the borough of BRENT is well known for the large Wembley Sports Stadium, built originally for the British Empire Exhibition of 1924.

Wemyss (Fife; Strathclyde) Place of the 'caves'. *Uamh-s* (Scottish Gaelic) 'caves'. In the case of both **East Wemyss** and **West Wemyss** on the Firth of FORTH, and **Wemyss Bay** on the Firth of CLYDE, there are many coastal caves to be found in their raised-beach cliff locations.

Wendover (Buckinghamshire) Place of 'the white waters'. *Winn* (Brythonic Celtic conjectural word) 'white'; *dover* (Brythonic Celtic derivative of root word dubro) 'water'. This small town, which nestles in a gap in the steep northern escarpment of the CHILTERN HILLS south-east of AYLESBURY, takes directly the name of the river here. The 'whiteness' of the water may reflect both the underlying chalk bedrock and the turbulent nature of the river at this point. Early records show: *Waendofran* c.970; *Wendoure* 1086 (Domesday Book). *Compare* ANDOVER; DOVER.

Wenlock Edge (Shropshire) 'Hill ridge by the white monastery'. *Winn* (Brythonic Celtic conjectural word) 'white'; *loc* (Old English) 'religious enclosure'. This distinctly long and narrow limestone ridge, which extends for 15 miles (24 km) southwestwards from **Much Wenlock**, derives its name from this small town. The latter is the site of a 7th-century Cuniac Benedictine abbey and a later priory, its name being noted as *Wynloca* around 1000, and *Wenloch* in the Domesday Book. The later 'Much' prefix is from *mycel* (Old English) meaning 'great'. The ridge name itself was recorded in 1227 as simply *Egge*.

Wensleydale (North Yorkshire) 'The valley of Waendel's clearing'. *Waendel* (Old English personal name) unidentified; *leah* (Old English) 'woodland clearing'; *dal* or *dael* (Old Danish or Old English) 'valley'. Probably the best known of the 'Yorkshire Dales' and the name of a famous cheese originally from here, this west-east valley of the upper River Ure takes its basic name from the village of **Wensley** at its lower eastern end. It was recorded as *Wandelesleydale* around 1150.

Wentworth (Surrey) The name of this residential district between ASCOT and VIRGINIA WATER, famous for its championship golf course, takes its name from the 19th-century Wentworth House (now the golf clubhouse) itself named after the owner, a Mrs Wentworth.

Wessex (England) 'Territory of 'the West Saxons'. *West* (Old English) 'west'; *seaxe* (Old English tribal name) 'Saxon'. This is the name of the former ancient Anglo-Saxon kingdom in the south and southwest of ENGLAND, which had its capital at WINCHESTER. It was the territory of the West Saxons, as distinct from that of the East Saxons (now ESSEX) and that of the South Saxons (now SUSSEX). Unlike these other kingdoms, it never became a county, although as a name it is still used by many organisations as a more meaningful term by which to promote their regional interests than broad descriptions such as 'the West Country'. It was recorded as *West Seaxna lond* in 709.

West Bridgford (Nottinghamshire) 'Ford by the bridge'. *Brycg* (Old English) 'bridge'; *ford* (Old English) 'river crossing'. The name of this town on the River TRENT, just south of NOTTINGHAM, implies that for some time after the building of a bridge here the ford was still in use. It appears in the Domesday Book as simple *Brigeforde*, the 'West' affix being added later to distinguish it from the village of East Bridgford, a few miles downstream and to the northeast.

West Bromwich (West Midlands) 'Farm where broom grows'. *Brom* (Old English) 'broom'; *wic* (Old English) 'farm'. The name of this town, northwest of BIRMINGHAM, was recorded as *Bromwic* in the Domesday Book. The distinguishing affix of *West* was added later in contradistinction to Castle Bromwich.

Westbury (Wiltshire) 'Western stronghold'. *West* (Old English) 'west', 'western'; *byrig* (Old English—dative of *burh*) 'fortified place'. The 'stronghold' here, by this town at the 'western' edge of SALISBURY Plain, is the Iron Age fort called Bratton Castle beside which is a large 'white horse' cut into the chalk hillside. The name is documented as *Westberie* in the Domesday Book of 1086.

Western Isles (Scotland) This self-explanatory name, given official recognition as the 'Island Authority' created in 1975, is a long-standing alternative term for the Outer HEBRIDES; the westernmost archipelago of 200-plus islands that stretches for 130 miles (200 km) in a crescent off the northwest mainland of Scotland.

West Glamorgan *see* **Glamorgan**.

West Ham (Greater London) 'Riverside land'. *Hamm* (Old English) 'riverside pasture'. This well-known district of LONDON's 'East End', north of the THAMES and east of the Lea rivers, represents the western counterpart of East Ham with which it forms the borough of NEWHAM. The Domesday Book entry is plainly *Hame*, the simple name used to describe the whole area before any geographical differentiation.

West Hartlepool *see* **Hartlepool**

West Kirby (Merseyside) 'Western church-village'. *West*

(Old English—later affix) 'western'; *kirkju-by* (Old Norse) 'village with a church'. The name of this residential town and resort on the western corner of the WIRRAL peninsula was recorded as simply *Kircheby* in 1154, but by 1289 a text showed it as *Westkirkeby*, probably so qualified on account of its location rather than distinction from an eastern counterpart.

Westmeath (Ireland) The name of this county in east-central Ireland came into being in 1542 when this western part of the former ancient territory of MEATH was formalised into the overall Tudor administrative structure for the island. Its Irish name is *An Iarmhi*, deriving from: *an* ('the'), *iar* ('west'), and *Mhi* ('Meath').

West Mersea *see* **Mersea, East** and **West**.

West Midlands (England) This is the self-explanatory name that was adopted in 1974 for the then new metropolitan county created to cover the large urban conurbation centred on BIRMINGHAM and extending from COVENTRY in the southeast to WOLVERHAMPTON in the northwest. There is no official administrative eastern counterpart, although the term 'East Midlands' is frequently used for the roughly triangular area encompassed by DERBY, LEICESTER and NOTTINGHAM; the airport serving this is called 'the East Midlands'. As a whole 'the Midlands' roughly corresponds to the ancient Anglo-Saxon kingdom of Mercia.

Westminster (Greater London) Place of 'the west monastery'. *West* (Old English) 'west'; *mynster* (Old English) 'monastery'. Recorded as *Westmynster* in about 975, the famous name of the district and borough, or City of Westminster as it is correctly known, stems from an 8th-century monastery founded here, to the west of the City of London, the site of which is now occupied by the 13th-century Westminster Abbey.

Westmorland (England) 'Land of the Westmoringas'. *Westmoringas* (Old English tribal name based on *west* + *mor* + *ingas*) meaning 'people west of the YORKSHIRE moors'; *land* (Old English) 'district'. This former county name applied to the area that is now represented by the southeastern part of CUMBRIA. It appeared originally as *Westmoringaland* in a document of 966. *See* APPLEBY-IN-WESTMORLAND.

Weston-super-Mare (Avon) 'Western farm on the sea'. *West* (Old English) 'west', 'western'; *tun* (Old English) 'farmstead'; *super Mare* (later Medieval Latin affix) 'on the sea'. The name of this well-known Bristol Channel resort, southwest of BRISTOL, originally appeared in a text of around 1266 as simply *Weston*, a very common place name, but in a record of 1349 it had become *Weston super Mare*, thus distinguishing it from **Westonzoyland** on Sedge Moor, some distance to the southeast.

Westport (Mayo) This small fishing port and resort on Clew Bay has a self-descriptive English name given to it by Peter Browne, 2nd Earl of Altamont, who laid out the town in the late 18th century with the intention of developing a small industrial textile community here. Its original Irish name is *Cathair na Mart*, meaning 'stone fort of the beef oxen'.

Westray (Orkney) 'West island'. *Vestr* (Old Norse) 'west'; *ey* (Old Norse) 'island'. Although this island is not the most westerly of the group, apparently it was to the Vikings on account of the fact that their compass cardinal points were set at a 45-degree difference from the current bearings.

West Sussex *see* **Sussex**.

Westward Ho! (Devon) This somewhat surprising place name, complete with an exclamation mark, was given to this late 19th-century coastal resort development as a special tribute to Charles Kingsley's novel of this name, published in 1855, and largely set in the locality here, near BIDEFORD. *Contrast* WAVERLEY.

West Yorkshire *see* **Yorkshire**.

Wetherby (West Yorkshire) Place of 'the wether-sheep farm'. *Vethr* (Old Scandinavian) 'wether', a castrated ram; *by* (Old Scandinavian) 'farmstead'. The name of this small market town, southeast of HARROGATE, was recorded as *Wederbi* in the Domesday Book of 1086.

Wexford (Wexford) 'Esker fiord'. *Escir* (Old Irish) 'esker', 'ridge'; *fjordr* (Old Norse) 'sea inlet'. The name of this county town and county in southeast Ireland describes the large sand spit at the fiord entrance here. The Irish name, *Loch Garman*, meaning the 'lake of the headland' may refer to the pool behind the spit.

Weybridge (Surrey) 'Bridge over the River Wey'. *Wey* (Brythonic Celtic river name) possibly 'the mover'; *brycg* (Old English) 'bridge'. The Domesday Book entry for this largely residential and aerospace engineering town, immediately southwest of WALTON-ON-THAMES, was *Webruge*.

Weymouth (Dorset) Place at 'the mouth of the River Wey. *Wey* (Brythonic Celtic river name) possibly 'the mover'; *mutha* (Old English) 'river mouth'. The name of this resort and Channel port, on the coast south of DORCHESTER, was noted as *Waimouthe* in 934.

Whaley Bridge (Derbyshire) Possibly 'woodland clearing by a road', with the later addition of 'a bridge'. *Weg* (Old English) 'road'; *leah* (Old English) 'clearing'; *brycg* (Old English—distinguishing affix) 'bridge'. The name of this town on the River Goyt by the western edge of the PEAK DISTRICT, northwest of BUXTON, was originally recorded as *Walley* in 1230.

Whalsay (Shetland) 'Whale's island'. *Hval-s* (Old Norse) 'whale's'; *ey* (Old Norse) 'island'. The meaning here may relate to the whale-like outline of this island lying off the east coast of SHETLAND'S MAINLAND. It was recorded in the mid-13th century as *Hvalsey*.

Whickham (Tyne and Wear) 'Homestead with a quickset hedge'. *Cwic* (Old English) 'quickset hedge'; *ham* (Old English) 'homestead'. The name of this heavy industries town, west of GATESHEAD, was recorded as *Quicham* in a document of 1196.

Whipsnade (Bedfordshire) 'Wibba's detached plot of land'. *Wibba* (Old English personal name) unidentified; *snaed* (Old English) 'detached piece'. The name of this village south of DUNSTABLE, famous for its zoo, has a name recorded as *Wibsnede* in a text of 1202.

Whitburn (Lothian) 'White stream'. *Hwit* (Old English) 'white'; *burna* (Old English) 'stream'. Near to this former mining town, southwest of BATHGATE, are to be found other places taking their names after river colours, i.e. Blackburn and Greenburn.

Whitby (North Yorkshire) 'Hviti's village'. *Hviti* (Old Scandinavian personal name); *by* (Old Scandinavian) 'village', 'farmstead'. The name of this historic port and resort, on the North Sea coast northwest of SCARBOROUGH, was documented as *Witeby* in the Domesday Book of 1086.

Whitchurch (Hampshire; Shropshire) Place of 'the white church'. *Hwit* (Old English) 'white'; *cirice* (Old English) 'church'. The name of both these places, one a small town east of ANDOVER, the other a larger town north of SHREWSBURY, has the sense of 'a stone-built church edifice, with limestone incorporated in its fabric'. The Shropshire town is on the site of the former Roman station of *Meliolanum*. Respective records show: *Hwitancyrice* 909; *Whytchyrche* 13th century.

Whitechapel (Greater London) Place of 'the white chapel'. *Hwit* (Old English) 'white'; *chapele* (Middle English) 'chapel'. The self-explanatory name of this east LONDON district, like WHITCHURCH, refers here to a white-coloured and stone-built chapel, which in this case was the chapel of *St Mary de Mattelfelon*, as recorded in 1282. The locality name itself was noted in 1340 as *Whitechapele by Aldgate*.

Whitehall (Greater London) Place of 'the white palace'. *Hwit* (Old English) 'white'; *heall* (Old English) 'hall', 'palace'. This famous LONDON area of the City of WESTMINSTER, which effectively is the seat of British government and which is centred on the thoroughfare of this name, is dominated by the Houses of Parliament, Downing Street and ministry buildings. It takes its name from the former 16th century Whitehall Palace, itself presumably so called because of its light-coloured building stone, evident now in the sole surviving Banqueting House. The name was noted in a text of 1530 as *Whytehale*.

Whitehaven (Cumbria) 'Harbour by the white headland'. *Hvitr* (Old Norse) 'white'; *hofuth* (Old Norse) 'headland'; *hafn* (Old Norse) 'harbour'. Located north of ST BEES HEAD, this elegant town, laid out in Wren style in the 17th and 18th centuries by the Lowther family, was given its name much earlier by Viking sailors who aptly described its original situation. Early records manifest the full name origin before the middle element was dropped for ease of pronunciation: *Qwithofhavene* c.1135; *Hwithothehavene* 1202; *Wytofthavene* c.1250.

Whithorn (Dumfries and Galloway) 'White house'. *Hwit* (Old English) 'white'; *erne* (Old English) 'house'. This small town, south of WIGTOWN, called *Candida Casa* (Latin for 'White House') from its foundation in 397 by St Ninian, was a leading religious centre for many centuries.

Whitley Bay (Tyne and Wear) Place on 'the bay by the white wood or clearing'. *Hwit* (Old English) 'white'; *leah* (Old English) 'wood', 'woodland clearing'; *baie* (Old French) 'sea indentation'. This coastal resort, north of TYNEMOUTH, takes its name from the small bay on which it lies, which in turn was named after the original settlement here, noted as *Hwyteleya* in 1198.

Whitstable (Kent) Place of 'the white post'. *Hwit-an* (Old English—dative form) 'white'; *stapol* (Old English) 'post'. Recorded as *Witenstapel* in the Domesday Book, the name of this coastal resort, northwest of CANTERBURY, suggests that this may have been originally a place of assembly for the local hundred (a medieval administrative council) that was marked by a post, or, as it was on the sea that there was some form of navigational landmark here. *Compare* BARNSTAPLE.

Whitworth (Lancashire) Place of 'Hwita's or the white enclosure'. *Hwita* or *hwit* (Old English personal name) unidentified; or 'white' ; *worth* (Old English) 'enclosure'. The name of this textiles town, north of ROCHDALE, was recorded as *Whiteworth* in the 13th century.

Wick (Highland) Simply the place on the 'bay'. *Vik* (Old Norse) 'bay'. This important administrative centre and fishing port in the extreme northeastern corner of Scotland takes its name from the fact that it stands on a sheltered bay. It was recorded as *Vik* in 1140. *Compare* UIG; VOE.

Wickford (Essex) Probably 'ford by a former Romano-British settlement'. *Wic* (Old English based on Latin *vicus*) 'site of earlier Romano-British settlement'; *ford* (Old English) 'river crossing'. The name of this town on the River Crouch, northeast of BASILDON, was noted as *Wicford* in a document of around 995.

Wickham Market (Suffolk) 'Homestead by a vicus, with later market-place status'. *Wic* (Old English based on Latin *vicus*) 'earlier Romano-British settlement'; *ham* (Old English) 'homestead'; *merket* (Middle English) 'market place'. This small town, northeast of IPSWICH, was originally recorded as simply *Wikham* in the Domesday Book of 1086. By the 15th century it was recognised as a market town of considerable importance.

Wicklow (Wicklow) 'Vikings meadow'. *Vikingr* (Old Norse) 'Viking', 'sea rover'; *lo* (Old Norse) 'meadow'. The name of this county town and county on the east coast of Ireland, implies a meadow favoured for settlement by the Vikings, probably at the mouth of the River Vartry here. The Irish name is *Cill Mhantain*, meaning the 'church of St Mantán', Mantán reputedly being a disciple of St Patrick.

Widnes (Cheshire) Place of 'the wide promontory'. *Wid* (Old English) 'wide'; *naess* (Old English) 'ness', 'promontory'. Recorded as *Wydnes* around 1200, the straightforward descriptive name of this industrial town reflects its location on a broad headland on the north bank of the MERSEY where the estuary narrows, the significance of which has resulted in this being the furthest downstream bridging place in modern times.

Wigan (Greater Manchester) Probably 'Wigan's homestead'. *Wigan* (Brythonic Celtic personal name). The name of this industrial town northwest of MANCHESTER, made famous in this century by George Orwell's essay *The Road to Wigan Pier*, was recorded in a document of 1199 with a form exactly as now. It may originally have had some form of generic affix that was lost at an early stage .

Wight, Isle of (England) Probably 'the place of the division'. The name of this well-known rhombic-shaped island and county, lying off the south coast of mainland BRITAIN, would appear to have an ancient Celtic origin, referring to its situation between two arms of The SOLENT and the need for ships to alter course on approach. Perhaps it stems from a Brythonic Celtic root word similar to *gwaith* (Welsh) 'to turn', and cognate with *vectis* (Latin) 'to lever'. Records show: *Vectis* c.150 (Roman name); *Wieht* 534; *Gueith c.*800; *Wiht c.*890. *Wit* 1086 (Domesday Book).

Wigston (Leicestershire) 'Viking's farm'. *Wicing* (Old English) 'pirate', 'Viking'; *tun* (Old English) 'farmstead'. Recorded as *Wichingestone* in the Domesday Book, the name of this town, just south of LEICESTER, was later attached by the affix *Magna* (Latin) 'great', to distinguish it from the village of **Wigston Prava**, some 10 miles (16 km) to the southwest.

Wigton (Cumbria) 'Wicga's farmstead'. *Wicga* (Old English personal name); *tun* (Old English) 'farmstead'. The name of this market town, on the lowlands southwest of CARLISLE, was recorded as *Wiggeton* in 1163.

Wigtown (Dumfries and Galloway) 'Wicga's farm'. *Wicga* (Old English personal name); *tun* (Old English) 'farm'. The derivation of the name of this small town, south of NEWTON STEWART, is the same as for WIGTON (Cumbria) across the SOLWAY FIRTH. Recorded as *Wyggeton* in 1283.

Willesden (Greater London) Place of 'the hill by a spring'. *Wiell* (Old English) 'spring'; *dun* (Old English) 'hill'. This district of northwest LONDON, in the borough of BRENT, has a name that is recorded as *Willesdone* in 939 and as *Wellesdone* in the Domesday Book and whose present form has evolved by association with the neighbouring Harlesden and NEASDEN.

Willington (Durham) 'Farm associated with a man called Wifel. *Wifel* (Old English personal name); *ing* (Old English connective particle) 'associated with'; *tun* (Old English) 'farmstead'. The name of this town, in the former coal-mining district north of BISHOP AUCKLAND, was documented as *Wyvelingtun* in about 1190.

Wilmslow (Cheshire) 'Wighelm's burial mound'. *Wighelm* (Old English personal name); *hlaw* (Old English) 'burial mound', 'tumulus'. Recorded as *Wilmesloe* in a document of around 1250, the name of this residential town, south of MANCHESTER, probably means that there was such a prehistoric mound found on the estate here at the time of its early Anglo-Saxon settlement. *See* WINSLOW.

Wilton (Wiltshire) 'Farm on the River Wylye'. *Wylye* (Brythonic Celtic river name) 'tricky one' in the sense of 'liable to flood unpredictably'; *tun* (Old English) 'farmstead'. The renowned name of this historic carpet-making town, lying on the River Wylye west of SALISBURY, was first recorded as *Uuiltun* in 838, and later as *Wiltune* in the Domesday Book of 1086.

Wiltshire (England) 'The dependant district of Wilton'. Following the customary practice of naming 'shires' after their chief centre, the name of this county in south-central England represents 'Wilton-shire', after the former county town of WILTON and with the addition of the suffix *scir* (Old English) 'district'. It was recorded as *Wiltunscir* in 870 and as *Wiltescire* in the Domesday Book of 1086.

Wimbledon (Greater London) Probably 'Wynnman's hill'. *Wynmann* (Old English personal name); *dun* (Old English) 'hill'. The name of this district of southwest LONDON, in the borough of MERTON, which is internationally famous for its annual lawn tennis tournament, was originally *Wunemannedunne*, as recorded in about 950, and its considerably changed present-day form is due to Anglo-Norman influences.

Wimborne Minster (Dorset) 'Nunnery by the meadow stream'. *Winn* (Old English conjectural word) 'pasture'; *burna* (Old English) 'stream'; *mynster* (Old English later monastic affix) 9th-century nunnery. This town on the River Stour, upstream and northwest of BOURNEMOUTH, takes its basic name from the former name of the tributary River Allen here. Records show: *Winburnan* 718; *Winburnan monasterium* c.894; *Winborne* 1086.

Wincanton (Somerset) 'Farmstead on the white River Cale'. *Wincawel* (Brythonic Celtic river name—former branch name) 'white Cale'; *tun* (Old English) 'farmstead'. The name of this small market town, with its well-known racecourse, to the northeast of YEOVIL, was recorded as *Wincaletone* in the Domesday Book of 1086.

Winchester (Hampshire) 'Roman town of Venta'. *Venta* (pre-Celtic) possibly 'favoured place'; *ceaster* (Old English) 'Roman station'. This ancient cathedral city and capital of the former Saxon kingdom of WESSEX was earlier the important Roman town of *Venta Belgarum*, to give the name in full, as documented in the 4th century. Subsequent records show: *Uintancaestir* c.730; *Wintanceaster* 744; *Wincestre* 1086 (Domesday Book). *See* GWENT.

Windermere (Cumbria) 'Vinand's lake'. *Vinand-ar* (Old Swedish personal name—genitive form); *mere* (Old English) 'lake'. The name of the largest lake in the LAKE DISTRICT was recorded as *Wynandremer* in about 1160, and the lakeside resort town of Windermere, now occupying a central location on its eastern shore, takes its name directly from that of the lake.

Windsor (Berkshire) 'Slope with a windlass'. *Windels* (Old English) 'windlass', 'winding gear'; *ora* (Old English) 'slope', 'bank'. The name of this famous town with its royal castle, on the south bank of the THAMES west of LONDON, somewhat surprisingly refers to the possible early use of an windlass here to pull carts up from the river. It was recorded as *Windlesora* in about 1050.

Winsford (Cheshire) 'Wine's ford'. *Wine* (Old English personal name); *ford* (Old English) 'river crossing'. The name of this town on the river Weaver, upstream and south of NORTHWICH, was first recorded in about 1334 as *Wyneford bridge* showing that its origin as a fording place had already been superseded.

Winslow (Buckinghamshire) 'Wine's burial mound'. *Wine* (Old English personal name); *hlaw* (Old English) 'burial mound', 'tumulus'. The name of this small town, south-east of BUCKINGHAM, was recorded as *Wineshlauu* in 795. *See* WILMSLOW. *Compare* WINSFORD.

Wirksworth (Derbyshire) 'Weorc's enclosure'. *Weorc* (Old English personal name); *worth* (Old English) 'enclosure'. The name of this small town, south of MATLOCK, was recorded as *Wyrcesuuyrthe* in a document of 835. *Compare* WORKSOP.

Wirral (Cheshire/Merseyside) Possibly the place of 'the nooks where bog myrtle grows'. *Wir* (Old English) 'bog myrtle'; *healum* (Old English—plural of *halh*) 'nooks'. Although recorded as *Wirhealum* in 984, the familiar name of this large peninsula, lying between the estuaries of the MERSEY and DEE, has a traditional derivation that is not totally convincing, and there may have been another meaning of *halh* originally used here.

Wisbech (Cambridgeshire) Possibly 'marshy-meadow valley or ridge'. *Wisc* (Old English) 'water-logged pasture'; *bece* (Old English—locative of *baec*) 'valley', 'ridge'. Recorded as *Wisbece* in the Domesday Book, the name of this agricultural town on the River Nene in the middle of The FENS, southwest of KING'S LYNN, has a confused origin and derivation, but it is reasonably certain that the meaning and sense relate to the nature of the low-lying topography here.

Wishaw (Strathclyde) Probably 'Willow wood'. *Withig* (Old English) 'willow'; *sceaga* (Old English) 'wood'. Such a description of this now industrial town, southeast of MOTHERWELL, is still evident in the wooded banks of the South Calder Water, on which it stands.

Witham (Essex) Probably 'the homestead on a bend'. *Wiht* (Old English) 'bend'; *ham* (Old English) 'homestead'. The name of this town on a bend in the River Brain, northeast of CHELMSFORD, was early recorded as it is now.

Withernsea (Humberside) Possibly a place by a 'lake near a thorn tree'. *Vith* (Old Scandinavian) 'near'; *thorn* (Old Scandinavian) 'thorn tree'; *saer* (Old Scandinavian) 'lake'. Recorded as *Widfornessei* in the Domesday Book, the name of this North Sea coastal resort, east of HULL, may have this complicated derivation, which could work equally with very close Old English equivalent elements. Either way, the explanation is not conclusive, and a personal name, such as the Old Norse *Vith-Forni*, may be the origin of the first element.

Witney (Oxfordshire) 'Witta's island'. *Witta-n* (Old English personal name—genitive form); *eg* (Old English) 'island'. Recorded as *Wyttanige* in 969, the name of this town, on the River Windrush west of OXFORD, indicates an elevated area of land surrounded by low-lying marshland, and certainly this description would have been apt here.

Wivenhoe (Essex) 'Wifa's spur of land'. *Wifa-n* (Old English personal name—genitive form); *hoh* (Old English) 'spur or low ridge'. The name of this small town, which is situated in front of a low ridge on the River Colne downstream of COLCHESTER, was noted in the Domesday Book as *Wiunhov* and as *Wyvenho* in 1246.

Woburn Abbey (Bedfordshire) Place of 'the crooked stream'. *Woh* (Old English) 'crooked', 'winding'; *burna* (Old English) 'stream'. A popular visitor attraction, this impressive 18th-century stately home of the Duke of Bedford, set in a great park north of LUTON, takes its basic name from the nearby village of Woburn, which in turn is named after the local stream; it was recorded in the Domesday Book of 1086 as *Woburne*.

Woking (Surrey) Settlement of 'Wocc's people'. *Wocc* (Old English personal name); *ingas* (Old English) 'people of'. The name of this residential satellite town, just southwest of the LONDON conurbation and north of GUILDFORD, was recorded as *Uucchingas* in 710.

Wokingham (Berkshire) 'Homestead of Wocc's people'. *Wocc* (Old English personal name); *inga* (Old English—genitive of *ingas*) 'people of'; *ham* (Old English) 'homestead'. This town, southeast of READING, is only 15 miles (24 km) away from WOKING, and almost certainly has a common origin of association through the same named individual. This town's name appears in a text of 1146 as *Wokingeham*.

Wolds, The (Lincolnshire; Humberside/North Yorkshire) 'Upland forest-land, later cleared'. *Wald* (Old English) as above explanation. The two principal areas subscribing to this term are the chalk upland ranges known as the **Lincoln Wolds** and the **Yorkshire Wolds**, with the former paralleling the coast just inland of GRIMSBY, and the other sweeping round in an arc from FLAMBOROUGH HEAD to HULL. Topographically, they are one, split only by the HUMBER at the point where the new road bridge effectively reconnects them. Many villages in the area take the distinguishing and locational suffix of '-on-the-Wolds', and early records of such include: *Garton in Wald* 1347; *Foston on le Wolde* 1609. *Compare* WEALD, THE.

Wolverhampton (West Midlands) 'Wulfrun's high farm'. *Wulfrun* (Old English personal name—later prefix) a lady to whom manor was given in late 10th century;

hean (Old English—dative form of *heah*) 'high'; *tun* (Old English) 'farmstead'. Situated on comparatively higher ground, to the northwest of BIRMINGHAM, this large industrial town originally was called *Heantune*, as recorded in 985, and only in a text of around 1080 do we see *Wolvrenehamptonia* as a forerunner of its current form.

Wolverton (Buckinghamshire) 'Farmstead associated with a man called Wulfhere'. *Wulfhere* (Old English personal name); *ing* (Old English connective particle) 'associated with'; *tun* (Old English) 'farmstead'. The name of this northwestern constituent town of MILTON KEYNES was recorded as *Wluerintone* in the Domesday book of 1086.

Wombourne (Staffordshire) Place of 'the crooked stream'. The derivation for this town southwest of WOLVERHAMPTON is the same as for WOBURN ABBEY , except that the first element is represented by *won*, the dative of *woh*. The name appears in the Domesday Book as *Wamburne*.

Wombwell (South Yorkshire) Probably 'the spring in a hollow'. *Womb* (Old English) 'womb', denoting 'a hollow'; *wella* (Old English) 'spring'. The name of this town in the coal-mining district southeast of BARNSLEY was recorded as *Wanbuella* in the Domesday Book of 1086.

Woodbridge (Suffolk) Either 'Wood by a bridge' or 'a wooden bridge'. *Wudu* (Old English) 'wood', 'wooden'; *brycg* (Old English) 'bridge'. Records of the name of this town, northeast of IPSWICH, show: *Oddebruge c.*1050; *Wudebrige* 1086 (Domesday Book).

Woodhall Spa (Lincolnshire) 'Manor house in or by a wood'. *Wudu* (Old English) 'wood'; *heall* (Old English) 'hall', 'manor house'. This latter-day spa town, southwest of HORNCASTLE, was recorded in the 12th century as *Wudehalle*.

Woodstock (Oxfordshire) 'Place in the woods'. *Wudu* (Old English) 'wood'; *stoc* (Old English) 'place'. The name of this historic town, which has the famous

Blenheim and which lies to the northwest of OXFORD, was recorded as *Wudustoc* in about 1000.

Wookey Hole (Somerset) Place of 'the animal snare by the cavern'. *Wocig* (Old English) 'trap', 'snare'; *hol* (old English) 'ravine', 'cave'. The name of this village at the foot of the MENDIP HILLS, to the northwest of WELLS, takes its basic name from the nearby village of **Wookey**; the 'Hole' of course is the famous limestone cavern here. The name was noted as *Wokyhole* in 1065.

Wool (Dorset) Place at 'the wells'. *Weilla* (Old English) 'wells' or 'springs'. The name of this large village on the River Frome, upstream and west of Wareham, was noted as *Wille* in the Domesday Book.

Wooler (Northumberland) Place of the 'hill spring'. *Wella* (Old English) 'spring'; *ofer* (Old English) 'hill'. Recorded as *Wulloure* in a text of 1187, the name of this small town aptly describes its elevated situation on the northeastern edge of the CHEVIOT HILLS overlooking the River Till valley, northwest of ALNWICK.

Woolwich (Greater London) 'Wool-handling port'. *Wull* (Old English) 'wool'; *wic* (Old English) 'harbour', 'port', 'specialised premises'. This eastern riverside district of the borough of GREENWICH, on the south bank of the lower Thames, has a '-wic' ending name that describes its particular original function; it was documented in 918 as *Uuluuich*. 150 years later, the Domesday Book entry of *Hulviz* shows how the Anglo-Normans had difficulty in pronouncing and transcribing the name of this place.

Wootton Bassett (Wiltshire) 'Farmstead by a wood, with later possession by the Basset family'. *Wudu* (Old English) 'wood'; *tun* (Old English) 'farmstead'; *Basset* (later Anglo-Norman manorial affix) Alan Basset, who held the estate from 1230. Recorded as simply *Wdetun* in a document of 680 and *Wodetone* in the Domesday Book, the very common basic name of this small town, west of SWINDON, was distinguished by its later affix of ownership to become *Wotton Basset* as noted in 1272.

Worcester (Hereford and Worcester) 'Roman town of the Weogora tribal territory'. *Weogora-n* (Brythonic Celtic tribal name—dative form, possibly based on river name) 'dwellers of the winding stream'; *ceaster* (Old English) 'Roman station'. The name of this well-known cathedral city and county town, on the River SEVERN upstream and north of GLOUCESTER, was recorded as *Uueogorna civitate* in 691, as *Wigranceastre* in 717, and appears in the Domesday Book of 1086 as *Wirecestre.* The old county name of **Worcestershire** was documented first in about 1040 as *Wireceastrescir*.

Workington (Cumbria) 'Estate associated with a man called Weorc'. *Weorc* (Old English personal name); *ing* (Old English connective particle) 'associated with'; *tun* (Old English) 'estate', 'farmstead'. The name of this former iron and steel-making centre and port, on the west Cumbrian coast midway between WHITEHAVEN and MARYPORT, was documented as *Wirkynton* around 1125.

Worksop Nottinghamshire) 'Weorc's valley'. *Weorc* (Old English personal name); *hop* (Old English) 'small enclosed valley'. This industrial town, in the coal- mining district northeast of MANSFIELD, originates from the same personal name as in WIRKSWORTH and WORKINGTON, although the same man is not necessarily involved, certainly not in the case of the latter. Its name appears as *Werchesope* in the Domesday Book.

Wormwood Scrubs (Greater London) 'Snake-infested wood' later cleared and 'overgrown with brushwood'. *Wyrm* (Old English) 'snake', 'reptiles'; *holt* (Old English) 'wood'; *scrubb* (Old English conjectural word related to *scrybb*) 'scrubland'. The unpleasant sounding name of this large open space in the borough of HAMMERSMITH, well known for its prison, has an even more repugnant and alarming meaning. Recorded as *Wormeholte* in about 1200 and *Wrmholt* in 1290, the original basic name was in use quite late, as *Wormholt Scrubs* was noted in 1819, since when the first word somehow has been misrepresented.

Worsbrough (South Yorkshire) 'Weorc's or Wirc's stronghold'. *Weorc*; *Wirc* (Old English personal name); *burh* (Old English) 'fortified place'. The name of this coal-mining community, south of BARNSLEY, was recorded as *Wircesburg* in the Domesday Book of 1086. *See* WORKSOP.

Worsley (Greater Manchester) Possibly 'clearing of a man, Weorchaeth, or a woman, Weorcgyth'. *Weorchaeth*; *Weorcgyth* (Old English personal name); *leah* (Old English) 'forest clearing'. Records of this town, west of MANCHESTER, show: *Werkesleia* 1196; *Wyrkitheley* 1246.

Worthing (West Sussex) Probably the settlement of 'Wurth's people'. *Wurth* (Old English personal name); *ingas* (Old English) 'people of'. The name of this well-known coastal resort and residential town, west of BRIGHTON, appears in the Domesday Book of 1086 as *Ordinges*. Subsequent records show: *Wurddingg* 1219; *Worthinges* 1246.

Wotton-under-Edge (Gloucestershire) 'Farmstead by a wood, at the foot of a scarp'. *Wudu* (Old English) 'wood'; *tun* (Old English) 'farmstead'; *under* (Old English related to Old Saxon, Gothic *undar*) 'below'; *ecg* (Old English) 'edge', 'ridge'. The common basic name of this small town, southwest of STROUD, is the same as that of WOOTTON BASSETT, and the later distinguishing suffix aptly describes its location below the western scarp slope of the CHILTERN HILLS. Records show: *Wudutune* 940; *Vutune* 1086 (Domesday Book); *Wotton under Egge* 1466.

Wrekin, The (Shropshire) The name of this isolated craggy hill, just west of TELFORD, which rises to a height of 1334 ft (407 m) and thus dominates the surrounding district, is thought to be one of ancient Brythonic Celtic origin and transferred from the nearby settlement of WROXETER. Its exact meaning is uncertain. The name was recorded as *Wrocene* in 975.

Wrexham (Clwyd) Probably 'Wright's pasture'. *Wryhtel* (Old English personal name) unidentified; *hamm* (Old English) 'water meadow', 'pasture'. Despite the fact that Wrexham, a town on the western edge of the Cheshire Plain, is not located on a river, there are sufficient indications to conclude that there must have been some form of watercourse here in early times. The current name appears to have been influenced by its Welsh corruption, *Wrecsam*, formerly *Gwregsam* in 1291. Records show: *Wristlesham* 1161; *Wreccesham* 1236.

Wroxeter (Shropshire) 'Roman fort of Viroconium'. *Virico* or *Uiroco* (Brythonic Celtic) obscure meaning; *ceaster* (Old English) 'Roman station'. The origin and meaning of the name of this village west of the WREKIN, capital of the Celtic Cornovii tribe and site of a former Roman town, remains a mystery. Records show: *Ouirokonion* c.150; *Rochecestre* 1086 (Domesday Book); *Wroxcestre* 1155.

Wymondham (Norfolk) 'Wigmund's homestead'. *Wigmund* (Old English personal name); *ham* (Old English) 'homestead'. The name of this small town, southwest of NORWICH, is noted in the Domesday Book as *Wimundham*.

Y

Yarmouth, Great (Norfolk) Place at 'the mouth of the River Yare'. *Yare* (Brythonic Celtic river name based on conjectural root element *gar* or *ger*) 'babbling stream'; *mutha* (Old English) 'river mouth'. Early records of the name of this well-known coastal resort and port at the mouth of the River Yare, east of NORWICH, show: *Gernemwa* 1086 (Domesday Book); *Gernemuda* 1130; *Gernemuta Magna* 1254, the latter representing the addition of the prefix 'Great' to distinguish this place from the former village of Little Yarmouth, which is now incorporated as a southern suburb.

Y Drenewydd *see* **Newtown**.

Yeadon (West Yorkshire) Probably place of the 'high hill'. *Heah* (Old English) 'high'; *dun* (Old English) 'hill'. This derivation aptly describes the elevated situation of this town, which is on one of the spurs of the hill ridge known as the Chevin to the northwest of LEEDS, near the site of its airport. The Domesday Book records the name as *Iadun*.

Yell (Shetland) 'Barren' place. *Geldr* (Old Norse) 'barren'. This old Viking name remains appropriately descriptive of Shetland's second largest island, lying between MAINLAND and UNST, which has a terrain of low rocky ridges and intervening bog, giving a generally heavy and cheerless aspect. In the *Orkneyinga Saga* of the 13th century the name was recorded as *Ala*; and in later documents as *Jala*; *Jella* and *Yella*.

Yeovil (Somerset) Place on 'the River Gifle'. *Gifle* (Brythonic Celtic river name possibly based on root element *gablo*) 'forked one'. Although this market town and light engineering industrial centre, southeast of TAUNTON, stands on the river known today as the Yeo, the latter was originally the *Gifle*, which subsequently in 878 was recorded as *Yevel*. Early records of the town name itself include: *Gifle* c.880; *Gyfle* c.950; *Givele* 1086.

Yes Tor (Devon) 'Eagle's craggy hill'. *Earn* (Old English) 'eagle'; *torr* (Old English) 'tor', 'rocky hill'. This well-known DARTMOOR hill, with its distinctive cap of eroded granite rock piles reaching a height of 2020 ft (619 m) above sea level, represents, together with its near and very slightly higher neighbour, High Whillays, the most elevated point in southern England. As such, its appropriately eerie (and eyrie) name was recorded as *Ernestorre* in 1240. *Compare* SNOWDON.

Yetholm (Borders) 'Village of the pass'. *Geat* (Old English) 'pass', 'gate', 'gap'; *ham* (Old English) 'village'. This ancient 'gateway' settlement, situated in the CHEVIOT HILLS just north of the border between SCOTLAND and ENGLAND, is split into **Kirk Yetholm** and **Town Yetholm**, on opposite banks of the Bowmont Water. It is famous as the long-established chief settlement of the Scottish Gypsies. Early records show more clearly the derivation of the current name form: *Gatha'n* c.800; *Jetham* 1233; *Yetham* 1297.

York (North Yorkshire) 'Estate of Eburos or of the yew trees'. The present name of this famous historic minster city, east of LEEDS, is a roundabout corruption of the original, through the influences of successive settlers here: Celts, Romans, Anglo-Saxons, Danes and possibly even the Normans. To begin with the first recorded name, which was *Eborakon* in about AD 150, and which, with the 4th-century version of *Eburacum*, was the Romans' name for their fortified town here. Both these names are held to be derived from the Brythonic Celtic personal name *Eburos*, which itself is believed to have origins in an ancient Celtic root word meaning 'yew tree'. The Anglo-Saxons, not fully comprehending the sense of the former latinised name, made association with their word *eofor* (Old English) for 'a wild boar', and, by adding *wic* (Old English) for 'dwelling place', and *ceaster* (Old English) as recognition of the former 'Roman station', created the name of *Eofor-wic-ceaster*, as recorded in 644, and subsequently adopted the simpler and shorter version, *Eoforwic* as documented around 738. Then, during the 9th and 10th centuries when Danish Viking power controlled the town, the name was modified to a Scandinavianised *Iorvik* or *Jorvik*, the latter being remembered today in its use as the title of the Jorvik Viking Centre here. Recording it as *Euruic* in the Domesday Book, the Normans played their minor part in consolidating the evolutionary process. Influenced by the latter rendering, the predominating Viking form was very quickly elided to *Iork* and re-adopted by the English to appear in its present form of *York* by as early as the 13th century, well before the famous minster was completed here. The long and complex story of the development of this name was to have a final and fitting twist in the 17th century when it was transferred to the 'New World' and adopted as the 'New York' that was to witness the immigration of so many of the peoples that had influenced its name originally.

Yorkshire (England) 'The dependant district of York'. This county name, which some would say is synonymous with the word 'cricket', first appeared in its Old English form as *Eoferwicscir* in about 1050. The original area of the county was so large that it was eventually divided into three divisions: the East, North, and West Ridings—the word 'riding' meaning 'thirding', derived from *trith-jungr* (Old Norse) 'third part'. More recently, under the major reorganisation of Local Government in England and Wales in 1974, Yorkshire was again carved up into three new administrative county units, this time as: **North Yorkshire**; **South Yorkshire**; **West Yorkshire**.

Youghal (Cork) 'Yew wood'. *Eochaill* (Irish Gaelic) 'yew wood'. Apparently in ancient times a large yew wood grew on the hillslope on the south side of the Blackwater River estuary where this market town was founded by the Anglo-Normans in the 13th century. Even yet some of the old yews remain.

Ystrad (Mid Glamorgan) Place in 'the valley'. *Ystrad* (Welsh) 'valley'. This 19th-century coal-mining town, at the centre of the RHONNDA Fawr, has a simple Welsh name that literally describes its typical South Wales 'valley' situation.

Y Trallwng *see* **Welshpool**.

Z

Zennor (Cornwall) Place of 'the church dedicated to St Senara'. The distinctive name of this village on the northwest coast of the PENWITH peninsula, west of ST IVES, was recorded in a text of 1291 as *ecclesia Sancte Senare*, a female saint about whom nothing is known.

Zetland *see* **Shetland**